Rethinking the Reentry Paradigm

Rethinking the Reentry Paradigm

A Blueprint for Action

SECOND EDITION

Kimberly A. Houser
ASSOCIATE PROFESSOR OF LAW AND JUSTICE STUDIES
ROWAN UNIVERSITY

Melinda Schlager Arnold
PROVOST AND VICE PRESIDENT OF ACADEMIC AFFAIRS
TEXAS A&M UNIVERSITY-TEXARKANA

CAROLINA ACADEMIC PRESS
Durham, North Carolina

Library of Congress Cataloging-in-Publication Data

Names: Houser, Kimberly A. (Professor of criminal justice), author. | Schlager, Melinda, author.
Title: Rethinking the reentry paradigm : a blueprint for action / Kimberly A. Houser, Melinda Schlager Arnold.
Description: Second edition. | Durham, North Carolina : Carolina Academic Press, [2023] | Includes bibliographical references and index.
Identifiers: LCCN 2023005486 | ISBN 9781611638684 (paperback) | ISBN 9781531000134 (ebook)
Subjects: LCSH: Parole—United States—Planning. | Criminals—Rehabilitation—United States. | Ex-convicts—United States—Life skills guides.
Classification: LCC HV9304 .S335 2023 | DDC 364.6—dc23/eng/20230310
LC record available at https://lccn.loc.gov/2023005486

Carolina Academic Press
700 Kent Street
Durham, North Carolina 27701
(919) 489-7486
www.cap-press.com

Printed in the United States of America

Contents

Acknowledgments

I am very grateful to Melinda Schlager Arnold for allowing me the opportunity to be a part of the work that she began. Melinda's heartfelt passion for addressing the importance of reentry and reintegration is inspiring. My passion for this subject was inspired by my mentor, Dr. Wayne Welsh. I will never forget the lessons learned as his student and research assistant. Wayne opened my eyes to the importance of reentry and reintegration and taught me that we can make a difference through research and education. There are people along the way that teach and inspire you in ways that you will never forget. Melinda, you allowed me to use that inspiration to be a part of your great and informative work on this subject, for which I will always be grateful.

I started my academic career later than most, having worked in the field of healthcare before going to graduate school. Perhaps that also helped me to look at much of the criminal justice system from a public health perspective. I am now an Associate Professor at Rowan University in the Department of Law and Justice Studies and have been so fortunate to have a department and college that supports and promotes the work of their faculty. I am particularly grateful to my colleagues and Dean for their support and encouragement in the writing of this book.

To my husband, Bob, who has supported me without reservation, I thank you. You knew the importance of this book to me and encouraged me every step of the way. Your love and support are beyond words. And, to my Aunt Barb, thank you for our standing dinner and game night on Friday where family is central and laughter is in abundance. Lastly, in recognition to my dear friend, Eric McCord, who passed far too young, you continue to inspire me to be the best that I can be. You believed that we can truly make a difference through research and knowledge, something that you practiced every day with great passion.

I'm a better educator, a better researcher, and most importantly a better person for having had you in my life.

I tell my students that one of the most important, yet under-addressed, subjects in criminal justice are the stories of the people leaving prison and returning home. Once the prison door shuts, the people inside and the obstacles they face within the institution and on reentry are rarely thought about and often forgotten. The impact on families and communities left behind are the collateral damage. As a society and as human beings, we owe people the opportunity to effectively reintegrate back into society and live fulfilling and productive lives. However, as this book lays out, that is often not the case. We must do better as a society in allowing people to be more than the sum of their mistakes.

Kimberly Houser
February 2023

Since the writing of the first edition of this book, much has changed—but also stayed the same. While I may have changed jobs a time or two, or three, since 2012, I remain surrounded by people who have invested considerable time and energy in helping me affect change despite strong headwinds. I have now had the privilege of working for four distinct higher education systems and have come full circle with the A&M System in finding an academic and geographic home in Texarkana.

As provost, one does not have much time to write or think. In fact, one does not have much time to do much of anything. But the opportunity to work on a new edition of this book and turn the reins over to my colleague Kim Houser, someone who believes as firmly as I do that reentry matters, has been invigorating as well as a humble reminder that we can never lose sight of why any of us got into the higher education business to begin with. We transform lives and make a difference—one person at a time. This reminder has helped me stay the course on more than one occasion. A heartfelt thanks to Emily Cutrer who as president and mentor (whether she realized it or not) has supported me in my provostian efforts to do good, make change, and move the dial. Enjoy your next chapter. You have certainly earned it.

A tour working for UNT Dallas and with the Dallas Police Department and other north Texas law enforcement agencies to broaden police leadership horizons resulted in some of the most challenging, meaningful, and rewarding work I have ever done. I have incredible respect for those who do the job right and who put their lives on the line every day to keep us safe. I applaud your willingness in the safe space that was our classroom to demonstrate your humanity, vulnerability, and desire for a better world. You are leaders who—on a daily basis—can affect change on the ground and in the communities you serve. Just remember that each citizen engagement is a chance to reframe the narrative.

A two-year detour to Montana as provost brought with it very big sky, beautiful sunrises, cold temperatures, rugged terrain, difficult decisions, and experiences that have forever shaped me as an academic and human being. Sadly, however, the 'take home' was not much different than the one I encountered when I worked for parole in New Jersey, probation in Dallas, and other organizations that shall remain nameless. In summary: change is difficult, so the status quo is satisfactory; people want change until they don't and then only when it applies to someone else; and most people do not have the intestinal fortitude to make the real change that is necessary to move the dial in a meaningful way. A profound thanks to Dan Edelman for his encouragement, trust, and confidence in me, my abilities, and my vision. We almost had it. Much gratitude to my soul sister and dear friend Christine whom I left behind but who continues to influence me in ways too numerous to count.

To my dear Cameron who remains in the arctic tundra, a young woman forging her own path despite significant obstacles that would discourage most, you truly amaze. You are as resilient, strong-willed, and as sweet and kind as they come. May you continue to ask "why," never settle for "because," and fully embrace that absolutely anything and everything is possible. I am so proud of you.

Settling in Texarkana was a homecoming of sorts for my now-retired husband Jeff, who spent 28 years in service to Dallas County helping those who struggled (often unsuccessfully and repeatedly) with helping themselves. A proud 1983 graduate of Texas High, his wish to spend more time in TXK with the grandkids was granted. You have treated the world so much better than it has treated you. You never complain despite numerous legitimate reasons to do so, the glass is always half full even when it usually isn't, and you love deeply and completely. Not that I am counting or anything, but only 11 short years to go. The time will pass far too quickly for my liking but with you by my side I know that anything is possible and that the future is bright.

Melinda Schlager Arnold
February 2023

Introduction

Ironically, the concept of offender reentry has encountered as many barriers and impediments to legitimacy as have the thousands of people who leave prison every day and reenter society. That neither has been overwhelmingly successful should not be surprising given society's wholesale ignorance of the former and overwhelmingly punitive approach to the latter. Those words graced the pages of the original edition of this book and are truer than ever today.

In the nearly 11 years since the first edition of this book was released, some things have changed but more things have stayed the same. A cursory review of the Bureau of Justice Statistics webpage reveals that statistical reports on prisoner counts remain current with *Prisoners in 2021—Statistical Tables* (published December 2022); that reports on recidivism are reasonably up-to-date, as seen in *Recidivism of Prisoners Released in 34 States in 2012: A 5-Year Follow-Up Period (2012-2017)* (published in July 2021 with results that indicate that little to no progress has been made in reducing recidivism, I might add); but that information on reentry is virtually nonexistent. The last official BJS report, *Reentry Trends in the United States*, was issued in October 2002.

Understandably, shifts in criminal justice funding priorities happen. An emphasis on homeland security and human trafficking, among a variety of high-profile concerns, has resulted in the redirection of substantial funds away from other priorities (such as drug enforcement). But one thing is consistent. The overwhelming majority of people who go to prison also, eventually, go home. Yet, neither the challenges they encounter nor the policies, processes, or the likelihood of their success have principally changed in the last decade. More concerning still is the sad reality that the barriers and impediments to reentering society after having spent time in prison haven't fundamentally changed since the first prison opened and the first person was released from prison to the community. Attention must continue to be paid.

Even today, our best efforts to address the offender reentry problem often result in the most deleterious and (un)intended of consequences. Some of the most well-intended reentry policies and practices have fallen prey to organizational missteps and implementation failures and have been co-opted for political gain at the expense of the people for which they were developed. That any offender is successful in the reentry process continues to be a testament to his or her fortitude and occurs despite the system, not because of it.

At this juncture, it is commonly accepted knowledge that at least 95% of all people incarcerated in state prison at this very moment will be released from prison at some point in the future. Put another way, 9.5 out of every 10 people sent to prison will leave either upon completion of their sentence or on parole supervision (Releases from State Prison, 2002). Until offender reentry became a household phrase in corrections circles in the early 21st century, most of us hadn't given it much thought. The criminal justice system has most often been concerned with getting the bad guys off the streets, not the notion that the bad guys at some point leave prison and return to the streets. But precisely because 95% of people in prison ultimately leave, this has required all of us in the business to reorient our thinking.

Thinking about offender reentry is more difficult than it sounds. We know basically what offender reentry is, but after more than one hundred years of releasing people from prison to the community, we still don't have a good handle on the breadth and depth of the practice nor have we been able to completely parse out the relationship between the reentry process and victims, offenders, and the community. One considerable obstacle to thinking clearly about the reentry problem is that it has no overarching theoretical construct or "glue" that holds it together (Bazemore & Boba, 2007; Maruna, 2006; Simon, 1993). In fact, scholars contend that current views of offender reentry include, "the rather bizarre assumption that surveillance and some guidance can steer the offender straight" (2001, p. 24). If it were only that easy.

The bulk of the literature on offender reentry evaluates and/or describes its direct (impact on recidivism) or indirect (reentry programming) ability to "work." While efforts to evaluate what works have been instrumental in determining what works best for whom in what circumstances, resultant policies and programs are generally geared toward addressing specific problems and/or deficits in individual offender skill sets but are absent a clear narrative that fuses individual-level offender problems with contextual, environmental, and social concerns. At base, reentry is comprised of a patchwork quilt of policies and programs that individual offenders may access, the outcomes of which can (at least to some degree) be quantified. What we lack, however, is a theoretical construct or narrative through which to understand offender reentry or implement effective policy that enhances the chances of better outcomes.

This book is divided into three distinct parts. Part I brings together disparate issues that, when viewed in tandem, provide the reader with an understanding of what comprises offender reentry. Where Part I explores the various dimensions of offender reentry, Part II provides several contexts within which to view it. Finally, Part III fuses together the dimensions of reentry with various contextual frameworks to provide an integrated narrative for moving the discussion and practice of offender reentry forward.

A word (or two) about some of the limitations of this book. First, when discussing the reentering offender, this book, unless otherwise indicated, is talking about people who leave prison and who return to the community on parole or some type of post-incarceration supervision. Keep in mind that plenty of people leave prison upon completion of sentence and without additional supervision. While these offenders need and require access to reentry services (perhaps more than anyone), the focus of this discussion is on those people under active supervision. One can reason that if it is difficult for people on supervision to successfully reintegrate, it is likely doubly problematic for those with no support.

Second, while this book attempts to be as inclusive as possible of all offender types, it does not specifically address sex offender populations. This is not an oversight but a calculated omission. Sex offenders encounter the same barriers and impediments to reentry as other offenders — and then some. Given page and content constraints, a decision was made to leave out any specific mention of sex offenders and to subsume them into the general conversation about reentering offenders.

Third, this text specifically addresses issues related to offender reentry at the state level. While a mention of federal statistics may occur here and there, the overwhelming focus of this book is to evaluate offender reentry at the state level. Federal release mechanisms and practices vary from those at the state level and for purposes of streamlining the discussion, the decision was made to concentrate on state-level offender reentry practice.

One cannot discuss any criminal justice topic without discussing race. Offender reentry is no exception. However, it was not possible to parse out issues solely relevant to race and reentry and to isolate them in a single chapter. Therefore, discussions of race permeate virtually every chapter of the book. Where relevant, racial distinctions between reentering offenders is made. Otherwise, the discussions in the book should be read as inclusive of all races and ethnic groups.

Observant readers will notice a variety of statistics in this book. Some of these numbers are more time-sensitive than others. That is, many of the official statistics provided in this book come from the Bureau of Justice Statistics and are not always available for the most recent year. In all cases, the data provided is the most recent data available. This issue is no more visible than in discussions of recidivism. National recidivism data always lags considerably because of the time that must pass in order to determine whether someone has become criminal justice involved again.

Finally, information on offender reentry is often fractured in its location and content. However, there are a few places where one can look to begin the process of understanding and further studying this most important criminal justice issue. First, any student of offender reentry should consult the mammoth body of work on the subject by The Urban Institute. This organization was one of the trailblazers with respect to identifying and studying offender reentry and students of the subject should start with a reading of some of the seminal reports written by Urban staff for a good primer on the subject. Specifically, and most relevant here, the Urban Institute has engaged in a series of studies as part of the *Returning Home: Understanding the Challenges of Offender Reentry* project. In fact, some of the work from these studies appears in chapters throughout this book. Access to this link (http://www.urban.org/center/jpc/returning-home/publications.cfm) should provide students of offender reentry with all of the ammunition they need to study this topic in earnest.

In 2001, the Serious and Violent Offender Reentry Initiative (SVORI) was born. This was the federal government's first attempt to bring together multiple governmental agencies to tackle the offender reentry problem. The first round of grants asked states to put together a reentry program that addressed the needs of adult and/or juvenile offenders being released from prison to communities around the United States. Most (but not all) states submitted proposals and grant monies to develop reentry programs were released. As part of this initiative, a series of evaluations of various offender reentry programs were conducted. A great place to read about SVORI and locate information on these evaluations is: http://nij.gov/topics/corrections/reentry/evaluation-svori.htm. Mention of the SVORI initiative occurs in this text. Hopefully these reports and information from the website can provide you with appropriate context.

Other information on offender reentry can be obtained from the National Reentry Resource Center at http://nationalreentryresourcecenter.org. Information on federal legislation that supports funding for many reentry initiatives including the Second Chance Act can be found at http://www.reentrypolicy.org/government_affairs/second_chance_act. Additional information can be located at www.reentrypolicy.org.

At the end of the day, offender reentry impacts everyone. We are naive and misinformed if we think otherwise. When someone is released from prison (regardless of the manner in which they are released), their departure from closed custody and subsequent arrival in the community has ramifications for them, their family, the community to which they return, and society at large. Therefore, we have a social and moral obligation as citizens not only to do reentry (because most offenders are coming home), but also to think reentry. Only when we attach the same level of importance to prison release as we do to prison admission will we affect any real change. Our collective—and continued—moral failure may be our insistence to glorify and publicize punishment while fostering and promoting ignorance and silence surrounding the reentry process and the human beings that engage and often fail in this herculean task.

"Correction does much, but encouragement does more."

— Goethe

Rethinking the Reentry Paradigm

Chapter 1

Understanding the Reentry Problem

All offenders leaving prison, regardless of the manner in which they are released, face significant challenges associated with successful reentry into society. Some may not have a place to stay, others may require medical attention, most may not be qualified for jobs, and many may expect their families and society at-large to embrace them upon their release. These challenges are not new. Since the first prison was constructed, offenders have come and gone. Why then is the issue of offender reentry of such monumental concern to us now?

Historical Context

In order to understand how offender reentry has become such a topic of interest, we must first appreciate how the United States finds itself at the point of incarcerating more people than any other industrialized nation (Walmsley, 2007). In 1975, the rate of incarceration per 100,000 residents began to increase in the United States. By the 1980s, the U.S. was incarcerating its citizens at an alarming rate of 275 per 100,000 residents, and by 2010, the rate had almost doubled: 500/100,000 residents (Carson & Sabol, 2012; Glaze, 2011). It was at this point that incarceration rates had peaked, and we began to see a gradual decline in prison populations with each consecutive year (Kaeble & Cowhig, 2018). By 2019, incarceration rates were at their lowest levels in 24 years, representing a 17% drop since 2009 (Carson, 2020). Although this reflects a shift in the mass incarceration trend that began in the mid-1970s, the U.S. continues to incarcerate its citizens at rates higher than any other Westernized country, with an imprisonment rate of 350/100,000 residents as of 2021 (Carson, 2022; Gramlich, 2018).

There is a complex set of factors that scholars call upon to explain the meteoric rise in rates of incarceration in the United States. Sentencing, politics, the War on Drugs, economics, and inequality are among the primary suspects in the mass imprisonment movement. Interestingly, it took the mass incarceration of thousands of people to force (only after the fact) criminal justice policymakers and practitioners to scratch their heads and wonder.

Sentencing

One primary explanation for the increase in U.S. prison populations is a seismic shift in sentencing policy. Until the 1980s, the primary sentencing structure for the majority of states was indeterminate. This means that sentences were not fixed. Instead, sentences were determined based on the assignment of a flexible term of incarceration by a judge. This method of sentencing was developed predicated on the idea that fixed terms of incarceration do not allow for adjustment of time in prison based on good behavior or any progress that offenders may make with respect to individualized treatment and case management (Walker, 1998). In an indeterminate sentencing schema, a judge assesses a minimum sentence, but it is the parole board—an administrative board—that makes the final determination about how long an offender spends in prison (Parsons-Lewis, 1972).

The indeterminate sentence model is an outgrowth of early beliefs in punishment that promoted the notion that people will make progress in prison at different rates and that an objective board—the parole board—is in the best position to review rehabilitative efforts on an individual basis and to make sound release decisions. What separates indeterminate sentencing from other sentencing options is that the foundation of indeterminate sentencing is the criminal, not the crime (Tonry & Petersilia, 1999). In this way, indeterminate sentencing with release by the parole board is intended to motivate offenders by promoting and encouraging good behavior in prison.

This is in stark contrast to determinate sentencing schemas that provide fixed terms of incarceration based on nature and type of crime as well as mitigating and aggravating circumstances. Determinate or fixed sentences were adopted in the 1980s in opposition to indeterminate sentences that were believed to be too lenient, not uniformly applied, and supportive of outmoded rehabilitative ideals (Garland, 2001; Tonry, 1996). Determinate sentencing was implemented by creating a set of sentencing guidelines that judges were required to follow. Judges could sentence offenders to terms outside of the recommended punishment, but they were required to clearly defend their decision to do so. Where indeterminate sentencing encouraged judicial discretion in the sentencing process, determinate sentencing squelched the ability of judges to move outside the established norms.

Not surprisingly, as state-level sentencing structures moved away from discretionary sentencing to determinate guidelines, the need for parole waned. Maine was among the first states to abolish parole in 1976. By the year 2000, 19 other states had abolished the practice of parole altogether or only for certain crimes (Petersilia, 2003). The federal system abolished parole in 1987 (Hoffman, 2003). The decrease in the ability of judges to set discretionary or indeterminate sentence terms and of parole boards to be able to modify offenders' terms of release based on rehabilitative goals also set the stage for the development of other punitive approaches to sentencing.

Mandatory minimum sentences were created wherein offenders were required to serve a mandatory period of incarceration before they could be released. This mode of sentencing was made most famous by John D. Rockefeller who, in his efforts to staunch the flow of drugs into New York, proposed mandatory life sentences for people caught selling or conspiring to sell heroin, LSD, or other drugs (Griset, 1991). After passage, mandatory minimum sentence laws in New York (and other jurisdictions) have been responsible for the incarceration of an increasing number of people on drug charges, but unfortunately the unintended consequences have been that the laws have not necessarily targeted the people for whom the laws were written. The laws have resulted in small-time dealers of color doing significant time for possession and trafficking of relatively small amounts of drugs instead of high-level drug dealers (Bova, 2009).

Other hard-line sentencing modalities such as three-strikes legislation (laws that enhance sentences for serious second-time offenders and require life in prison for offenders who commit a third felony) have also resulted in unintended outcomes. While states jumped on the bandwagon to adopt these stringent sentencing measures, the end result has often been the incarceration of offenders for life for the commission of a third felony that does not include crimes against the person (Abramsky, 2002).

Truth-in-sentencing legislation, another punitive sentencing response, was geared toward providing transparency to the public regarding the actual amount of time that offenders served in prison. Truth-in-sentencing legislation required that offenders serve a specific percentage of their sentence (say 85%) before being eligible for release (Ditton & Wilson, 1999). The shift from indeterminate to determinate sentencing along with all of the other additional restrictive sentencing schemas mentioned above resulted in an increased number of offenders remaining behind bars for longer—a practice that resulted in large increases in prison capacity and ultimately prison population.

Politics

While there is support for the contention that changes to sentencing schemas are responsible for the mass incarceration movement, others argue that politics is to blame. Prior to the 1960s, prisons were islands unto themselves; they were hands-off. Traditionally, prisons were institutions that were managed by wardens, and few people took any interest in their form or function. However, looming social issues of the 1960s, including riots, the civil rights movement, and desegregation were contextualized by politicians in the framework of social disorder, and these issues resulted in increased fear of crime and feelings that more needed to be done to fight social instability (Western, 2006). These fears culminated in a more hands-on approach, particularly by the judiciary.

Increasing rates of violent crime didn't help matters. Criminal justice decision-making, once the sole jurisdiction of criminal justice professionals, became political. "The judgment of experts was questioned by the voice of the people" (Travis, 2005, p. 220). Punishment became a political concern marked by political responses that included firm and unyielding support for policies and programs that cracked down on those whose behavior was not socially acceptable. Specifically, Travis (2005) argues that social instability fueled political will to the point that state and federal lawmakers were instrumental in marshalling support for a shift from indeterminate to determinate sentencing (as discussed above), and expanding the use of punishment to include additional funds for the building of more prisons, increasing community corrections capacity (i.e., parole), and encouraging the creation of additional collateral consequences to incarceration. Crime and criminal justice issues became a fulcrum by which political leaders gained traction, stumped for reelection, and changed social policy and law.

The politicization of crime has impacted other areas of civic life, including census counts and political representation. When census counts are taken, prisoners are counted as "residents" of the jurisdictions in which they are incarcerated. Given that most prisons are located in rural areas or minimally in locations somewhat far from the offenders' actual place of residence, census counts that include prisoners are not accurate reflections of population. Moreover, since allocations of various federal funds are often predicated on census count, some rural areas ultimately receive artificially high levels of funding while others (usually the large, inner cities; places where prisons are not usually located but places from which most offenders originate) receive proportionately low levels of funding (Lawrence & Travis, 2004).

Census counts also impact political representation. Rural and other areas that house prisons are able to count prisoners as residents for the purposes of keeping or expanding political representation, but are essentially counting people who cannot vote and do not have a stake in the issues of the community in which they are incarcerated (see the discussion later in this chapter on voter disenfranchisement). Conversely, large, urban centers often lose representation or are minimally redistricted based on census counts that reflect lower numbers of residents. Where rural areas gain political representation as a result of being able to count prisoners as citizens, urban areas are often victims of decreased political representation precisely because they cannot count the large numbers of offenders who technically reside there but are imprisoned elsewhere (Travis, 2005).

War on Drugs

One result of the process of politicizing crime was a concerted political effort to combat a perceived serious crime problem: drugs. Certainly, the social disorder of the 1960s and ensuing increase in drug use (perceived or otherwise) did nothing to temper general beliefs that drugs were a nemesis. Once Richard Nixon dubbed drugs a serious national threat, the call for comprehensive anti-drug policy at the state and federal level was heeded without question (Nixon, 1969). By 1970, Richard Nixon implemented the Comprehensive Drug Abuse Prevention and Control Act. Nixon used this law to justify a full-fledged attack against drug use, drug manufacturing, and drug distribution. A consequence of this act was the creation of the Drug Enforcement Agency (DEA) in 1973 (DEA History, n.d.).

Understandably, the War on Drugs has been identified as having considerable impact on the expansion of prison populations in the United States. There is no question that incarceration rates for several crime categories increased dramatically from 1980 to 2001: murder (201%), sexual assault (361%), robbery (65%), assault (306%), and burglary (66%). However, nothing challenges the 930% increase in incarceration rates for drug crimes during this time (Travis, 2005).

An increase in arrests for drug crimes (from 300 per 100,000 U.S. residents in 1980 to almost 700 per 100,000 U.S. residents in 1996) coupled with more arrests resulting in harsher punishments and longer prison sentences reflected a shift in state and federal drug policy. Prison admissions for drug crimes increased (from two admissions for every 100 drug arrests in 1980 to eight admissions per 100 drug arrests in 1996) as did time served (from under two years in 1980 to over three years in 1996). At the height of the War on Drugs, substantially large numbers of offenders were in prison for drug offenses for exceedingly long periods of time (Travis, 2005).

The War on Drugs resulted in a large number of minorities sentenced to prison for drug-related offenses, largely the result of law enforcement practices that targeted large, urban inner cities and sentencing measures that provide enhanced penalties for drug crimes as part of the get-tough, truth-in-sentencing mantra, not increased criminal activity on the part of people of color (Petersilia, 2005). Research indicates that police tend to be proactive in their management of drug offenses as opposed to other offenses (such as robbery or burglary) due to the fact that they tend to target drug dealing in urban areas because it is more visible (Walker, 2002). Moreover, people of color were more likely to be convicted for crack-related offenses that carry harsher penalties than crimes involving cocaine (Petersilia, 2005). Given that people of color tend to live in large, urban centers where proactive drug enforcement generally takes place, and that in the 1980s and 1990s crack cocaine was the drug of choice for inner-city, minority youth to deal and dabble in, it is no wonder that large numbers of minority offenders were arrested for drug crimes.

Recent data indicates that among Hispanic offenders in federal prison or privately run facilities, 62% are serving time for drug related offenses compared with 42% of black offenders and 40% of white offenders

(Carson, 2022). At the state level, the percentage of black and Hispanic offenders incarcerated for drug crimes has declined in recent years; the percentage among white offenders has remained relatively static (Carson, 2020, Carson 2022; Carson & Sabol, 2012). For example, among incarcerated black offenders at year end 2008, approximately 23% were incarcerated for drug crimes compared with 11% at year-end 2020. Similarly, we see that among Hispanic offenders, 18% were sentenced for drug crimes in 2008 compared with 6% in 2020. These changes may be reflective of softening views on drug laws and policies by politicians and the general public, as evidenced in part by the legalization/decriminalization of cannabis in many states throughout the U.S. Despite this, drug abuse violations still lead in arrests (Drug Policy Alliance, n.d.). In 2019, there were more than 1.5 million arrests for drug violations reported to the FBI's Uniform Crime Report; this is more than any other offense category (Federal Bureau of Investigation, 2019). Moreover, we still find that almost half (47%) of federal offenders are incarcerated for drug related offenses (Carson, 2022).

Economics

Some scholars argue that economic factors encouraged the mass incarceration movement. Proponents of this school of thought argue that crime stems from economic necessity and that only when punishment exceeds poverty will crime decrease (Rusche, 1933/1978). Extending this argument, contemporary scholars contend that the poor do not just pose a criminal threat, they represent the marginal class and are viewed as a social threat that encourages social instability and volatility—acts that undermine the larger social order (Quinney, 1974).

Methods of containing the marginal classes are multi-faceted. Western argues that laws are often created to criminalize behaviors (e.g., vagrancy laws written to criminalize homelessness). He also suggests that the police often monitor the behaviors of citizens in poor, urban communities more frequently and carefully not necessarily because more crime occurs in these areas but because their daily lives play out in public (i.e., in homeless shelters, at food kitchens, etc.) He further argues that judges often mete out harsher sentences to the economically disadvantaged compared with others (Western, 2006).

A study that evaluated the impact of economic marginalization on the rise of mass incarceration found that rapid growth in rates of incarceration is a function of ethnicity and education in addition to the collapse of urban labor markets. Economic inequality targets people of color and results in decreased opportunities for economic advancement for lower-educated black men, and the resulting unemployment and poor wages may have driven these men to crime (Western, 2006). Western (2006) further contends that mass incarceration grew out of a shift from indeterminate to determinate sentencing methods that adversely penalized young, black, uneducated men living in inner cities.

Other research contends that the prison boom was a function of allocations in state spending driven by factors outside economic marginalization. Spelman (2009) suggests that states spend more on prison when violent crime increases and when more offenders are housed in county jails. He is a proponent of the "build it and they will come" philosophy. Spelman argues that prison populations are a function of capacity and funding. "Populations only increase when the beds and the money are available" (Spelman, 2009, p. 55).

When money is available, prison capacity will increase, and when beds are available the system will figure out a way to fill them. The economy of prisons is best understood in light of the dramatic increase in the number of prisons built in the years that coincide with get-tough approaches to managing the crime problem. Data indicate that the number of state prison facilities increased from 600 in the mid-1970s to just over 1,000 by the year 2000 (Lawrence & Travis, 2004). Moreover, prison expansion was pervasive. Prison growth became the hallmark of strategic plans for every state department of corrections. Not only did every state participate in the prison-building binge, they did so with an eye toward expanding the geographic arm of corrections by expanding prison sites to include rural as well as metropolitan areas (Lawrence & Travis, 2004).

In the 1980s, the expansion of prisons throughout the U.S. were furthered by the growth of the modern private prison industry. In lieu of reforms to reduce the prison population, states sought private companies to help house the burgeoning offender population. Corrections Corporations of America (CCA) (currently known as CoreCivic) and Wackenhut (currently known as the GEO Group) led the way for the expansion of for-profit private prisons (Gotsch & Basti, 2018; Harding et al., 2019; Tartaglia, 2014). Since then, private prisons have become a lucrative and growing industry. By 2021, 7% of the state prison population (up 4% from end of year 2020) and 14% of federal prisoners were housed in privately operated facilities (Carson, 2022). By 2018, Core-

Civic was operating in 19 states with 73,000 beds and had an annual revenue of $1.8 billion (CoreCivic, 2018; Harding et al., 2019). In other words, filling beds is profitable.

While efforts to fill prison beds involve increasing prison admissions, other creative attempts to fill prison beds include overcriminalizing crimes already on the books (e.g., taking a misdemeanor and making it a felony punishable by a term of incarceration in state prison) or creating crimes where they did not exist before (Luna, 2005).

Still other innovative approaches to managing the economics of prisons include manipulating prison releases. This includes releasing fewer people, releasing people more slowly, and bringing back to prison people who have already been released (i.e., incarcerating more offenders for parole violations). Offenders returned to prison for violating parole represent an ever-growing segment of the prison population. States admitted approximately 27,000 parole violators to prison in 1980. By 2000, those same states admitted approximately 203,000 parole violators—a sevenfold increase. Put another way, the number of admissions to state prisons for parole violations in 2000 approximates the total number of state prison admissions in 1980 (Travis & Lawrence, 2002). As of 2019, approximately 29% of parolees and 16% of probationers were removed from community supervision to serve a period of incarceration (Oudekerk & Kaeble, 2021).

Building, operating, and populating prisons comes at an extraordinary cost to state and federal budgets. In 2020, state governments allocated $65.9 billion dollars to corrections spending; a 3.9% increase over the prior year. This figure represents a two-year consecutive increase in spending and a significant slice of state budget pies (National Association of State Budget Officers, 2020). One would expect that if prison populations decline so too would correctional budgets. The Vera Institute of Justice examined whether a direct relationship does in fact exist between a state's prison population and their fiscal budget (Mai & Subramanian, 2017). Thirteen of 45 responding states in their survey were able to reduce both their spending and their prison population. Over a period of five years (2010 through 2015), the combined spending among the 13 states was reduced by $1.6 billion and their prison population by 31,090 people. The savings were achieved primarily through the closing of facilities and reduction in employees. Despite concerns of rising crime rates with prison closures, all 13 states noted a decline in crime with the majority seeing a double-digit drop in their crime rates.

Inequality

While the Unites States incarcerates significantly larger numbers of people than other countries, it does so discriminately. As you will see later in more detail, prisons are almost exclusively a minority man's world. Over 90% of the prison population is male, and minority men are incarcerated at rates disproportionate to the larger U.S. population. Recent data indicate that black men had the highest rate of incarceration at 1,807 per 100,000 U.S. residents at year-end 2021, more than double that of Hispanic men (810100,000) and greater than five times the rate of white men (327/100,000) (Carson, 2022). Black males ages 18 to 19 saw the largest differences in imprisonment rates for males by race or Hispanic origin at 381/100,000, 11.6 times the rate for white U.S. residents (33/100,000) (Carson, 2022). This observed inequality is not limited to race. Most incarcerated men of color are un- or under-educated. Over 32% of black men aged 20–40 who were dropouts were also incarcerated in a prison or jail in the year 2000 (Western, 2006). This is in comparison to 6.7% of white and 6% of Hispanic men incarcerated during the same time period. Furthermore, the rate of black men who were not in college, aged 20–40, and incarcerated was 17%, in contrast to 5.5% of Hispanic, and 3.2% of white men (Western, 2006).

When viewing the issue of inequality through a different lens, the differences are even more apparent. In Western's study of punishment and inequality in America, he calculated the likelihood that a man would go to prison by the age of 35. To calculate these lifetime probabilities, Western evaluated two cohorts of white and black men in 1940 and 1960. His findings indicate that white men aged 30–34 from the 1940s cohort were 1.4% more likely to go to prison compared with white men of the same age from the 1960s cohort (2.9%). This is in stark contrast to both cohorts of black men. When calculating the risk of imprisonment for black men, Western found that black men aged 30–34 were 11% more likely to have been imprisoned in 1940 compared with 20.5% of black men of the same age from the 1960s cohort (Western, 2006).

When education is factored into the equation, the results change significantly. Lifetime risks of imprisonment for both the white and black cohorts decreased as educational attainment increased. Both white and black men with some college were less likely to be imprisoned than male high school dropouts. However, disparities by race still remain. White males with some college were 0.7% more likely to be incarcerated compared with 4.9% of black men presenting with some college education. White males who were high school dropouts were 11.2% more likely to be incarcerated in 1960 compared with 58.9% of black male high school dropouts (Western, 2006).

Abnormally high rates of imprisonment and reduced levels of educational attainment translate into high rates of unemployment for black offenders. Western found that the jobless rate for black males who were dropouts but who had not been incarcerated increased from 34% to 49% between 1980 and 2000. When factoring in offenders incarcerated in a prison or jail or out of work, the rate increased from 41% to 65% for the same time period (Western, 2007).

How might imprisonment be responsible for this significant jobless rate? First, there is some agreement amongst researchers that with a criminal record comes stigma that may discourage employers from hiring offenders. Second, incarceration often limits the ability of people to enhance or improve their skills. Lack of access to educational or vocational programming prior to incarceration or while in prison limits access to these opportunities once they leave. Third, incarceration may inhibit offenders' ability to network and find jobs, even menial ones, after release from prison (Travis, 2005; Western, 2007).

In sum, history suggests that there is likely not just one reason why the United States has assumed the dubious distinction of being the mass incarceration nation (Ridgeway, 2010). Changes on multiple fronts including sentencing, politics, and economics created a situation ripe for the taking. Throw in the War on Drugs and inequality (not only with regard to color, but education and employment as well) and it is not surprising that imprisonment has become a way of life for a significant number of people. Whether we wish to acknowledge the reality or not, prisons are social institutions that have and will continue to shape the lives of a considerable number of U.S. citizens both inside prison walls and out (Western, 2007).

Current Trends

The incarceration rate in the United States exceeds that of Western Europe and other democracies (National Research Council, 2014). Over 1.2 million offenders were under state or federal institutional corrections authority at year-end 2021 (Carson, 2022). This equates to an imprisonment rate of 350 per 100,000 US residents, as mentioned above. Since peaking in 2009, there has been a marked decline of 11% in the prison population (federal and state correctional authority) between 2009 and 2019 (Carson, 2020) and a 24% decline between 2011 and 2021(Carson, 2022). Factors such as declining crime rates, changes in prosecutorial and judicial sentencing patterns, and criminal justice reform measures have largely contributed to this reduction (Gramlich, 2018). Moreover, as recidivism rates remained high among released offenders, public sentiment was waning on the use of incarceration and punitive policies in favor of more rehabilitative approaches to addressing crime (Mai & Subramanian, 2017). Despite the changing trends, the pendulum swings slowly; the United States continues to have the highest incarceration rate in the Westernized world (Gramlich, 2018).

Prison Admissions and Releases

In recent years, the number of releases from state prison have surpassed admissions. Despite releases declining by 19% from 2020 to 2021, they still exceeded state prison admissions (Carson, 2022). In 2009 prison releases exceeded prison admissions for the first time in more than three decades (Carson & Golinelli, 2013). As Figure 1-1 indicates, prison releases since 2010 have regularly outpaced the decline in admissions. That is, more offenders have routinely been released from prison than admitted to prison in any given year. By year end 2021, the imprisonment rate fell for the thirteenth consecutive year—down 29% from year end 2011 (Carson, 2020; Carson 2022). The imprisonment rate decline between 2020 and 2021 were for both women and men, as well as across all racial and ethnic groups; black adults declined 4% and imprisonment rates for Hispanic adults decreased by 3% (Carson 2022). In fact, the overall rate of correctional supervision has steadily declined from 2008 to 2020 (Kluckow & Zeng, 2022; Maruschak & Minton, 2020). These changes are reflective of two factors—a decrease in the number of people under correctional supervision and an increase in the number of U.S. residents aged 18 and older (58% and 42% respectively) (Maruschak & Minton, 2020).

Overall, 404,346 offenders were released from state prison year end 2021, a 19% decline from 2020 as noted above (Carson, 2022). Offenders were released one of two ways: conditionally and unconditionally. Approximately 77% of state (312,726) prison releases were post custody conditional releases on community supervision or other requirements (Carson, 2022). Similar to state prisons, the federal prison system reported a decline in prison releases between 2020 and 2021 at 16%. Due to the

Sentencing Reform Act of 1984 eliminating federal parole and requiring the court to impose a term of supervised release following incarceration as part of the initial sentencing, only 144 federal prison releases were reported as conditional (Carson, 2020; Carson, 2022).

Figure 1-1. Number of Sentenced Prisoners Admitted to and Released from State Prison, 2010–2019

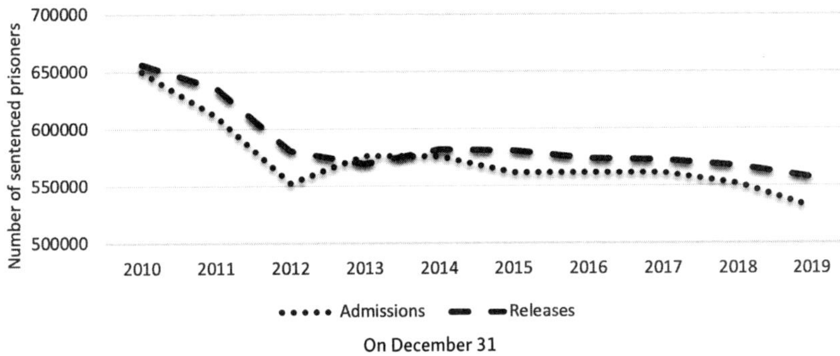

Adapted from Bronson & Carson, 2019; Carson & Sabol, 2012; Carson, 2014; Carson, 2015; Carson, 2018; Carson, 2020.

When we turn our attention to an evaluation of prison populations by crime type, we find that despite the declining average lengths of stay in prison that were observed in the early 2000s, expected lengths of incarceration have been increasing in recent years. Overall, two-thirds of offenders released in 2018 served less than two years in prison, with the average time served of 2.7 years (Kaeble, 2021). Moreover, offenders were serving an average of 44% of their maximum sentence prior to their initial release. When we consider specific offense types, the average length of incarceration for violent offenses has been steadily rising, with state prisoners released in 2018 serving an average stay of 56 months, more than double the average of all other offense type (Kaeble, 2021). This compares with an average stay of 46 months in 2000 and 44 months in 2008 for violent offenses (West et al., 2010). Similarly, property, drug, and public order offenders can expect an additional six months in prison compared with average expected stays in 2008 (21 months and 15 months respectively) (Kaeble, 2021; West et al., 2010).

When considering the number of offenders under some form of community supervision, the numbers are staggering. As of 2019, more than 4.3 million people were on community supervision of some kind (probation or parole) of which close to 3.5 million were on probation (Oudekerk & Kaeble, 2021). While the number of people on community supervision remains extraordinarily high, there has been a steady decline of this population since 2007. By end of year 2018, community supervision was at its lowest since 1998 and down 14% since 2008 (Kaeble & Alper, 2020). As Figures 1-2 and 1-3 show, the probation population has been driving the decline in community supervision (Kaeble & Alper, 2020). The number of people released from probation in 2018 outpaced the number of people being placed on admission for the tenth consecutive year, with a 17% overall reduction in the probation population since 2008. The parole population, on the other hand, rose 6% between 2008 and 2018. During this same time period, there were eight years observed where parole admissions outpaced parole exits (Kaeble & Alper, 2020). Overall, the rate of adult probation fell 25% between 2000 and 2019, while the adult parole rate stayed constant (Ouderkerk & Kaeble, 2021).

Figure 1-2. Adults Under Probation Supervision, 2008–2018

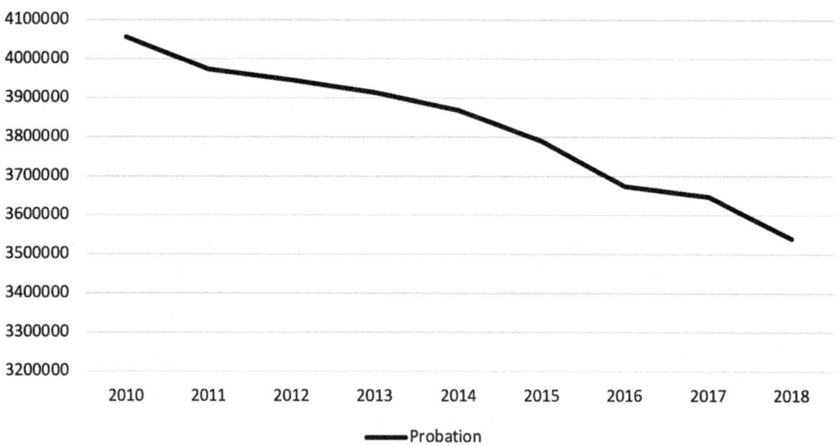

Source: Adapted from Kaeble & Alper, 2020.

The most recent recidivism data available from over 30 states indicates that 83% of offenders were arrested within nine years of release from prison, with approximately 44% arrested at least once during the first year of release (Alper et al., 2018). Over the nine-year follow-up period, released prisoners had an average of five rearrests (Alper et al., 2018). Having extended the standard three-year recidivism follow-up to

Figure 1-3. Adults Under Parole Supervision, 2008–2018

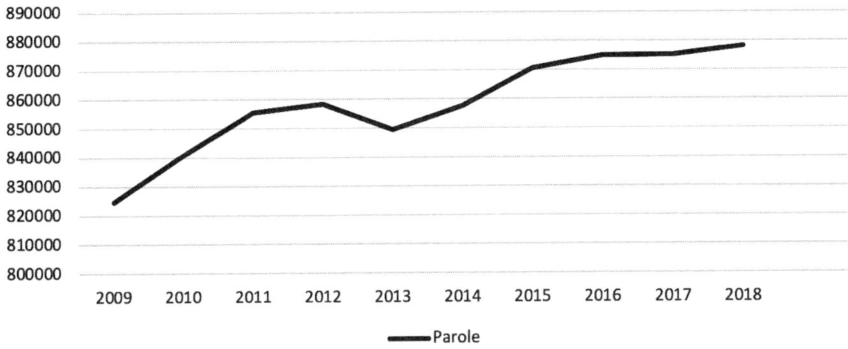

Source: Adapted from Kaeble & Alper, 2020.

nine years, the Bureau of Justice Statistics reported a cumulative increase in arrests of 15 percentage points, from 68% to 83% respectively. There is some variability in this rate of recidivism by crime type as indicated in Figure 1-4. When considering cumulative arrest percentages over the nine year period, property offenders had the highest rates of rearrest at 88%, compared with 84% for drug offenders and 82% for public-order offenders. Violent offenders had the lowest overall rate of rearrest at 79% (Alper et al., 2018).

Offender Characteristics

Figure 1-4. Annual Arrest Percentage of Released State Prisoners by Most Serious Commitment Offense Type, 2005–2014

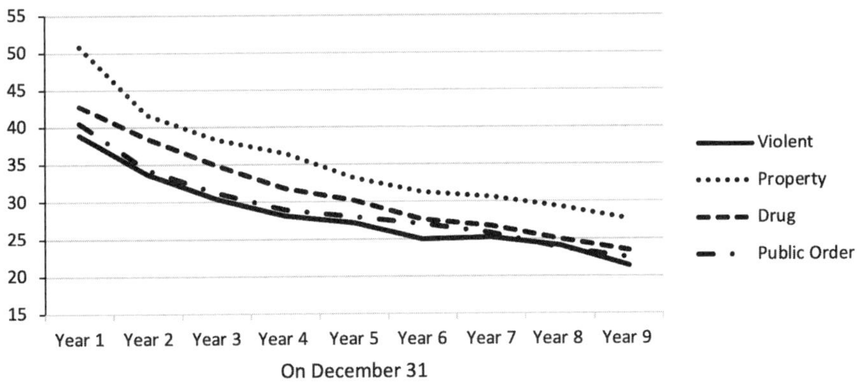

Source: Adapted from Alper, Durose, & Markman, 2018.

The information presented thus far provides us with some general knowledge about prison admissions and releases and the trends we have observed over time. However, these data do little to inform us about who specifically resides in prison and, subsequently, who is likely to be released. The bulk of the information we have regarding characteristics of offenders in prison and soon-to-be-released prisoners comes from the Bureau of Justice Statistics National Inmate Surveys and National Prisoner Statistics Program.

As Table 1-1 indicates, historically, offenders in prison have been predominantly male. While we have always incarcerated female offenders, traditionally they have comprised a very small percentage of the total inmate population. However, between 2000 and 2010, women constituted the fastest growing segment of the prison population, increasing at double the annual rate of male prisoners (1.6% & 0.8% respectively) (Glaze & Kaeble, 2014). Women now represent approximately 7% of the total prison population, up from 4% in 1978 (Carson, 2022). Each year from 2003 to 2019, women represented more than 100,000 prisoners housed in state or federal correctional facilities (Carson, 2022) Moreover, almost half (47%) of incoming prisoners have at least one minor child (Maruschak et al., 2021a).

Race has always been and continues to be a significant issue relative to offender reentry. When we look at parole, approximately 45% of offenders reentering the community are white, while 38% are black, and 15% are Hispanic (Oudederk & Kaeble, 2021). Put another way, a little more than half of offenders leaving prison at any given time are black or Hispanic; however, they only represent 32% of the general U.S. population (United States Census Bureau, 2019). This finding is not unexpected given that the rate of imprisonment among black adults is more than five times greater than that of white adults despite imprisonment rates of black adults decreasing 32% between 2009 to 2019 (Carson, 2020a).

The incarceration of significant numbers of minority offenders poses unique challenges for the communities and families from whence these offenders came. We must consider that plucking large numbers of young, minority men from their communities for the purposes of incarcerating them, only so that they will be released at some point in the future, has consequences. We must also accept that the reasons behind why there is such racial disparity amongst incarcerated offenders are not easily understood (Mauer, 2011; Western, 2006).

Table 1-1. Selected Demographic Characteristics of Offenders

Characteristic	Percentage
Gender	
Male	93
Female	7
Race	
White, non-Hispanic	35
Black, non-Hispanic	37
Hispanic	27
Other	14
Age	
18–24 years of age	8
25–39 years of age	45
40–54 years of age	33
55 and above	16
Most Serious Instant Offense	
Violent	62
Drug	13
Property	14
Public Order	11
Drug abuse/dependence	58
Parents of at least on minor child	47
Mental health	
Any mental health problem	37
Major depression	24
Bipolar	18
Anxiety disorder	12
Post-traumatic stress disorder	13
Personality disorder	13
Schizophrenia/other psychotic disorders	9
Physical health*	
Ever had a chronic health condition	44
HIV/AIDS	1.3
STDs excluding HIV/AIDS	6
Hepatic C	10
Tuberculosis	6

* indicates estimates for state and federal prison populations; all other estimates include state prison populations only.

Adapted from: Bronson et al., 2017; Bronson & Berzofsky, 2017; Carson, 2022; Maruschak et al., 2021a; Maruschak et al., 2015.

When considering the age of offenders, the prison population has been shifting towards an increasingly aging population. Sentence enhancements and other get-tough sentencing legislation have led to longer prison stays without regard to age. Indeed, there was a 31% increase in offenders age 55 and older serving 10 years or more for new court commitments between 1993 and 2013; there was a 10% increase for those offenders age 65 and older (Carson & Sabol, 2016). Moreover, longer sentences were imposed on older offenders convicted of violent offenses compared with younger offenders. By way of example, in 2013 offenders aged 55 and older received an average sentence of 128 months for a new violent offense compared with 100 months for offenders 18 to 39 years of age and 111 months for those aged 40 to 54 (Carson & Sabol, 2016). In the span of 20 years (from 1993 to 2013) we saw the number of offenders aged 55 and older admitted to prison increase by 308% (Carson & Sabol, 2016). According to the most recent available data, 24% of the state and federal incarcerated population is aged 50 or over, with 4% aged 65 and older; an increase from 21% and 3.2% in 2019 (Carson, 2020; Carson, 2022). Overall, older prisoners accounted for the majority of growth (106%) in the prison population between 2003 and 2013 (Carson & Sabol, 2016).

Data regarding the instant offense, or the offense for which offenders were most recently incarcerated, reveals some interesting results. Not surprisingly, violent offenders continue to make up the majority (62% of sentenced prisoners, up 7% from end of year 2018 (Carson, 2020; Carson 2022). In contrast to violent offenders, the estimated percentage of state-sentenced drug offenders has been declining since 2000. Although arrests for drug offenses remain higher than all other offense categories, incarceration rates at the state level have been going down over the past 20 years. Between 2000 and 2010 there was an 8% reduction in state-incarcerated drug offenders, with new court commitments declining 22% between 2006 and 2011(Carson & Golinelli, 2013; Carson & Sabol, 2012). As of end of year 2020, 13% of state prisoners were incarcerated for drug offenses, which was down 1% from 2018 and 19% from 2008 (Carson, 2022; Carson & Sabol, 2012). Although state prison systems have seen declining numbers, drug-involved offenders continue to make up approximately half (47%) of the federal prison population, of which more than 99% are serving time for drug trafficking (Carson, 2020; Carson, 2022).

The decline in state-incarcerated drug offenders over the past two decades may, in part, be a reflection of criminal justice reform measures, including the rapid expansion of problem-solving drug courts beginning in 1989. Drug courts were designed to relieve heavy drug-related court case backlogs while keeping non-violent drug-involved individuals out of the prison system and in the community (Saum et al., 2019). Although few existed in the early years of their development, there are currently more than 3,000 operating drug courts in the U.S., representing one of the fastest growing intervention approaches for substance-involved offenders (National Institute of Justice, 2016; Saum et al., 2019).

Offenders returning home are not first timers. Petersilia indicates that only 22% of state inmates released from prison have not served a prior sentence either as a juvenile, or in jail, on probation, or in prison. Conversely, Petersilia (2005) reports that 46% of state prisoners will have served three or more probation, jail, or prison terms.

Inmates soon to be released from prison are not well educated. Nearly 41% of offenders do not have a high school diploma or a general equivalency diploma (GED). This is in comparison to the general U.S. population, in which 18% of people do not complete the twelfth grade (Harlow, 2003). More revealing is the fact that 17% of offenders preparing to leave prison do so with an eighth-grade education (or less), reducing their likelihood of successful reentry. Indeed, studies suggest that offenders who participate in adult basic education, GED programs, and postsecondary correctional education are less likely to return to the criminal justice system (Cecil et al., 2000; Layton-Mackenzie, 2012).

No doubt, low levels of education further impact the ability of offenders to obtain jobs once released. People who have spotty employment histories prior to incarceration will likely have an even harder time securing employment after release. Petersilia (2005) notes that 33%, or one-third, of state prisoners indicated they were not working in the month before their arrest. Moreover, difficulty finding a job after release is compounded by employers who are reticent to hire ex-offenders at all or who provide a wage penalty when they do (Holzer, 1996). That is, if an employer agrees to hire an offender, they usually do so through offering them lower wages compared with workers who have no previous record of offending. In their examination of labor market outcomes of released prisoners, Looney and Turner (2018) noted that only 55% of ex-prisoners reported any earned income within the first full year of release. Moreover, among those with jobs, their median annual earning was $10,090, with just 20% reporting earnings of more than $15,000.

Research indicates that offenders who are married or who maintain consistent relationships with their families do better (i.e., recidivate less) than their counterparts (Nelson et al., 1999). Yet, data indicate that over 25% of offenders are either divorced or separated. While offenders may not be married, a significant number of them (47% of state offenders and 57% of federal offenders) do present with children or have a sibling or spouse that is also incarcerated (Maruschak et al., 2021a; Petersilia, 2005). Between 1991 and 2007, there was a 79% increase in incarcerated parents, with the number of incarcerated mothers more than doubling in that time (up 131%) (Glaze & Maruschak, 2010). Prison can be and often is a family affair.

In addition, offenders have disproportionately high rates of drug abuse and dependence disorders. The majority (58%) of state prisoners meet the criteria for a substance use disorder compared with 5% of the adult general population (Bronson et al., 2017). Data from the 2004 *Inmate Survey* found that 82% of inmates report having used illegal drugs in their lifetime, with more than two-thirds having used illegal drugs regularly (Belenko et al., 2012). Offenders overwhelmingly report being involved with or using drugs or alcohol at the time of the offense that led to their incarceration. Thirty-nine percent of state-involved offenders reported using drugs in the month prior to their instant offense, and 42% reported drug use at the time of their current offense (Bronson et al., 2017).

Compared with drug and property offenders, violent offenders are less likely to report drug use in the month prior to their arrest or to have committed the crime to get money to obtain drugs (Bronson et al, 2017). It is noteworthy, however, that alcohol is more closely linked to the commission of violent crime than any other illegal drug (National Council on Alcoholism and Drug Dependence, Inc., 2015). Not unexpectedly, 39% of property offenders reported committing their crime to buy drugs with property offenders also being more likely to meet the criteria for drug abuse and dependence (Bronson et al., 2017). Moreover, female offenders have a greater likelihood of being diagnosed with a drug abuse or dependence disorder and are more likely to report drug use in the month prior to their most recent offense compared with their male counterparts (Bronson et al., 2017).

Offenders reentering the community from prison are also likely to be mentally ill. The incidence of significant mental health problems in the offender population is high compared with the general U.S. population. Forty-three percent of state prisoners have a history of a mental health disorder, with 14% reported to have serious psychological distress (SPD) compared with 5% of the general population (Maruschak et al., 2021b). The most common disorder reported by prisoners was major depression (27%) followed by bipolar disorders (18%). An estimated 14% of prisoners had post-traumatic stress disorder, and 11% had a personality disorder. Moreover, the majority (69%) of female state prisoners met the diagnostic threshold for a mental health disorder; this compares with 41% of male prisoners. For many offenders, their mental health conditions are exacerbated by the co-occurrence of a substance use disorder. Research is limited on the prevalence rates of co-occurring disorders (COD); however, the Bureau of Justice Statistics (BJS) estimates 54% of female and 41% of male state prisoners have a COD (these numbers were obtained by extrapolating data from a national survey of state and federal inmates and were not specifically measured in the original survey (James & Glaze, 2006).

Offenders also tend to be less physically healthy compared with the general public. Forty-four percent of prisoners reported having a chronic health condition (e.g., cancer, hypertension, kidney problems) in their lifetime, compared to 31% of persons in the general population (Maruschak et al., 2015). Similar to mental health disorders, female offenders are more likely to experience chronic health problems compared with male offenders. Rates of infection with communicable diseases are also higher in the offender population than in the general population, making the need to address healthcare concerns in prison and upon release a priority (Hammett, 2000). Almost one quarter (21%) of offenders reported having an infectious disease (e.g., tuberculosis, hepatitis B and C, or other sexually transmitted diseases [STDs]) in their lifetime (Maruschak et al., 2015). Prisoners also have higher rates of HIV/AIDS than the general population (1.3% compared with 0.4% respectively). Although alarmingly high, this statistic could be a conservative measure since not all prisons require HIV/AIDS testing on admission. Hepatitis C is the most commonly reported infectious disease (10%) among offenders, with approximately 3% reported to have Hepatitis B. The prevalence of tuberculosis among prisoners is twelve times higher than that of general population estimates (6% compared with .05%, respectively) (Maruschak et al., 2015).

In addition to the disproportionately high prevalence rates of chronic health conditions and infectious diseases among the general offender population, the unprecedented growth of older inmates is placing additional healthcare demands on correctional facilities. Prisoners aged 50 and older are approximately three times more likely to have a chronic health condition or infectious disease than their younger counterparts (Maruschak et al., 2015). The Pennsylvania Department of Corrections (2020–2021) report medication costs are 3.5 times higher for inmates over the age of 50 (average annual medication costs per inmate under age 50 is approximately $1,000 compared with $3,600 for inmates over 50). Departments of correction are estimated to spend $8.1 billion collectively on healthcare services, approximately one-fifth of the overall prison budget expenditures (Pew Charitable Trust, 2017).

Unstable housing is yet another hurdle that affects the offender population both prior to incarceration and on return to the community. National estimates suggest upward of 15% of the prison population experienced homelessness in the year leading up to their incarceration (Couloute, 2018). Those offenders who are mentally ill are more likely than not to be homeless. Indeed, 13% of mentally ill offenders were reported homeless prior to arrest compared with 6% of non-mentally ill offenders (James & Glaze, 2006). It is therefore reasonable to assume that at the time of release, offenders often present with unstable housing opportunities. Parole restrictions, reluctant landlords, and lack of affordable housing make it difficult for returning offenders to find stable housing (Wiltz, 2019). Greater than half (54%) of released prisoners in New York City were released directly to the shelter system in 2017, a 23% increase from 2014 (Coalition for the Homeless, 2018). In the majority of cases, offenders leaving prison return home upon release, whether or not they are welcome. Parole violations and the incidence of rearrest have also been found to be higher for offenders who have poor housing prospects at the time that they are released from prison. Of 49 offenders followed in New York at their time of release from prison, 38% who reported that they did not have stable housing absconded from parole, compared with 5% of offenders who indicated they would not live in a shelter (Nelson et al., 1999).

Prison and Pre-release Programming

Virtually every prison provides some prison programming. Whether it is substance abuse counseling or educational/vocational programming, nearly 97% of all prisons provide some form of prison programming opportunity (Stephan, 2008). Data from the BJS *Inmate Survey* indicate that while most prisons provide some programming, few prisoners participate. Approximately 10% of state or federal inmates report participating in alcohol treatment while only 12% of offenders indicated that they participated in drug treatment of any kind (Petersilia, 2005). Only 25% of inmates admit that they participate in prison-based peer or self-help groups. When evaluating offenders within 12 months of release from prison, the *Inmate Survey* indicates that only 12% of state inmates had participated in a prerelease prison program of any kind (Petersilia, 2005).

Program participation is in large part driven by program capacity. There are fewer prison program opportunities offered today than before. Therefore, prison personnel are forced to prioritize participation in programming, usually based on need. As Petersilia indicates, inmates with the most severe issues report significantly higher rates of treatment and program participation than offenders with moderate problems. Thirty-seven percent of inmates with a high alcohol index score, 40% of inmates with a high drug index score, 63% of offenders with a high mental health needs index, and 52% with a high educational/vocational needs index score received treatment in state facilities in 1997 (Petersilia, 2005).

In one sense, this is good. A significant number of people who have treatment needs are receiving services. However, a closer look at these numbers suggests that while a majority of offenders with mental health and educational/vocational needs are receiving treatment, only between 36–40% of high needs offenders with alcohol and drug problems are being treated. Therefore, nearly half of offenders are not receiving mental health or educational/vocational programming and nearly 60% of offenders are not able to take part in alcohol and drug programming (Petersilia, 2005). Many offenders have co-occurring mental health and substance use disorders requiring an integrated treatment approach to address each disorder simultaneously. However, correctional treatment services are often fragmented in their treatment approach, offering either mental health or substance use services, excluding this large population from receiving needed treatment (Wexler, 2003). Moreover, only three-quarters of correctional facilities provide assistance for continuity of care to the community for the mentally ill nearing release, and less than a quarter of parole agencies have access to specialized mental health programs (Petersilia, 2003).

Despite the clear need for programming for offenders who are soon to return to the community, funding for pre-release programming has been drastically curtailed. At the national level, states have been forced to close large budget deficits by diverting spending from corrections budgets to other state agencies. In many instances, corrections budgets have been slashed or remained flat, as states struggle to provide only the most necessary programs to offenders in prison.

While corrections program budgets are subject to reallocation and reduction due to looming budget deficits, they are also affected by public sentiment and political rhetoric, as well as the belief in the principle of least eligibility: the notion that offenders should not receive services that are not currently available to law-abiding citizens (Petersilia, 2003). Consequently, corrections departments have been forced to carefully balance public sentiment with the pressing need for programs that will even minimally prepare offenders for release. Budgetary concerns aside, the fact remains that fewer opportunities to manage mental health and substance abuse problems and educational/vocational deficits of offenders in prison translates into more people being less prepared to negotiate these same challenges upon release.

Reentry Considerations

The general public has been led to believe the following about the criminal justice system. The system is set up to manage people who break the law. Once a law has been broken, people are adjudicated and sentenced to a variety of sanctions ranging from probation to prison. Those who are sent to prison serve some if not most of their sentence, and then they are released from prison to the community either on parole or upon completion of their sentence, where they are free to reintegrate, reconnect, and pick up with their lives where they left off. Unfortunately, this scenario is far from the truth.

In most instances, prison is merely one component of the punishment process. While a general understanding of punishment has most of us believing that the punishment is the sentence, this is simply not the case. There are a variety of additional restrictions and informal punishments that plague offenders long after they leave prison; these sanctions often preclude offenders from successfully reintegrating into society. These sanctions are often referred to as the collateral consequences of incarceration.

Prisons are clear and visible structural manifestations of society's disdain for people who break the law. Prisons look like mean and nasty places. Yet, there are other ways to punish people, ways that are much more subtle and much less visible than the prison gate. Ironically, these invisible punishments are in some instances more pervasive and injurious in the long term to the people upon whom they are placed than the formal sentence they receive from the court (Travis, 2002).

Collateral consequences or invisible punishments have been around for some time. They are the residual effects of civil death laws that were imported from England and imposed upon criminals during the colonial period (Ewald, 2002). However, contemporary collateral consequences are unique compared with colonial sanctions in that they place a punishment burden on the offender long after their sentence has expired (Pinard, 2010).

What is so unique (and so problematic) about invisible punishments is that they are not a function of a sentence passed down by the judge but are "imposed by operation of law" (Travis, 2002, p. 16). These invisible punishments are sanctions that are applied to offenders as a result of civil law. Collateral consequences of imprisonment civilly disable the offender long after criminal sanctions resulting in physical restraint (prison) have ceased.

Of particular concern is the fact that most offenders have no idea what collateral consequences are and how they may be impacted by these sanctions upon release from prison. This is because these consequences are not customarily discussed or addressed during the criminal court process (Pinard, 2010; Travis, 2002). Unfortunately, information regarding how these invisible punishments work and what these punishments "do" is not openly discussed or universally understood. These punishments are imposed in the shadows but play out in the open and have a firm grip on the ability of an offender to move forward once they return to the free world.

Reliance on collateral consequences as an adjunct to formal punishment is an outgrowth of get-tough sentencing policies and feelings (mostly by lawmakers) that punishment for the crime itself is not long or harsh enough (Travis, 2002). In an effort to increase the severity of punishments without having to restructure sentencing policy, adversely impact already overcrowded prisons, or raise taxes, lawmakers expanded the number and type of collateral consequences of imprisonment as a means to further differentiate between "us" (law-abiding citizens) and "them" (law breakers). This has resulted in the practice of social exclusion of offenders from critical resources and services that assist them in the reintegration process (Tonry & Petersilia, 1999; Travis, 2002).

There seems to be no rhyme or reason behind how lawmakers developed and passed legislation related to collateral consequences. These add-on punishments seem to have been blindly created with little thought to how they would work, who they would impact, and the unintended consequences that would result (Tonry & Petersilia, 1999). Justifications for imposing collateral consequences of any kind generally fall into two categories. One camp claims that people who violate the law are not trustworthy and that they have demonstrated themselves to be liars. As a result, society at-large cannot trust offenders to vote honestly or not bilk the government out of public assistance money they might receive (Thompson, 2008).

The other argument for supporting collateral consequences is grounded in social contract theory. The social contract is a tacit agreement that we all make to live by the laws that have been created to keep us safe. Offenders rationally and willingly break this contract when they engage in criminal activity. As a result, they should not have the ability to take part in activities or receive services in the same way as the rest of us who are law-abiding citizens, even after they have served their time (Thompson, 2008).

Collateral consequences include the following: not allowing offenders to vote, terminating parental rights, using a felony conviction as legal grounds for a divorce, not allowing offenders to ever hold public office or public employment/government jobs, permanently barring offenders from serving on juries or owning a firearm, requiring offenders to register with law enforcement, denial of all federal assistance including food stamps and housing, and inability of offenders to access student loans (LaFollette, 2005; Wheelock, 2005).

> Civil penalties, which, unlike fines, prison time, or probation, are not specified in the criminal law and are rarely mentioned during sentencing. These penalties are imposed not just while a felon is incarcerated or paroled or on probation, but after completion of her sentence—and often permanently (LaFollette, 2005, p. 241).

Voter Disenfranchisement

While a detailed discussion of the panoply of different collateral consequences of imprisonment is beyond the scope of this book, it is important to understand just how devastating application of these invisible punishments can be to offenders attempting to reenter society. To that end, the issue of voter disenfranchisement is discussed in some detail.

The Sentencing Project estimated five million Americans were either currently or permanently unable to vote because of a felony conviction in 2020 (Uggen et al., 2020). Of this number, black individuals were disproportionately impacted, with 1 in 13 black citizens unable to vote. These data are representative of the scope of the problem associated with disallowing people who have been to prison the right to vote. Inhibiting large numbers of people, primarily minority men, from engaging in the fundamental process of voting strips a significant number of people of a basic right of citizenship (Thompson, 2008).

Furthermore, this practice further alienates offenders from engaging in mainstream behaviors. Refusing to allow significant numbers of offenders to vote effectively silences them from having a say in the political process. By virtue of the fact that a disproportionate number of people incarcerated are of minority status and therefore represent a majority of the number of people released from prison, voter disenfranchisement actively reduces the ability of minority groups to participate in the political process (Wheelock, 2005). Exclusion from the political process translates into the belief (and likely reality) that offenders' civic interests are not being properly represented (Thompson, 2008).

No doubt, the inability of large numbers of people (minority or otherwise) to participate in the political process only because they have been incarcerated could and likely has shifted the balance of political power in this nation. "The interaction of incarceration and disenfranchisement can skew the balance of political power within a state between those who have power in the electoral process and those seeking access to the franchise" (Thompson, 2008, p. 136).

Given the tenacity with which lawmakers have expanded and implemented collateral consequences, surely they did this based on support and prodding from the public? Not entirely. Research that assesses public opinion about felony disenfranchisement indicates that the issue is more complicated than it seems. A study by Pinaire and colleagues (2003) indicates that the public is not in favor of policies that permanently limited offenders right to vote. Approximately 82% of respondents rejected the idea that offenders should never be able to vote. Results from a similar study suggest that the public does not agree with giving incarcerated offenders the right to vote, but believes that people on probation and parole should have the ability to vote (Manza et al., 2004). Follow-up polls have found that the public does not understand or see the necessity of restrict the voting rights of offenders (Heumann et al., 2005).

If the public does not condone voter disenfranchisement, offenders don't either. Research evaluating felony offender perceptions of voter disenfranchisement provide interesting insight into a complicated issue. When asked, offenders emphatically disagree with the practice of voter disenfranchisement. It is "the salt in [my] wounds" (Uggen & Manza, 2002, p. 17) notes one female offender; I am but a "fraction of a citizen" indicates another (Cardinale, 2004, p. 7). "You know, to me it seems like they want to penalize you for the rest of your life for a mistake that you've made" (Wahler, 2006, p. 11).

When asked their opinions, other offenders noted that voter disenfranchisement policies are a constant reminder that they are not viewed as full citizens in the eyes of society and that as long as they are not allowed to vote, they will never be able to fully reintegrate into society (Cardinale, 2004; Uggen & Manza, 2002). Moreover, respondents indicate that the inability to vote results in disdain for the political process itself (Cardinale, 2004). Perplexing then is that while research supports the contention that feelings of belonging and engagement in the civic process assist in transforming offenders into pro-social citizens, we promote laws and practice policies that reinforce offenders' feelings of being "less than the average citizen" (Uggen et al., 2004, p. 261).

In the past few years, many states have begun to address the issue of voter disenfranchisement through policy and legislative changes. For example, in 2020, the state of California restored the voting rights of citizens on parole through Proposition 17. Also in 2020, Washington, DC joined Maine and Vermont in allowing convicted felons to vote while incarcerated. Iowa restored voting rights to felons (excluding certain conviction types), and New Jersey now allows persons released from prison with felony convictions and those on probation and parole to vote (National Conference on State Legislatures, 2021). Changes in state disenfranchisement laws along with population growth have led to a small decline in voter disenfranchisement rates since 2016. There was an estimated .15% decline in total disenfranchisement and 1% decline in black disenfranchisement between 2016 and 2020 (Uggen et al., 2020). Although several states are responding to the issue of voting disenfranchisement through legislative changes, there still remains a large number of Americans who are unable to vote.

In July of 2009, the National Conference of Commissioners on Uniform State Laws (NCCUSL) approved model legislation entitled *The Uniform Collateral Consequences of Conviction Act* (Periman, 2011). This act would assist states in uncovering and mitigating due process issues that result in collateral consequences of incarceration and that by extension impact offender reentry. Components of the act require states to identify, collect, and publish all laws regarding collateral consequences, provide notice of collateral consequences in pretrial proceedings and at guilty plea, sentencing, and release, and support a certificate of restoration of rights (Periman, 2011). While this act does not carry the force of law, the mere fact that the NCCUSL, in existence since 1892 with the mission to improve state law and promote uniformity of legislation, voted its passage speaks volumes. In sum, if punishment never ends, if it is meted out long after the offender leaves prison in ways collateral to imprisonment, then successful reintegration is never possible.

Why Reentry, Why Now?

Obviously, offender reentry is a matter of some concern and consequence. First, despite declining rates of incarceration over the last decade, the U.S. still incarcerates more than 1 million adults. This means that we also have more offenders being released each year back to communities that are often ill-quipped to respond to the needs and demands of returning offenders (Hipp et al., 2010a). Essentially, the issue has become one of an economy of scale. Returning offenders are often geographically concentrated in disadvantaged urban neighborhoods with limited resources to meet the needs of its residents, yet alone the vast needs of high numbers of returning offenders (Hipp et al., 2010a; Lynch & Sabol, 2001; Visher & Farrell, 2005). The large numbers of people incarcerated resulting in substantial numbers of people being released from prison to the community at one time is taxing systems and processes to the hilt, not to mention garnering the attention of those who work within the system as well as the attention of politicians and the public.

Second, more than ever, offenders are returning to society after having spent more time in prison without the benefit of institutional programming and pre-release preparation (Travis et al., 2003). Recent research evaluating the Serious and Violent Offender Reentry Initiative indicates that offenders leaving prison do so with high levels of need (Petersilia, 2003; Travis, 2005). A survey of SVORI participants suggests that nearly everyone who responded reported needing at least one of ten transition services: legal assistance, financial assistance, public assistance, health insurance, a mentor, documents for employment, housing, transportation, driver's license, clothes, or food (Lattimore et al., 2010). More people in need of more intense services have created a glut of need and insufficient capacity, a dangerous combination.

Third, the irony is that criminal justice policy often espouses rehabilitation and the need for offenders to leave prison and "go straight," and we attempt to provide services in the prison system to support that notion, but the very system that sends people forth to the community has erected invisible barriers to reentry, making attainment of successful reintegration illusory at best.

Chapter 2

Parole

There are only a handful of ways in which people leave prison. Short of dying there, people will either leave prison early or upon completion of their sentence. Given that the first alternative occurs rather infrequently, most people exiting prison do so either through parole or upon completion of sentence. Parole is generally defined as the conditional release of an offender from prison so that they may serve the remainder of their sentence in the community under supervision. This means that people who apply for and are granted parole leave prison with time remaining on their sentence—time that must be completed in a community setting with the benefit of supervision. Offenders who leave prison upon completion of their sentence do so with no restraints, literally or figuratively.

Historical Context

Parole has been the lynchpin of corrections practice for some time. Yet as correctional practice goes, parole is a chameleon whose purpose and goal has shifted as easily as the trade winds. Alexander Maconochie, a prison warden in Australia in the 1840s, is routinely credited with developing the modern-day idea of parole. In fact, Maconochie was rather radical in his thoughts about how to encourage offenders to behave. Faced with managing a violent offender population on Norfolk Island, an island off the coast of Australia where some of the most difficult prisoners were sent by Britain (when transportation was their primary method of offender management), Maconochie sought to develop a method of prison discipline that would keep the peace and foster offender accountability (Newman, 1963).

This method of prison discipline included stages wherein offenders earned their freedom based on good behavior (Morris, 2002; White, 1976). The marks system allowed offenders to earn credits on a daily basis depending on their behavior and the amount of labor they performed. As offenders demonstrated their ability to engage in good behavior over time, the number of freedoms and privileges they were awarded increased. In essence, the marks system as implemented by Maconochie allowed offenders to move along a continuum from strict imprisonment with no freedoms, to labor, through conditional release, to the point where offenders ultimately earned the ability to gain complete restoration of their liberty (Morris, 2002; Rubin et al., 1963). In this way, offenders controlled their own destiny through hard work and following the rules.

By the mid-1800s, Sir Walter Crofton, a penal reformer in Ireland, expanded Maconochie's practices through the use of the Irish System. Generally thought to have influenced the modern-day corrections classification process, the Irish system was comprised of three levels: strict imprisonment, indeterminate sentence, and ticket-of-leave. Offenders were classified into one of these three categories based on a series of criteria. Over time, offenders earned marks for good conduct. Those offenders who earned ticket-of-leave classification status were allowed to leave the prison and were supervised in the community (Alarid et al., 2008).

In the United States, Zebulon Brockway was the first to experiment with parole at the Elmira Reformatory in New York in 1876. He did so by expanding the use of the Irish system by not only classifying offenders and rewarding them for good conduct, but also by prioritizing them for parole. For those offenders who were paroled, volunteers in the community agreed to supervise the newly released prisoners. The volunteers were required to file written reports that testified to an offender's adjustment in the community, including their work ethic (Abadinsky, 1997). By the mid-1940s, virtually every jurisdiction in the U.S. had adopted some form of what had become known as parole release (Clear & Cole, 2000).

As parole became a fixture on the corrections landscape, a fundamental shift in punishment philosophy took place in the United States. This shift in philosophy, however, did not occur in a vacuum; it was part of a series of larger changes that occurred in American society between 1890 and 1920. Commonly known as the Progressive Era, this period in American history highlights a series of rapid and significant transformations in the areas of industry, professionalism, and social concerns. As a result of this period of unchecked and rapid growth and uncertainty, efforts to control a world seemingly spinning out of control resulted in the rise of unprecedented social control and social regulation (Simon, 1993; Walker, 1998).

Most scholars agree that the Progressive Era sought to better understand and mediate social issues through the use of the social sciences. As more people graduated from college, they became experts or "professionals" in their specific area of study. A professional was a person who acquired a distinct set of skills and was qualified to perform job-specific tasks. The desire for professionalism evolved because people were looking for skill sets to differentiate themselves from others. The Progressive Era is often credited with professionalizing such disciplines as social work, medicine, and law through the creation of professional associations such as the AMA and ABA (Rothman, 1980).

Progressives believed the world to be full of a variety of social problems and injustices (e.g., poverty and crime) that required swift and far-reaching action. The Progressives also believed that government intervention would be necessary and even required in order for sweeping change to occur. It is in this context that people began to transform the way they thought about social issues and began to expect that changes in behavior—criminal or otherwise—would only take place if an individualized approach to reformation and rehabilitation was adopted.

Nowhere is manifestation of the philosophy of reform and rehabilitation more noticeable than in the resultant twentieth-century practice of parole. Modern-day parole was seen as a natural extension of the rehabilitative ideal; a belief that finds its roots in the notion that humans are imperfect beings who make mistakes that can be corrected with assistance. The realization of the rehabilitative ideal came in the form of the medical model and the belief that criminal behavior was the result of environmental and psychological factors (not individual factors) that if diagnosed properly could be "cured." The medical model was designed to individualize the treatment of crime and criminality by using a case management plan that, if followed, could treat bad behavior and restore an offender's health.

An underlying assumption of the medical model was that specialists in the area of crime and punishment would be able to diagnose an offender's problems and develop a plan that would help cure an offender's ills. The primary tools that this specialist would use to accomplish this goal were the indeterminate sentence and parole. The indeterminate sentence would allow an objective board to make decisions about an offender's rehabilitative progress, and parole would provide the mechanism by which the offender could be released from prison prior to completion of sentence.

Parole's legitimacy as a useful correctional tool has been strongly influenced by offender release practices. For the purposes of our discussion, offenders are released from prison through discretionary, mandatory, or unconditional release. Discretionary and mandatory releases are conditional methods of release. That is, discretionary and mandatory release are predicated on the decision of either a parole board or a statute, but in either case result in the release of offenders from prison early so that they may complete their sentence in the community.

Discretionary release is conditional release granted by a parole board after offenders have served some portion of their sentence in prison. This is the most established method of release and has been used since the late 1800s. However, get-tough policies and practices have resulted in a shrinking number of jurisdictions that use discretionary release and have resulted in increased reliance on mandatory release practices.

Jurisdictions that continue to support discretionary release practices have parole systems that establish a timeframe within which an offender is eligible for parole. The primary function of paroling authorities in those jurisdictions is to determine an offender's readiness for release into the community and their likelihood of success once there (Paparozzi & Caplan, 2009). Discretionary release practices emphasize rehabilitation and the management of the offender rather than the offense. Parole eligibility is also usually crime specific. Some offenders are not eligible for release to parole because they have been convicted of a crime for which parole is not an option.

Discretionary release is possible because of the adoption of an indeterminate sentencing structure. Indeterminate sentencing provides the judiciary with the flexibility to sentence a range rather than a fixed period of time (e.g., 15–25 years in prison). This sentencing practice also empowers parole boards with the authority to weigh the risks and benefits associated with releasing an offender early, and then to determine whether or not to release, when, and under what conditions.

Using the example above, offenders who are sentenced under an indeterminate sentencing schema would be minimally eligible for parole after 15 years in prison but would not have to be released then, if at all. The maximum amount of time an offender with a sentence of that kind could serve is 25 years. Parole boards essentially modify the term of sentence by allowing offenders to leave prison early provided that they take part in supervision for a specified period of time (determined as the difference between when an offender is released and the maximum amount of time they are required to serve minus good time and other sentence credits). Not surprisingly, discretion is the hallmark of this method of release.

Almost as soon as jurisdictions began using discretionary release, critics of the process led calls to abolish it. (Turpin-Petrosino, 1999). Criticisms of discretionary release include the belief that the practice often results in prolonged incarceration, that paroling authorities do not always make informed decisions, and that this practice might adversely impact public safety (Kuziemko, 2007; Paparozzi & Caplan, 2009; Rothman, 1980). Further concerns suggest that this practice results in unchecked discretion and sentencing disparity (Sieh, 2005), and that a determinate method of sentencing wherein judges sentence offenders to specific periods of incarceration produces a more rational, equitable, and just system (Turpin-Petrosino, 1999). In addition, the belief that parole and indeterminate sentencing are inhumane, particularly because they are imposed on unwilling participants and because rehabilitation has not been shown to be effective (Glaser, 1969), coupled with public perception of the criminal justice system as too lenient in its management of offenders, are additional concerns that have been lodged against discretionary release practice (Flanagan, 1996; Flanagan & Longmire, 1996; Green & Doble, 2000).

A push to replace discretionary release with a release process less subject to disparate outcomes gained momentum in the 1970s at a time when the merits of rehabilitation were being seriously questioned (Martinson, 1974) and when sentencing inequities and arbitrary and capricious parole release decisions were believed to be undermining the foundations of rehabilitative theory (Cullen & Gilbert, 1982). Data on sentencing practice reflects this shift in sentencing policy. Since 1990, the use of discretionary release in the United States has decreased significantly, from 39% to 24%, while 15 states along with the federal system have replaced discretionary release with mandatory release and either replaced or severely curtailed parole board decision-making (Hughes et al., 2001).

In contrast to discretionary release, a practice designed to ensure that the offender is ready for release, mandatory release is primarily concerned with deterring future crime by punishing the offense. Mandatory release is a means of granting parole after an offender serves her sentence minus any good time credits. In most cases, mandatory release is automatically calculated and generally dictated by statute. The statutes that codify mandatory release usually outline a range of punishment with a mid-range sentence most often selected. Judges who choose a low- or high-range sentence are normally required to identify what mitigating or aggravating circumstances justified the modified sentence (Ireland & Prause, 2005).

Philosophically, mandatory release practices are grounded in principles of just deserts: the idea that punishment should reflect the culpability of the offender and the harm associated with the crime committed, not the offender's rehabilitative prospects (von Hirsch, 1976). Consequently, offenders who are released from prison via mandatory release normally spend a proscribed period of time on parole (sometimes this is crime-dependent) after release from prison. Mandatory release employs little or no discretion and obviates the need for human intervention—from parole boards or anyone else—in the release process. Moreover, and perhaps more importantly, mandatory release does not factor offender readiness for release into the release decision-making process. Mandatory release decisions are driven by statute and little else.

Unconditional release is the act of releasing someone from prison with no supervision. Unconditional release is reserved for those offenders whose sentence expires and who, upon release, are no longer under the auspices of the criminal justice system. Offenders who complete their time and are not paroled are said to "max out" and are released from prison on their "max date." While these offenders reenter as others do, offenders released in this way do not access parole services. This does not mean that these offenders cannot take part in community-based programs to which parolees might avail themselves, it just means that if they do it is because they locate the services themselves as they are not required to do so as a condition of parole. One can surmise that if reentry/parole services are difficult to locate for people on parole who are required to take part in program and treatment, the challenges that offenders who max out face in attempting to access services are considerable.

Current Trends

From the beginning, the purpose of parole has been elusive. Messinger and colleagues (1985) in their work on the foundations of parole in California indicate that parole was utilized for a variety of purposes with no clearly delineated goal. Not only was parole utilized to provide early release to offenders who may have been assigned excessive terms of incarceration, but parole was also utilized as a method of executive clemency.

Other scholars have argued that parole was created as a back-door option to assist in controlling the size of the prison population (Simon, 1993) and that parole was a means by which administrators were able to maintain institutional control and discipline (Bottomley, 1990). Yet these claims are in direct conflict with other work that suggests that parole was part of a broader effort by many states to rehabilitate prisoners (McKelvey, 1977) and that Progressive ideals formed the basis of parole (Rothman, 1980). Ultimately, threads of the rehabilitative ideal and Progressive Era along with other, less altruistic reasoning have defined the function and purpose of parole and have found their way into contemporary parole policy and practice.

Today, the purpose of parole is varied and includes supervision of offenders in the community, rehabilitation of offenders, and public safety (Caplan, 2006; Morgan et al., 1997; Seiter & West, 2003). In some instances, these goals might seem at odds with one another, minimally creating what Caplan describes as a "weak collective consciousness and anomie" (2006, p. 3).

There is no question that parole has had to adapt to changing times. A program or process that may have initially emphasized rehabilitation has, in contemporary times, evolved into something quite different as paroling authorities struggle to maintain their primacy and their very existence. As Messinger and colleagues suggest in their work on California, as times have changed, so too has it become necessary for a "revised justification" of parole (1985, p. 103). While modifications to the function and purpose of parole have occurred as a result of external forces (e.g., changes in sentencing legislation), internal and organizational changes have no doubt also impacted parole policy and practice (e.g., use of technology, reliance on surveillance, specialized caseloads).

Essentially, the lack of a clear purpose for parole has created an environment in which no clear parole identity exists. The absence of a clearly defined goal and purpose of parole has likely impacted parole success, in part because parole has never been adequately defined for either parole officers or the offenders they serve (Caplan, 2006). Consequently, parole outcomes have historically been difficult to measure and assess, and a determination of parole success out of reach. Other scholars suggest that differing goals and purposes of parole have made it difficult for parole to isolate its core values and that this has resulted in parole often being used as a scapegoat when problems (particularly as they relate to public safety) arise (Paparozzi, 2003).

Parole Boards

At the heart of parole lies the parole board, the administrative body responsible for making decisions about whom to release from prison, when, and under what circumstances. Yet, for entities whose decisions wield so much influence, parole boards have received relatively little attention in research and scholarship. The singular lack of attention that has been paid to parole boards has allowed them to function relatively independently and free from oversight and evaluation.

The ability to fly under the radar has in no way diminished the ability of parole boards to escape criticism (Petersilia, 1999; Turpin-Petrosino, 1999). In fact, almost as soon as they were created, parole boards became the subject of intense derision. The complaints against these powerful administrative boards have been profuse. Rhine (1996) argues that indeterminate sentencing and the rehabilitative ideal provided parole with legitimacy that manifested itself in the formation of parole boards that became self-described "experts" in behavioral change and rehabilitation, despite having no real qualifications in those areas. Others contend that parole board members are selected based on political patronage and that professional qualifications of parole board members are important, but are not generally considered when people are appointed to parole board positions. At the crux of this discussion is the belief that, "parole boards have enjoyed unfettered power to make vital decisions without procedural considerations of due process and without independent review" (Bixby, 1970, p. 27).

Parole Board members are appointed by governors for fixed terms of office, (usually staggered), and have the ability to modify judicial orders (i.e., sentences) even though they have no judicial authority (Clear & Cole, 2000; Gottfredson & Gottfredson, 1988). Moreover, as offenders have no constitutional right to parole (i.e., it is a privilege, not a right), parole board members have the ability to exercise unregulated discretionary authority when making parole release decisions (Bonham et al., 1986; Del Carmen & Louis, 1988; Parsons-Lewis, 1972). In addition, parole boards also have additional authority to establish, change, or rescind parole dates, issue warrants and subpoenas, set conditions of parole, restore the civil rights of offenders, and grant final parole discharge (Petersilia, 1999).

Understandably, the unique position held by parole boards makes them particularly vulnerable to criticism regarding their inherent use of discretion and their decision-making process. The use of discretion is an issue raised by both supporters and detractors of parole boards as a means to either justify their existence or discredit them. The primary argument in favor of parole board discretion is that these administrative bodies are in the best position to make decisions about the release potential of an offender precisely because they are an objective entity that was not involved in sentencing and is not currently involved in managing the offender in prison.

The argument against parole board discretion is the belief that the level of discretion that the board possesses is unprecedented and dangerous. "No other part of the criminal justice system concentrates such power in the hands of so few" (Rhine(a) et al., 1991). Detractors also believe that parole decisions are made on fairly subjective grounds, therefore increasing the possibility of bias in decision-making (Pogrebin et al., 1986). In fact, a study by Hawkins (1972) notes that very little consistency exists between the stated criteria used for parole board decision-making and their actual behavior. This is particularly problematic in light of *Greenholtz v. Nebraska* (1979) and *Board of Pardons v. Allen* (1987) that despite their being no constitutional right to parole, states may create a protected liberty interest wherein offenders may be entitled to parole if they meet certain conditions. If states create a presumption that offenders who meet specific requirements will be paroled, this raises the question of how parole decisions can (and do) remain arbitrary.

Turpin-Petrosino (1999) explored this very question in her work on parole board decision-making in a presumptive parole state. The study suggests that the rise of presumptive parole legislation at the state level after the passage of *Greenholtz v. Nebraska* (1979) and *Board of Pardons v. Allen* (1987) was specifically devised to limit discretion in the parole decision-making process. With the passage of presumptive parole policy, states pushed the burden of proof of parole suitability from the offender to the parole board, making it more difficult for states to arbitrarily refuse parole (Turpin-Petrosino, 1999). However, results of this particular study indicate that despite the efforts of one state, parole board decision-making behavior was not modified significantly with the implementation of presumptive parole policy. Instead, there was, "bureaucratic resistance in forgoing discretionary decision making for a restricted formula approach" (Turpin-Petrosino, 1999, p. 329). Given the extraordinary use of discretion by parole board members, it is no wonder that parole boards possess extraordinary power. This power is nowhere more evident than in the parole decision-making process.

Research indicates that the primary factors considered during the parole release decision-making process include institutional behavior, crime severity, criminal history, incarceration length, mental illness, and victim input. Carroll and Burke (1990) in their work on factors in parole decision-making evaluated case information provided to board members when deciding parole release. Results of their work indicate that institutional factors were the single greatest predictor of parole release. These authors found that institutional conduct, sentence length, and prison program participation along with past criminal record were the best predictors of future criminal conduct (Carroll & Burke, 1990). West and colleagues (2000) sought to expand the work on the relationship between institutional factors and parole release by interviewing offenders who were parole eligible, but who had been denied parole. Results from this study further confirmed the work by Carroll and Burke (1990) indicating that while offenders believed institutional factors and program participation were critical for parole release, only misbehavior and noncompliance were critical factors in parole denial. Recent research further supports the importance of institutional conduct in parole decision-making, reporting that inmates charged with infractions in the year preceding their parole hearing were 92% less likely of being paroled (Houser et al., 2019a). Moreover, noncompliance with institutional programs was strongly related to parole denial, whereas successful completion of programs tripled and participating in antiviolence programming nearly tripled the likelihood of being granted parole.

Where Carroll and Burke's work touched on the importance of sentence length as a primary factor in the parole decision-making process, work by Turpin-Petrosino (1999) explored crime severity and crime type as a mitigating release factor. Results from this study on the implementation of presumptive parole policy in New Jersey suggested that the crime type for which an offender was originally incarcerated was the single greatest predictor of parole release. Nonviolent offenders were more likely to be released to parole than offenders who presented with violent or sexual crimes (Turpin-Petrosino, 1999). A recent study by Vilcica (2018) also reported the nature of the original offense to be a significant predictor of parole release. The researcher suggested that the parole board is

> averse to granting release to inmates serving sentences for offenses generally regarded as heinous crimes, regardless of anything else that may help assess those inmates' readiness for reentry into society (e.g., successful institutional programming and behavior). If a person is in prison for a sex offense, there seems to be little that he or she can do to improve the likelihood of gaining release. (Vilcica, 2018, p. 1372)

While Vilcica's (2018) research did not find length of time served to be predictive of parole decisions, she did find that inmates must experience at least one parole denial to increase their likelihood of future release. This finding, as the researcher notes, suggests that parole boards use the parole process in a punitive manner.

When considering the impact of mental health on parole decision-making the research is limited and mixed. Several studies suggest that offenders who present to the parole board with histories or evidence of mental illness are less likely to be released than those who do not (Caplan, 2007; Feder, 1994; Hannah-Moffat, 2004). Other research, however, suggests that mental health status is not associated with the likelihood of being paroled (Houser et al., 2019a; Matejkowski et al., 2011). In a recent study examining more than 1,000 parole decisions over a period of four months, researchers suggested mental health status on parole decision-making may be indirectly associated with risk assessment instruments used by parole boards (Houser et al., 2019a). Along with being more likely to have risk factors unique to their mental health disorder, the mentally ill often have significantly more general risk factors for recidivism compared with non-mentally ill inmates (Houser et al., 2019a; Skeem et al., 2014). Therefore, the mentally ill tend to perform poorly on general criminal justice risk assessments used by parole boards, suggesting an indirect effect of mental health in parole decision-making (Carrol et al., 1982). In other words, parole boards appear to adhere to official policy guidelines of risk assessment rather than using subjective assessments that mental health disorders should negate parole release.

Offenders who receive recommendations from institutional parole officers and departments of correction are significantly more likely to be paroled (Houser et al., 2019a; Morgan & Smith, 2005). Houser and colleagues (2019a) noted that a favorable recommendation from the department of corrections almost tripled the likelihood of release. While race does not seem to play a role in whether an offender is granted or denied parole (Anwar & Fang, 2015; Mechoulan & Sahugue, 2015; Morgan & Smith, 2005), age does appear to be a significant predictor. Recent studies found inmates over the age of 35 were significantly less likely to be paroled (Houser et al., 2019a; Vilcica, 2018).

Victim input has also been evaluated as a factor that may impact the parole release decision-making process. Work by Parsonage and colleagues (1994) indicated that victim statements did have a statistically significant impact on parole decisions when other institutional factors were controlled for. Adding to the work of Parsonage and colleagues, Morgan and Smith (2005) found the greater the amount of victim input, whether by written statement or oral allocution, the more likely parole will be denied (assuming the input was opposed to parole). This is in stark contrast to more recent work by Caplan (2010) that indicates that victim input was not a statistically significant predictor of parole release.

There is some empirical evidence to support the idea that extra-legal or institutional, political, and economic factors—variables not directly tied to the offender or the offense—significantly impact the parole decision-making process (Morgan & Smith, 2008). This body of research supports the contention that organizational and administrative concerns (often driven by economic factors) do impact who is paroled and at what rate (DeGostin & Hoffman, 1974; Pogrebin et al., 1986).

Simon (1993) argues that transformations to parole policy and practice can be linked to shifts in emphasis away from rehabilitation to a more surveillance-oriented approach, and that these changes are in large part related to political and economic developments at the time. In essence, the rehabilitative ideal was usurped by more management-oriented concerns that gave rise to alterations in parole release decision-making and practice (Simon, 1993).

In an effort to mediate some of the problems associated with the broad use of discretion in the parole decision-making process, there has been a push for a more structured approach to parole decision-making. The purpose of the structured decision-making process is to provide more rational and consistent parole decisions; allowing the use of discretion when necessary, but providing some fixed parameters within which parole board members must operate (Hoffman & DeGostin, 1974). Structured guidelines of this type were adopted by the federal parole system in the 1970s.

At the state level, Runda and colleagues (1994) found that it wasn't structured guidelines, but the professionalism of parole board members that impacted decision-making. Runda and colleagues (1994) suggest that as parole boards have become more professional (e.g., their credentials rather than politics were considered for appointment) a greater degree of standardization of policy and practice (e.g., a decrease in the amount of discretion) is evident. Paparozzi and Caplan (2009) argue that the professionalism of the parole board should be taken into consideration when evaluating the parole decision-making process. In fact, Paparozzi and Caplan note that,

> There has been no documented discussion or literature on the makeup of paroling authorities on matters such as credential requirements, work experience requirements, training requirements, the manner in which members of paroling authorities are appointed to their positions, or the ability of paroling authority members to lead and administer a criminal justice system component that potentially affects the lives and well-being of virtually all citizens. (2009, p. 402)

While there is a paucity of scholarly information regarding the credentials of such an important decision-making body, it is widely known within the profession that parole board members present with widely varied educational and professional backgrounds; some have no knowledge of criminal justice and/or the behavioral sciences (Sieh, 2005). That some parole board members have no experience or understanding of social behavioral issues is somewhat disturbing given that one of the parole board's primary responsibilities is to ensure that an offender's release from prison will not jeopardize the safety of the general public (Paparozzi & Caplan, 2009; Runda et al., 1994).

Given that many parole board members are appointed rather than elected, it is not a stretch to say that politics plays an important role in the parole process, oftentimes to the exclusion of professionalism (Burke, 1995; Petersilia, 2003). Parole board opinions may be swayed by political influence. Parole decision-making is often less a function of board qualifications or determination of specific offender risk factors and more an administrative response to policies, practices, and prison capacity (Luthar, 1995; Paparozzi & Caplan, 2009). Moreover, responses to administrative issues are oftentimes reactive rather than proactive and predicated on political considerations rather than fact or need (Wilson & Royo Maxwell, 2005).

Yet, Paparozzi and Guy argue that parole boards are perfectly aligned with the criminal justice system to display leadership, provide advocacy, and inform current corrections policy if they so desire (Paparozzi & Guy, 2009). Parole boards can and should redefine their mission and impact by being proactive, engaging participants in the parole process, rather than making release decisions based on less-than-optimal information. Parole board members can be gatekeepers to the reentry process, rather than merely unilateral decision-makers (Paparozzi & Guy, 2009).

Parole Officers

Talk of parole cannot occur in a vacuum. That is, one must not only consider the people who make the parole release decisions, but also the people—the parole officers—who actively make parole "work." Parole officers wear a multitude of "hats": cheerleader, social worker, parent, authoritarian, and taskmaster. Research on parole officers is prolific, but somewhat disjointed, and can generally be grouped into categories that address role conflict/adaptation, burnout/stress, use of discretion, officer supervision styles, caseload/workload size, contact standards, and the use of weapons.

Role Conflict/Adaptation

Sigler (1988) in his work on role conflict in probation and parole indicates that role conflict and role adaptation are different. Role conflict occurs when different people may hold different expectations for a role or set of roles performed by an individual or when a person may be required to play several different roles simultaneously. Role adaptation occurs when a person is expected to adopt or vacillate between two or more different behaviors in a single context (Sigler, 1988). Interestingly, Sigler found that officers likely adapt to different roles to reduce role conflict and that those officers who are unable to adapt accordingly, more often than not, leave the profession (Sigler, 1988).

The majority of the research on officer role adaptation locates the discussion about parole officers in the context of a social work–surveillance dichotomy (Seiter & West, 2003). Work done by West and Seiter (2004) found that while officers spend more time engaging in activities that are considered casework, they perceive themselves as being surveillance oriented. Other research confirms the ongoing struggle that officers seem to have in reconciling treatment-oriented approaches to supervision with control- or surveillance-based methods of supervision (Fulton et al., 1997).

This conflict has also been established in Clear and Latessa's work wherein they established two sometimes diametrically opposing functions of parole officers: to enforce the law and to help the offender (Clear & Latessa, 1993). Still other work has suggested that officers vacillate between the two roles of caseworker and supervision officer by adapting their behaviors to fit the particular situation at hand. McCleary (1975) contends that officers will often change their role orientation and adapt their focus based upon an offender's behavior and a specific situation. Dembo (1972), on the other hand, found that officers with a greater propensity to punish were often more likely to take formal action against technical violations and propose prison time. Evidently, there is some support for the idea that officer role/job orientation directly affects officer behavior on the job and offender outcomes in the community (Dembo, 1972).

Of course, those of us on the outside looking in are certain that role adaptation must be bad. This may not be the case. Clear and Latessa (1993) explored this idea in their work on probation officers and found that it is possible, to some extent, to reconcile the two seemingly opposing roles of "social worker" and "law enforcer" but that organizational factors such as agency philosophy and job assignments may be directly related to the extent to which officers are able to carry out multiple job roles.

This position is further supported by work from Lynch (1998), who in her discussion on parole officer identity argues that parole officers are uniquely situated between the push to socialize and train based on the organizational mission and vision of a paroling agency and the pull of broader social norms and needs. While organizational dicta may govern practice, those policies and practices must be interpreted and implemented by staff. Therefore, officer orientation is a blend of organizational demand and individual officer preference.

> In the end, they [parole officers] shape their role within the constraints of management demands, legal requirements, and implicit public demands in such a manner that they have their own vision of who they are and what they should do as parole agents. (Lynch, 1998, p. 854)

Furthermore, Lynch (1998) notes that differing views and perceptions between management and line staff further cloud officers' abilities to establish clear role identities. When management and staff view problems, solutions, and organizational missions and visions differently, role confusion and diffusion are bound to occur. This author also found support for this position in work on parole officer and administrator attitudes (Schlager, 2008). A lack of consistency in attitude and orientation between line staff and management creates instability and confusion; these problems will impact how an officer interacts with offenders as well as offender outcome (Schlager, 2008).

Several other scholars have addressed bureaucratic agency dynamics and the potential impact they have on job perception and job function. When perception of agency goals and purpose differed significantly from individual officer ideology, feelings of anomie and stress were high. Research by Donnellan and Moore (1979) indicate that altruistic goals are generally the reason why people become a parole officer, but over time, these goals are often hard to reconcile due to the "disconnect" that often exists between practice and initial job perception. Furthermore, the initial goals and orientation of people new to working in parole are significantly influenced by their goals, attitudes, and belief systems as well as bureaucracy and agency policies and practices that, over time, can and sometimes do alter role orientations (Donnellan & Moore, 1979).

Burnout/Stress

Given the confusion surrounding role conflict/adaptation in parole it is not unreasonable to expect some measure of job burnout or apathy in the job. Burnout in this context has been defined as, "a syndrome of emotional exhaustion and cynicism that occurs frequently among individuals who do 'people work' of some kind" and likely impacts officer attitudes about the clients they serve, the job they do, and the organization within which they work (Maslach & Jackson, 1981, p. 99). Moreover, the push and pull that Lynch (1998) describes likely extends past external variables (i.e., organization and society) to internal conflicts within organizations that make performing the job of parole officer very stressful.

Stress and job burnout has been associated with departmental size. Larger paroling agencies tend to have more difficulty clarifying organizational goals, thereby creating a work environment where officers feel judged not by the quality of the work they do, but the quantity they produce (Seiter & West, 2003). Murky organizational goals, coupled with job responsibilities that are not clearly defined, can create an environment where officers feel forced to define their own jobs because it has not been done for them (Seiter & West, 2003). Furthermore, stress in the workplace, especially for parole officers, manifests itself in individual-level stressors associated with interactions between offenders and staff as well as organizational stressors related to trying to fulfill the obligations and requirements of the job (Finn & Kuck, 2003).

A study by Whitehead (1985) on burnout extended the definition of burnout established by Maslach and Jackson (1981) to suggest that burnout is, "a failure to cope successfully with the chronic stress of client contact" (p. 95). In this context, Whitehead (1985) found a curvilinear relationship between feelings of depersonalization and burnout. Officers on the job for six months or less presented with the lowest burnout scores, while officers on the job three years or more expressed the highest burnout scores. Interestingly, the most experienced officers (e.g., those with 15 years or more of experience) indicated burnout scores as low as those on the job six months or less.

Stress, burnout, and general confusion regarding job roles and orientation can take their toll on officer attitude. Taxman (2002) alludes to the importance of attitude when she discusses deportment, and this author suggests in her work on officer attitudes about community corrections that, "underlying attitudes and orientations that officers have about where they work, how they view supervision, and who they serve may be intrinsically tied to issues of deportment (i.e., how they interact with offenders) and ultimately supervision outcome" (Schlager, 2008, p. 275).

The way in which parole officers interact with offenders is as much about the attitude they have about crime and criminality as how they feel about their jobs. By and large, parole officers do not feel appreciated and respected for the work that they do. These feelings of organizational anomie (Caplan, 2010) can only impact officer attitudes about their jobs as well as their job performance (McCleary, 1975; Lawrence and Travis, 1984). In turn, attitudes about the job and the role orientation they adopt may be just as responsible for influencing offender outcome as actual offender performance (McCleary, 1975; Schlager, 2008).

Discretion

Where role orientation influences attitude, attitude and orientation toward the job can and does impact how and in what ways officers utilize discretion. Yet, other factors may have bearing on the extent to which officers utilize discretion including a paroling agency's philosophical orientation (rehabilitation v. surveillance), laws, and formal organizational policies and practices (Jones & Kerbs, 2007). In general, the administration of justice relies on a set of independent decisions made by individual actors throughout the course of the criminal justice process. Parole is no exception. The argument supporting the use of discretion in parole practice is similar to that used for promoting the use of discretion in parole decision-making. An environment that provides officers with the flexibility to make decisions predicated on the individual needs of the offender is one that will foster rehabilitation of the offender and enhance public safety (Barklage et al., 2006).

On the other hand, arguments against the wholesale use of discretion by officers include the position that discretion, when not limited in some way, will result in great discrepancies in the interpretation and administration of justice, not to mention agency policy and procedure. Too much discretion can result in differing methods of parole practice (i.e., supervision) that make assessing the efficacy of these practices difficult, if not impossible (Jones & Kerbs, 2007). Furthermore, in his study on structural variables and how they constrain parole officers' use of discretion, McCleary notes that inconsistent, differing, and sometimes counter-productive management by supervisors instills limits on the ability of officers to appropriately manage offenders and creates opportunities for officers to co-opt discretion. "In short, the PO often does what he *has* to do, not what he *wants* to do" (1975, p. 210).

Officer Supervision Styles

The work on officer supervision styles is an extension of much of the research on role conflict/role adaptation, research that locates the job of the parole officer within a casework/social work-surveillance continuum. Casework is generally defined as supervision that places an emphasis on assisting offenders with problems, counseling, and the brokering of services. Surveillance, on the other hand, is a supervision style that emphasizes monitoring and compliance with the conditions of supervision and detecting violations.

The research on officer supervision styles plays an increasingly important role in the conversation regarding the purpose of parole. If the purpose of parole is rehabilitation, then many would argue that casework should be the focus of parole practice. However, if enforcing the conditions of parole and monitoring behavior is the priority, then surveillance-oriented methods of supervision should be promoted. Yet, what is apparent is that neither casework nor surveillance alone results in "successful" supervision (Petersilia, 1999). An approach to supervision that has shown some promise in empirical studies is a balanced approach to supervision—one that integrates components of both casework and surveillance into the supervision process (MacKenzie, 2000).

But, the agency mission and vision, its philosophy, is what sets the tone for the officers who work there. If a parole organization emphasizes a casework or surveillance or integrated supervision approach to the handling of offenders, then those are the tasks that officers will perform. West and Seiter (2004) reinforce the contention that casework and surveillance function more along a continuum, than operate as a dichotomy. West and Sieter (2004) evaluated officer supervision styles by asking officers to self-report how they spent time on their jobs. Generally, women spent more time on casework than men, but in all cases, both men and women engaged in both casework and surveillance-type job activities. Moreover, in all cases, both men and women recognized the need for surveillance as well as casework in the supervision process (West & Seiter, 2004).

Other work by Seiter (2002) supports the findings of West and Seiter (2004). Seiter (2002) found that officers view the most important component of their job as close monitoring of offender behavior and brokering services or referring offenders to community providers for assistance. Moreover, Seiter indicates that officers believe that the shift in agency philosophy from casework to surveillance is part of a larger shift in correctional policy that is the result of increased numbers of people in prison and other get-tough sentencing policies (Seiter, 2002).

Caseload/Workload Allocations

The "right" caseload size is one of the most elusive numbers and best kept secrets in parole. Historically, while a casework style of parole has placed an emphasis on helping offenders with problems and brokering services, the surveillance approach to supervision emphasizes monitoring and compliance (Seiter, 2002). As jurisdictions have begun to focus more closely on surveillance and other compliance efforts, the size of the caseload has become a bone of contention. Petersilia notes that caseload sizes in the 1970s were usually set at 45 parolees per officer, but that by 2002, parole caseloads of 70 or more were common (Petersilia, 2000). In the early 1990s, some caseloads in California reached 500 per officer (Beto et al., 2000). Caseloads of that size mean that there is only limited time to work with offenders. Not surprisingly, monitoring and surveillance-oriented supervision are the norm in these instances and manifest themselves in the practice of urine testing, perfunctory questions, and minimal offender–officer interaction (Seiter & West, 2003).

Logic follows that the larger the caseload, the more difficult it is for an officer to provide a high-quality, high level of individualized service. Increased reliance on and enforcement of compliance-driven methods of supervision (e.g., drug monitoring) results in officers who have less time to devote to meaningful case management and who must spend their time monitoring offenders and enforcing rules in order to do their jobs at all.

Many believe that finding the right caseload size is the panacea to many of the problems within community corrections. In 2006, in an effort to evaluate caseload size, the Manhattan Borough president surveyed parole officers working in Manhattan and the Bronx. Results from the survey indicated that 89% of officers characterized their caseloads as being too high, that 87% of officers believed they were supervising too many parolees, and that 93% of officers did not believe they had enough time to devote to the needs of the parolees they served (Stringer, 2006).

The basic premise is understandable. Theoretically, smaller caseloads would allow more time for officers to properly manage/supervise offenders. Yet, several studies have illustrated that caseload size—in and of itself—does not and will not significantly alter offender outcomes. Clear and Hardyman (1990) in their work on intensive supervision note that closer supervision results in reduced caseload size and does not always achieve greater success. Work by Latessa and colleagues (1998) found that offenders that were supervised in smaller caseloads than average had similar arrest rates to offenders on average caseloads (75+).

How can this be? In many instances, researchers and practitioners interchange the concepts of caseload and workload, a distinction that is very important. A caseload is comprised of the total number of offenders supervised by any given officer. Caseloads can rise or fall depending on the number of offenders on parole and the number of officers available to supervise. Workload, on the other hand, is the amount of time that an officer must commit to managing each offender on a caseload. As with caseloads, workloads may vary significantly depending on the needs and requirements of each offender (DeMichele & Payne, 2007).

There are only a finite number of hours in a day, days in a week, and weeks in a year that are available for officers to work with offenders. Therefore, if officers provide the same level of service to all offenders, a "one-size-fits-all" approach will result in a standardized method of offender management that does not consider individual needs and minimizes the amount of time that an officer has to spend with any client on their caseload. In fact, this approach enforces and even promotes surveillance-style supervision and results in a "piling up of sanctions" that supports punitive supervision (Lucken, 1997, p. 367).

A caseload-based approach to parole supervision and offender management flies in the face of risk/needs-based literature that argues that offenders who are treated and who participate in programming predicated on risk have better outcomes than those who receive case management and treatment regardless of risk. Moreover, supervision that ignores the management of criminogenic needs is not successful because it is not expressly working to reduce risk (Schlager & Pacheco, 2011).

A study by Taxman and colleagues indicates that reduced caseload size coupled with supervision strategies that support evidence-based practice can be effective (Taxman et al., 2006). Their work evaluated Maryland's Proactive Community Supervision (PCS) program. In this study, moderate- and high-risk probationers and parolees (as determined by risk/needs assessment) were supervised in reduced caseloads of 55 compared with the agency norm of 100 cases/officer. The evaluation was comprised of 274 randomly selected cases for PCS matched with 274 cases supervised using traditional methods (non-PCS).

Results indicated that offenders assigned to the PCS caseload had significantly lower rearrest rates (32.1% for PCS vs. 40.9% for non-PCS) and significantly lower rates of technical violations (20.1% for PCS vs. 29.2% for non-PCS). Moreover, the PCS offenders presented with a 38% lower chance of being rearrested or being charged with a technical violation, when compared with the non-PCS offenders (Taxman et al., 2006). Not only does the Maryland study consider caseload size but it also considers workload requirement and does so utilizing risk/needs-based approaches to supervision and case management. In this way, caseload sizes were reduced, workload was better distributed, and improved offender outcomes were achieved.

Similar to Maryland's PCS program, the specialized needs caseload model uses an approach that limits caseload sizes and groups offenders based on similar criminogenic risks and needs in one caseload (e.g., mentally ill and/or drug- and alcohol-addicted offenders, gang members, and sex offenders) (Burrell, 2005). Officers are specially trained to respond to specific high-risk/need populations using comprehensive, collaborative, and targeted treatment approaches. While specialized needs caseloads are relatively commonplace in agencies throughout the U.S., there is a paucity of research on their effectiveness; findings, however, have been generally favorable (see Lurigio et al., 2012; Wolf et al., 2014). Although considered an effective management approach for high-risk and high-need parolee populations, smaller caseloads, specialty training, and additional treatment services stretch already limited resources, making it difficult for some agencies to employ this management strategy (Burrell, 2005).

Comparing supervision approaches of specially trained officers (STO) working with seriously mentally ill parolees and probationers to officers without special training, Matejkowski and colleagues (2015) found STOs were more likely to be familiar with risk/need and recovery-oriented mental health approaches. Moreover, STOs voiced a stronger belief in the effectiveness of comprehensive treatment approaches, including the effectiveness of mental health treatment (Matejowski et al., 2015). However, in an unexpected finding, almost half of STOs believed the threat of a technical violation was more effective than personal motivation in getting mentally ill offenders to engage in services, suggesting a more confrontational than rehabilitative approach.

Contact Standards

Contact standards are another topic of intense discussion and are an extension of the discussion surrounding the shift from casework to surveillance. Contact standards are surveillance-related, "countable" items that provide a means by which officers are able to tangibly monitor whether or not an offender is complying with supervision. Those facets of supervision that are often defined as contacts are the number of times an offender sees their officer. Other types of contacts can include collateral contacts (e.g., contact with family, treatment providers, employers). Contacts are generally considered to be a very important component of supervision precisely because they are countable and because theoretically it is assumed that the more contacts an officer has with an offender, the more closely they are supervising the offender. Unfortunately, studies that have evaluated the efficacy of increased contacts on supervision outcome have found that the number of contacts did not result in reductions in recidivism (Gottfredson & Gottfredson, 1985; MacKenzie, 2000; Petersilia, 1998; Petersilia & Turner, 1993). Instead, more contacts resulted in closer surveillance that in turn revealed more technical violations (Seiter, 2002). As noted above, these same evaluations also concluded that smaller caseloads were not, in and of themselves, responsible for reductions in recidivism.

Weapons

The appearance of weapons on the community corrections landscape has also been tied to the shift in emphasis in parole from casework to surveillance. Certainly, many jurisdictions have argued for the need to carry a weapon given the dangerous conditions under which they work. But Keve (1979) determined that agencies whose officers carry weapons do not do so because of the danger they may face, but do so because of an overall agency philosophy and mission that emphasizes law enforcement to the exclusion of casework.

Yet, in some cases, it seems plausible that jurisdictions have adopted the use of weapons in an effort to shore up their job/role orientation. Cohn (1997) found that jurisdictions that supported the arming of officers also presented with support for law enforcement caseload management strategies. These findings are in contrast to what Sigler and McGraw (1984) found in their work on the influence of weapons and role perceptions and role conflict. These scholars indicate that those officers who perceive their role as law enforcement were more likely to use weapons than those who saw their role from a treatment perspective.

Parolees

No discussion of parole would be complete without tapping into the perspective of those whose liberty hangs in the balance. Some might suggest that parolees should have no say in a process that is meant to protect the public from crimes that they have committed, but this discussion posits otherwise. In fact, there is much to be learned from those who are the consumers of parole supervision and services.

> Only when we adopt a consumer perspective are we able to perceive the practical significance of our institutions, laws, and public transactions in terms of their impacts upon the lives and homely experiences of human beings. (Cahn, 1961, p. 30)

Because parole is a privilege and not a right, the decision to grant parole is immune from many legal protections, including due process. While *Morrissey v. Brewer* (1972) provides some minimal due process rights in the parole revocations process, the parole hearing itself remains exempt from due process protection (West-Smith et al., 2000). Moreover, many states are presumptive parole states (i.e., the presumption that offenders who meet certain requirements will be granted parole) and use discretionary release. Therefore, the actual decision to release an offender to parole lies within the discretion of the parole board (West-Smith et al., 2000). As previously discussed, the decision to parole is often secret, arbitrary, and no doubt misunderstood, not only by the general public but also by the people to whom these decisions mean the most.

There is a paucity of literature that evaluates the offender perspective of parole, but what research does exist is very interesting. A study by Cole and Logan (1977) may be the first study that actually considered the offender's perspective of the parole decision-making process. Results from this study indicated that offenders did not believe that they had any agency or control in the parole decision-making process. Moreover, offenders did not perceive themselves as having the ability to influence the parole board, since they believed that parole decisions were made based on factors outside their control (Cole & Logan, 1977). Furthermore, offenders saw themselves as having very little control over what they could do in prison to improve their chances of parole, especially given the small number of treatment and/or educational/vocational programs available in the prison (Cole & Logan, 1977).

More often than not, offenders are denied parole. Consequently, it is not unreasonable to expect that many offenders are dissatisfied with the decisions of the parole board. The question remains, why? Many offenders indicate that decisions made by the parole board are arbitrary. Some of this dissatisfaction may also come as a result of a singular lack of understanding of the process (West-Smith et al., 2000). A study by West-Smith and colleagues (2000) solicited letters from offenders who were denied parole in an effort to determine what variables offenders thought were most relevant to their parole being denied. As a matter of course, offenders believe that institutional adjustment (i.e., the lack of any institutional infractions), completion of education and treatment programs, and passing their parole eligibility date are the usual and customary prerequisites for parole (West-Smith et al., 2000). Results from the study indicate that offenders believe that the criteria for release decisions utilized by parole boards are not uniform and are often hidden from the offender.

Moreover, offenders believe that the parole board uses criteria other than those that are officially stated and that parole release decisions have little to do with offender accomplishments while in prison and more to do with whether the parole board feels the offender has been punished enough (West-Smith et al., 2000). If, as West-Smith and colleagues suggest, release decisions are subjective to the point that they do not follow established guidelines but are driven more by "latent norms" that emerge over time, it is no wonder that offenders do not understand why their parole is rejected, despite compliance with the rules (West-Smith et al., 2000, p. 9).

Other work evaluating offender perceptions of parole release indicates that many offenders do not spend time engaging in activities that might impress the parole board precisely because they do not believe that these activities (e.g., education, treatment, and the like) will make a difference in the parole decision outcome (Muhammad, 1996). This is particularly relevant for offenders who have spent long periods of time in prison.

Reentry Considerations

Leaving prison and returning to the community may be a process that is as old as the hills, but it is also a process that has evolved over time and one that has been significantly influenced not only by offenders themselves but also by personnel who are employed by the corrections system to assist with the transition. Undoubtedly, parole board composition impacts parole board decision-making that in turn determines who reenters society on parole and when, and under what specific conditions. How a parole officer views their job, including the role orientation that they adopt, will likely significantly impact their job performance as well as offender outcome. The extent to which offenders engage and interact with their parole officers (for better or for worse) and the level of guidance and assistance (or resistance) they receive while on parole can only influence the degree to which offenders are able to successfully navigate the reentry endeavor.

Good, bad, or indifferent, parole is the organizational construct through which the majority of offenders reenter the community from prison. Therefore, while offenders must take responsibility and be held accountable for their actions and behaviors, the attendant issues associated with parole practice and process must also be considered as influential variables in evaluating offender reentry.

Part I

The Dimensions of Offender Reentry

Chapter 3

Housing and Reentry

In his seminal work, the psychologist Abraham Maslow establishes that human beings have needs that are ordered in a hierarchy from basic to complex. Maslow's theory identifies five levels of need: physiological, safety, love, self-esteem, and self-actualization (Maslow, 1943). Where physiological needs are human beings' most basic needs, other needs such as safety, love, self-esteem, and self-actualization evolve over time as lower-order needs are satisfied. Examples of physiological needs include food, clothing, and shelter.

It is not difficult to understand why housing is a physiological need and why it is so critical for offenders leaving prison and returning to the community. Without shelter, one has little else. In fact, one scholar has determined that housing is the "lynchpin that holds the reintegration process together...and that in the end, a polity that does not concern itself with the housing needs of returning prisoners finds that it has done so at the expense of its own public safety" (Bradley et al., 2001, p. 1).

Given the primacy of this need, one would expect that criminal justice practitioners would have a clear plan in place to address this paramount concern, but this is not so. Managing the housing needs of reentering offenders has proven to be one of the most fundamental and challenging reentry issues to address. Even returning offenders recognize the importance of having a place to live upon release. A recent report indicates that offenders view housing as a critical component if they are to achieve any reentry success (LaVigne et al., 2004).

Historical Context

Everyone leaving prison needs a place to go, but the reality is that not everybody has one. The number of offenders leaving prison with no specific address varies significantly by jurisdiction and is in many cases uncountable due to differing definitions of homelessness and the invisibility of homelessness (i.e., if a homeless person does not visit a soup kitchen, shelter, or some other place where they can be counted, they are not known to be homeless). Moreover, rates of homelessness can be calculated in a variety of different ways, making an exact count virtually impossible.

Data limitations aside, an understanding of homelessness estimates in the offender population are important. Research by Ditton suggests that 9% of state prisoners lived on the street or in a shelter in the 12 months prior to arrest (1999). Hughes and colleagues (2001) report that among those leaving state prison in 1999, 12% were homeless at the time of arrest. Other available estimates of homelessness prior to incarceration vary significantly from 8% to 25% (Greenberg & Rosenheck, 2008a; McNiel et al., 2005). A study by Greenberg and Rosenheck found that 9.2% of criminal justice-involved state and federal prisoners were homeless prior to incarceration. Interestingly, 7.2% of state and federal prisoners were homeless in the previous year although not at the time of arrest, while 1.7% of offenders were homeless at the time of arrest (2008b). Homelessness disproportionately impacts mentally ill offenders with 13% of mentally ill state prisoners reported as homeless in the year prior to arrest compared with 6% of non-mentally ill offenders (James & Glaze, 2006). Nine percent of incarcerated parents report being homeless in the year before their arrest, with mothers being twice as likely as fathers to have been homeless (Glaze & Maruschak, 2008).

A somewhat dated study of homelessness and time spent in jail/prison indicates that 18% of the homeless population served time in prison for a felony conviction, and approximately 33% of homeless people were jailed on misdemeanor crimes (Shlay & Rossi, 1992). In a recent study of homeless adults living in 6 shelters across Oklahoma City, Gonzalez et al. (2018), found more than three-quarters (76%) of the 581 participants had a history of arrest with greater than half (57%) having been in jail more than 3 times. The most prevalent offense type was drug possession (35%) followed by driving under the influence (31%) and disorderly conduct or public drunkenness (28%); violent offenses were the least prevalent. Although estimates vary as indicated above and are not easily attainable for myriad reasons, research has evidenced a relationship between homelessness and involvement with the criminal justice system (Gonzalez, et al., 2018). Travis projected that approximately 25% of the general homeless population has served time in prison (Travis, 2005).

Estimates suggest offenders with one prison experience are nearly seven times higher than the general population to be homeless; with more than one incarceration experience the rate of homelessness almost doubles (13 times higher than the general population) (Couloute, 2018); a cycle often referred to as the "revolving door" of homeless incarceration (Gonzalez et al., 2018). A study by Prison Policy Initiative argued that measuring housing insecurity (lack of stable housing) of the formerly incarcerated provides a more accurate measure of the scope of the problem (Couloute, 2018). Findings of their study of formerly incarcerated men and women in 2008 revealed that 105 out of every 10,000 formerly incarcerated persons was homeless; however, the rate increased to 203 out of every 10,000 when including those persons living in a shelter, and 570 out of every 10,000 when marginal housing (living in a rooming house, hotel, or motel) was included in the measurement. Their results suggest that if we consider housing insecurity rather than homelessness as our measure, the rate is more than three times higher. Regardless of the measurement, one cannot deny the salience of homelessness/housing insecurity as a reentry concern.

In their work concerning state and federal inmates, Greenberg and Rosenheck review the literature and determine that there are four approaches to explaining the nexus between homelessness and crime (2008b). The first approach argues that homelessness is criminogenic in that people often try to survive on limited resources, many of which are not obtained legally (McCarthy & Hagen, 1991). The second perspective suggests that poor physical and mental health and substance abuse are common among the homeless and are issues that increase the likelihood that homeless individuals become criminal justice-involved (Greenberg & Rosenheck, 2008a; Kushel et al., 2005). Criminal justice research supports this contention. In their study on a national sample of jail inmates, Greenberg and Rosenheck found that poor physical health was a significant contributor to homelessness (2008a). The most recent available data from the Bureau of Justice Statistics reports 14% of drug-abusing or drug-dependent state prisoners were homeless prior to their most recent incarceration; more than double that of other inmates. Moreover, 42% of prisoners with substance use disorders reported receiving public assistance in their lifetime (Mumola & Karberg, 2006).

The mentally ill are also more likely to find themselves homeless prior to incarceration. Estimates suggest mentally ill state prisoners are more than twice as likely to be homeless compared with their non-mentally ill counterparts (13% compared with 6%) (James & Glaze, 2006). A retrospective study by McNiel and colleagues of more than 12,000 adults booked in a San Francisco County jail found mentally ill inmates were more likely to be homeless or living in shelters at the time of their arrest. Moreover, homelessness was found to be an even greater problem for the severely mentally ill with co-occurring substance use disorders (McNiel et al., 2005). This finding is consistent with the exacerbated nature of comorbid disorders, including poorer treatment and medication compliance (Volavka & Citrome, 2008).

Although estimates regarding the state of the homeless population are difficult by virtue of their transient nature, the Housing and Urban Development (HUD) Continuum of Care Homeless Assistance Program estimates approximately 116,000 homeless persons to have a serious mental health disorder and greater than 88,000 to have a chronic substance abuse disorder (Housing and Urban Development, 2020). For many of this vulnerable population their crimes are a by-product of their homelessness (e.g., panhandling, vagrancy, sleeping on the street) (Marcil et al., 2016).

Third, scholars contend that there are socio-demographic characteristics that are empirically proven to be associated with both homelessness and crime. Studies indicate that being male, single, young, poor, of minority status, or poorly educated significantly increases the likelihood that an individual will be homeless and that they will engage in crime (DeLisi, 2000; Solomon & Draine, 1995a). Finally, research indicates that the relationship between homelessness and incarceration is complex in that prior incarceration increases the risk for homelessness by eroding family and communal ties, employment opportunities, and access to public housing (Metraux & Culhane, 2006). The geographically remote locations of prisons, along with institutional policies and other hardships of visitation as discussed in chapter 5, make it difficult to maintain relationships outside of the institution (Arditti, 2003; Christian, 2005). The majority of inmates receive few to no visits from family or friends (Bales & Mears, 2008; Derkzen et al., 2009). A former Executive Director of the Pennsylvania Prison Society noted that "families tend to drift away. Parents may die and spouses go on" (Razzano, 2001, p. 1).

Using survey data of urban families to examine housing hardships experienced by formerly incarcerated men, Geller and Curtis (2011) found recently incarcerated males were twice as likely to experience housing insecurity and homelessness than non-incarcerated males controlling for sociodemographic characteristics including pre-incarceration housing. Moreover, incarcerated men were significantly more likely to experience housing instability, moving more than once per year and relying on others to help support them. Expecting that employment and income may influence housing insecurity, the researchers reported that while greater annual earnings five years post-prison release did serve as a protective factor reducing housing insecurity and homelessness, ex-offenders making equal money to non-incarcerated men were still at significantly greater odds of being insecure in housing. Unsurprisingly, men coming out of prison having lived in public housing prior to their incarceration were at a greater risk of eviction in keeping with HUD's one-strike policy, which is discussed in more detail at the end of this chapter (Geller & Curtis, 2011).

Current Trends

As offender release decisions made by parole boards have been usurped by decisions mandated through truth-in-sentencing legislation, fewer offenders are leaving prison with a housing plan in place (Visher & Travis, 2003). The consequence of this practice is an increasing number of offenders leaving prison often not knowing where they will sleep (Geller & Curtis, 2011). Offenders who are fortunate enough to leave prison with an address or place to lay their head, more often than not, go home to a friend or close family member.

A VERA Institute report evaluating the dynamics of offenders leaving prison and jail in New York determined that the majority of offenders leaving prison and/or jail went to live with their families upon release and that those who did not were three times more likely to abscond on parole (Nelson et al., 1999). Two days after release, 82% of offenders (40/49) interviewed in the VERA study were living with a relative or significant other (Nelson et al., 1999). In a series of Urban Institute studies evaluating housing options for soon-to-be or just-released prisoners, between 63% and 78% of offenders in Ohio and Texas indicated that they would live with a family member or close friend upon release, while 88% of offenders in Illinois and almost 60% in Maryland indicated that were actually living with family since release (LaVigne & Thompson, 2003; Visher et al., 2004).

While being released from prison to a family member or close friend may be an optimal housing solution from an offender's perspective, in some instances it is not always the best option and is not always celebrated by those with whom the offender goes to live. In some instances, family and friends may be fearful for their safety and/or the safety of loved ones when the offender comes to live with them. In other circumstances, the returning offender may serve as a fiscal drain on family and friends (Roman & Travis, 2006).

The offender may also be perceived as being a destabilizing force in the home (Roman & Travis, 2006). A study on returning offenders in Illinois indicates that 20% of offenders left home within two years of release from prison precisely because of conflicts with family (LaVigne & Parthasarathy, 2005). Moreover, family and friends may face possible legal liability for agreeing to house an offender. Conditions of parole may limit or prohibit with whom offenders can live, as conditions or parole often specify that offenders cannot live or associate with anyone who has a criminal record (Rhine(a) et al., 1991).

In some instances, going home is not an option, particularly for sex offenders. In many instances, sex offenders have conditions of parole that restrict their access to family members or friends. Furthermore, many states place restrictions on where sex offenders can live once they leave prison, requiring that sex offenders remain some distance away from schools and other places where children are present (Levenson & Cotter, 2005). Limited housing options put sex offenders at an extreme disadvantage and often create a scenario of forced homelessness. Increased homelessness in sex offenders can then make it difficult for law enforcement to track and monitor these offenders because they are in a constant state of transience (Levenson, 2005). In a recently published study on the impact of South Carolina's sex offender residence restriction (SORR) law on homelessness, researchers found the homeless rate of released sex offenders increased each year following the implementation of SORR (Cann & Isom-Scott, 2020). Within four years of its implementation, the rate of homelessness increased by more than 600%, which as the authors suggest, is counterproductive to the policy's intended aims, particularly as there is no evidence to suggest a link between residential proximity to locations often restricted to sex offenders and recidivism (Cann & Isom-Scott, 2020; Maguire & Singler, 2011; Zandbergen, Levenson, & Hart, 2010).

Clearly, going home is not always an option for every offender. In these situations, the shelter system picks up the slack. Emergency shelters are places where people go to live when other living arrangements are not available. Typically, shelters are short-term solutions to acute housing needs. These facilities do not assist homeless people with finding more permanent or long-term housing (Roman & Travis, 2006). According to the U.S. Department of Housing and Urban Development, an emergency shelter is, "any facility with overnight accommodations, the primary purpose of which is to provide temporary or transitional shelter for the homeless in general or for specific populations of the homeless" (U.S. Department of Housing and Urban Development, 2007).

Although dated, data from the Bureau of Justice Statistics indicates that approximately 13% of offenders released in 1998 had been homeless at some point in the year prior to arrest and were documented as living either in homeless shelters or on the street (Mumola, 2000). The Prison Policy Initiative estimates that released offenders are ten times more likely to be homeless compared with the general public (Couloute, 2018), suggesting that this population is going to be disproportionately utilizing the services of shelters and other forms of temporary housing. Indeed, as noted above, Geller and Curtis (2011) found previously incarcerated men were more than twice as likely to be living in a shelter than non-incarcerated men. Data from the Nelson and colleagues report (1999) indicates that two days after release, 14% (7/49) of offenders were living in a temporary shelter or on their own while another reentry study in New York State found that 11% of prisoners released to New York City between 1995 and 1998 entered a homeless shelter within two years of their release (Metraux & Culhane, 2004). Recent data finds more than half (54%) of prisoners in New York City were released directly to the shelter system in 2017, up 21% in just three years (2014) (Routhier, 2018).

While emergency shelters are meant to provide temporary housing to people in acute need, data from 2008 indicates that the average length of stay in an emergency shelter was 69 days for single men, 51 days for single women, and 70 days for families (U.S. Conference of Mayors, 2008). If offenders are utilizing shelter resources, they are doing so for some time at a great cost. New York City's Independent Budget Office estimated a $1.7 billion budget in 2017 to meet their shelter capacity needs (Stefanski, 2017). The Los Angeles Homeless Services Authority (LMHSA) budgeted $335 million dollars in interim housing alone for fiscal years 2022–23 (LHMSA, 2022). The likelihood of recently released offenders using shelters is greatest in the first few months following release (Remster, 2019). A recent study following ex-offenders over a period of eight years noted approximately 39% of released offenders who stayed at a shelter did so only one time (Remster, 2019). While this finding would indicate that shelters are serving their intended goal of helping during the transition from prison to the community, this also means that more than half (60%) of ex-offenders using shelters stayed on more than one occasion (the average number of shelter stays was two), suggesting a slow and difficult reintegration process back into the community. The average time spent in a shelter was approximately two months and the average total time in shelters (combining all shelter stays per individual) was over five months. Among those who used a shelter, 49% had their first stay more than two years following their release. Although this first stay was delayed, the average time between stays was just over one year, reducing the amount of time until they entered the shelter again by more than half (Remster, 2019).

There are significant public safety costs associated with increased numbers of offenders living in emergency shelter situations. A study conducted on Georgia parolees found that the likelihood of arrest increased 25% each time a parolee changed their address (Meredith et al., 2003). Another study suggested that 38% of offenders who indicated that they were going to live in a shelter absconded from parole, compared with 5% of offenders who did not report going to live in a shelter (Nelson et al., 1999). A later study using a large cohort of persons released from state prison in New York indicated that offenders with histories of shelter use prior to the index prison stay were more likely to reenter a shelter and to be reincarcerated (Metraux & Culhane, 2004). Thus, the highest risk of homelessness for returning offenders was having a history of pre-incarceration residential instability. These findings support homelessness as a risk factor for future criminal justice involvement and, as Metraux and Culhane suggest, "the hiatus spent in prison fails to alleviate, and likely exacerbates, residential instability" (p. 151).

Private and public housing options are available for offenders who require stable housing. Private housing options for offenders usually include buying or renting houses or apartments and are often very difficult to locate, let alone afford. Moreover, criminal backgrounds pose significant obstacles in obtaining access to private housing. A 1997 study indicates that 43% of property managers and owners were inclined to reject an applicant with a conviction (Helfgott, 1997). Research by Clark contends that traditional assessments of housing and reentry view the problem from the offender's perspective. However, an evaluation of landlords' attitudes toward renting to released offenders could be very informative in informing reentry housing policy and practice (Clark, 2007).

Clark contends that landlords do not universally dismiss rental applications from people with criminal backgrounds. Data indicates that landlords are more willing to accept applications from and rent to people who have committed misdemeanors over felonies. Moreover, survey results indicate that landlords base their decision to rent on many factors including credit, income, employment, and rental history (Clark, 2007). Results also suggest that landlords are very interested in whether or not offenders are rehabilitated. From their perspective, landlords interpret attempts to rehabilitate as trustworthiness (Clark, 2007).

Given the difficulty associated with securing private housing, most offenders are forced to seek housing from public sources (Page & Travis, 2010). To qualify for public housing options, offenders must meet certain HUD criteria. Public housing can include transitional or more permanent housing options. As defined by HUD, "the movement of homelessness individuals and families to permanent housing within a reasonable amount of time (usually 24 months)," is called transitional housing (National Coalition for the Homeless, 2009). Data for the general homeless population indicates that those staying in transitional housing do so for an average of 175, 196, and 223 days for single men, single women, and families, respectively (U.S. Conference of Mayors, 2008).

Most transitional housing facilities available to offenders are halfway houses that are typically run by corrections departments or contracted private companies. Halfway houses are small group homes where offenders live together so they may more smoothly transition from prison to the community. These houses provide offenders with the opportunity to work, save money, and to locate and secure more permanent housing options if necessary. Halfway houses often also provide access to treatment and other transitional services. A recent meta-analysis examining the effectiveness of halfway houses on recidivism found that they are an effective community-based strategy to reduce recidivism with positive benefits extending long term (two to three years post release) (Wong et al., 2019). Generally, access to halfway houses is reserved for drug users, while other types of transitional housing programs are most often reserved for the general public (Roman & Travis, 2006).

Data on the numbers of state and federal offenders released to halfway houses is sorely limited. Daniel and Sawyer (2020) contend that information is often not made publicly available, due largely to the fact that the majority of facilities are privately owned and therefore not mandated to furnish information to the public in the same way as government run facilities. CoreCivic Corporation, the largest owner of "partnership correctional, detention and residential entry facilities" across the nation, was operating 29 halfway houses in 2020, up from only 2 in 2014 (CoreCivic, n.d.; Lartey, 2020). Based on available data, halfway house capacity is unfortunately a fraction of the total need. Although dated, estimates indicate that less than half of 1% of all inmates released from prison in 1999 had access to a halfway house (American Correctional Association, 2000). Further limiting access to federal prisoners, in November 2017, the Bureau of Prisons announced that they would be ending contracts with 16 halfway houses throughout the country for budgetary reasons (Watkins, 2017).

Still other public housing options include permanent supportive housing: a housing option that is particularly beneficial to offenders who require long-term housing and includes supportive services for homeless individuals who present with some sort of disability. This type of supportive housing enables special needs populations to live as independently as possible in a permanent setting. The U.S. Conference of Mayors (2008) indicates that the average stay for a homeless person in permanent supportive housing was 556 days for single men and 571 days for single women: just over a year and a half. While this type of housing option is very relevant for offender sub-populations such as mentally ill or substance-abusing offenders who may require intensive programming and services as an adjunct to housing, housing options of this type are the exception rather than the rule (Black & Cho, 2004).

Other public options include the Housing Choice Voucher Program (Formerly Section 8 Housing). This is a federal program that assists low-income families or individuals to afford housing in the private market (Roman & Travis, 2006). Participants in this program find their own housing (i.e., single-family homes, townhouses, and apartments). Housing choice vouchers are administered locally by public housing agencies (PHAs) that receive federal funds from HUD to administer the voucher program. A housing subsidy is paid to the landlord directly by the PHA on behalf of the participating family/individual. The family/individual then pays the difference between the actual rent charged by the landlord and the amount subsidized by the program.

Program eligibility for these types of programs is determined based on minimum federal and local requirements. Wait times for housing of this type are often extreme and the precise eligibility criteria for offenders is not known, as it varies based on jurisdiction. Moreover, as Travis notes, very little is known about whether and to what extent offenders take part in or make use of this and other types of federal housing programs, primarily because federal laws ban offenders convicted of felonies from taking part in such programs because of their crime (Roman & Travis, 2006).

As Roman and Travis indicate, barriers to finding viable housing opportunities upon release from prison include not only minimal housing capacity but also myriad rules and regulations that severely restrict access to any public housing options that might be available (2006). The scarcity of housing options significantly impacts all homeless people, resulting in substantial wait times. As of February 2022, close to 255,000 families were on the waiting list for public housing in New York City; 17,200 families were on the waiting list for Section 8 housing with more than 6,000 on the waiting list for both public and Section 8 housing (New York City Housing Authority, 2022). Any Section 8 housing assignments are being made from the waitlist. There is no indication as to when the list might reopen. Families with children on these waitlists usually receive first consideration. Offenders generally receive none (Roman & Travis, 2006).

In addition to housing supply, legislative barriers also limit offenders' chances of living in public housing. Passed as part of the Housing Opportunity Program Extension Act of 1996, the "one strike and you're out" component of the act was designed to protect people living in public housing projects from crime by giving public housing agencies the authority to evict tenants involved in drug or other criminal activity (Housing Opportunity Program Extension Act, 1996). The one-strike rule also permits housing authorities to terminate the leases of those with criminal histories or individuals harboring people in their apartments who are not listed on the lease and have criminal records (Roman & Travis, 2006).

Moreover, local housing authorities are required to deny admission to convicted sex offenders, anyone who has ever been convicted of producing methamphetamine on public housing premises, and anyone who has been evicted from public housing within the past three years because of illegal drug activity or alcohol abuse (Roman & Travis, 2006). Furthermore, public housing leases can carry a provision that states that a tenant can be evicted if he or any member of the household or guest engages in drug-related criminal activity on- or off-site (Bradley et al., 2001). This lease provision was affirmed by the U.S. Supreme Court in *HUD v. Rucker*, No. 00-1770 in March 2002.

Of note is that these one-strike policies are not automatic or universal. Local authorities have the ability to exercise leeway in enforcing these rules. For example, local authorities can take applicants' efforts at rehabilitation (i.e., read as participation in drug/alcohol treatment) into account when making housing assignment decisions. However, given the demand for public housing resources, these one-strike rules are often used by housing authorities as filters to deny housing to a significant subset of people waiting for services (Fleischer et al., 2001). Moreover, these policies are also used to deny housing to people who have been arrested for, but not convicted of, drug-related offenses (Legal Action Center, 2004). Research that assessed the degree to which local housing authorities use the one-strike rule indicates that 75% of housing authorities used the rule and that application of the rule was responsible for 43% of housing application rejections (U.S. Department of Housing and Urban Development, 1997).

Reentry Considerations

The use of the one-strike policy as a means to exclude offenders from accessing public housing is only trumped by obstacles within the community that limit where released offenders can live. Even in jurisdictions where money for housing of offenders is available, community opposition can make building or providing transitional and supportive housing difficult, if not impossible. Known as NIMBY (Not In My Backyard), this communal opposition is single-handedly responsible for stopping many an offender-based housing development project in its tracks.

Communities often see the benefit of providing housing services to offenders leaving prison, but do not want these services offered near them. Interestingly, this opposition is not solely reserved for wealthy neighborhoods. Disadvantaged communities often have concerns about what the location of offender housing will do to their already compromised neighborhoods. Residents in all areas not only fear for their lives but also express concern over how offender-based residential facilities will impact their property values (Dear, 1992; Lake, 1996). One way that localities circumvent providing housing for offenders is to impose zoning restrictions that make breaking ground on housing of this type virtually impossible (Roman & Travis, 2006). Community organizers also often protest, appeal to politicians, and even engage in court proceedings to shut down projects or significantly delay them (Page & Travis, 2010).

Research indicates that resistance to housing released offenders in the community is particularly great for drug-using offenders (Roman & Travis, 2004). Moreover, for offenders who are able to find housing on their own, landlords can and often do discriminate against them. Criminal background checks are a routine part of many apartment applications. People with criminal histories are often summarily rejected despite meeting other leasing requirements (Helfgott, 1997). Clearly, NIMBY significantly restricts the supply of offender-based housing to the point that offenders are forced to access other services (legally or otherwise) generally reserved for the non-offending public (Roman & Travis, 2004). Of course, the irony is that efforts to rid neighborhoods of crime and criminals through NIMBY often achieve just the opposite outcome as homeless offenders often access needed housing illegally.

In addition to policy and practice that seeks to exclude offenders from accessing public housing, the fragmented nature of the housing system in the United States does nothing to help matters. Housing services at the national level are managed by multiple agencies, and there is no one agency specifically tasked with ensuring that offenders who leave prison have safe and affordable housing upon their release. Corrections authorities do what they can to link offenders with housing at the local level, but demand far outweighs capacity, and many offenders are left out in the cold.

Promising Practice

The reentry challenges associated with housing are seemingly insurmountable. However, within the last few years, some effort has been made to address these issues in a meaningful way. The Second Chance Act was in large part responsible for bringing the housing concerns of offenders to the fore. Prior to passage of this bill, little thought was given to where offenders lived after they were released from prison. Passage of this legislation has also encouraged the creation of a variety of new programs and collaborative approaches to housing offenders, including involving corrections personnel in the identification of offender housing needs. In addition, funding through grants has encouraged private and public organizations alike to rethink housing programming and to engage in partnerships that stretch traditional boundaries.

For example, some jurisdictions have expanded transitional and supportive housing capacity specifically for offenders who present with drug or mental health problems. These housing options provide comprehensive and individualized services, including education and vocational training, substance abuse treatment, employment assistance, and access to medical and mental health care (Black & Cho, 2004). Programs of this type have been initiated in New York (Heritage Health and Housing), California (Delancey Street Foundation), and Illinois (St. Andrew's Court) and aim to provide residents with housing stability and access to services (Page & Travis, 2010). Retention rates for programs of this type range between 75 to 85 percent after one year (Barrow et al., 2004). Offender-based intensive service-driven supportive housing programs of this type also reduce reliance on third-party treatment and service programs often frequented by substance abusers and the mentally ill (Fontaine & Biess, 2012). As a result, this opens up access to community-based programming for other citizens in need.

An example of a specific supportive housing model developed for offenders with histories of substance abuse is Oxford House. Oxford House is predicated on principles of self-governance and mutual support and is unique in that it operates without professional staff. Each house includes 12 residents who agree to pay rent, help with house chores and maintenance, and refrain from drug and alcohol use. There is no required or maximum length of stay. Research shows that Oxford house participants are less likely to abuse drugs or alcohol, more likely to be employed, and spend less time engaged in criminal activity (Jason & Ferrari, 2010). In addition, peer-led, mutual help housing models such as Oxford House have been shown to reduce recidivism (Olson et al., 2005).

Efforts to combat NIMBY are possible, although not easy. Communities' fears regarding safety and concerns regarding the impact of offender-based housing on property values are understandable, although not always rational (Dear, 1992). Emotions and fear drive NIMBY and are grounded in a lack of understanding of fact. Research indicates that NIMBY reactions are heightened when residents have not participated or been engaged in the proposed project (Page & Travis, 2010). Fears associated with housing offenders in the community also correlate with the size of the facility, the number of residents to be served, the nature and type of the offenders' criminal history, and the degree to which the community might come in to contact with the residents (Doble & Lindsay, 2003). If the community feels exploited or taken advantage of in any way, or if they feel that offenders will receive more and better services than they do, they are likely to reject the placement of offender-based community housing in their community (Doble & Lindsay, 2003; Page & Travis, 2010).

Meaningful engagement of the community can help mitigate NIMBY. If the community feels that their fears and concerns are being legitimately addressed, they usually become more invested in the process and more accepting of it. Involving local stakeholders in the siting of offender-based community housing and developing trust between the housing provider and the community are efforts that can go a long way toward assuaging community concerns regarding the placement of offender-based housing in their midst. Moreover, educating the public about the residents and the benefits they will derive from taking part in the offender-based housing project can further placate community fears (Page & Travis, 2010).

Offenders who leave prison without a place to live exact a heavy toll on the housing and homeless service systems, the criminal justice system, and the communities to which they return. These offenders tax already broken housing systems by reducing the amount and type of housing services available to non-offending homeless people. In addition, offenders who return to the community without stable living arrangements are more likely to recidivate than those who do have stable housing options.

Any effective reentry policy must not only address public housing restrictions such as the "one strike and you're out" policy but also expand housing capacity. The hard reality is that society must recognize that the majority of offenders who go to prison eventually return to the community, and when they do, they need a place to rest their heads—and they will find one, one way or another.

Chapter 4

Education and Employment and Reentry

Education and employment are inexorably linked. Level of educational attainment directly impacts job prospects, job placement, and opportunities for job promotion for all citizens. If it is difficult for a law-abiding citizen to improve their level of educational attainment and job prospects in today's economy, one can only imagine the roadblocks that offenders must encounter in achieving the same end. Herein lies the irony. For offenders, education and employment are critical for success upon release from prison. For offenders, education and employment are difficult, if not impossible, to obtain.

Education

Educational attainment is defined as the highest level of education that an individual has completed (U.S. Census, 2011). Generally speaking, society uses educational attainment as a barometer by which to judge the degree to which a person is educated. In today's world, we generally assign people who have completed a bachelor's degree or higher the moniker "educated," while we award the label "uneducated" to those who have not. These distinctions take on added meaning when considering them in the context of offender populations. Data from the most recent national study on education and correctional populations indicates that 40% of state prisoners and 31% of offenders on probation had not completed high school or obtained a GED compared with 18% of the general population (Harlow, 2003). Clearly, education is a pressing issue with respect to offender reentry.

Historical Context

The belief that education is fundamental to transforming those who break the law is supported by the fact that providing educational opportunities to offenders in prison has been a priority for more than 200 years (Coley & Barton, 2006). At their inception, prisons were recognized as places where offenders would engage in thoughtful reflection and repent for their sins. In most cases, this reflection took the form of moral and religious instruction provided to offenders by prison authorities (Gehring, 1997). By the late 1800s, Zebulon Brockway was integrating educational programming into Elmira Reformatory, placing emphasis on literacy and communication skills instead of religious instruction (Crayton & Neusteter, 2008).

The early 1900s were marked by an increase in the number and type of educational programs offered to offenders in prison, primarily because of the rise of the indeterminate sentence and the emphasis placed on the relationship between personal achievement and parole eligibility. During this time, education was one primary means by which offenders were able to prove themselves and their desire to rehabilitate, thereby making them particularly good candidates for parole consideration (Gehring, 1997). In 1965, Congress passed legislation allowing offenders to apply for financial aid (Pell Grants) to attend college while in prison (Hrabowski & Robbie, 2002). By the 1970s, prison education programs were considered the cornerstone of all correctional programming (Ryan & McCabe, 1994). Education was and continues to be viewed as the primary conduit through which rehabilitation would and can occur. Consequently, prisons throughout the United States significantly enhanced educational opportunities for offenders, adding Adult Basic Education (ABE) and General Education Development (GED) program offerings. By the 1980s, vocational, post-secondary education programs, and literacy and GED programs were available in virtually every prison (Ryan & McCabe, 1994).

However, a series of misplaced evaluations on the impact of education programs on recidivism coupled with get-tough-on-crime attitudes resulted in waning support for educational programs (Lillis, 1994). The public became increasingly antagonistic toward offenders who received Pell Grant support for education when they themselves could not always obtain access to these same funds. By the mid-1990s, public disdain for offender access to post-secondary education had risen to such a level that Congress voted to eliminate prisoner eligibility for Pell Grants in the Violent Crime Control and Law Enforcement Act of 1994 (Marks, 1997). With the elimination of Pell Grants, large numbers of prisons closed all access to college courses, while others significantly reduced their programs (U.S. Department of Education, 2019; Taylor, 2004). As expected, immediately following the loss of funding, correctional education participation was greatly reduced, with a 44% decrease in the number of incarcerated people receiving post-secondary educational programming (Tewksbury et al., 2000). While the number of prisoners who now take part in post-secondary education has returned to pre-1994 levels, more of these offenders are taking part in vocational programming than in academic courses (Erisman & Contardo, 2005).

More recently, having acknowledged the benefit of education on post-release outcomes, the Department of Education established a new initiative-based experiment, the Second Chance Pell Grant (U.S. Department of Education, 2015). Starting in 2015, the Second Chance Pell Grant allowed for the waiver of Pell Grant Fund restrictions to incarcerated populations in federal and state penal institutions on a limited basis (U.S. Department of Education, 2015). The initiative allows a limited number of Institutions of Higher Education (IHE) to partner with federal or state correctional facilities to provide funding to inmates who would otherwise be eligible students and who are due to be released from prison within five years (U.S. Department of Education, 2015). The most recent numbers find 130 IHE in 42 states and the District of Columbia participate in the program (U.S. Department of Education, 2020). According to the Vera Institute of Justice (2020), each year of the initiative has seen an increase in enrollment, with nearly 17,000 people over the first three years participating. To date, more than 4,500 certificates, postsecondary diplomas, associate degrees, and bachelor's degrees have been earned (Vera Institute of Justice, 2020). In December 2020, Congress passed the Consolidated Appropriations Act, 2020, making "permanent the change to allow incarcerated individuals access to Federal Pell Grant Funds for qualifying prison education programs" (United States Department of Education, 2021).

Current Trends

General research supports the notion that education is important for offenders and that it can mitigate recidivism (Crayton & Neusteter, 2008). Yet, scholarship indicates that offenders entering prison are less educated than the general population. This is not surprising given that individuals who drop out of high school or do not complete a GED are three times more likely than college-educated persons to enter the criminal justice system (Sickmund & Puzzanchera, 2014). As the data above suggest, over one-third of state prison inmates and offenders on probation did not complete high school or its equivalent at the time they were incarcerated/adjudicated to probation (Harlow, 2003). When disaggregated, these numbers are even more pronounced, as minority rates of high school non-completion are 44% and 53% for black and Hispanic offenders, respectively (Harlow, 2003). When evaluated according to gender, we see that women tend to be more educated than men, with 36% of women having graduated from high school or equivalent compared with 32% of men (Harlow, 2003).

These data are careful to mention "high school degree or its equivalent." The General Educational Development test or GED is the most commonly accepted equivalent to a high school diploma. Developed by The Center for Adult Learning and Educational Credentials of the American Council on Education, the GED is a test given to people who are not actively enrolled in school but who wish to test their knowledge of information expected of high school graduates. Not surprisingly, offenders often take the GED. At last count, approximately 26% of inmates took the GED while in prison, while 11% took the GED while on probation (Harlow, 2003).

The fact that offenders often lack a high school diploma or GED represents only the tip of the iceberg with respect to the educational deficits that offenders face. A 2003 national assessment of adult literacy in prison conducted by Greenberg and colleagues indicates that significant numbers of offenders from around the United States are either illiterate or functionally illiterate. Greenberg and colleagues (2007) found that 39% of offenders present with below basic literacy compared with 21% of the general population. Ryan indicates that almost half of offenders in the prison system in 1990 were illiterate when using sixth-grade achievement as the standard (Ryan, 1990). A recent study of female state inmates by Houser and colleagues (2019a) found the women to have on average an eleventh-grade education, but were only reading at an eighth-grade level. Gaps in educational attainment for offenders are more pronounced when considering that nearly 17% of offenders have been diagnosed with a learning disability compared with only 6% of the general population (Greenberg et al., 2007). High rates of learning and intellectual disabilities reveal are very apparent in youth detained in the juvenile Justice system. While estimates vary, it is reported that somewhere between 33% and 41% of detained or incarcerated juveniles have a special education disability compared with approximately 10% of students in the general population (Miller et al., 2019). The majority of these youth will not return to school and are likely to end up in the prison system (Miller et al., 2019).

Reentry Considerations

At base, offenders are under-educated compared to the population at large and generally present with lower levels of literacy, resulting in a group of people who are less able to cope with daily activities and daily life (Gaes, 2008). Consequently, it is no wonder that education programs are the most commonly offered programming options for offenders who are incarcerated. Education programs most commonly offered in the prison setting include adult basic education (ABE), general education development (GED), and vocational/technical programs. As Table 4-1 indicates, access to college coursework is also available in some prisons. In addition, special education courses are available for offenders who present with learning disabilities.

The majority of state prisons (84%) offer some type of educational programming opportunity to offenders, with 84% of state prisons offering adult secondary education, 80% providing adult basic education programs, and 50% offering vocational training opportunities (Layton-Mackenzie, 2012; Stephan, 2008). Educational and vocational opportunities are somewhat greater in federal prisons than state institutions (Layton-Mackenzie, 2012). Despite the growing number of offenders housed in private prisons, only 61% offer adult basic education, 70% offer secondary education, and 44% offer vocational training programs (Layton-Mackenzie, 2012). Interestingly, while adult basic education is offered in most prisons, as of 2004, relatively few (less than two percent) of offenders in state prison are actually receiving basic education services.

Table 4-1. Institutional Educational Programs by Type

Type of Education	Definition
Adult Basic Education (ABE)	Basic skills training in math, reading, writing, and English as a Second Language (ESL)
General Education Development (GED)	High school equivalency instruction
Vocational Education	Hands-on training to prepare offenders for specific jobs/and or industries
Post-Secondary Instruction	College-level coursework that allows offenders to earn credit that may be applied toward an associate, bachelor, or master's degree.
Special Education	Educational training for offenders who have learning disabilities

Conversely, 20–30% of offenders are receiving adult secondary education and vocational life skills training. Not surprisingly, a significant gap exists between need and provision of service (Brazzell et al., 2009).

Institutional educational programs are important to consider in the context of total prison populations. In 1991, out of a total of 792,535 offenders in state prisons, 57% of prisoners participated in prison education programming. This is in contrast to 1997, where participation in educational programming dropped to 52% at the same time that state prison populations grew to 1,176,564 (Western et al., 2003). Of the state prisoners participating in programs in 1997, over half participated in vocational and high school/GED programs.

Completion rates for offenders who take part in prison education programs are difficult to calculate and not generally available. Because prison programs differ greatly between number and type of programs offered, a determination of completion rates by program type (i.e., ABE, GED, etc.) is not possible. However, a study by Erisman and Contardo (2005) found that during the 2003–2004 academic year, 85,000 prisoners had access to postsecondary programming, less than 5% of the incarcerated population. Moreover, a small number of prison systems were responsible for the largest number of enrolled offenders in postsecondary programming (90%). Fifteen prison systems were responsible for providing 96% of all of the degrees and certificates awarded to offenders nationwide (Erisman & Contardo, 2005).

Because it is generally accepted that basic reading, writing, and math skills are required to function in everyday life, and because the United States prison population is generally considered to be, "the most educationally disadvantaged population in the United States," many states mandate that basic education skills be taught to those who do not meet state-mandated education minimums (Klein et al., 2004, p. 1). A study conducted in 2002 by McGlone indicates that 22 of 50 states and the federal government have adopted legislation or implemented policies that mandate education for offenders. These educational programs usually require offenders to participate in programming until such time as they are able to achieve a state-determined education minimum. In 10 states that minimum standard is the GED. Other states require offenders to function at a sixth-grade level (McGlone, 2002). The Federal Bureau of Prisons requires inmates without high school diplomas or GED certification to participate in a literacy program for a minimum of 240 hours or until they've earned their GED (Federal Bureau of Prisons, n.d.) Once the required level of achievement has been obtained, offenders have the option to continue taking part in educational program offerings or to withdraw.

Participation in educational programs, whether required or volunteer, can result in numerous benefits and/or consequences for the participants. Offenders who are mandated to attend educational programming can often obtain earned release credits and parole eligibility for their participation and not be required to have a job assignment. Conversely, offenders who decide not to take part in educational programming may adversely impact the parole decision-making process. Good time credits can also be withheld for nonparticipation (Coley & Barton, 2006).

There is some disagreement about whether compulsory prison education policies are effective and beneficial to offenders. Those who support mandatory prison-based education argue that momentum will encourage offenders who begin taking education courses to continue (Ryan & McCabe, 1994). Detractors of compulsory prison-based education suggest that forced participation in education programs results in poorer performance than if the offender volunteered (Jenkins, 2002). While the research is limited, Ryan and McCabe's (1994) comparison of voluntary versus mandatory participation in a South Carolina prison-based literacy program found no significant difference in an inmates' level of achievement based upon whether their participation was mandated or voluntary.

Regardless of whether educational programs in prison should be compulsory or volunteer, the fact remains that the fiscal resources necessary to fund such enterprises are great and that they come from a variety of different sources (Brazzell et al., 2009). Funding for correctional education programs usually comes from state and federal sources. At the state level, funding for correctional programming comes from general fund appropriations to state departments of corrections, departments of labor and education, or from special revenue sources (Brazzell et al., 2009). In addition, money for funding of these programs comes from Title II of the Workforce Development Act (for ABE and GED programs), the Carl. D. Perkins Vocational and Applied Technology Education Act (for vocational and technical training), and grants (Brazzell et al., 2009).

Funding for corrections programming is difficult to track because state funding streams are sometimes difficult to follow, but what we do know is that declines in funding for educational programming began in the 1990s and that this trend continues to present (Coley & Barton, 2006). The 2008 recession led to even further budget cuts in corrections programming (Davis et al., 2013). For example, California's 2009 fiscal budget reduced correctional education spending by 30%, resulting in the elimination of 712 teaching positions and a 50% reduction in vocational programs. The Texas Legislature reduced their prison education budget by $35.6 million over a period of two years, with the elimination of almost 300 full-time positions and reductions in salary. During this same time, Oklahoma reduced funding for academic and vocational programs, closing vocational training in five of its prisons (Davis et al., 2013). Not only have corrections budgets shrunk overall, but targeted resources allocated for educational programs in prison have been significantly impacted. In some instances, funding for teachers in prisons has been so drastically reduced that educational programs are taught by corrections staff (Klein et al., 2004).

Research on the efficacy of correctional education programs is generally of two types: research that assesses the impact of prison-based education programs on recidivism (i.e., rearrest, reconviction, and reincarceration), and research that evaluates the degree to which these programs impact employability. The nature and type of the relationship between prison-based education programs and recidivism is not clear (MacKenzie, 2008). Scholarship indicates that increased education while in prison results in improved cognitive skills of offenders (MacKenzie, 2006), impacts moral development (Duguid, 1982), and enhances problem-solving abilities that encourage offenders to mediate their own criminogenic needs, thereby reducing their likelihood of reoffending (Andrews et al., 1990).

Moreover, increased educational attainment may bolster executive cognitive function (that level of functioning required to plan and to regulate goal-directed behavior)—functioning necessary to mediate antisocial behavior (Giancola, 2000). Still other researchers suggest that education encourages maturity (Batiuk et al., 1997), increases coping mechanisms for offenders who have been prisonized while also promoting pro-social behaviors (Harer, 1995), and allows for more critical thinking to assess the consequences of actions and behaviors (Harer & Langen, 2001). In a rare qualitative study, Pelletier and Evans (2019) noted that offenders participating in higher education programs (e.g., college, master level) developed greater confidence and integrity, better communication skills, and a more positive self-image; factors associated with recidivism. On reentry, "these relational attributes enabled participants to connect to social institutions that have provided them with employment opportunities, access to prosocial networks, and the ability to have a positive influence over others" (pp. 55–56).

It is also possible that the act of engaging in educational programs while in prison may enhance other program participation. The more educated an offender is, the more likely they are to engage in other institutional programming that may have additional potential long-term benefits (Gaes, 2008). Layton-Mackenzie (2012) suggests that while many correctional education programs "are consistent with the principles of effective programs... there are still many unknowns about correctional education"—what curriculums are the most effective and "what works for whom, when, why and in what circumstances" (p. 513).

Although it is generally held that education reduces criminal involvement and contributes to desistence from crime (Esperian 2010; Kim & Clark, 2013; Lichtenberger & Onyewu, 2005; Machin et al., 2011; Pompoco et al., 2017; Taheri & Welsh, 2016), research suggests that the relationship may not be straightforward. A recidivism study conducted by

Steurer and colleagues (2001) determined that offender participation in educational programming reduced the likelihood of future incarceration by 29%. Other recidivism studies reveal similar outcomes. Recidivism studies in Texas, California, and New York indicate that recidivism rates for offenders who participated in prison education programming were lower than for offenders who did not participate (Chase & Dickover, 1983; Duguid, 1981; Thorpe et al., 1984).

Findings from the Bureau of Justice Statistics indicate that less educated offenders (40% without a high school diploma and 45% with a GED) were more likely than more educated offenders (26% with a high school diploma and 21% with some college) to have been sentenced as a juvenile (Harlow, 2003). Lochner (1999) estimated that graduating from high school reduced the probability of criminal involvement by 86%. In their three-year recidivism study of adult parolees, Houser and colleagues (2019b) reported that while pre-incarceration education levels were predictive of reincarceration for a new crime, when they controlled for individual- and neighborhood-level characteristics, education was no longer significant, suggesting that while education is important, other factors may play a stronger role in predicting the likelihood of returning to prison.

Abeling-Judge (2019) examined the impact of re-enrolling in educational programs on criminal desistance among individuals who left formal education prematurely. Overall findings suggested resuming education to have a partial desistance effect, varying by offense type and specific degree attainment. More specifically, the results of GED certification were somewhat inconsistent but suggested that individuals completing their certification were less likely to commit property crimes, but no significant differences were noted in violent offending. Completing high school was found to be generally supportive of reduced offending; however, similar to GED certifications, differences were noted in property crimes, but not violent offending (Abeling-Judge, 2019).

Work by Jancic (1998) evaluated the efficacy of correctional educational programming in multiple states. Results indicate that offenders in the Texas program who received more than 200 hours of academic and/or vocational programming were reincarcerated less often than offenders who received less than 200 hours of programming or no programming at all. Moreover, offenders in New York who successfully completed GED requirements while incarceration were reincarcerated 5.1% less often than offenders who did not. When evaluated by program type, a review of six studies that assessed prison-based ABE, GED, and secondary education programs found that correctional educational programs were responsible for reducing recidivism in five of six studies (Jensen & Reed, 2006). However, research evaluating New Jersey inmate populations suggests that a GED did not predict post-release arrest (Zgoba, 2008), and a study from Florida did not find that a GED improved recidivistic outcomes (Tyler & Kling, 2003).

In their meta-analysis of prison education programs over a period of 32 years, Davis and colleagues found, on average, that participants were 43% less likely to recidivate than non-participants. Focusing solely on GED programs, since they are the most common educational approach in correctional facilities, the researchers found participants had 30% lower odds of recidivating, though the researchers were not able to disentangle if participants were involved in other programs that may have also contributed to reducing recidivism (Davis et al., 2013). Similarly, Pompoco and colleagues (2017) reported that participants of GED, vocational training, apprenticeship programs, and college classes were less likely to return to prison three years post release; these findings did not hold true, however, for inmates who started programs but failed to complete them.

When considering the impact of post-secondary prison-based education programs on recidivism, it is apparent that disparate findings exist. Various studies indicate that post-secondary educational attainment while in prison reduced recidivism (Steurer et al., 2001; Taylor, 1992). Still other work indicates that post-secondary education impacted offender behavior positively while in prison and resulted in less recidivism for those who participated in programming the first year after release compared with a similar group who did not participate (Winterfield et al., 2009). Moreover, a meta-analysis evaluating prison-based post-secondary education programs conducted by Wilson and colleagues (2000) evaluating 33 experimental and quasi-experimental education, vocation, and work programs found that program participants in all of these programs recidivated less than nonparticipants. Other meta-analyses by Chappell (2004) and Aos and colleagues (2006) found similar results.

Education studies on inmate misconduct (infractions of institutional rules) have yielded disparate findings. For example, using the Survey of Inmates in State Correctional Facilities, Houser and colleagues (2012) reported no association between an inmate's level of pre-incarceration educational attainment and their likelihood of being charged with prison misconduct. Gover and colleagues, to the contrary, found an inverse relationship between education and prison misconduct, but only for females; no significant findings were reported for males (2008). Yet, another study by Lahm (2009) found that for each additional year of pre-incarceration education, the number of prison misconduct charges decreased.

Lahm (2009) further examined prisoner misconduct across four types of correctional education programming. Interestingly, Lahm's findings revealed participation in college programs significantly reduced the likelihood of being charged with misconduct; however, participation in GED, high school, or vocational programs had no impact. Similar to Lahm's findings, Pompoco and colleagues (2017) found completion of college classes during an inmate's first year of incarceration lowered their chances of engaging in violent misconduct; however, unlike Lahm, they found this to be true of GED completers as well; vocational training and apprenticeship programs were not found to have any effect on violent misconduct.

Few analyses of the costs and benefits of prison-based education exist. Studies by Taylor (1992) and Hrabowski and Robbi (2002) attempted to assess the fiscal impact of providing prison-based education, but they did not employ econometric methods to handle issues of marginal costs and other cost–benefit consideration (Gaes, 2008). To date, the most complete cost–benefit analysis of prison-based education was conducted by Aos and colleagues (2006). In this study, as Table 4-2 demonstrates, the authors suggest that prison-based vocational training and general education programs provide the single largest net benefits in adult correctional education. Based on their meta-analytic findings that participation in correctional education programs is associated with a 13-percentage point reduction in reincarceration over a 3-year period, Davis and colleagues (2013), using a hypothetical pool of 100 offenders, estimated 3-year reincarceration costs for inmates who received correctional education and those who did not. Their findings indicated that reincarceration costs of inmates who did not receive correctional education would be between $2.94 million and $3.25 million; reincarceration costs of inmates who did receive correctional education would be between $2.07 million and $2.28 million. Thus, correctional education would reduce reincarceration costs over 100 inmates by $0.87 million to $0.97 million. The costs estimated were conservative as they were estimated on direct costs only (the cost of education programming and the cost of incarceration itself).

Table 4-2. The Financial Benefits of Prison-Based Education

Prison-Based Education Type	Expenditure per Offender	Future Criminal Justice Cost Savings	Future Cost Savings Including Victim Savings
Vocational Training	$1,182	$6,806	$13,738
General Education	$962	$5,306	$10,669

Adapted from Aos et al., 2006.

When considering the savings attained from reduced victimizations and all of the other attendant costs associated with managing victims, overall reductions in cost abound while reductions in recidivism rates of 9% and 7% for vocational training and general education, respectively, are possible (Aos et al., 2006).

The impact of prison-based educational programs can be further felt when employment prospects post-prison are considered. Research indicates that offenders who are able to achieve educational improvement while in prison tend to find more jobs compared with offenders who don't (Gerber & Fritsch, 1995). For example, a study by Wolf and Sylves (1981) indicated that 75% of inmates who obtained their college degree while in prison found employment after release from prison. Additional research by Taylor (1992) and Jenkins and colleagues (1995) indicate that post-secondary correctional education had beneficial effects on post-release employment and that the higher the level of education achieved in prison, the more likely the offender was to obtain employment upon release. Work by Tyler and Kling (2007) argues that participation in GED programming affects labor market outcomes by increasing offender skill levels and by making offenders more marketable. Davis and colleagues (2013) found inmates participating in education programs were 13% more likely to be employed following release. A survey of employers in

Florida reported formal education, training, and job readiness certification were important factors associated with their willingness to hire ex-offenders (Swanson et al., 2014).

If, in fact, offenders are leaving prison less educated than the general population, this likely translates into reduced access to job opportunities for offenders. Minimal job opportunities result in increased competition for existing jobs, but also jobs that are likely to pay less than a living wage (Hanneken & Dannerbeck, 2007). This effect is further felt when considering that simply having a criminal record decreases an offender's ability to find employment at all, let alone employment that pays reasonably (Bushway, 1998; Western et al., 2001).

Promising Practice

Several interesting programs targeting improving the educational attainment of offenders while in prison hold promise. One such promising initiative includes involving community colleges in the prison-based education process. Historically, community colleges are more educationally accessible to a greater number of non-traditional students and tend to cost less (Contardo & Tolbert, 2008). Moreover, community colleges can sometimes offer more program flexibility as they often seek out new client bases and program offerings based on societal needs (Contardo & Tolbert, 2008). Research indicates that 68% of all postsecondary correctional education programs were provided by community colleges (U.S. Department of Education, 2009). In 2014, California passed law SB 1391, allowing community colleges to deliver on-site classes in prisons and to receive full-time equivalency funding for incarcerated students. Within three years of the law being implemented, 34 out of the state's 35 prisons had degree-building college courses, with an enrollment of almost 4,500 students per semester (Corrections to College California, 2018).

There are a variety of reasons why partnerships between prisons and community colleges make sense. First, community college tuition and fees are more affordable than traditional colleges/universities. Second, community colleges are generally more conveniently located, although distance education offerings now make physical proximity to colleges almost a non-issue. Third, community colleges are accredited as post-secondary educational agencies and therefore qualify for a variety of federal grants and programs, including the U.S. Department of Education's Grants to States for Workplace and Community Transition Training for Incarcerated Youth. Moreover, the Higher Education Act of 1994 ensures that money is available through grants to state correctional agencies to fund literacy, life skills, and job skills programs through community colleges (U.S. Department of Education, 2009).

What the current literature also reveals is the importance not only of participating in prison-based education programs but doing so at the correct dose (Cho & Tyler, 2008). Cho and Tyler indicate in their work on prison-based adult basic education (ABE) and post-release labor market outcomes that offenders who participate in ABE have better employment outcomes compared with non-participants only if they received a minimum amount of program exposure. Offenders also experienced better outcomes when there were minimal interruptions in program participation (i.e., fewer prison moves, lockdowns, etc.).

To this point, our conversation has focused on prison-based educational programs with an eye toward understanding how and in what ways offenders are prepared for release. But, because we know that 95% of people who go to prison eventually leave, it only makes sense to focus on what post-prison educational opportunities are available for offenders.

Certainly, offenders have access to the same educational opportunities outside prison walls as do ordinary citizens, but as we have discussed previously, access to grant funding and other forms of financial aid can be restricted depending on the type of crime committed (Crayton & Lindhal, 2007). More often than not, the problem seems to be related to offenders' inability to navigate the free world when it comes to figuring out how to access educational programs, how to apply for admission, and how to register, not to mention the practicalities associated with going to class and studying, rather than the availability of educational opportunities.

In an effort to make the process associated with furthering one's education understandable to offenders, a recent publication seeks to provide practical, real-world information to those who are interested in furthering their education after they have been released from prison (Crayton & Lindhal, 2007). This how-to guide provides information from how to use the internet to what documentation is required for application, to the different types of educational options available (i.e., GED, vocational programs, and college). In addition, this guide provides valuable tips on how to pay for college and highlights important challenges that offenders (particularly those with drug offenses) will face with respect to obtaining financial aid (Crayton & Lindhal, 2007). What is not included in this guidebook is information related to basic literacy programs.

Of particular interest is a program in Seattle, Washington, called Post-Prison Education Program that was created specifically to assist high-risk offenders leaving prison and returning to communities in Washington State with furthering their education (Post-Prison Education Program, 2022). Interested offenders can apply to the Post-Prison Education Program where they will be assisted in achieving a higher education while also being provided wraparound services that will help them achieve this goal including mentoring, transportation, daycare, legal aid, substance use/mental health treatment and help finding housing and employment (Post-Prison Education Program, 2022). All applicants must apply for traditional financial aid and use all other fiscal resources available to them to pay for their education. The Post-Prison Education Program then provides scholarships to cover the balance of costs associated with tuition, books, transportation, and rent. According to the program, an independent audit completed by the University of Washington found a 92% success rate over 11 years for participants staying out of prison.

Interestingly, while information on how to access and take part in educational programming after release from prison is difficult to obtain for offenders, it appears that they also are not always encouraged by parole officers. Rhine and colleagues reported in 1991 that only one in six paroling agencies required offenders on parole supervision to participate in educational or vocational training (Rhine(a) et al., 1991). Hopefully, this practice has changed since the early 1990s, but more recent data is not available. In any event, it seems antithetical to scholarship that clearly suggests that educational attainment is important for all, and a necessity for offenders if they have even a remote chance of obtaining and maintaining gainful employment upon release.

Employment

It has been empirically proven that work works. Work directly and positively impacts recidivism. Research indicates that offenders who are able to get and maintain employment recidivate less and are better able to navigate the reentry process (Apel & Horney, 2017; Laub et al., 1998; Welsh & Zajac, 2013). Even offenders agree that employment is beneficial. First-hand accounts from offenders seeking employment indicate that finding and maintaining employment facilitates positive adjustment to life after prison (Uggen et al., 2005). Exactly how or why this is the case is not fully understood. Some scholars argue that work serves as a turning point or transition in the life course of criminal behavior (Elder, 1985). Proponents of this position argue that important life events such as marriage, employment, or having a child can positively impact behavior in such a way as to reduce the likelihood that people will engage in crime (Sampson & Laub, 1993).

Work and other traditional, pro-social behaviors (i.e., getting married, having a child, etc.) allow for frequent contact with people who subscribe to conventional behaviors, and these experiences "rub off" or encourage conformity (Sampson & Laub, 1993). Results from one study note that work is the most effective turning point in the life course of criminal offenders over the age of twenty-six (Uggen, 2000).

While employment may be most beneficial to facilitating successful offender reentry, it is extraordinarily difficult, if not sometimes impossible, for offenders to obtain. As mentioned earlier in this chapter, offenders face significant educational deficits that put them at a disadvantage in the job market compared with their non-offending, better-educated, job-seeking counterparts. Lack of education coupled with spotty or nonexistent work experience, not to mention the stigma associated with being an offender, make getting and maintaining employment very challenging under the best of circumstances and impossible under the worst (Holzer et al., 2006; Western, 2007).

As Figure 4-1 indicates, the employment history of many offenders is meager in the years leading up to their incarceration (Looney & Turner, 2018). A large national study conducted by the Brookings Institute reported 56% of individuals in the two years prior to incarceration had "essentially no annual earnings (less than $500)," with 30% earning between $500 and $15,000, and a mean salary among those that were employed of $12,780 (Looney & Turner, 2018, p. 8). Additional findings showed unemployment rates rose just prior to incarceration—"probably a direct result of criminal activity, such as incarceration before trial or sentencing" (2018, p. 8). The lack of employment prior to incarceration further limits critical opportunities for offenders to return to jobs on their release.

Figure 4-1. Employment Prior to and Post Incarceration

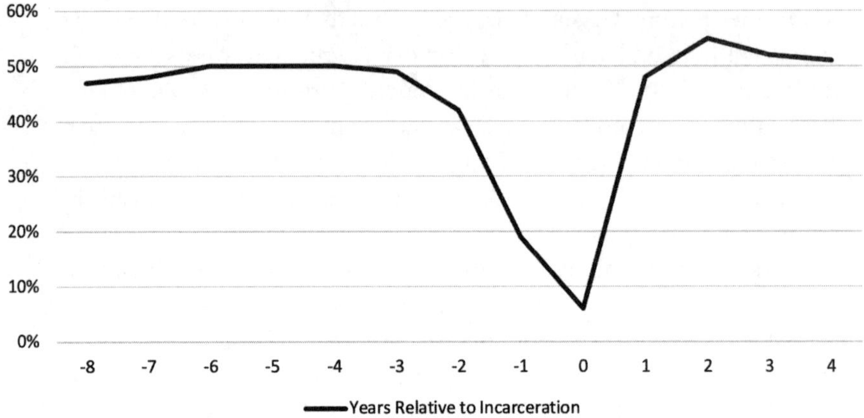

Adapted from Looney & Turner, 2018
Note: Sample includes individuals aged 18-64 incarcerated between 2009 and 2013
"(Year 0 denotes year of incarceration, year -1 is the calendar year of entry into prison, year 1 is the calendar year leaving prison, year 2 is the first full calendar year after release.)" (Looney & Turner, 2018, p. 6).

In an effort to mitigate these challenges, offenders are often forced to utilize familial ties and exploit social networks at their disposal to achieve positive employment outcomes, rather than to rely on more formal job search efforts (Berg & Huebner, 2011). Informal social networks are often able to facilitate a positive employment outcome for offenders precisely because offenders have friends and family or extended acquaintance networks who are willing to vouch for them. This is in contrast to more formal hiring practices that often result in the offender being turned away, not called for an interview, or otherwise not contacted because they may have admitted to having a criminal record on the job application.

Assuming an offender is able to find employment, no matter the method, they tend to earn less than others with similar backgrounds who have not been incarcerated (Bushway & Reuter, 2002). This wage penalty can result in significant hardship for people who have, in addition to regular expenses, fiscal obligations such as child support payments, fines, fees, restitution, driver's license surcharges, etc. Moreover, collateral consequences, including occupational licensing limitations, make gainful (and legal) employment even more elusive (Legal Action Center, 2004).

Historical Context

Work has always been a fundamental component of prison life. In fact, work and punishment have often been synonymous. Early prisons reinforced this notion by requiring hard labor and by viewing work as punishment (Garvey, 1998). The more severe the punishment, the harder offenders were expected to work. The prevailing belief was that through work, offenders would repent of their sins. Whether working alone in their cells or with others, many early prison administrators viewed work as the means by which offenders would be rehabilitated (Travis, 2005).

Nineteenth-century prison administrators also viewed prison labor as a means to employ large numbers of people for cheap wages. Furthermore, outsourcing prison labor to private businesses meant that prisons would realize some of the profit—a very appealing thought for many. Contract labor practices allowed state prisons to sell prison labor to private industry that in turn made goods that were sold on the free market. By the time of the Civil War, "the contract labor system had become the dominant organizational form of prison labor throughout the North" (Garvey, 1998, p. 352). In the South, convict labor was leased; a situation wherein prisons provided the labor to companies who were responsible for producing goods and for the care and custody of the inmate (Friedman, 1993).

By the end of the nineteenth century, the contract labor system was in jeopardy. Stakeholders from all sides were convinced that prison labor was a form of unfair labor practice as companies paid lower wages to inmates and produced goods at a higher profit all while free market labor was denied access to the same jobs (Garvey, 1998). As a result, labor unions took a lead role in discouraging the use of convict labor contracted out to private industry.

Ultimately, convict labor became the ward of the state through the rise of state's use industries or goods produced in prison by prisoners only for government entities. License plates, furniture, and food are examples of goods produced under state's use industry, then as now (Travis, 2005). Prisoners became employees for the state, making goods and providing services that did not compete with the free market, and performing duties that offset government expenditures (Garvey, 1998). Not surprisingly, work performed in prison for the prison was paid at wages infinitely lower than wages paid to employees in the free market who might perform the same or similar jobs.

In 1979, Congress passed the Justice System Improvement Act that was designed to encourage states to partner with private businesses to employ inmates. Out of this legislation came the Prison Industry Enhancement (PIE) Certification program that allowed prisons to receive an exemption from the ban on interstate commerce for prison-made goods (passed under the Hawes-Cooper Act of 1929). The primary purpose of PIE was to establish public–private ventures between prisons and private companies wherein inmates could work prison jobs provided by private business (Garvey, 1998). Unfortunately, this program has not been successful in developing these public-private linkages, primarily because of the costs associated with doing business in a prison environment and the requirement that private business pay inmates fair-market wages (Travis, 2005).

While prison and work have been inexorably bound together, the outcomes have not usually been favorable, especially for the offender. Those in prison who do work, do so for reduced wages and in positions that will not always provide them with marketable skills once they leave prison. Moreover, any skills that offenders may possess prior to incarceration are often not maintained while they are incarcerated, and upon release, these offenders are often not able to compete in the job market with people who have never been incarcerated (Travis, 2005).

Current Trends

Research indicates that most offenders are working prior to incarceration, even if that work is in low- or un-skilled positions, part-time work, or work that supplements legal employment with illegal activity (Kachnowski, 2005). Sixty percent of respondents who took part in the *Returning Home* study in Illinois indicate that they worked in food service, construction, or maintenance jobs. The median income for offenders working prior to incarceration was $8.50/hour (Kachnowski, 2005).

As noted above, work in prison does not always build or maintain skills. Most job assignments in prison are maintenance, janitorial, or food service work that assists the prison with day-to-day operations, but it does not build or maintain skill sets that are transferrable to the outside world (Travis, 2005). Prison-based employment programs aimed at enhancing skills and/or improving academic achievement do exist, but capacity does not in any way meet demand.

Roughly two-thirds of offenders do not participate in prison-based employment/vocational activities, this despite research that argues that in-prison work/vocational programs do impact recidivism. Gerber and Fritsch note that there is "a fair amount of support for the hypothesis that adult academic and vocational programs lead to... reductions in recidivism and increases in employment opportunities" (Gerber & Fritsch, 1995, p. 11).

Prison administrators generally support prison work programs. First, these programs help keep the peace. Inmates who work while in prison are less likely to engage in misconduct or have idle time and are more likely to learn workplace habits (e.g., arrive to work on time) and job readiness (e.g., minimal skills for employment) skills that are transferrable to the outside (Atkinson & Rostad, 2003; Solomon et al., 2004).

A study conducted by the Urban Institute as part of the *Returning Home* study sheds some light on post-prison employment for offenders. From a sample of 740 men, 65% were employed in the eight months after release in primarily semi- or un-skilled labor jobs. Twenty-four percent of study participants indicated that they held construction or general manual labor jobs, while 12% held food service positions, and 10% found work in maintenance (Visher et al., 2008). Despite the fact that the median monthly income for this sample was $700/month, most respondents in this study did not work a legitimate job and relied on family and friends for support rather than legal employment (Visher et al., 2008). Results also indicate that individuals with weak prior employment histories or educational deficits required significant additional assistance finding a job.

Respondents to the *Returning Home* employment study also indicate that they used multiple strategies for finding employment that included talking with friends/relatives, responding to newspaper advertisements, asking for assistance from their parole officer, and contacting former employers. Over 70% of offenders indicated that their criminal record impacted their ability to obtain employment. The best job leads and employment opportunities came from previous employers, further strengthening the notion that informal social networks are critical to finding post-prison employment (Visher et al., 2008).

The Brooking Institute's study on labor market outcomes further supports the assertion that the "incarcerated fare poorly in the formal labor market after they are released" (Looney & Turner, 2018, p. 7). In the first full year after release, almost half (49%) of ex-offenders earned less than $500, 32% earned between $500 and $15,000, and only 20% earned more than $15,000. Among those with jobs, the median annual salary of ex-offenders was $10,090, compared with median annual earnings of $19,492 for individuals with less than a high school diploma but no criminal record. Moreover, the majority of released offenders have few ties with the Internal Revenue Service (IRS) or other tax-generating agencies, suggesting "little attachment to the formal sector" (p. 7).

When considering individual-level factors that impact offenders' ability to get and maintain employment, interesting results emerge. Not surprisingly, offenders who used drugs or had physical or mental health conditions were employed fewer months than those that did not. Conversely, offenders who were married and who had strong relationships with their children were likely to be employed longer than offenders who did not (Visher et al., 2011). Clearly, pre-incarceration work experience, participation in prison work/vocational programs along with in-prison work experience, the ability to arrange work prior to release, reconnecting with old employers, and stable, pro-social influences (i.e., marriage) maximize the chances that an offender will be able to find and maintain employment once they return to the community setting (Visher et al., 2011).

When considering recidivism, men from the *Returning Home* study who were employed and who made more than $10/hour were half as likely to return to prison than those making less than $7/hour (Visher et al., 2008). Predicted probabilities of reincarceration for this sample were 8% for men who earned over $10/hour, 12% for those who earned $7–$10/hour, and 16% for those earning less than $7/hour. The predicted probability of recidivism for those respondents who were unemployed was 23% (Visher et al., 2008). In their study on post-release outcomes of offenders who participated in prison-based therapeutic community drug treatment programs, Welsh and Zajac (2013) found employment on release not only reduced rearrest and reincarceration, but it also reduced drug relapse.

Reentry Considerations

Upon release, offenders face a variety of problems in the labor market, problems that began long before incarceration. As noted earlier, many offenders were working prior to incarceration. However, in a study conducted by the Bureau of Justice Statistics (2000), 31% of offenders reported that they were unemployed in the month prior to arrest, compared to a 7% unemployment rate in the general U.S. population over the age of 18; findings are similar to those of the Brookings Institute that found higher unemployment nearer incarceration.

Offenders have a difficult time obtaining and maintaining employment in the community due to unstable work histories or limited legitimate work experience. When evaluating employment rates of offenders, data indicates that in the 1980s, the employment rates in any given week averaged approximately 60% for all offenders who had been previously incarcerated, but only 45% for black men (Holzer et al., 2003a). As has been established elsewhere, a disproportionate number of people in prison are people of color (nearly one-third are African American and nearly one-quarter are Hispanic). Given reduced employment opportunities for minorities, it is not surprising that access to post-prison employment is severely diminished (Bellair & Kowalski, 2011) and that minorities continue to be the targets of labor market discrimination (Holzer et al., 2003a); limitations that drastically impact the ability of offenders to obtain jobs, legitimate or otherwise.

Moreover, most offenders return to low-income and predominantly minority communities. These communities generally have few jobs available, especially to people with few contacts and/or little experience in legitimate work environments (Holzer et al., 2003a). Employment opportunities are also not always evenly distributed across neighborhood and community lines, making access to employment difficult (Bellair & Kowalski, 2011).

Furthermore, offenders' own attitudes about work and the types of available jobs are also likely to impact their employment choices. Many of the jobs available to offenders pay low wages, provide few benefits, and limit upward mobility. Offenders are less likely to engage in these types of jobs, choosing to forgo legitimate employment opportunities in favor of illegal options that pay more despite the risk these jobs often pose

(Holzer et al., 2003a). Examining correlates of parole success and failure in Pennsylvania, Bucklen and Zajac (2009) found parole violators were more likely to refuse low-end jobs and were more likely to report dissatisfaction with work. The researchers noted that violators were unrealistic in their expectations, disregarded their criminal records, and expressed a sense of entitlement—"I won't work at [a fast food restaurant] no matter what," indicating refusal to start with a "survival job" and work up to a "career job" (p. 253). Conversely, successful parolees were committed to their jobs and willing to work their way up to a higher position. Violators were also less likely to have a bank account, once again reinforcing limited ties to the formal sector.

In addition, offenders have trouble securing jobs because they never developed the skills required to hold a job. While in-prison job-training programs for ex-offenders have increased significantly in the last few years, they generally focus only on providing offenders with the skills they need to perform a job, rather than the additional life and cognitive skills that are also necessary to function in the workplace and in society (Bushway & Reuter, 2002).

One of the central discussions regarding offenders and employment has to do with whether offenders are lazy and unwilling to find employment or whether their criminal record impacts their ability to find a job. Some argue that poor employment outcomes for offenders are a function of personal characteristics and their unwillingness to do meaningful work (Piehl, 2003). Yet, businesses that do hire ex-offenders indicate that they do so because of the quality of the employee and their level of productivity. Business owners argue that potential employees from the free world are not always as invested or hungry for work as those who have been to prison and that this motivation works to the employer's advantage (Atkinson & Rostad, 2003). For many offenders, work is more than a needed paycheck, it is a requirement of their release: "their freedom may depend on it" (Swanson et al., 2014, p. 104). Still, others argue that if offenders are able to jump through the hoop requiring evidence that they are qualified for the jobs to which they are applying, they are often circumvented in their employment search by the "mark of a criminal record" (Pager, 2003, p. 937).

More than ever, personal information about individuals is widely available. This is no more apparent than for offenders at the time that they apply for employment. The degree to which a criminal record impacts an offender's ability to get and maintain employment is central to research conducted by Devah Pager (2007). Pager's research indicates that the "negative credential" or stigma associated with a criminal record plays out in unique ways when offenders attempt to seek employment (2003, p. 932). Her central research question assesses to what degree a criminal record affects the chances of an offender being selected by an employer for work given two equally qualified job candidates (Pager, 2007).

In an effort to evaluate this question, Pager developed a sophisticated study design that included two pairs of testers who applied for real job openings. One pair of testers was white and the other was black. Each tester in each group alternated possessing a criminal record with the other so that each tester had equal opportunity to play both criminal and noncriminal (Pager, 2007). Data from Pager's study evaluating the effect of a criminal record for white offenders indicated that 34% of white applicants without criminal records received callbacks for job interviews compared with 17% of white applicants with criminal records. In this instance, a criminal record reduced the likelihood of receiving a job callback by 50% (Pager, 2007).

Data are even more revealing for the black testers. Overall callback rates for black applicants were significantly lower than for white applicants. Moreover, the effect of a criminal record is more apparent for black applicants than for white applicants. Fourteen percent of black applicants with no record received callbacks compared with 5% of black applicants that had a criminal record (Pager, 2007). Callback rates for non-offenders relative to offenders for white applicants were 2 to 1 and nearly 3 to 1 for black applicants (Pager, 2007). Results from this study certainly support the contention that having a criminal record is an official status or marker that provides employers with an easy and obvious sieve through which to filter potential employees.

The question remains, to what extent are employers willing to hire people with criminal records? Traditionally, employers are unwilling to hire people with a criminal record for a variety of reasons. Some occupations are not legally available to people who have felony records (Hahn, 1991), some employers place a premium on trustworthiness of employees and do not feel that people who have broken the law can be trusted (Holzer et al., 2001; 2002), and employers can sometimes be held legally liable for the criminal actions of their employees under the auspices of negligent hiring (Bushway, 2004). If an employer knows or should have known that an employee had a criminal history and that employee engages in criminal activity, the employer may be held liable (Connerley et al., 2001).

Given these considerations, it is not surprising that research indicates that employers are very unwilling to hire ex-offenders, even more so than other disadvantaged groups such as welfare recipients. In a 2003 survey of employers, over 90% of employers were willing to consider filling their most recent job vacancies with welfare recipients, while only 40% considered filling the vacancy with an offender (Holzer et al., 2003a). Employees who do hire offenders seem more willing to do so if that work does not require direct contact with customers, such as in unskilled manufacturing, construction, or transportation positions. Moreover, employers seem more amenable to hiring offenders with drug or property convictions than those charged with a violent crime or those released from prison with little or no work experience (Holzer et al., 2003b). A survey of potential employers found 60% were willing to hire ex-offenders; however, almost 70% of those willing employers also said that certain crimes would automatically disqualify someone from consideration (Swanson et al., 2014). Other research indicates that employers who actually conduct background checks are more likely to hire African Americans but that in the absence of these background checks (generally due to cost), employers will use other traits such as age, gender, and race to assess employability (Holzer et al., 2006).

In an effort to incentivize employers to hire ex-offenders, federal programs in all 50 states along with some individual state programs have been implemented using incentives such as tax credits and fidelity bonds. By way of example, Congress passed the Work Opportunity Tax Credit Program (WOTC), providing employers the opportunity to earn federal tax credits for hiring ex-offenders and other "targeted populations that have consistently faced barriers in the workplace" (Internal Revenue Service, 2020, p. 1). When Swanson and colleagues (2014) asked employers if available tax credits would make them more willing to hire an ex-offender, only 10% said that it would influence their decision. A recent study by the Rand Corporation found a 37% increase in the number of employers willing to consider hiring a non-violent ex-offender if they had a post-conviction certificate verifying work performance history, and 77% were willing to hire an offender if baseline tax credits were increased to 40% of a worker's wage (up to $5,000) (Hunt et al., 2018).

If offenders can find and actually get a job, any motivation an offender might have to maintain employment is tempered by the fact that there is a greater likelihood that he or she will encounter a "wage penalty" compared to people with similar skills who do not have a criminal record (Pettit & Lyons, 2007). The economic impact of incarceration on the wage-earning potential of offenders is striking. Regardless of age, men coming out of prison can expect between 4.6 and 6.8 percent less in wages than the general population (Petit & Lyons, 2009). As Figure 4-2 indicates, men who have been incarcerated have significantly lower wages, employment rates, and annual earnings than their crime-free counterparts.

Figure 4-2. Reduction in Employment, Wages, and Earnings Associated with Incarceration, 1983 to 2000

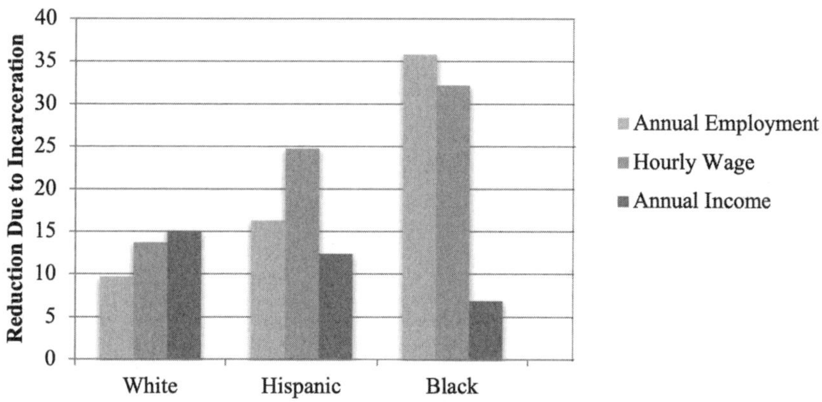

Adapted from Western, 2006.

Apparently, wage penalties that existed at the time of incarceration are exacerbated once offenders begin the reentry process and then only magnified by race and ethnicity. If all incarcerated men possessed significantly fewer job skills at the time they were imprisoned compared with non-incarcerated men, African American and Hispanic offenders possessed even fewer marketable job skills upon release compared with Caucasian offenders (Western, 2006). Furthermore, data suggest that incarceration reduces hourly wages, on average, 15% but that the net loss is particularly great for Hispanic offenders (24.7%). The incarceration effect for black offenders is that they are likely to be paid 12.4% less than black men who never went to prison (Western, 2007). Overall, men with criminal records who have gone to prison earn approximately 30–40% less per year than men who have not been incarcerated.

In concrete terms, a 30-year-old black man who is a high school dropout earns an average of $9,000 per year. For a black male with a criminal record, his yearly earnings are reduced by $3,000 (Western, 2007). The disparity between black and white offenders who are dropouts is palpable. White males who are 30 years old and who are high school dropouts earn an average of $14,400 each year. The earning potential for a white male with a prison record is reduced by $5,200 (Western, 2007).

For women leaving prison, the struggle of finding work can have even greater challenges. Employers are more willing to hire ex-offenders for construction and manufacturing positions, typically male-dominated industries (Sered & Norton-Hawk, 2019). Women typically seek positions in industries that have greater contact with people (e.g., retail, daycare) and are therefore more likely to require criminal background checks (National Employment Law Project, 2016). Women are also more likely to require childcare for their minor children while at work. The conundrum being that the majority of the women can't afford childcare, yet they need the work to support themselves and their child(ren). Following a group of released women over 10 years, Sered and Norton-Hawk (2019) noted that despite being enthusiastic about finding work, the jobs that the women could secure were low wage with poor working conditions. Employers expected the women to work erratic hours with no guarantee of a minimum number of hours and therefore no guarantee of a minimum pay. Moreover, the women reported that employers made no provisions for them to check in with their parole officers or submit to urine tests as a required condition of their supervision.

Yet, even if an employer is willing to hire an ex-offender, and even if the offender is willing to accept a wage penalty just to be employed, competition for legitimate work among offenders and law-abiding citizens still exists. And the bigger question remains, will the offender be able to maintain employment in the long term? Prison records divert offenders from getting and maintaining long-term jobs due to the adverse effects that incarceration has on skill sets, stigma, and social connections (Western, 2006). And while getting a job is certainly difficult, the types of jobs available to offenders are even more problematic. If jobs available do not pay a living wage, it may well be that offenders feel that they have no choice but to supplement legal work with illegal activity (Western,

2006). Keeping in mind that the monetary benefits of a criminal lifestyle will likely always outweigh the income from a legitimate job, getting a legitimate job often does not pay.

Kelly and Fader (2012) suggest that adding to the already formidable challenges that ex-offenders face getting a job is the current trend by employers to use computer- and internet-based application processes. Some of the biggest employers, such as Walmart, Target, Lowes, Home Depot, and Best Buy, use exclusively electronics-based job applications. Kelly and Fader noted that three-quarters of the retailers required a criminal background check, with 40% requesting a release of the applicant's credit history and 54% drug test results. Unlike paper applications that typically ask for this information in fine print at the end of the form, electronic applications are more likely to request permission at the beginning, often before asking personal information such as name and address. If an applicant refuses permission, the application process is terminated. While not exclusive to electronic applications, personality tests of up to 150 items are also part of the application process. The researchers note, however, that electronic applications make the use of personality tests easier and less expensive. Moreover, unlike paper applications hindered by length, electronic applications are able to include more personality test questions and therefore place greater weight on these responses in their hiring decisions (Kelly & Fader, 2012).

Promising Practice

There are a variety of programs that attempt to mitigate the problems associated with offenders finding work. These programs attempt to provide support for both the employer and the employee and are generally discussed in the context of supply-side and demand-side program options. Supply-side programs usually provide some level of job training and educational enhancement and run the gambit from in-prison vocational and educational programs to apprenticeship opportunities, job skills training, peer support networks, and life skills training.

One program is particularly interesting because it attempts to fill the gap in transitional employment for offenders who have just left prison. New York's Center for Employment Opportunities (CEO) program was recently evaluated with interesting results (Redcross et al., 2009). CEO is a transitional jobs program that pays offenders to work in jobs on a short-term basis. During their employment, these offenders are provided with support services and after a period of time, if they perform well, CEO works with the offender to find more permanent employment.

Transitional jobs programs for offenders are viewed as being beneficial because they allow the offender to accumulate work experience in a controlled environment and to demonstrate accountability, timeliness, trustworthiness, and other important job skills (Redcross et al., 2009). Programs like CEO also allow offenders to earn wages at a critical time in the reentry process and enable staff to address issues related to job performance before offenders attempt to seek jobs in the open labor market (Redcross et al., 2009). Results from the evaluation indicate that the CEO program generated increases in employment for transitional jobs, but less so for more permanent positions. The CEO program also reduced recidivism during the first year of the study, affecting a recidivism rate of 31% for the program group compared with 38% for the control group (Redcross et al., 2009).

Another program of promise is the Ready4Work program developed by Public/Private Ventures focusing on offenders with the greatest needs and at high risk for recidivism. This program provides employment services via partnerships with local faith, justice, business, and social service organizations nationally. Offenders interested in participating in the program voluntarily enroll within 90 days of release from prison and have the opportunity to take part in a 12-month program that provides job skills and employment services as well as mentoring. Results from an outcomes analysis of the program indicate that program retention was good; offenders who enrolled in the program remained engaged in the program for a median of eight months. Moreover, offenders who sought out mentors were more likely to remain in the program than offenders who did not. Approximately 56% of all program participants held a job for at least one month while in the program, and 33% of offenders were able to maintain jobs for six months or more. Recidivism data finds 2.5% of participants returned to prison for a new offense within six months of release and 6.9% within one year; these percentages are lower than national averages (Farley & McClanahan, 2007).

Demand-side programs include bond and wage supplement programs, enterprise zones, community development, and weed and seed grants. Bond programs are subsidized by the government and provide employers with bonds or insurance against possible crimes that an ex-offender might commit while on their payroll. Wage supplements are government-sponsored programs that reduce employer's wage payments through subsidy or tax credit. This program encourages employees to hire offenders because it reduces the amount of money employers must pay in labor costs (Bushway & Reuter, 2002). In both instances, these programs are designed to encourage employers to hire ex-offenders by providing them with a sense of security and financial incentive to do so.

Other demand-side program options are community-based efforts to promote neighborhood cohesion through encouraging interactions between employers, their new employees, and the community at large. Enterprise zones provide tax incentives to small, economically depressed communities. The programs offer investment, labor, and financial incentives to employers to locate their businesses in these communities in an effort to promote job development and economic growth in the community (Erickson & Friedman, 1991). Community development block grants are similar in scope to enterprise zones, but in this instance money is provided to local governments through block grants to revitalize distressed neighborhoods (Bushway & Reuter, 2002).

Finally, the federal government through the Department of Justice developed a program called "weed and seed." This program is also aimed at revitalizing economically depressed neighborhoods, but does so through fighting crime and developing community-based employment linkages. The idea is that criminal activity that deters local residents from participating in the legal job market (e.g., through selling drugs) must be "weeded" from the community and other, legal employment opportunities must be "seeded" or made available and be attainable to those in the community (Bushway & Reuter, 2002).

The overriding belief is that work programs and work opportunities for ex-offenders must increase legal earnings and the potential for legal jobs. The relationship between work and crime must change so that offenders do not look upon crime and work as choosing one career over another. Instead, offenders must change the way in which they evaluate the consequences of their actions, and only then legitimate work for legitimate work's sake will prevail (Piehl, 2003).

Chapter 5

Families and Children and Reentry

The family is a little recognized but very critical component of the reentry process. When crimes are committed and adjudicated, it is the perpetrator who is directly punished, but the family is often indirectly affected in the process. Family dynamics are significantly altered by the incarceration of a loved one. Parents who are incarcerated are removed from the day-to-day activities and lives of their children, parenting dynamics are modified sometimes permanently, and children are forever impacted by their parents' law-breaking behaviors.

Families

Until relatively recently, offenders were sentenced to terms of imprisonment with little or no thought as to how the incarceration of a family member would impact/alter the family dynamic. After all, the offender committed the crime and the offender should do the time. This lack of concern or interest in the family as a dimension of the reentry process extends to practitioners and scholars alike. Practitioners have generally not been willing to embrace the idea that families and family structures are or should be their concern. In fact, some corrections authorities assert that families do not play significant roles in encouraging criminal behavior (i.e., they do not believe that families are criminogenic factors that can influence risk/recidivism). The role of a correctional institution is to incarcerate the offender, not to consider family dynamics (Christ & Bitler, 2010). Conversely, scholars such as Hairston (2001a) argue that families are especially worthy of study and evaluation precisely because families can impact how offenders adjust to incarceration and how well they do upon release. Still other research supports increasing the focus on, and support provided to, families of the incarcerated, contextualizing this within the boundaries of good social conscience (Foster & Hagan, 2009).

Accepting the notion that families are impacted in some way by incarceration, one important issue to consider is who or what the family is. Traditional notions of family composition (a mother, father, and children) no longer apply when evaluating families and the offenders to whom they are related (Fishman, 1990). The notion of family is more complex and broad in its nature and scope when considering it in the context of incarceration. Families may be defined as single parents/mothers with children (Baunach, 1985; Martin, 2001), caregivers of children of incarcerated parents (Bloom & Steinhart, 1993), and extended kin networks that include biological as well as other family and friends (Codd, 2007; Mumola, 2000).

Current Trends

Who exactly are the family members of retuning prisoners? A recent study of family members of returning offenders to Houston, Texas, provides some insight. As Table 5-1 indicates, family members in the Texas study were usually female, African American, and older than their returning relatives (Shollenberger, 2009).

The median age of family members of returning prisoners to Houston, Texas, was 51, with the largest share of family members represented in the sample being grandmothers or mothers. Three-quarters of family members of returning offenders were African American (61%) or Hispanic (14%). Seventy-five percent of family members interviewed were either married or had been married at the time of interview. A majority of family members had minimally attained a high school education or equivalent (Shollenberger, 2009). Family members of returning prisoners in Texas received income from a variety of sources including gainful employment (53%), government subsidy, including Medicare/Medicaid, supplemental Social Security Income/Social Security Disability, and food stamps (88%), and a household member's income (25%) (Shollenberger, 2009).

Table 5-1. Demographic Characteristics of Family of Incarcerated Offenders

Demographic Characteristic of Family Member	Percentage
Gender	
Female	77
Male	23
Ethnicity	
Black/African American	61
White	26
Hispanic	14
Other Race	12
Multiple Races	.6
Marital status	
Married or living as married	40
Single, never married	25
Divorced	15
Widowed	15
Separated	5
Relationship of respondents to returning relatives	
Parents	39
Grandparents	5
Friends	11
Siblings	19
Partners/spouses	13
Adult children/grandchildren	4
Other	9
Educational attainment	
High school	71
Some college	37

Adapted from Shollenberger, 2009.

Interestingly, the acute incarceration of a family member was not a seminal event in these family members' lives, but one of a series of familial incarcerations the family had to manage. Most of the family members interviewed had had personal contact with the criminal justice system or knew at least of one other family member who had been incarcerated. Thirty-six percent (36%) of family members had themselves been arrested as an adult, and 21% had served time in an adult correctional facility (Shollenberger, 2009). At the time of interview, 30% of family members reported having at least one family member incarcerated in addition to the family member for whom they were being interviewed (Shollenberger, 2009).

Family members indicated that there were several obstacles that made staying in touch with their family member in prison difficult. Specifically, family members identified distance from prison (59%), difficulty arranging transportation (38%), restrictive telephone policies (35%), restrictive visitation policies (24%), and the cost of visiting (19%) as rate-limiting factors in maintaining constant contact with their incarcerated family member (Shollenberger, 2009).

Visitation/Contact

Prison policies and practices do not generally promote or support maintaining family ties. Complex and difficult rules and regulations often discourage family visitation and other methods of contact (Hairston, 2001a). Long waits, rude treatment by corrections personnel, and dirty facilities often limit families' willingness to visit loved ones in prison. Specifically, the frequency and type of visits varies significantly by prison and is particularly difficult when visits include children. Children are often required to sit in crowded visiting rooms without the benefit of touching or interacting with the person they are there to visit (Hairston, 2001a). In many instances, institutional rules and regulations mandate that only biological children of inmates may visit (Bauhofer, 1987). Moreover, lack of information from prison personnel and feelings of being "guilty by association" make family members feel unwelcome when they visit and therefore less likely to do so. Visitation is also impacted when fathers must rely on the mother of their child/children to facilitate visitation. In some cases, mothers are not willing to broker visits between father and child; in other cases they are not able (Hairston, 2001a).

Contact with children and family by inmates is also made difficult because of heavy surcharges that are placed on phone calls made from prison. Although the Federal Communications Commission (FCC) has made progress at reducing the abusive costs associated with calls from prison over the past decade, a phone call made from prison or jail is still higher than it would be for anyone else (Wagner & Jones, 2019). For example, a 15-minute call from a Michigan jail costs on average $12 and can go as high as $22. Providers have also been able to circumvent the FCC's rate caps by charging additional fees including opening, maintaining, and funding accounts that can increase the cost of a phone call by as much as 40% (Wagner & Jones, 2019). This, coupled with extra charges tacked on by prisons and telephone companies, makes this kind of communication with loved ones fiscally prohibitive for many families (Hairston, 2001a). Furthermore, the number of calls that an inmate can place is often limited. Correspondence through mail is often an option for incarcerated family members, but this too can be problematic. Some institutions put stickers on mail indicating that the letter is from someone in prison (Hairston, 2001a).

In an effort to help maintain family relationships, some states have recently taken steps to implement virtual visitation programs. By way of example, the Pennsylvania Department of Corrections offers family members the option to schedule virtual visits at no cost. Inmates are allowed up to 45 minutes per visit and up to five visits per month (Pennsylvania Department of Corrections, 2020). While this program offers families a more convenient and affordable visitation with their loved one, it may still be cost prohibitive for families living in poverty since the family member must have internet access and a computer that has both audio and video capabilities. While not all prison and jail systems offering these programs provide the services for free, the costs are greatly reduced compared to the cost of a phone call and/or traveling to the institution. Virtual visitation provides family members a means of visitation when it might otherwise not be possible; however, these are relatively new programs and are not yet widely available.

The strength of family relationships in existence prior to and during incarceration do correlate with successful adjustment to the prison setting and subsequent release (LaVigne et al., 2004). The research on this association has been fairly consistent. Whether or not families have contact with loved ones in prison and the extent to which they do so has been empirically tied to recidivism rates. Offenders who have greater contact with their families while incarcerated tend to recidivate less than those who have less or no contact with family members (Arditti et al.,

2003; Hairston, 2002a). Whether contact is through personal visit, mail, or telephone, contact of some kind makes a meaningful difference (Naser & Visher, 2006).

Geography

There are other significant barriers to remaining in touch with one's family while incarcerated, barriers unrelated to visitation policy or institutional rules. Oftentimes, prisons are located far away from where families live, requiring families to travel significant distances for a visit. Overnight visits and other expenses often make personal visits impossible or an infrequent event (Braman, 2002; Hickert et al., 2018; Travis & Waul, 2003a). Men's prisons are typically located an average distance of 100 miles from their home; women's prisons 160 miles (Travis et al., 2005). In addition, access to transportation (public or otherwise) is difficult to find (Mumola, 2000). Furthermore, even if families are able to find transportation to take them to the prison, because of the distance between prisons and the large, urban areas from which most prison visitors come, there is not ample time to visit. Time is a commodity in short supply for families that have had to renegotiate employment and finances because wage-earning family members may be incarcerated (Christian, 2005). For incarcerated people with strained family ties, the many hardships associated with visitation and distance to travel further weakens already tenuous relationships (Arditti, 2003; Christian, 2005).

Maintaining social ties with family members provides emotional and instrumental support on release and is generally associated with more successful post-release outcomes (Bales & Mears, 2008; Barrick et al., 2014; Meyers et al., 2017; Mitchell et al., 2016). Despite this, the majority of offenders receive few to no visits, further isolating them from conventional society (Bales & Mears, 2008; Derzken et al., 2009; Duwe & Clarke, 2011). A study of 7,000 inmates by Bales and Mears (2008) found less than half (42%) of inmates received any form of visitation during their incarceration. Following a group of inmates over a period of one year, Cochran noted 75% of inmates had no visits from family or friends (Cochran, 2012). Research has also found disparities in who gets visited; young, educated, female, white, or Latino inmates are more likely to receive visits, unlike older, African-American inmates and those with more extensive prior records and gang affiliations (Cochran et al., 2017; Tewksbury & Connor, 2012).

Financial Hardship

Families of the incarcerated often have significant financial problems as a result of the incarceration of a family member. In some instances, the primary financial provider of the family is incarcerated (Davis, 1992; Hairston, 2003). In addition to the loss of income, the incarcerated family member may have provided in-kind services such as home repairs and childcare, creating additional hardships and financial burdens (Braman, 2004). In other instances, families go in to debt in an effort to support their incarcerated relative (Davis, 1992). Still other financial hardships are encountered by grandparents and other extended family members who may be taking care of children if the parent was receiving welfare benefits or other public support prior to incarceration and is ineligible to do so after imprisonment (Bloom & Steinhart, 1993).

Moreover, family members may also augment an incarcerated family member's prison experience by providing clothes, books, money for commissary, etc., oftentimes putting themselves in serious financial straits as a result (Christian, 2005; Comfort, 2002). Family members may also end up paying for prison fees, health care charges, and in some instances, child support (Hairston, 2003). Family members also incur significant costs to visit their family members in prison (Naser & Visher, 2006). As might be expected, there are significant costs associated with travelling to prisons to visit loved ones, including overnight stays, bus tickets, and food. These expenses, in addition to the geographic location of the prison itself, often negatively impact families' ability to visit at all or severely curtail the frequency with which they do visit (Naser & Visher, 2006).

Emotional Trauma/Stigma

Regardless of the type of relationship that family members had prior to incarceration, imprisonment is a very emotional experience not only for the person going to prison, but also for the family and children they leave behind. Feelings of loneliness, separation, anger, guilt, relief, and a host of other emotions often complicate already difficult familial relationships (Lanier, 1993). Incarcerated parents are particularly vulnerable to feelings of loss, depression, and other mental health problems because of constant concern and worry regarding their children (Lanier, 1993).

In addition, families of the incarcerated often experience social stigma and increased hostility from the community (Codd, 2007). In some cases the fear of this stigma is actually greater than the reality, but the fact remains that family members are often reticent to tell others about an incarcerated family member and are often fearful of reprisal from those who may find out (Davies, 1980; Fishman, 1988). This stigma, real or imagined, is most clearly felt when considering children of incarcerated parents. In many instances, children are not told of a parent's incarceration or are lied to about where their parents are for fear of the teasing and ostracism they may face at school (Codd, 2007). Conversely, in some neighborhoods, because of the sheer number of people who have left the community for prison, stigma is not a problem. In fact, in some instances, imprisonment is seen as a rite of passage (Schneller, 1976).

Information Gathering

Most families navigate their way through the criminal justice system by word of mouth. Understanding and accessing information related to their family member's imprisonment or any other aspect of the system is neither easily accessed nor routinely divulged. Family members are often left to figure it out on their own by piecing together information obtained from multiple sources or remain uninformed (Hairston, 2003). This lack of knowledge and/or understanding of the criminal justice process results in feelings of uncertainty and anxiety amongst family members on either side of the prison wall (Fishman, 1990).

Furthermore, many families of offenders do not understand the parole process or what happens to their family members when they are released from prison. They have no idea what is expected of their family member with respect to reporting and so on and often feel alienated from the parole and release process. In other cases, families work very closely with parole officers to provide information about their family member and to seek advice about how to manage the transition from prison to the community and how to assist with employment, drug treatment, and the like (Naser & Visher, 2006).

Reentry Considerations

Research strongly suggests that families play a significant role in whether and to what extent offenders who leave prison are successful in the reentry process. Research indicates that social support (from family and other support networks) reduces or mitigates the impact of stress and strain on individuals who may be experiencing it (Irwin & Austin, 1994). Certainly, those leaving prison have high hopes in their abilities to turn things around (Irwin & Austin, 1994), but what they hope for and reality may be starkly different (Richards, 1995). Therefore, it is not surprising that offenders leaving prison rely very heavily on family support for housing, employment, and encouragement (Naser & LaVigne, 2006). There appears to be some recognition that offenders cannot go it alone, or go it alone for long. Returning offenders seem to appreciate the need for family and/or social support in the reentry process.

Families provide a multitude of services to the reentering offender. Families often act as sounding boards for offenders who are looking for guidance or who may be feeling fearful about the future. In addition, family members of offenders are often required to be loyal while reconciling their own hurt and anger (Shapiro & Schwartz, 2001). These varied role responsibilities often result in family members who may want to assist the returning offender and others who do not. Ultimately, "family members who have been hurt and who are dealing with their own problems will try again to help a loved one if they believe that something has changed or if they find an outlet for their own anxiety and a source of ongoing support" (Shapiro & Schwartz, 2001, p. 54).

The role of the family in assisting offenders in prison and out is empirically supported, but is not equivocal. Studies that have evaluated both tangible and emotional support indicate that higher levels of both types of support result in positive reentry outcomes related to employment, decreased substance abuse, and reduced incidence of post-release depression (Ekland-Olson et al., 1983; LaVigne et al., 2004; Visher et al., 2004) as well as lower rates of physical, emotional, and mental problems and lower rates of reconviction (LaVigne et al., 2004; Sullivan et al., 2002). Still other research suggests that while social support (defined as a network of family and friends and even organizations that provide support for the offender) can ease the reentry process, it must be tempered with specific attention to assisting the offender with reorienting to the outside world and settling into different lifestyles (Breese et al., 2000).

Some studies note that increased levels of stress and fear on the part of the family is often related to whether or not the family member is able to reenter successfully (Zamble & Quinsey, 1997). Certainly, offenders returning from prison to the community may feel pressured to contribute financially, emotionally, or otherwise to the family unit when they are not always able to (Breese et al., 2000). However, research indicates that families encounter tangible stressors associated with having to try to support or at least contribute financially to the support of the offender returning to the community while simultaneously trying to support themselves (Breese et al., 2000; Sullivan et al., 2002). Still other scholarship indicates that there are "disconnects" between offender expectations of what reentry will be like as it relates to family dynamics and the reality associated with the release process, although recent research supports the contention that expectations and realities of offenders are generally met or exceeded (Naser & LaVigne, 2006).

In the end, the offender who leaves the family unit fulfilling one set of familial responsibilities when they enter prison likely leaves prison and reenters the community and the family with different roles, responsibilities, and expectations. Undoubtedly, conflicting feelings and concerns make the process of reentry difficult not only for the offender but for the family itself, as both parties attempt to renegotiate relationships and family roles (Hagan & Dinovitzer, 1999). The extent to which these familial roles are defined, differentiated, and renegotiated has not been fully addressed in the literature (Martinez, 2006; Shapiro & Schwartz, 2001).

Promising Practice

The fundamental premise is that reentry programs that engage the family and emphasize family involvement result in better outcomes (i.e., offenders who recidivate less and who reconnect with their families in a positive way). Literature from the substance abuse field supports the contention that families who are committed to helping their loved ones fight alcoholism and/or drug use results in increased commitment to treatment and programming and fewer relapses after treatment (Bobbitt & Nelson, 2004; Knight & Simpson, 1996). One program that has had some success in achieving this goal is La Bodega de la Familia, a program facilitated by Family Justice, Inc.

La Bodega de la Familia (The Family Grocery) has been developed to support the notion that strengthening family ties of substance abusers under parole supervision can improve treatment success, reduce relapse, and decrease the amount of substance abuse within families (Shapiro & Schwartz, 2001). La Bodega specifically serves families in which one or more members are on probation or parole for abusing alcohol or drugs. In addition to providing advocacy and crisis intervention services, La Bodega provides opportunities for family and individual counseling with a case manager who also works closely with probation and parole officers to holistically manage the needs of the drug-abusing offender (Bobbitt & Nelson, 2004).

The foundation of the La Bodega program is strengthening bonds between family members. It accomplishes this goal through encouraging new and different relationships with community supervision personnel and through providing strengths-based support for the family unit. A strengths-based approach emphasizes family strengths in a way that can facilitate positive offender reentry. The key is to discover assets within the family unit that can encourage successful reentry and family reunification (Shapiro & Schwartz, 2001). Examples of these assets include successful ways of coping, skills and talents within the family network that can encourage or assist the returning offender with finding employment and making a smooth transition, and methods of empowering the offender to "go straight" (Shapiro & Schwartz, 2001). A family-focused, strengths-based approach to managing the return of offenders from prison to the community requires a partnership built on trust, respect, and collaboration between community supervision officers, families of offenders, and the offender themselves (Shapiro & Schwartz, 2001).

Recently, Family Justice developed a case management tool that collects information on offenders' social networks and how these networks and relationships impact reentry (DiZerega & Shapiro, 2007). The Relational Inquiry Tool is comprised of a series of questions related to family dynamics and family composition that can be utilized by case managers and other personnel for the purposes of developing a family-focused, strengths-based approach to reentry (DiZerega & Shapiro, 2007). This tool also emphasizes positive behaviors as well as personal strengths as they relate to families in the case management effort. This instrument has been pilot tested in programs such as La Bodega across the county with good results (DiZerega & Shapiro, 2007).

An evaluation study of La Bodega found that the family-focused approach to offender reentry reduced recidivism and drug use from 80% to 42% and overall improved family wellbeing (Sullivan et al., 2002). Moreover, interviews with participants in the program indicate that families were instrumental in helping drug abusers through difficult periods and providing moral and emotional support for the continuation of treatment, thus minimizing relapse (Sullivan et al., 2002). Clearly, family involvement in the reentry process can and does have a positive effect on offender performance and outcome. Neglecting to consider the family dynamic in the reentry process only promotes unnecessary barriers to success.

Children

When parents are adjudicated and sentenced to prison, children are often left behind. It is estimated that more than five million children have had an incarcerated parent, or nearly 7% of children in the U.S. (Murphey & Cooper, 2015). By way of context, the number of children of incarcerated parents increased 80% between 1991 and 2007 (Glaze & Maruschak, 2010). Specifically, black children were 7.5 times more likely than white children (0.9%) to have a parent in prison compared with Hispanic children, who were 2.5 times more likely than white children to have an incarcerated parent (Glaze & Maruschak, 2010). Moreover, half of children with an incarcerated parent in 2007 were age nine or younger, and most children lived with their mothers prior to her incarceration (Glaze & Maruschak, 2010). Sixty-four percent of incarcerated mothers and 46% of incarcerated fathers lived with their children prior to imprisonment (Glaze & Maruschak, 2010). Young children living with the loss and stigma of a parent to incarceration has become so commonplace in our society that the well-known children's show, *Sesame Street*, created a resource kit, *Little Children, Big Challenges: Incarceration*, for parents and caregivers of young children with an incarcerated parent (Reilly, 2013).

Sadly, these figures are conservative estimates of the number of children who may have incarcerated parents, as this information is not systematically collected by correctional agencies, child welfare agencies, or schools (Poehlmann et al., 2010). However, we can extrapolate from the information above that high rates of incarceration have resulted in large numbers of children growing up (for at least a while) without the benefit of a mother and/or father. Moreover, children's lives are interrupted several times when a parent goes to prison; once when the parent leaves and once when the parent returns. If the parent is in and out of prison, these interruptions are more frequent (Gabel & Johnston, 1995). More than three-quarters (77%) of state inmates with minor children reported prior criminal histories; 60% had served multiple sentences prior to their most recent incarceration and almost half (49%) were on some form of conditional release (i.e., probation or parole) at the time of their arrest (Mumola, 2000). The parent may have committed the crime, but both the parent and the child are forced to do the time (Boudin, 2011).

Mandatory minimum sentencing policies, particularly those related to the "war on drugs," led to an unprecedented growth in the number of persons incarcerated and, in turn, disruption of families (Bush-Baskette, 2000). The "war on drugs" disproportionately impacted women, who are more likely to be the primary caregiver of minor children (Bush-Baskette, 2000; Glaze & Marushak, 2008; Mumola, 2000). Since the "war on drugs" began, there has been a 100% increase in the rate of children with incarcerated mothers and a 75% increase in incarcerated fathers (Martin, 2017). Not unexpectedly, the number of children in foster care also more than doubled, an unintended consequence of the "war on drugs" policies (Swann & Sheran-Sylvester, 2006). Research suggests that the mass incarceration of females was the largest contributor to the growth in foster care caseloads from 1985 to 2000 (Swann & Sheran-Sylvester, 2006). Children experiencing the instability of placement in foster care are more likely to show poorer inhibitory controls, have higher levels of oppositional behaviors, and are more likely to engage in delinquency (Hu et al., 2020).

Although reunifying children with parents is one of the primary goals of the foster care system, Halperin and Harris (2004) note that the child welfare policies have not been "tailored to the circumstances of parental incarceration" (p. 340). For example, caseworkers in New York City often misinterpret the 75-mile limit policy/procedure. The policy calls for caseworkers to file for travel reimbursement using a different source if they travel more than 75 miles; caseworkers, however, often interpret this policy to mean that they are not obligated to arrange prison visits if travel to the prison exceeds 75 miles. "This is an example of how the system's failure to train caseworkers in managing such cases impedes these mothers' ability to parent from prison" (Halperin & Harris, 2004, p. 343).

Current Trends

Children whose parents are in prison are one of the most at-risk populations and are negatively impacted in a multitude of ways, including enduring psychological and emotional trauma as well as financial strain (Adalist-Estrin, 1994; Hairston, 1989; Hairston, 2009; Murray & Farrington, 2005; Phillips et al., 2002; Springer et al., 2000). According to one evaluation, 70% of children whose mothers were incarcerated presented with emotional or psychological problems, including anxiety, fear, hypervigilance, depression, and shame or guilt (Parke & Clarke-Stewart, 2002). There is also a greater likelihood of familial and emotional disruption as children of incarcerated mothers are often placed with relatives or in foster care as discussed above (Hagan & Dinovitzer, 1999; Hairston, 2008).

Adverse behavioral symptoms, such as a decline in school performance, truancy, drug and alcohol use, aggressive behaviors, sadness, withdrawal, and low self-esteem, can also manifest themselves (Dallaire, 2007a; Murray et al., 2009). Boys are more likely to exhibit externalizing behaviors (i.e., anger, hostility), while girls are more likely to display internalizing behaviors (i.e., anxiety, shame, withdrawal, guilt) (Parke & Clarke-Stewart, 2002). Adult children of incarcerated parents have been found to be at an increased risk of violent behaviors (Muftic & Smith, 2018). Environmental factors such as poverty and care-giving concerns also impact children whose parents are incarcerated (Murray & Farrington, 2008). Moreover, these children are more likely to associate with delinquent peers (Cochran et al., 2018). An estimated 70% of children with incarcerated parents become criminal justice-involved (Jucovy, 2003). There are also strong indications that children with incarcerated mothers are at higher risk for delinquency compared with children of incarcerated fathers. Studies show that adult children with incarcerated mothers are 2.5 times more at risk for incarceration compared with adult children with incarcerated fathers (Dallaire, 2007b).

In a survey of teachers discussing their experiences with children of incarcerated parents, several themes emerged further supporting these assertions (Dallaire et al., 2010). Teachers reported emotional and academic problems, with many of the children having a low threshold for frustration and easily "fall[ing] apart" (p. 284). Half of the respondents noted that younger children and/or those with incarcerated mothers had a more difficult time coping. When it came to the issue of stigmatization, some of the teachers reported that their colleagues were the source of the stigma. They indicated that some teachers were not supportive of the children and had lower expectations of their abilities (Dallaire et al., 2010).

What is most difficult to ascertain is whether parental incarceration is the causal factor associated with children's outcomes in these various domains, or whether the incarceration of parents serves as a risk marker (DeHart & Altshuler, 2009; Murray & Farrington, 2008). Recent scholarship suggests that parental incarceration, in and of itself, does not directly correlate with psychosocial disturbances in children (Hanlon et al., 2005). Rather, through no fault of their own, children of incarcerated parents are a part of families who present with risk factors for criminal behavior, including substance abuse, poverty, crime, few educational and vocational opportunities, family instability, and intergenerational violence. In their study of children with an incarcerated parent, Murphey and Cooper (2015) found more than half of the children experienced substance abuse in the home, and one-quarter lived in a home where mental health disorders were present. It was common for these children to come from broken homes, with more than one-third witnessing and/or experiencing violence in their neighborhood. As Murray and Farrington (2005) suggest, "prisoners' children are a highly vulnerable group with multiple factors for adverse outcomes. Parental imprisonment appears to affect children over and above separation experiences and associated risks" (p. 1269). Hence, parental incarceration is another in what is often a long list of adverse childhood events (Murphey & Cooper, 2015).

Interpersonal Contact

There is no question that parent–child separation due to incarceration can adversely impact a child's interpersonal development if the child lived with the parent prior to incarceration (Miller, 2006, 2007; Murray & Farrington, 2006). Understandably, the disruption caused by parental incarceration can result in negative effects on the quality of the child–parent attachment while simultaneously impacting a child's peer relationships (Hairston, 2008, 2009; Parke & Clarke-Stewart, 2002). Research suggests that even if the child has already bonded with their parent, the disruption associated with the incarceration will likely adversely affect the quality of the bond (Parke & Clarke-Stewart, 2002).

Certainly, the level and type of contact that children require from parents varies depending on age. Logically, infants and very young children require more contact and interaction with their parents than older children. Unfortunately, infants of incarcerated parents do not routinely receive the nurturing and close contact that they need from their parents if their parents are behind prison walls. Incarcerated women often express that they are no longer able to fulfill their role of being a mother (Arditti, 2012; Arditti & Few, 2008). Instead, attention, nurturing, and daily care are provided by other caregivers such as grandparents, other family members, and foster care. While the nature and scope of contact between parent and child changes as the child gets older and often includes personal visits, letters, and telephone calls, the fact remains that caregivers are the gatekeepers of contact between the child and the incarcerated parent and therefore exercise significant influence regarding whether or not and the degree to which contact between parent and child takes place (Enos, 2001).

Of course, contact between the child and incarcerated parent is also governed by institutional rules and regulations as well as parental wishes. Some prisons do not provide "child friendly" environments. In these instances, children are expected to endure long waits for visits, to sit still, and oftentimes they are not allowed to touch or actively engage with the parent whom they are visiting (Sturges & Hardesty, 2005). After enduring long waits and traveling long distances, visits may also be cut short due to institutional procedures delaying the parent getting to the visitation room (Dixey & Woodall, 2012). Some prisoners make the conscious decision to not have their children visit in order to spare them the emotional and procedural hardships associated with such visits (Dixey & Woodall, 2012). This does not mean that contact between parent and child does not take place, it just means that sometimes this contact is relegated to the exchange of letters and telephone calls (Poehlman et al., 2010). Ultimately, research indicates that it is the quality, not the quantity of the visits with the incarcerated parents that matters. Positive contact no matter the format yields optimal results (Poehlmann, 2005).

Children who come from families with minimal economic resources are at a significant disadvantage when it comes to being able to visit or have contact with their incarcerated parents. Because children must rely on caregivers or other family members or kin networks to bring them to prisons to visit their parents, oftentimes these visits are not possible and, if they are, do not occur frequently (Baunach, 1985). As noted previously in this chapter, the distance of prisons from areas where these children live makes routine travel to these prisons difficult and costly. Consequently, many children must rely on alternative forms of communication with their parents (Poehlman et al., 2010). Geographic and financial hardships are often only exacerbated when the mother is the incarcerated parent (Hagan & Dinovitzer, 1999). Because there are fewer prisons for women, female inmates are more likely to be incarcerated farther from family, making it difficult, if not impossible, for many children to visit or maintain a relationship with their mother while they are in prison (Hairston, 1991a).

Violence/Trauma

Scholarship indicates that children with incarcerated parents often come from homes where violence is present (Hagan & Dinovitzer, 1999). Children's exposure to violence ranges from being a witness to violence to being a victim (DeHart & Altshuler, 2009). Given that between 60 and 73% of incarcerated mothers report prior sexual and physical abuse and that approximately 66% of children lived with their mothers prior to incarceration, it is likely that a significant number of children whose parents are now incarcerated were exposed to or were victims of violence prior to their parents' imprisonment (DeHart & Altshuler, 2009).

In open-ended interviews among incarcerated mothers, the women revealed that "their children were often direct witnesses to verbal or physical abuse" (DeHart & Altshuler, 2009, p. 471). The children were often in the path of danger, and for those that did not directly witness the violence, they were aware of the violence in the home. Mothers spoke of the psychological, behavioral, and physical harms that their children endured. Children's behaviors manifested both passively by hiding and crying, and aggressively by attempting to verbally and/or physically intervene. Children experienced physical and sexual abuse, with some of the children becoming pregnant or contracting sexually transmitted diseases. Some of the mothers reported that their child was permanently disfigured or injured from their abuse, while some reported their child died as a result of their injuries (DeHart & Altshuler, 2009).

Moreover, children who come from homes where violence is prevalent tend to display more difficulty in managing aggression, exhibit problem behaviors in school, and tend to present with higher rates of depression, anxiety, fearfulness, low self-esteem, difficult concentrating, low test scores, and social incompetence (Fantuzzo & Mohr, 1999). As children age, these behaviors are further manifested in at-risk behaviors such as sexual promiscuity, drug use, and oftentimes truancy. Intergenerational explanations of violence are also relevant here as they argue that people who are victimized as children are more likely to grow up to victimize as adults (Widom, 1989). Consequently, research supports the contention that people who were the targets of physical violence as children or who saw their parents fighting may be more likely to engage in subsequent violence towards their children and spouses as adults (Chatterji & Markowitz, 2001; Heyman & Slep, 2002).

Other researchers have also found that children who experience violence are more likely to approve of violence as an appropriate form of punishment for misconduct and accept violence in dating relationships, especially when they become adults. In a study by Chatterji and Markowitz (2001), a high percentage of women suffered some form of abuse as a child, witnessed violence and abuse, and had families who were involved with drugs or alcohol; sixty-two percent (62%) of these women reported recollections of drug or alcohol abuse in their homes, while 43% of women recalled memories of their mother under the influence of drugs or alcohol. Furthermore, 55% percent of women were able to recall moments when their father was under the influence of drugs or alcohol. Still other women admitted that their parents were responsible for introducing them to drugs and/or alcohol (Greene et al., 2000).

Stigmatization

In addition to the issues noted above, stigmatization is oftentimes a significant problem for children of incarcerated parents. Stigmatization is a process that formally labels differences, associates these formally labeled differences in a negative way, and creates an atmosphere where labeled individuals are devalued and receive discriminatory treatment, all of which occur to encourage differences in "social, cultural, political, and economic power" (Link & Phelan, 2001; Phillips & Gates, 2011, p. 286). For example, the term "children of incarcerated parents" once used as a means to describe a group of people is now often used as a derogatory label by which this particular group is ostracized and often discriminated against. Children of incarcerated parents are often distinguished from all children or other children who may face similar problems related to family adjustment and social and psychological problems (Phillips & Gates, 2011).

For these reasons, it is understandable why some families engage in the "conspiracy of silence" and choose not to tell children that their parent is incarcerated (Johnston, 1995, p. 59). These families are often afraid of the social stigma that will occur as a result of divulging the family secret, including teasing and bullying of children, shunning of the children and family by neighbors, and the undue stress that this knowledge might cause the child (Phillips & Gates, 2011). Moreover, the incarcerated parent may wish to protect the child by not worrying them and may choose not to divulge where they are (Goozh & Jeweler, 2011).

However, failure to inform children of their parent(s) incarceration makes discussion about the issue virtually impossible as a family and intentionally (or not) may harm children who believe that their parent(s) have left them (Hairston, 2007). Conversely, children who know about the incarceration of a parent may be unwilling to discuss the issue with anyone because of fear of what others will think or the need to defend their parent or pretend that everything is all right (Goozh & Jeweler, 2011). Furthermore, these children may be embarrassed by their parents' mistakes. Yet, research indicates that children who were informed about their parents' incarceration and who were told in an open and honest way were more likely to feel lonely rather than angry. This research suggests that telling children about the incarceration of their parents will have tangential effects, but that the effects may be more manageable than if the child is left in the dark (Poehlmann, 2005).

Resilience

Thus far, the discussion of children of incarcerated parents has focused on the usually negative effects of parent–child separation; that is, the negative consequences that many children encounter as a result of the incarceration of their parent. However, just because a child's parent has been or is incarcerated does not mean that they will absolutely suffer from or encounter the panoply of problems and issues discussed previously. In fact, "while it is critical to be cognizant of predisposing cumulative environmental risks, it is just as important to acknowledge the strengths that individuals inherently possess and the strengths within their environments" (Miller, 2007, p. 27).

Resilience has been found to exist as an internal trait and presents itself as an understanding and insight of internal strengths that encourage personal growth. Resilience is also the positive outcome of a traumatic event (Richardson, 2002; Sameroff & Seifer, 1990). Children who own resilience as an inherent trait usually possess an easy temperament and have a sense of humor. These traits enable children to roll with resistance and to develop good problem-solving skills (Kirby & Fraser, 1997). In children where resilience is a process that requires insight and understanding of one's capacity for personal growth, children learn to adapt or cope in pro-social ways during times of significant stress and adversity. They are introspective enough to learn how to grow and learn from stressful events or situations (Miller, 2007). Children in whom resilience is an outcome tend to bounce back without much trouble from traumatic events (Miller, 2007).

Protective factors are those specific factors that decrease the likelihood of a negative outcome in high-risk populations, enhance the likelihood of resilience, and are associated with successful outcomes from children of incarcerated parents (Miller, 2007). Assets or protective factors that are associated with resilience include close family and kin networks. The collective responsibility that these extended family and kin networks share (especially for African-American children) offer stability, consistent care, and exposure to family traditions and social norms (Chipman et al., 2002). In particular, African-American families tend to emphasize kinship and extended family care of children of incarcerated parents due to the likely termination of parental rights that occurs if children are placed in foster care (Miller, 2007). Additional protective benefits of the extended family and/or kinship networks are the intergenerational coping skills that are transmitted from one generation to another. Furthermore, cultural identities and reliance on religion for support help children and families cope with the stress of an incarcerated parent together (Walsh, 1998).

A study by Nesmith and Ruhland (2008) reinforces the notion that some children do not fall prey to at-risk behaviors. In this study, despite harboring feelings of loneliness, fear, and anxiety, children found pro-social outlets for their feelings and concerns and were creative in developing coping mechanisms. The primary protective factors that assisted these children in being resilient to at-risk behaviors were sports, theater, and church (Nesmith & Ruhland, 2008). Many children searched for a place where they could feel normal, where they could fit in, and where they were able to excel at a skill (Nesmith & Ruhland, 2008).

Promising Practice

Research indicates that contact between children and their incarcerated parents is important and can be beneficial, but it is also impacted by a series of interrelated factors that must be considered. The scholarship suggests that the benefit of child contact on incarcerated parents is significantly positive, whereas literature evaluating children's outcomes in relation to the nature and type of parental contact is mixed (Poehlmann et al., 2010). A variety of factors, including relationships with caregivers, type of contact, age of child, and emotional and psychological issues for both parents and children must be evaluated and considered when determining whether and how contact between children and incarcerated parents occurs (Poehlmann et al., 2010). Visits that occur as part of a larger intervention process (i.e., are structured to address psychological, emotional, and behavioral concerns of incarcerated parents and children) tend to be more effective than visits that are not part of a formal intervention process (Byrne et al., 2010). Interventions may include anything from better preparing parents and children for the visit to working on relationships between caregivers and incarcerated parents to encouraging child-friendly visitation environments (Arditti, 2003; Poehlmann et al., 2010).

In an effort to promote honesty with children who have an incarcerated parent, Goozh and Jeweler (2011) developed a booklet that they make available to children who have an incarcerated parent. This pamphlet is presented in an easy-to-read format and helps answer children's questions about incarceration by providing information about the criminal justice process from arrest to incarceration. "Providing children with reliable, dependable information allows them to begin to make sense of their situation and to start the dual process of grieving the loss of their parent and coping with their new life circumstances" (Thombre et al., 2009, p. 69). Moreover, children can obtain information that is helpful to them in a nonthreatening way; this information can assist in smoothing the transition for them while their parents are imprisoned and help prepare them for the time when their parents are released.

Some mentoring programs focus primarily on the needs of children of incarcerated parents. These programs link children of incarcerated parents to mentors (oftentimes through Big Brothers/Big Sisters) who provide emotional and often financial support to these children who have one or more parents in prison. A recent study evaluating a mentoring program for children indicates that if matches between mentors and mentees extended beyond six months the matches were more likely to remain solvent in the long term (Shlafer et al., 2009). Nearly one-third of the matches were dissolved in the first six months of participation in the program, generally due to scheduling conflicts, realization regarding the time commitment involved, and match incompatibility (Shlafer et al., 2009). Interestingly, the more interactions between mentor and mentee, the more likely the match was to continue.

Ultimately, the extent to which families and children are involved in the reentry process must be mediated by circumstances to ensure that the experience for the family and the offender is a positive and safe one (Nelson et al., 1999). Sadly, there are instances in which it is in the best interest of all parties for families, children, and offenders not to communicate or visit. Families should be evaluated for domestic violence and other possible issues that may impact the family dynamic and endanger family members or the returning offender. However, more often than not, communication and visitation by families and children has been shown to be an effective motivator for the offender while in prison and a critical element in the success of the offender after they leave. Coupled with the benefits that families and children most often derive from continued communication with their family member/parent, programs and policies that more comprehensively include and involve families and children will likely encourage better reentry outcomes.

Chapter 6

Incarcerated Parents and Reentry

Parents recognize that incarceration has a significant impact on their children, and this awareness manifests itself in a variety of ways. In an effort to manage the stress, emotional burden, and fear associated with being away from their children, some parents reject their children entirely by cutting off all communication and contact. Others attempt to maintain a connection with their children at any cost. Some parents believe that frequent communication with their children (whether it be in person, by mail, or over the telephone) is preventative in that it can minimize the possibility that their children will also be incarcerated at some time in the future (Thombre et al., 2009).

Incarcerated men and women who are parents are generally clear about the lessons they hope their children will learn as a result of their imprisonment. Parents want their children to understand the value of education, possess knowledge of the law and their constitutional rights, and be aware of the realities of prison life. In addition, parents recognize the need for their children to engage in good, pro-social decision-making, especially as it is relates to interactions they have with their peers (Thombre et al., 2009). Parents want their children to be better educated and more aware of the consequences of their actions. Parents want for their children what they didn't or couldn't have for themselves.

Current Trends

This parental desire to stop or at minimum disrupt the cycle of criminal behavior is informed by empirical research that supports several intergenerational theories to explain parental incarceration. The first intergenerational explanation of parental incarceration is rooted in discussions of selection and self-control. The foundational hypothesis of this theory is that certain traits, including genetics and weak self-control, predispose incarcerated parents and their children to engaging in criminal behavior. Gottfredson and Hirschi (1990) identify these traits as low self-control, high impulsivity, and low conscience. People who present with these traits have an increased likelihood of engaging in criminal activity that results in their incarceration as parents and the potential imprisonment of their children in the future.

The second intergenerational explanation of parental incarceration is located in notions of stigma. Where stigma associated with imprisonment usually results in offenders' exclusion from the normative social group, it also creates a sense of alienation wherein parents and subsequently their children are excluded from pro-social activities and lifestyles. This results in downward social, legal, and economic trajectories that result in generations of illegal behavior (Foster & Hagan, 2009; Hagan & McCarthy, 1997).

The third explanation of parental incarceration includes socialization and strain theories that argue that economic deprivation and family disruptions lead to decreased opportunities for educational attainment, more social exclusion, and ultimately criminal involvement (Cloward & Ohlin, 1960). Reduced opportunities for children's exposure to education, economic advantage, and family stability due to the incarceration of their parents ultimately excludes these children from adopting conventional norms and encourages criminal behavior (Foster & Hagan, 2009).

As discussed in the prior chapter, the number of incarcerated men and women who are parents is staggering. According to the most recent data, more than 684,000 prisoners were parents of more than 1.4 million minor children (Maruschak et al., 2021). Approximately 47% of men and 58% of women in state or federal prison were a parent of at least one minor child as of 2016. An estimated 51% of minor children with a parent in state prison and 44% with a parent in federal prison are under the age of ten (Maruschak et al., 2021). Between 1991 and 2007, there was a 79% increase in the number of incarcerated parents in state and federal prisons (Glaze & Maruschak, 2010). Mothers accounted for the majority of this growth as their numbers more than doubled between 1991 and midyear 2007 (up 131%) compared with a 77% increase among fathers (Glaze & Maruschak, 2010).

In a 2004 survey on parenting, women were more likely to report having more than one child and to indicate that their children were living with them at the time of their present arrest (Glaze & Maruschak, 2010). Eighty-four percent of fathers noted that their minor child was living with his/her mother during his incarceration; mothers were more likely to report grandparents as the current caregiver. Mothers (52%) and fathers (54%) were equally likely to report providing financial support to their minor child(ren) prior to incarceration (Glaze & Maruschak, 2010).

Mothers and fathers who are incarcerated are often thwarted in their attempts to remain engaged with their children. For example, while the Adoption and Safe Families Act of 1997 (ASFA) seeks to provide stability to children in the foster care system, the law actually makes it difficult for incarcerated parents to be actively involved in their children's lives. As the law stands, ASFA requires that proceedings to terminate parental rights be initiated whenever a child has been in foster care for 15 of the previous 22 months. When applied to parents who are not incarcerated, this law might make sense, but this term of separation of parent and child is exceedingly difficult for incarcerated parents to manage given that average terms of imprisonment are five years (or 60 months) in length. Parents who place their children in foster care prior to incarceration will likely lose custody of their children and face termination of their parental rights because their prison sentence separates them from their child/children for 15 months or more (Genty, 2002). It is no wonder parents try to make alternative living arrangements for their children outside of the foster care system prior to incarceration.

As Table 6-1 on the next page indicates, incarcerated women who are parents tend to be young, white, less educated, and present with a prior history of criminal activity compared with men who are parents. Eighty-one percent of incarcerated women aged 25–34 were mothers, while 63% of incarcerated men in the same age range were fathers.

Table 6-1. Demographics of Incarcerated Parents, 2004

	Total (%)	Male Parents (%)	Female Parents (%)
Age of inmates who were parents of minor children			
<24 years of age	44	44	55
25–34	64	63	81
35–44	59	58	66
45–54	31	31	26
>55 years of age	13	13	*
Ethnicity of incarcerated parents			
White, non-Hispanic	46	45	62
Black, non-Hispanic	54	54	61
Hispanic	57	57	64
Other**	52	51	60
Marital Status			
Married	71	71	71
Widowed	36	35	41
Divorced	55	55	59
Separated	64	64	66
Never Married	45	44	61
Education			
<8th grade	50	49	62
Some high school	55	55	64
GED	51	51	64
High school graduate	52	52	59
Some college or more	49	47	59
Current offense			
Violent	48	47	57
Property	50	48	65
Drug	60	59	63
Public order	60	60	65
Prior criminal history			
None	48	47	58
Prior history	53	53	64

* Estimate not reported.
** Other race includes American Indians, Alaska Natives, Asians, Native Hawaiians, other Pacific Islanders, and persons identifying two or more races.
Adapted from Glaze and Maruschak, 2010. Percentages rounded.

Furthermore, 62% of incarcerated mothers surveyed in 2004 identified themselves as white, non-Hispanic, compared with 45% of fathers. While an equal number of men and women (71%) were married at the time of incarceration, women were less educated than men as 62% of women surveyed reported having less than an 8th grade education compared with 49% of men. With respect to prior criminal history, women were more likely (64%) to present with prior histories of criminal activity compared with men (53%). Incarcerated fathers and mothers were almost as likely to have committed violent (48% and 47%), property (50% and 48%), drug (60% and 59%), and public order offenses (60% and 60%), respectively.

Incarcerated parents in state prison reported contact with their children in a number of ways, including by telephone, mail, and visits. Overall, more than three-quarters (79%) of incarcerated parents reported having some contact with their children; hence 21% of parents had no contact with their children. Mothers were more likely to report visits with their children than fathers (85% and 78% respectively). Not surprisingly, parents who lived with their child(ren) in the month before arrest or just before incarceration were more likely to report visits with their children. More than half (56%) of mothers in state prison and 39% of fathers had at least weekly contact of some kind (Glaze & Maruschak, 2010). More parents reported contact via letters (70%) with their children than speaking by phone (53%) and less than half (42%) had a personal visit. This is not unexpected given the hardships and costs associated with prison visits and telephone calls discussed elsewhere in this book (Glaze & Maruschak, 2010).

Incarcerated mothers were more likely to have contact with their children via mail at least weekly (35%) compared with men (23%), and men were more likely never to have mail contact with their children (31%) than women (22%) (Glaze & Maruschak, 2010). The frequency of personal visits was more evenly distributed. Incarcerated men and women received similar visits at least weekly (12% compared with 15% for men and women, respectively), but men (59%) and women (58%) were almost equally likely never to receive visits (Glaze & Maruschak, 2010).

As Table 6-2 indicates, for parents who lived with minor children prior to imprisonment, women were more likely than men to have experienced physical and/or sexual abuse (60%), present with a current medical problem (50%), and be diagnosed with any mental health problem (73%), while men were more apt to have substance abuse/dependency issues (65%) than women. When comparing mothers and fathers who lived with their children prior to incarceration with those mothers and fathers who did not, interesting differences are observed (Glaze & Maruschak, 2010).

In virtually every category of assessment, the percentage of men who were homeless, ever suffered physical/sexual abuse, presented with a current medical problem, or had mental health or substance abuse/dependency problems was almost identical between the two groups. However, significant differences between mothers who lived with their children prior to incarceration and those that did not are evident.

Table 6-2. Incidence of Homelessness, Abuse, Health Problems, and Substance Abuse of Incarcerated Parents Who Lived with Their Children Prior to Incarceration, 2004

	Total (%)	Male Parents (%)	Female Parents (%)
Homeless in year before arrest	9	4	9
Physical/sexual abuse	20	16	60
Current medical problem	41	40	50
Any mental health problem	57	55	73
Any substance abuse/dependence	67	65	64

Adapted from Glaze & Maruschak, 2010.

As Table 6-3 reflects, women who did not live with their minor children prior to incarceration were much more likely than women who did live with their children and always more likely than men to be homeless in the year before arrest (29%), to have ever experienced physical/sexual abuse (72%), to present with a current medical problem (58%), to have been diagnosed with a mental health problem (75%) and to have substance abuse/dependence (82%).

Table 6-3. Incidence of Homelessness, Abuse, Health Problems, and Substance Abuse of Incarcerated Parents Who Did Not Live with Their Children Prior to Incarceration, 2004

	Total (%)	Male Parents (%)	Female Parents (%)
Homeless in year before arrest	9	12	29
Physical/sexual abuse	20	16	72
Current medical problem	41	40	58
Any mental health problem	57	55	75
Any substance abuse/dependence	67	69	82

Adapted from Glaze & Maruschak, 2010.

In many instances, parents who are incarcerated rely on other family members and friends to "parent" while they are away. As 75% of children with incarcerated mothers also have fathers who are criminal justice-involved, most fathers are not actively involved in the parenting of their child when mothers are incarcerated (Phillips et al., 2006). Consequently, in many instances this results in grandparents and other kin taking on additional (or new) parenting responsibilities for children that are not theirs. As noted above, alternative parenting arrangements are often made prior to the imprisonment of the mother or father in hopes of minimizing the exposure of the child to foster care and the possibility of the eventual termination of parental rights (Baunach, 1985; Enos, 2001).

The natural consequence of making alternative parenting arrangements outside the confines of the formal foster care system is that co-caregiving or co-parenting takes place; children of incarcerated parents are parented by several people simultaneously. As Cecil and colleagues (2008) note, adaptive family structures work collaboratively as a team to intervene and co-parent when the biological parents are unable to do so. As the chapter on families and children suggests, kinship networks are invaluable in maintaining and perpetuating the family unit when a family member is incarcerated, and multiple-parenting dynamics can work well when the alliance between co-caregivers is strong and uniform. In some cases, the alliance formed by co-parents can be stronger and more influential than traditional nuclear parental arrangements (McHale et al., 2002). When co-parenting relationships are poor, however, children can develop behavioral and other problems that often mimic those problems encountered by biological parents (Cecil et al., 2008).

Fathers

Since 1991, the number of children with an incarcerated father has grown 77% (Glaze & Maruschak, 2010). In 2007, more than 40% of incarcerated fathers were black, approximately 30% were white, and 20% were Hispanic (Glaze & Maruschak, 2010). Imprisoned fathers also tend to come from families where criminal behavior is common and where contact with the criminal justice system is frequent (Arditti et al., 2003; Carlson & McLanahan, 2002). The implications associated with the sheer number of fathers who are incarcerated cannot be overstated. More fathers inside prison walls means fewer fathers in the community to provide food, shelter, and economic support (Hairston, 2001b). Given the number of men in prison today, it is not hyperbole to suggest that, "prison-based parenting could easily become a normative phase of child rearing and development" (Hairston, 2001b, p. 114).

Ironically, while men may comprise the overwhelming majority of inmates in prison, they have not routinely been viewed in a paternal context. Upon incarceration, men are seemingly out of sight and therefore out of mind as both members of society and as fathers. Research suggests that identities and roles are malleable and are often modified, adopted, and/or discarded when circumstances dictate (Dyer, 2005). Understandably, incarceration is a circumstance that has the capacity to severely impact and alter parental identity and the ability of fathers to perform their parental role.

The parental role is further compromised when we consider that incarcerated men are twice as likely to divorce or separate than non-incarcerated men, with the divorce often occurring during incarceration (Lopoo & Western, 2005). This is particularly salient in light of findings that suggest single fathers are five times less likely to have frequent contact with their children compared to married fathers or those involved in a relationship (Laquale et al., 2018). In his survey of incarcerated fathers, Pierce (2015) noted that some fathers report that the mother of their child(ren) cut off all contact with them and they "no longer knew where their children were or how to contact them" (p. 380).

Arditti and colleagues argue that how fathers define and view themselves (fatherhood) impacts the extent to which they are able to provide for or are involved in parenting (father involvement) (Arditti et al., 2005). Unfortunately, stereotypes of men in prison precede thoughtful evaluation of the impact of incarceration of fathers and their attendant children (Hairston, 1998). Men in prison who are fathers have hopes and dreams for their children just like other fathers. The difference is that these hopes and dreams are often influenced by the incarceration experience (Hairston, 1998).

Imprisonment often impacts the ability of men to father in a meaningful way and often erodes their sense of self because they do not believe that the contributions they make are good enough or effective (Hairston, 1998). Not surprisingly, relationships that fathers have established with children prior to incarceration are at minimum interrupted and at maximum severed while the father is away from home. Fathers not able to take part in the day-to-day caregiving (including protection and discipline) of children may feel emasculated and "less than" in their children's eyes (Day et al., 2005).

Arditti and colleagues (2005) noted that incarcerated fathers in their study reported feelings of "impotence and the inability to carry out fathering functions" (p. 276). Feelings of helplessness and paternal role ambiguity further reduce men's confidence in themselves as fathers while in prison. Efforts to reestablish or maintain relationships with children are often hampered by the frustrations and stresses associated with being incarcerated and the realities of the reentry process—issues that require realignments of roles in the family unit by both the father and child (Arditti et al., 2005; Dyer, 2005).

Many men who are incarcerated openly acknowledge that they have not been good fathers or could have been better fathers (Lanier, 1993). Men who may not have been good fathers prior to incarceration may adopt aspirations (sometimes unrealistic) for the future. Sometimes they see incarceration as an opportunity to reinvent themselves as fathers and caregivers. Internal shifts in thought about what a father is and what a father is supposed to be may result in tangible changes in the present or beliefs that post-release behavior will change (Arditti et al., 2005). Regardless, these role transformations (however long-lasting) are driven by insecurities related to helplessness and feelings of lack of control and are attempts to aspire to socially conceived notions of what the perfect father is, even though these notions are not realistic (Doherty et al., 1998; Fox & Bruce, 2001). Laquale and colleagues (2018) suggest that incarcerated fathers often have a less optimal perception of their parental role. Although the men may be invested in being a good father, the forced separation of incarceration makes them feel less competent and satisfied in their role, particularly as they are not able to exert their parental control in the daily lives of their children. Additional issues that influence incarcerated men's paternal views of self, include the fact that children may not know their father is incarcerated, or they may have mixed feelings about their father's imprisonment and feel generally anxious about their father's return home (Johnston, 1995; Mazza, 2002). Moreover, children's attitudes toward their fathers may be shaped (at least in part) by their mother's feelings (Roy & Dyson, 2005). These and other dynamics may require that children renegotiate their role both within the family and with their father while the father is away and upon his return (Dyer, 2005; Lindquist et al., 2009).

Notably, father– close child relationships are mutually beneficial. Research indicates that fathers who are able to remain to their family and children tend to do better (i.e., recidivate less) than fathers who do not have the same opportunity (Patillo et al., 2004). Families and children serve as protective factors against recidivism and other attendant problems related to reentering the community from prison (Dyer, 2005). Conversely, research indicates that fathers who are present in their children's lives are instrumental in positively impacting their child's development (Gadsden & Rethemeyer, 2003; Pleck & Masciadrelli, 2004). When fathers are not present in their child's lives (no matter the cause), children are more likely to engage in a range of behaviors, including delinquent acts, acting out at school, experiencing depression, exhibiting aggressive behavior, and engaging in risky behaviors such as drug use and sex (Gable & Shindledecker, 1993; Heimer, 1996).

Data from the Returning Home Study finds fathers who had contact with their children nearing the end of their incarceration served shorter stays of incarceration and expressed strong levels of spirituality and control over their lives (Visher, 2013). Fathers who perceived their families as supportive were also more likely to establish strong attachments with their children following release. Moreover, fathers who experienced a positive relationship with their minor children were less likely to report feelings of depression, were less likely to reoffend (including technical violations), and were found to work more hours at their job (Visher, 2013). While the benefits associated with a father–child relationship are clear, maintaining the relationship is not always possible. One of the most challenging issues for men in prison is negotiating the family network. Family networks tend to be rather complex in composition, and this impacts the ability of men to interact with their children. Most incarcerated fathers are not married to the mother of their child/children at the time that they are incarcerated (Hairston, 1995; Lanier, 1993). Furthermore, fathers in prison are likely to have more than one child from more than one mother (Hairston, 1995). This dynamic results in men managing different roles with different children, in part depending upon the relationship that the man has with the child's mother (Arditti & Few, 2008). Co-parenting (whether with the other parent or through kin networks) is difficult enough without the added complication of prison. Fathers who attempt to co-parent often feel a loss of control not only because they are physically not able to be with their children but because the mothers or kin of their children often engage in "gatekeeping," wherein they filter and regulate fathers' contact with children (Roy & MacDermid, 2003).

Furthermore, men in prison suffer from some of the same insecurities as women in the sense that they worry about their children and do not want someone else to replace them in their children's lives while they are away (Lanier, 1993). If the father was living with a child and the child's mother prior to incarceration, the father was more likely to provide financial support and day-to-day care-giving. If the father was not living with a child prior to going to prison, they were also likely to provide financial support (Hairston, 1998). Interestingly, while fathers are generally willing to provide monetary support, they do not seem fully aware of the impact that their emotional support has in the development of their children (Hairston, 2001a).

Imprisoned fathers are not routinely considered either by the society that has deemed them incarcerable or by the system that houses them. Generally speaking, correctional policy and practice does not encourage men in prison who are fathers to develop, maintain, or improve relationships with their children (Hairston, 2001b). However, as this discussion indicates, current policy and practice is short-sighted. Research indicates that the majority of fathers who are incarcerated care deeply for their children and often become better members of society as a result of their ability to maintain relationships with their children. While the feelings they have for their children may be more difficult to express, they are no less meaningful or important when formulating effective reentry practice.

Mothers

By way of context, since 1991, the number of children with an incarcerated mother has more than doubled, up 131% (Glaze & Maruschak, 2010). In 2007, 48% of incarcerated mothers were white, 28% where black, and 17% were Hispanic (Glaze & Maruschak, 2010). Mothers were more likely than fathers to receive government assistance; 36% of incarcerated mothers received Social Security or other compensation from the government as income (Glaze & Maruschak, 2010).

Incarcerated mothers continue to grow in number, are primarily minority in status, and generally did not support themselves prior to incarceration. Moreover, where fathers struggle with navigating changing paternal identities and roles with the realities associated with incarceration, mothers who are imprisoned face the added challenge of reconciling parental identities and roles with societal expectations of what it means to be a woman, a mother, and a felon.

Many of the beliefs about women and the roles that they play in society are grounded in role theory (Mead, 1934). The notion that people are the products of the society in which they live and the social interactions in which they engage suggests that society both constructs roles for people and reinforces those roles in an effort to manipulate or mold behavior (Blumer, 1969). Moreover, society's efforts to manage behavior through social interactions are predicated on the belief that the behaviors that society wishes to reinforce are acceptable social norms (Biddle, 1986). Scholars also suggest that role transformations are a necessary function for people as they are required to modify and change their role behavior as they work through transitional life events (Herrschaft et al., 2009).

Role transformation is directly related to concepts of self and role identity and is gender-specific (Miller, 1976). Herrschaft and colleagues (2009) noted that women's constructs of self consist of ongoing attachments to important people in their lives. The strength of these attachments may change over time, but a woman's role identity is driven by the nature and content of the connections that they have established with family, friends, spouses, significant others, and children. Brown and Bloom (2009) indicate that for many women, motherhood is central to gender identification, and this may be even more pronounced for incarcerated women who have violated societal norms and gender role expectations. Arditti and Few (2006) suggest that the act of mothering is indeed fundamentally impacted by incarceration and that personal and social identities are changed and roles are transformed during this time.

Some scholars argue that in an attempt to mitigate societal critique of their poor choices, women in prison or who are criminal justice-involved often create "good mothering" self-constructs that attempt to reinforce or recreate what they perceive to be society's positive view of that idea while simultaneously eschewing women in prison who are viewed as unfit (Enos, 2001). Moreover, attempts to reconstruct and renegotiate role identities may be directly related to coping mechanisms that an incarcerated mother may use in an effort to come to grips with the loss of her child/children.

Celinska and Siegel (2010) examined this very issue. This study defined coping as "constantly changing cognitive and behavioral efforts to manage specific external and/or internal demands that are appraised as taxing or exceeding the resources of the person" (Lazarus & Folkman, 1984, p. 141). Results indicate that incarcerated mothers employ several specific coping strategies to manage the separation from their children during incarceration, including being a good mother, mothering behind prison walls, role reconstruction, disassociation from the prisoner identity, self-transformation, and self-blame (Celinska & Siegel, 2010).

The separation of women from their children brought on by imprisonment has multiple dimensions. Feelings of inadequacy and fear associated with loss of control over the well-being of their children along with guilt, anxiety, depression, and remorse for the impact their crimes have had on their children affects women's abilities to mother even marginally from inside prison walls (Sharp & Marcus-Mendoza, 2001; Snyder et al., 2001; Young & Smith, 2000). Incarcerated mothers find the separation brought on by imprisonment deeply isolating and one of the most difficult aspects of being incarcerated (Dodge & Pogrebin, 2001; Hairston, 1991a).

Scholars have defined this complex presentation of symptoms as maternal distress, a concept that is defined as depression, physiological malaise, and unhappiness (Arendell, 2000) and that has been associated with a series of negative parenting, social, and economic outcomes (Arditti & Few, 2008). A study evaluating maternal distress in mothers who were incarcerated indicates that not only was the concept validated, but that it was central to incarcerated mothers' adaptation to prison life and to the prospect of successful reentry to the community (Arditti & Few, 2008).

Still other research suggests that some women who are imprisoned view the separation from their children as a motivating factor for life change (Enos, 2001; Ferraro & Moe, 2003). They see their incarceration as an opportunity to "make good" and make up for the mistakes they may have made in the past. Other scholarship notes that women may seek to romanticize the nature and scope of the relationship they had/currently have with their children as a mechanism for coping with incarceration and separation from their children (Hairston, 2001a). This research suggests that erroneous perceptions or misconceived notions of the relationship with their children lead women to set unreasonable goals related to family reunification upon their release (Hairston, 2001a; Stanton, 1980). While mothers may plan to reunite with their children upon release from prison, the act of "doing time" often interferes with their ability to actually do so (Hairston, 2001a).

Brown and Bloom (2009) observed something quite different in their work on reentry and motherhood, suggesting that while women's concerns about their children may be foremost in their minds while in prison, they are often a source of consternation when they leave. Mothers' thoughts of their children being without them and fears associated with what to expect upon release from prison can be stressful and often impact their ability to successfully cope with their problems and the multiple issues that they face. In many cases, incarcerated mothers are left wondering how they are supposed to adhere to the multiple demands of adapting to prison and release at the same time they are supposed to fulfill society's requirements for being a good mother (Richie, 2001; Snyder, 2009). "Parenting women not only negotiate reentry, but they often must renegotiate the terms and conditions of their relations with children" (Brown & Bloom, 2009, p. 314).

There are specific ways in which the reentry process plays out for mothers who have been incarcerated and who are being released to the community. Many of these issues are related to the pathways that led these women to crime in the first place (i.e., lack of employment, poverty, drug use, trauma, victimization, etc.) as well as to the children they left behind at the time of imprisonment and will now interact with, to some extent, upon release.

Women often have significant problems finding employment due to spotty or nonexistent legitimate work histories prior to release. Moreover, many of these women have significant debt at the time of release (Levingston & Turetsky, 2007). Furthermore, reliance on informal methods of support from children's fathers as well as federal subsidies prior to incarceration makes it difficult, if not impossible, for some women to find gainful employment after release. Lack of basic employment skills and poor educational attainment stack the deck against these women. The best that most of these women have to look forward to are positions as low-wage workers (Ehrenreich, 2001). Obviously, their inability to find fruitful employment inhibits many mothers' ability to reunite with their children, let alone regain custody. In many cases, women simply cannot afford it.

Upon release, women who were incarcerated and who have children are anxious to rejoin and reconnect with their children, but sometimes these reunions are not positive, and in many cases these reunifications are not immediate. While many women are paroled to households where their children had been living, some are not. Delayed reunions with children can be positive in the sense that it can give women the opportunity to find a job, get settled, and prepare themselves for the challenges of being a mother and being on parole or released from prison (Brown & Bloom, 2009). In other instances, the added pressure of seeing children, attempting to redefine maternal roles, and meeting the challenges associated with reentry can be overwhelming. Women transitioning to the community who have children encounter the "co-occurrence of multiple demands" as all women do, but do so with the added dimension of being an ex-offender, a woman, and a mother (Richie, 2001, p. 380).

Hopefully, women were able to visit and communicate with their children while they were incarcerated. However, institutional policies often limit or make communication with children difficult (Snyder et al., 2001). In contrast to policies regarding visitation for fathers, visitation between mothers and children in the prison setting is generally viewed as vital for maintaining mother–child attachments while in prison and facilitating opportunities for reunification after prison (Hairston, 1991b). Similar to some incarcerated fathers, some imprisoned mothers only occasionally or never receive visits from their children due to geographic distance of the prison from the child's home, lack of an available adult to bring the child to visit, and disagreements with caregivers regarding what is in the best interest of the child (Baunach, 1985; Hairston & Lockett, 1987).

The extent to which women communicate with their children on the inside definitely impacts their willingness, ability, and motivation to reconnect with them on the outside. Whether communication is impeded by institutional barriers or caregivers, the maternal experience is impacted. The degree to which women rewrite, reformulate, or otherwise reinvent themselves as mothers upon their release from prison is complex. On the one hand, women have some semblance of control over how they wish society and their children would view them as mothers, but significant damage to the previously incarcerated mother's identity has often been done and is sometimes irreversible (Brown & Bloom, 2009).

The research on the impact of incarceration on mothers is by no means equivocal. There are layers of issues and concerns that impact the physical and mental health of women in prison who are mothers. However, the research does reveal and is consistent in noting that cultural constructs of femininity and motherhood that are superimposed on women by society along with the pressures associated with being a woman and attempting to reenter society after having been to prison complicate relationships between women and their children (Baunach, 1985; McMahon, 1995; Owen, 1998).

Reentry Considerations

Most prison programs do not address parenting issues/concerns, and the majority do not provide information in assisting incarcerated parents with the parenting challenges that face them as they prepare for release (Frye & Sawe, 2008). To add insult to injury, if parental programming in prison is offered, these programs tend to be reflections of mainstream society's beliefs about what is the right way to parent, and do not necessarily take into account cultural or other issues that may impede the ability of incarcerated mothers or fathers to parent (Mumola, 2000).

A review of the literature indicates that experts suggest that parenting programs (regardless of whether they are for mothers or fathers) should focus on a number of different conceptual domains, including:

- **Attachment Theory:** this theory suggests that attachments between mother/parent and child that are developed early and that are strong and healthy will result in better relationships between parents and child. Programs that are based on this theory usually incorporate frequent parent–child visitation and activities that encourage togetherness (Blinn, 1997).
- **Parenting Skills Training:** this training focuses on providing parents with skills for learning how to communicate with and maintain close relationships with their children while they are incarcerated and after release. These skills include active listening, empathy, and understanding and acceptance of a child's behaviors (Palm, 2003).
- **Self-Esteem and Self-Development:** incarcerated parents must also learn how to care for themselves. This includes working on self-esteem issues—issues that often impede their ability to be effective and loving parents (Blinn, 1997).
- **Social Support and Empowerment:** incarcerated parents must learn how to rely on social supports as a means to assist them with the problems associated with trying to parent while incarcerated (Turner & Eichenlaub, 1998). Peer support groups that bring incarcerated parents to talk about the stressors associated with being a parent in prison help mediate some of the fear and trepidation they feel.
- **Parenting Beliefs and Attitudes:** parents who are incarcerated should think about assessing their beliefs about children and child-rearing before they think about adopting new or different parenting skills (Powell & Eisenstadt, 1988).

While corrections personnel do not always provide the proper programming for parents while they are in prison, they also do not always inform these parents of the practical parenting challenges that await them when they are released. For example, a very practical consideration that significantly limits relationships with parents and children is unpaid child support. Most fathers in prison are not custodial fathers and therefore owe and are responsible for providing child support. Obviously, payment of child support is impossible while behind bars and made doubly difficult upon release given that many offenders are unable to get and maintain gainful employment.

Even if offenders are able to find employment, they are not often able to pay all or even some of the child support owed because of the large amount assessed and unrealistic expectations about what they are able to pay (Cammett, 2005). Currently, the child support "clock" continues while offenders are imprisoned. Parents leaving prison are often faced with repaying monetary obligations of various types but because the child support amount owed has continued to mount during their incarceration, oftentimes child support arrears for offenders incarcerated for long periods of time can reach hundreds of thousands of dollars. Offenders who owe large amounts of child support feel overwhelmed and are provided with little or no advice about how to manage this outstanding debt except to pay it.

Efforts on the part of state governments to be aggressive in the enforcement of payment of child support have resulted in a lack of flexibility with respect to the amount and frequency of payment. Wage garnishment occurs routinely and can equal up to 65% of one's salary. Garnishment of 65% of anyone's salary would be crippling, but is particularly so for offenders (Cammett, 2005). In addition to wage garnishment, offenders who do not actively pay child support may have their driver's license suspended, be re-arrested for non-payment, and be in violation of the conditions of parole.

The parent or other person caring for the child/children of offenders in prison has a right to receive compensation from the noncustodial parent for providing care. On this there is no dispute. However, jurisdictions have been historically intransigent in their willingness to work with offenders to develop payment plans/other options for reducing the child support debt. Very punitive approaches to obtaining payment for back child support have resulted in most offenders paying little or no child support at all.

Realistically, to enhance the likelihood of payment of any child support, it is likely necessary to readjust expectations. To that end, some jurisdictions have suggested capping or freezing child support arrears while offenders are imprisoned. Other have promoted providing a sliding scale for low-wage workers wherein a reasonable percentage was garnished; an amount that would most likely encourage payment and allow for the payee to continue working and bring home a living wage (Cammett, 2005). Understandably, more realistic monies owed would likely result in more efforts to pay. Research indicates that child support payments are more likely to be made when the amount due is a reasonable sum and one that is in line with the income of the child support provider (Roberts, 2002).

Promising Practice

Correctional programs do exist that attempt to assist fathers in prison with maintaining contact with their children. In particular, Idaho has a program entitled *Inside Out Dads* that is a 12-week, peer-taught program that encourages fathers to learn/strengthen communication skills with their children and caregivers. This program also addresses issues related to family roles and what to expect when the offender leaves prison and returns to the community (Idaho Department of Corrections, 2011). Other programs, such as *Books Beyond* in Rhode Island, allow offenders (mothers and fathers) to record the reading of a book for their children on audiotape or CD. The recording is then mailed to the child. In this way, the offender and child maintain contact and the child can hear the parent's voice (Rhode Island Department of Corrections, 2012).

Interestingly, while some institutional programs for fathers in prison do exist, there is little or no research that evaluates the efficacy of these programs. Program evaluation of parenting programs seems primarily reserved for programs that cater to mothers. Programs that have been developed to strengthen the mother–child relationship and that provide women with the opportunity to practice these skills have shown favorable outcomes (Kaminski et al., 2008). A program entitled *Parents Under Pressure* (PUP) developed and implemented in Queensland, Australia has shown some efficacy in helping mothers post release with reconnecting and forging meaningful relationships with their children. Researchers contend that this program was particularly successful because of the amount of time offenders spent with a therapist. Moreover, scholars argue that intensive interventions such as this one can improve child-parent relationships and help derail intergenerational pathways to crime (Frye & Sawe, 2008).

Another program, *The Extended Visitation Program*, has also been associated with positive experiences (Schubert, Duininck, & Schlafer, 2016). Mothers participating in the program live in specially designed residency units where their children can visit for extended periods of time. Mothers are able to show natural physical affection for their children and enjoy more privacy than the standard visitation rooms. Mothers reported the program allowed them to build and strengthen their relationships; they were "able to reassume their roles as mothers" (Schubert, et al., p. 223). Caregivers likened the program to therapy for the kids reporting that it let the kids know that their mother was still in their life and to feel connected with their mother.

Recent research also suggests that children want a relationship with their fathers both in and outside prison walls (Boswell, 2002; Nesmith & Ruhland, 2008; Yocum & Nath, 2011). Given fathers' desires for establishing or maintaining relationships with their children, and the potential benefit that is derived by both the parent and the child, encouraging these relationships is necessary (Yocum & Nath, 2011). Being able to spend time with children after release has been associated with reduced recidivism primarily because it reinforces prior family roles between parent and child (Hairston, 2002b).

Regardless of gender, the fact remains that parents, whether they are incarcerated or not, care very deeply about their children and want the best for them. This often serves as a motivating factor for parents who are imprisoned to change their behaviors, but even if it does not, their continued engagement in criminal behavior does not mean that they do not love their children (Palm, 2003). Research has shown that the needs of imprisoned mothers and fathers are different and therefore, parenting programs should address these differences in meaningful ways. Any programs that are developed should be sensitive to parents' cultural values and beliefs. Attempting to superimpose one set of values on another will not have any impact and will likely result in parental ambivalence (Cheng et al., 1997). Furthermore, parent education must become part of a larger effort to engage families and children in the parental educational process. In the end, if incarcerated parents are to become better parents, the programs that they participate in must cater to their needs and be inclusive of family and child.

Chapter 7

Physical Health and Reentry

Not surprisingly, offender populations are usually less healthy and suffer from mental health conditions more frequently than the general population. Indeed, state and federal inmates are nearly three times more likely to report at least one disability compared to the general population (Bronson et al., 2015). More than one-third (37%) of prisoners report a mental health disorder, and an additional 14% are considered to have a serious psychological disorder (Bronson & Berzofsky, 2017). In financial terms, the cost of managing offenders who are ill is staggering. States spent $8.1 billion on prison health care in fiscal year 2015 alone—about one-fifth of overall prison expenditures (Pew Charitable Trust, 2017). Inmate populations tend to suffer from more physical health problems, such as asthma, diabetes, and hypertension as well as HIV and communicable diseases, when compared with the general public (National Commission on Correctional Health Care, 2002). While these impairments may vary in severity, even minimal physical or mental impairments seem to impact offenders' ability to work and find employment once they are released. Indeed, 21% of state and federal inmates reported some condition that limited their ability to work once released (Maruschak & Beck, 2001).

Historical Context

Prior to the 1970s, policymakers and practitioners expressed little concern regarding the health care of individuals incarcerated in state or federal prisons. If healthcare was available inside prison walls it was delivered to inmates by staff with little or no medical training and almost always with poor outcomes (McDonald, 1999). Until this time, the courts remained "hands off" with respect to their intrusion into correctional affairs in general, and to prison healthcare issues in particular. The judiciary's position was that they lacked sufficient expertise to rule on correctional matters and that if they interfered in the day-to-day operations of correctional facilities, they would undermine corrections officials' authority (McMullan, 2011).

The judicial practice of being hands off was ultimately abandoned in the 1970s as a result of a series of Supreme Court cases that established basic rights of offenders in areas of due process, visitation, search and seizure, religion, legal services, and health care. The ultimate involvement of the courts in prison healthcare came as a result of a series of studies and evaluations that suggested that correctional facilities had the worst healthcare systems in the U.S. and that poor living conditions, overcrowding, and unsanitary conditions were responsible for increased numbers of offenders who were sick and left un- or under-treated (National Commission on Correctional Health Care, 2002; Shervington, 1974).

When considering specific judicial rulings regarding healthcare, *Newman v. Alabama* (1972) was one of the first court decisions that held the correctional system of Alabama in violation of the Eighth and Fourteenth Amendments for failing to provide inmates with adequate and sufficient medical care. However, *Estelle v. Gamble* (1976) may be the most significant court case addressing prison healthcare because it established a set of standards regarding medical care in all U.S. prisons (McMullan, 2011). *Estelle v. Gamble* (1976) established the threshold of "deliberate indifference to serious medical needs" while *Farmer v. Brennan* (1994) clarified the concept of deliberate indifference to require that a prison official or healthcare professional must be aware of and purposefully disregard an offender in order to be held liable (McMullan, 2011). As a result of these rulings, inmates now have three fundamental rights as they relate to healthcare in a prison setting: the right to have basic access to healthcare, the right to take part in care that is recommended for them, and the right to professional medical judgment (National Commission on Correctional Health Care, 2002). These rulings established access to healthcare in prison and are a protected right enforceable under Section 1983 of the U.S. Code.

Interestingly, increased legal attention to prison health issues has brought with it a new emphasis on prison healthcare by medical professionals. As a result, several professional organizations were created to specifically address prison healthcare needs, including the Academy of Correctional Healthcare Professionals, the American Correctional

Health Services Administration, the National Commission on Correctional Healthcare, and the Society of Correctional Physicians. Even the American Correctional Association has developed a Healthcare Professionals division within the organization.

A focus on setting professional standards for those who treat people in correctional environments has resulted in an increasing number of doctors, nurses, physicians' assistants, and pharmacists who practice medicine inside prison walls (McDonald, 1999). Moreover, the American Public Health Association was the first organization to develop national health care standards for correctional institutions (American Public Health Association, 1976). The most recent set of prison health standards were issued in 2008 by the National Commission on Correctional Healthcare (National Commission on Correctional Health Care, 2008).

Prisons have become one of the most expansive and expensive healthcare delivery systems in the nation, dramatically impacting healthcare policy and practice both inside and outside prison walls (McDonald, 1999). Moreover, it took judicial intervention in the correctional management of prison health issues to drive this expansion, and it has not come without a struggle. Differing standards for healthcare on both sides of the prison wall have made it challenging for health practitioners to do their jobs effectively and efficiently. Coupled with the volume of patients and serious medical problems with which many offenders present, prison healthcare continues to be a significant resource concern for the medical and corrections fields alike (McDonald, 1999).

Current Trends

A recent study highlights the extent of medical services offered in correctional jurisdictions. At time of admission, over 85% of prisoners were asked screening questions related to their health or medical history, and 64% were checked to determine if they were sick, injured, or intoxicated (Maruschak et al., 2015). Subsequent to prison admission, 94% of prisoners reported being tested for tuberculosis, 57% for Hepatitis B, 54% for Hepatitis C, 71% for HIV, and 33% for a sexually transmitted disease (STD) (Maruschak et al., 2015).

Communicable diseases are of particular importance to prison officials. An estimated 21% of prisoners reported ever having tuberculosis, or hepatitis or other STDs, more than four times the rate reported in the general population (Maruschak et al., 2015). These types of diseases are easily spread in situations where people live in close proximity to one another, such as prisons and jails. This was strongly evidenced with SARS-CoV-2, the coronavirus that causes COVID-19. The Centers for Disease Control and Prevention noted that containment of the highly infectious pathogen in correctional and detention centers was fraught with challenges, noting overcrowded living conditions, shared bathrooms, limited medical and isolation resources, and the constant flow of people in and out of the institutions (Centers for Disease Control and Prevention [CDC], 2020a). Indeed, more than half a million prisoners and institutional staff (526,534) contracted COVID-19 as of the writing of this book, with the majority of those infected being prisoners (CDC, 2020b).

High-risk behaviors within correctional institutions pose additional risk of communicable disease transmission, such as continued intravenous drug use, unprotected sex, sexual victimization, syringe sharing, and tattooing (Gough et al., 2010). While the rate of HIV among prisoners in 2015 was the lowest observed in the 25 years of data collection by the Bureau of Justice Statistics, an estimated 1.3% of female and 1.3% of male prisoners are known to be HIV positive or have confirmed AIDS (Maruschak & Bronson, 2017). Research suggests that most inmates with HIV were infected in the community before incarceration (Hammett, 2006; Rosen et al., 2015). This finding is supported in a systematic review and meta-analysis of HIV incidence in U.S. correctional inmates, which found the highest HIV incidence was among inmates released to the community and subsequently re-incarcerated (Gough et al., 2010). These finding reinforce the importance of testing on admission to further limit the spread within the institution.

HIV testing practices of incoming prisoners, however, vary by state, with only 15 states requiring testing (Maruschak & Bronson, 2017). Seventeen states and the Federal Bureau of Prisons use "opt-out" testing methods that automatically test prisoners for HIV unless the inmate chooses to "opt-out," with eight states employing "opt-in" protocols that require the inmate to request to be tested (Federal Bureau of Prisons, 2017; Maruschak & Bronson, 2017). Connecticut is the only state that does not test for HIV according to the most recent National Prisoner Statistic's Survey. The few remaining states either did not provide their testing methods or did not provide specific information. The majority of states and the Federal Bureau of Prisons will also mandate HIV testing if the inmate has been involved in an incident that may have exposed them to transmission of the virus (Federal Bureau of Prisons, 2017; Maruschak, 2010). Not surprisingly, the highest percentage of reported HIV cases among new prison admissions are in jurisdictions that have mandatory testing procedures (34%) and "opt-out" policies (31%) (Maruschak & Bronson, 2017), suggesting that HIV/AIDS rates are likely under-estimated among the prison population. While generally not in favor of mandatory HIV testing protocols in correctional institutions over concerns of discrimination, stigma, and victimization, public health organizations advocate for the use of "opt-out" strategies (Centers for Disease Control and Prevention, 2009; Rosen et al., 2015).

A recent study of adult prisoners in North Carolina addressed the question of whether prisoners understood the voluntary nature of "opt-out" HIV testing protocols (Rosen et al., 2015). Less than 40% of prisoners understood the test was voluntary with the proportions differing significantly across the seven intake facilities, suggesting that the clarity of instruction given to inmates differed by institution. Younger inmates (25 years old and younger) and those that believe HIV testing should be mandatory were less likely to perceive the test as voluntary. Interestingly, 84% of surveyed prisoners believed HIV testing should be mandatory, and 89% wanted to be tested on admission.

Examples of other communicable disease include hepatitis and tuberculosis. Hepatitis is a viral infection that infects the liver and can cause significant long-term health problems, including death. There are five types of hepatitis infection, identified as Hepatitis A, B, C, D, and E. The B, C, and D forms of the virus are most communicable because they are found in blood and other body fluids (Weinbaum et al., 2003). In prison settings, inmates are most likely to contract Hepatitis B or C. Prevalence rates of Hepatitis B infection in prison inmates are 1.0–3.7% compared with 0.5% in the general population. Approximately 16–41% of inmates may also have Hepatitis C.

Tuberculosis (TB) or *Mycobacterium tuberculosis* is a bacteria that is spread primarily through coughing and sneezing. Tuberculosis is more prevalent in the offender population due to poor healthcare prior to admission, poor living conditions, drug use, and compromised immune systems (McDonald, 1999). According to the most recent data collected by the Bureau of Justice Statistics, prisoners were about 12 times more likely than persons in the standardized general population to report ever having TB (Maruschak & Bernofsky, 2015). Moreover, unlike HIV testing as discussed earlier in this chapter, almost all prisoners (94%) reported having been tested for tuberculosis at the time of intake. It is important to note, especially when addressing the offender population, that increased incidence of tuberculosis is also attributed to drug-resistant strains of the disease that occur when people with active TB do not complete their treatment regimen (McDonald, 1999). Treatment for tuberculosis is lengthy and requires most patients to take medications for several years. Adherence to lengthy treatment regimens and medication compliance will likely prove more difficult for those in the offender population.

Data also indicate that the prevalence of sexually transmitted diseases is high for people in correctional facilities compared with the general population (Heimberger et al., 1993; Maruschak & Bernofsky, 2015). This is due to increased risky behaviors such as drug use, high-risk sexual behavior, and limited access to health care prior to incarceration (Kraut-Becher et al., 2004). Moreover, the importance of managing STDs in prison is significant, as these diseases impact not only the person infected, but the partners and others with whom the person comes into contact (Travis, 2005); yet only 33% of prisoners report being tested for STDs on admission (Maruschak & Bernofsky, 2015) Most recent data indicate the percentage of prisoners with sexually transmitted diseases (6%) is almost double that of the general population (3.4%) (Maruschak & Bernofsky, 2015). More specifically, prevalence rates of syphilis are 2.6–4.3%, compared with chlamydia and gonorrhea that are 2.4% and 1.0% in the corrections population (National Commission on Correctional Health Care, 2008). Other than Hepatitis C, tuberculosis and STDs are the most commonly reported infectious diseases among prisoners (Maruschak & Bernofsky, 2015).

A study evaluating jail populations in large urban areas indicates that the rate of syphilis in Los Angeles County jail was found to be 11 times higher than for the general population (Kraut & Haddix, 2008). A study published in 2007 that surveyed correctional health providers regarding HIV and sexually transmitted diseases indicates that approximately 76% of inmates are tested for syphilis at entry to prison. However, testing for gonorrhea and chlamydia is relatively low, with only 17% and 20% of inmates tested on a mandatory or routine basis respectively (Hammett et al., 2007).

High prevalence rates of chronic health conditions, among them asthma, arthritis, diabetes, and kidney-related problems, also pose significant issues for prisoners and institutions (Maruschak & Bernofsky 2015). Forty-four percent of prisoners report ever having a chronic health condition, compared to 31% of persons in the general population. Older prisoners and females are more likely to report a chronic health condition and/or infectious disease (Marushack & Bernofsky, 2015). High blood pressure is the most common condition among prisoners (30%), with almost three-quarters (74%) of prisoners considered to be overweight, obese, or morbidly obese. It is therefore unsurprising that prisoners are also more likely to report heart-related problems (Maruschak & Bernofsky, 2015). A national survey of prison healthcare found majority of states conduct limited cardiovascular risk testing during admission on some incoming inmates or when clinical indications warrant (Chari et al., 2016).

Prisoners also report significantly higher rates of cirrhosis of the liver than the general population (1.7% vs. 0.1%, respectively) (Maruschak & Bernofsky, 2015). Cirrhosis is a late-stage liver disease resulting in permanent liver damage and can lead to death (Cleveland Clinic, 2020). It is not unexpected to see the high prevalence of cirrhosis among prisoners, as the common causes include prolonged alcohol use, viral hepatitis, diabetes, obesity, injected drug use using shared needles, liver disease, and unprotected sex (Cleveland Clinic, 2020), all risk factors commonly found in the offender population as discussed earlier in this chapter.

Currently, most correctional facilities provide some form of screening for pre-existing medical conditions. The purpose of screening exams for health issues particularly in a prison setting is to identify risk factors for health problems or disease that can be managed through early intervention. Early intervention is much more cost-effective than full-blown disease management (Lee et al., 2007). Once these conditions are recognized, a treatment plan is developed for an offender. Some prisons have their own hospitals and medical personnel onsite, while others contract out their medical care to local and regional hospitals (McMullan, 2011). Some states, such as Texas, actually collaborate with state medical schools to provide medical care for inmates (Travis, 2005).

A 2006 survey by the American Correctional Association on inmate health care and communicable diseases provides us with the most current picture of the nature and scope of healthcare in a correctional setting. This survey evaluated staffing, budgets, and an assessment of general and specialized services provided (American Correctional Association, 2006). Forty-three of 50 states responded to the survey.

Data indicate that 14.8% percent of states' total corrections budgets were allocated to prison healthcare. The average annual per inmate expense was $3,755 (American Correctional Association, 2006). Service provision varies considerably by state. All states provided some level of service for the elderly (defined as 55 and older), women, and the chronically and terminally ill. Services ranged from providing specialized housing and medical units, to hospice and nursing home care for the elderly, to gynecological and pre/postpartum exams, pap smears, mammography, and reproductive counseling for women (American Correctional Association, 2006). In addition, chronic care clinics were the most common special provision for the chronically ill, while hospice, infirmaries, and conditional medical release or medical parole programs were reserved for the terminally ill (American Correctional Association, 2006). Some state correctional institutions, such as Pennsylvania's Laurel Highlands, are specifically designed to respond to inmates with special needs, including long-term care, personal care, dialysis, and inmates who are geriatric or confined to a wheelchair (Pennsylvania Department of Corrections, n.d.).

In an attempt to keep medical costs to a minimum, many correctional jurisdictions have implemented managed care-like practices within prison walls. These include requiring offenders to make "co-pays" for services, creating strict protocols for healthcare management and utilization, and instituting specific limits on the amount and type of services provided (McDonald, 1999). Of 43 respondents to the 2006 American Correctional Association survey on inmate healthcare and communicable diseases, 86% required inmates to provide a co-pay in the range of $2–$10 depending on the jurisdiction (McDonald, 1999).

Although a co-pay of $2–$10 may not seem like a lot of money, prisoners earn on average 14 to 63 cents per hour if they have a work assignment at all, making healthcare costs prohibitive for inmates without additional financial support (Sawyer, 2017). Sawyer (2017) likened a $4 copay for an inmate in Oklahoma earning about five cents per hour as the equivalent of a $580 co-pay charged to a non-incarcerated minimum-wage earner in the same state. Some states charge annual fixed healthcare fees of $100, debiting the inmate's account until the service fee is paid. Inmates with families unable to fund their accounts will receive a bill at the time of their release (Sawyer, 2017). Some states have recently begun to address these high costs. California and Illinois, for example, passed legislation in 2019 removing co-pays, and the state of Texas has replaced their $100 annual service fee with a $13.55 per visit fee (Sawyer, 2017).

While the demand for healthcare service provision is high in correctional settings, prison administrators often have a difficult time recruiting healthcare practitioners to work in a prison environment. The work is difficult and often seen as low status, and the pay is not in line with jobs these practitioners might hold in hospitals and doctor's offices in the community (Thorburn, 1995). In many instances, doctors and other healthcare providers are not used to working with offenders and find the clientele difficult to manage. To address the challenges of having on-site physicians and rising healthcare costs, corrections facilities have been increasingly turning to the use of telemedicine in patient care (Senanayake et al., 2018). Telemedicine allows physicians to meet with prisoners via videoconferencing while maintaining a nurse at the facility. The use of telemedicine has largely been confined to tele-psychiatry in correctional institutions over the past several years (Slate et al., 2013), suggesting a natural extension of this practice to physical healthcare. Prisons suffer from some of the same limitations of medical practices large and small. Oftentimes, prisons can only provide generalized medical care and must send patients with serious or specialized problems out to nearby hospitals for care. Moreover, prisons often do not have adequate treatment facilities or infirmaries, and medical records data systems are often antiquated (McDonald, 1999).

Eighty-six percent of deaths in prison were attributable to medical conditions such as heart disease, cancer, liver disease, and AIDS (Carson & Cowhig, 2020). In 2016, more than half of illness-related deaths were attributed to cancer (30%) and heart disease (28%). Between 2001 and 2016, male prisoners were on average about twice as likely to die of cancer, heart disease, or liver disease than female prisoners (Carson & Cowhig, 2020). Two-thirds of deaths in prison were the result of medical conditions that were present at time of admission to prison (Mumola, 2007). When comparing mortality rates of inmates to the general U.S. population, for inmates between the ages of 15 and 64, the overall mortality rate for prisoners was 19% lower than the general population between 2001 and 2004 (Mumola, 2007). In contrast, the inmate mortality rate was 56% higher than the general population for inmates in the 55–64 age group (Mumola, 2007).

Geriatric Inmates

While the age at which prison inmates are considered to be geriatric is somewhat flexible (no one quite agrees on what the magic age is), most practitioners view offenders over the age of 55 as qualifying as geriatric. Although it is not surprising that inmates over the age of 55 account for a significant percentage of the total inmate population, the number of state prisoners 55 and older tripled from 2001 to 2016 (Carson & Cowhig, 2020). In 2019, 13% of the total prison population were aged 55 and older, an increase of 2% in only four years (Carson, 2020; Carson & Anderson, 2016). Most contributive to the growing aging prison population are longer sentences and the number of older persons being admitted to state prison—an increase of 308% between 1993 and 2013 (see Figure 7-1) (Carson & Sabol, 2016). The number of older prisoners sentenced to more than one year in state prison increased 400% during this same time period, representing a change in the geriatric population from 3% of the total state prison population to 10% in two decades (Carson & Sabol, 2016).

Figure 7-1. Sentenced State Prisoners Aged 55 and Older

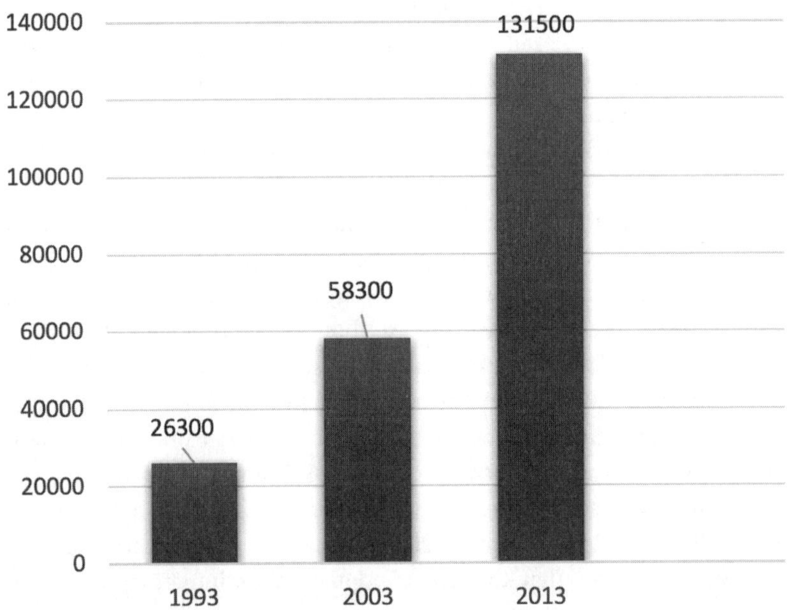

Adapted from Carson and Sabol, 2016.

As the corrections population ages, an already fragmented prison healthcare system sags under the weight of an increasing number of older offenders who present with more and more profound medical conditions that require the allocation of significant resources. Scholars contend that the healthcare needs of older inmates are many and complex due to an accelerated aging process that occurs in prison and a lack of basic medical care received prior to incarceration (Aday, 2003). By way of example, the Pennsylvania Department of Corrections (DOC) reported that 23% (10,697) of their total inmate population by end of year 2019 was over the age of 50. Most of these inmates are on medications at a cost to the DOC of $3.2 million per month. Moreover, the DOC requires three special long-term care units employing both skilled and personal care workers with a daily cost of $500 per inmate (Pennsylvania Department of Corrections, 2020–2021).

A survey of correctional officers assigned to random geriatric inmates reported 5% of known geriatric prisoners had active daily life impairments (Williams et al., 2009). The two most common impairments were bathing and transferring. Nineteen percent had mobility impairments, 6% had hearing impairments, 3% were incontinent, and 7% had memory problems. Officers further identified 3% of their geriatric prisoners as being unsafe in their current housing assignment. Perhaps more telling was that "nearly one-third of geriatric prisoners were completely unknown to their assigned officer, making assessment and provision for their disability unlikely" (p. 1288). Among those unknown geriatric prisoners, the California Department of Corrections and Rehabilitation designated 12% as disabled.

Not only is the number of geriatric offenders requiring medical care in prison growing steadily, the costs associated with caring for these inmates is astronomical. Because of lack of access to or receipt of medical care prior to imprisonment, many older offenders either present with increased chronic illness at entry to prison or are diagnosed with these ailments while incarcerated. For these inmates, all of the expenses usual and customary to caring for geriatric people are incurred, including nursing home care, increased hospitalizations, and multiple medication regimens (Hill et al., 2006). In California, inmates 55 and over account for 5% of the inmate population but more than 22% of the off-site hospital admissions costs (Hill et al., 2006). This figure will only increase as the number of geriatric inmates in California prisons and other jurisdictions continues to grow.

Geriatric patients generally present with more than one ailment and increased likelihood of chronic illnesses compared with the general population (Anno et al., 2004). Heart disease, arthritis, diabetes, hepatitis, HIV, hypertension, and liver disease are just a few examples of the types of ailments plaguing geriatric offenders. Given the nature of these illnesses, geriatric offenders generally take multiple medications, resulting in increased hospitalizations due to adverse events (Landefeld et al., 2004).

Other problems such as vision impairment, tendency to fall, urinary incontinence, and cognitive impairments make managing geriatric patients in prison particularly difficult. Often, special accommodations to prison buildings must be made to allow for the visually impaired and those inmates who may be prone to falls (Williams & Abraldes, 2007). Moreover, staff must be educated regarding inmates who may suffer cognitive impairment such as Alzheimer's Disease or dementia. Inmates with urinary incontinence suffer from issues related to stigma and ridicule (Hill et al., 2006).

Some jurisdictions offer geriatric inmates the ability to be housed in segregated housing units. This allows prisons to provide services to these inmates in a localized setting, maximizing resource allocation. This also results in decreased victimization of older inmates by younger ones (Aday, 2003). In some institutions, older inmates are cared for by other inmates (Williams et al., 2006), particularly when geriatric inmates may require hospice care (Aday, 2003). Many older inmates will die in prison. Eighty percent of state prisoner deaths in 2016 (the period for which the most recent data are available) were 45 years or older; 61% were aged 55 or older (Carson & Cowhig, 2020). As figure 7-2 indicates, overall mortality rates for prisoners age 55 or older between 2001 and 2016 were more than three times as high as any other age group.

In sum, geriatric inmates suffer from many of the same ailments and illnesses as the rest of us, but do so at alarmingly higher rates with the likelihood of multiple confounding factors. With correctional healthcare resources already stretched thin, geriatric patients in correctional facilities are consuming a large percentage of prison healthcare budgets with no relief in sight. Estimates of cost of care for these inmates reach $70,000 per year; two to three times the cost of healthcare for younger prisoners. Given the large increase in the number of older inmates requiring care, correctional departments face tough decisions regarding allocation of resources and the real possibility of a medical system that could easily

Figure 7-2. Percent Prisoner Deaths by Age

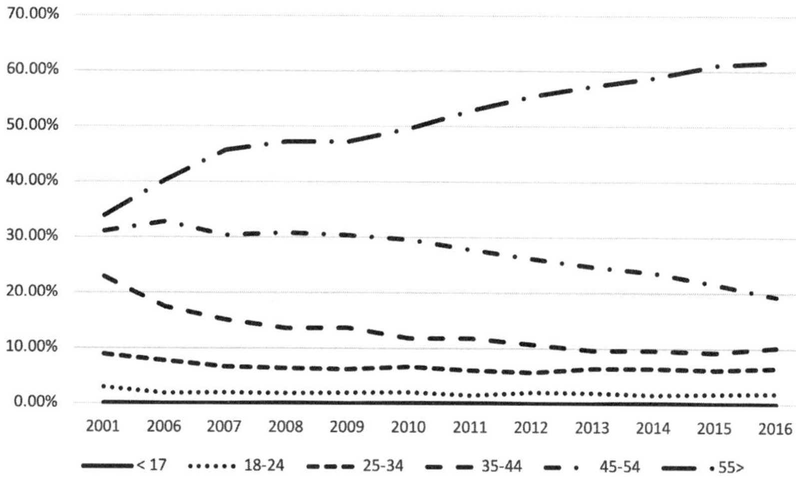

Adapted from Carson & Cowhig, 2020.

bankrupt even the largest corrections department (Anno et al., 2004; Mitka, 2004).

Reentry Considerations

While physical disabilities and chronic health conditions pose significant challenges to inmates within the institution, these impairments further compromise an offender's successful reentry to the community. Using data from the Serious and Violent Offender Reentry Initiative, Link and colleagues followed offenders within 30 days of release from prison up to 15 months after their release to the community (Link et al., 2019). Controlling for other factors, the researchers found a strong and significant relationship between physical health limitations and depression. Physical health and depression were further found to effect reentry outcomes. Specifically, the more physical limitations experienced by an offender, the less likely they were to maintain employment and the more likely they were to experience depressive symptoms. Depression was further associated with family conflict, which was a significant predictor of re-offending behaviors. Overall findings suggest both physical health and mental health are implicated in the reentry success of prisoners. Mallik-Kane and Visher (2008) call for policymakers and practitioners "to adopt a new paradigm that recognizes health as a universal rather than a special needs concern among returning prisoners" (p. 3).

While prisons are mandated to provide medical care to all in prison, the community is not. Once an offender leaves prison, any medical advances made behind prison walls are often not maintained in the community. Offenders who are prescribed medications for the treatment of diseases often do not refill the prescriptions or adhere to dosing regimens, creating an environment where drug-resistance strains of some diseases are prevalent (Aday, 2003). In other instances, offenders do not know where to go to seek medical care or are embarrassed and will not do so (Flanagan, & Bue-Estes, 2005).

Of particular concern is the lack of access to Medicare and Medicaid for offenders leaving prison. In most cases, these benefits are suspended while a person is incarcerated and are often the only available health benefits that offenders may be able to receive. Moreover, it takes months to reinstate these benefits after an offender is released. This often results in serious delays in treatment and medication; sometimes delays that can be fatal to the offender and detrimental to the public (Hornung et al., 2002).

The issues facing most inmates upon release are doubly daunting for geriatric offenders. Older offenders may be released to residences or programs that cannot adequately manage the needs of older offenders, they may not be employable due to chronic illness, and, similar to other offenders, they may lack medical insurance or other social assistance (Williams & Abraldes, 2007). Furthermore, older offenders, especially those that have been incarcerated for long periods of time, may be unable to function in society because of their lack of independent living skills (i.e., ability to cook, balance a checkbook, self-manage) and ability to assimilate into a society that does not tell them what to do and when to do it (Crawley & Sparkes, 2006). In addition, older prisoners generally suffer from higher rates of anxiety related to release from prison and their ability to reintegrate and function in the free world, as evidenced by their increased risk of post-release suicide (Crawley & Sparks, 2006; Pratt et al., 2006).

The Project for Older Prisoners (POPS) program was developed to assist older offenders (particularly those with terminal illness) in seeking early release from prison. Allowing early release to these offenders opens up prison space, reduces medical expenditures, and allows offenders to spend their final days in the community rather than behind prison walls. The POPS program, facilitated by legal scholar Jonathan Turley, engages law students as volunteers to assist low-risk offenders over the age of 55 to help them obtain parole or request a pardon. Students are usually tasked with preparing an extensive background report complete with an assessment of the offenders' likelihood of recidivism. If the offender is determined to be a worthy risk, students assist with reentry planning and help prepare the case for a parole hearing (George Washington University School of Law, 2012).

While most states have some form of compassionate release mechanism for the elderly or infirm to be released prior to their statutory or parole dates, compassionate releases are rarely used due to strict criteria, such as statutory exclusions, restrictive medical requirements, difficult application processes, and protracted hearing processes (Silber et al., 2017). More recently, however, a number of states through the Justice Reinvestment Initiative "have created or expanded release policies designed to reduce the number of elderly or infirm people in their custody" (Silber et al., 2017, p. 3). The Justice Reinvestment Initiative is a collaborative partnership between agencies and states to use data-driven approaches to design and implement innovative and comprehensive strategies to reduce crime and recidivism, as well as curb corrections costs using evidence-based strategies (Silber et al., 2017).

Promising Practice

Because 95% of people who go to prison leave at some point, public health officials have begun to recognize the immense opportunity to impact disease in the community by managing medical problems in prison (Lincoln et al., 2007). To that end, corrections agencies and public health organizations have begun to work together to formulate a continuum of service wherein disease prevention and management initiated in the prison setting is continued in the community upon release (Hammet et al., 2001).

To be blunt, correctional populations are captive audiences. Therefore, the ability to diagnose, treat, and educate large numbers of people who are often more sick and more susceptible to illness than the general population is unmatched. Furthermore, inmates have families. Public health/corrections collaborations that target offenders' family networks have the ability to reinforce important public health messages related to communicable diseases and HIV to a far broader audience than their captive patients (Lincoln et al., 2007).

Community health models view prisons and jails as clinics, places where healthcare providers can make substantive inroads in fighting communicable diseases including HIV/AIDS, initiate or continue treatment from chronic illness, and provide health education. In this model, a seamless transition from prison to community occurs when the same practitioner who treats offenders in prison also provides medical services in the community (Lincoln et al., 2007). In this way, medical information is shared between prison and community provider whenever possible and a continuity of service is maintained.

Continuity of service is only one component of successful medical management of offenders. In many cases, offenders do not understand their medical conditions let alone what medications to take, how often to frequent the doctor, etc., because they either do not leave prison with a medical discharge plan or do not understand what it says. This is not surprising given that research from the medical field indicates that the general public does not often understand their discharge plans either (Isaacman et al., 1992).

Studies indicate that patients with a poor understanding of discharge plans do not always follow doctor's orders and often do not adhere to medication regimens and other treatment requirements that can result in an increased risk to public health and safety (Makaryus & Friedman, 2005). Consequently, doctors and medical practitioners have determined that clear, concise discharge plans that are understandable to the patient will likely result in increased compliance with medication and treatment protocols (Moult et al., 2004).

Interestingly, very few inmates are released from prison with a pre-release plan, let alone a medical discharge summary (Angiello, 2005; Mellow, 2007). This is a considerable problem given that significant numbers of offenders leave prison with multiple health-related problems that likely require follow-up care and service provision. To that end, scholars suggest implementing specific medical discharge plans into the overall discharge process for offenders leaving prison. In Mellow's work on providing discharge plans for offenders leaving prison, he suggests that individualized healthcare plans be developed that clearly identify medical health issues, are written at a fifth- to sixth-grade literacy level, include short sentences that directly address the reader, are easy to read and understand, and are respectful and provide specific problem-solving strategies (Mellow, 2007). In this way, the medical discharge plan can serve as a roadmap for offenders in finding treatment once they are in the community. However, some community-based medical providers refuse to provide services to inmates. A discharge plan that makes community-based referrals will only be meaningful if providers are willing to accept and work with offenders (Flanagan & Bue-Estes, 2005; Mellow, 2007).

Travis notes that one of the most significant barriers to overcome in treating the physical health needs of offenders is the stigma that accompanies their release from prison. While in prison, offenders have had access to healthcare they likely would not have accessed otherwise. If prisons are making better efforts to treat and educate offenders inside prison walls, it becomes a significant public health concern if providers in the community are unwilling to treat offenders leaving prisons as they would any other patient (Travis, 2005).

Poor medical management of offenders prior to incarceration (self-imposed or otherwise) has been mitigated to some extent through the constitutional mandate that correctional authorities provide basic health care to all in their custody. However, any gains that are achieved in managing a population that presents with higher incidence of sexually transmitted diseases and other significant and costly medical conditions will be lost if community-based health care for offenders is not accessible. Given the overwhelming cost that the population incurs through the allocation of tax dollars to correctional health care, continuity of care between prison and the community for returning offenders should be the norm rather than the exception. While in some cases this means that offenders receive better health care benefits than the general public, the social and public health costs associated with under- or not treating returning offenders is much more significant. Once out of prison, offenders who require health care and who seek it will receive it one way or the other, often by taxing public hospitals and emergency rooms as charity care patients who drain the system. To date, most communities have been unwilling to accept this reality, with the potential for serious public health consequences too close for comfort.

Chapter 8

Mental Health

The physical health of inmates is not the only concern of prison officials. Nationwide, nearly one in seven state and federal prisoners suffer from a serious mental illness, with just over half of these offenders actually receiving mental health treatment while in prison and less than half (42%) receiving therapy from a trained professional (Bronson & Berzofsky, 2017). More curious is that a 2005 survey published in *Corrections Compendium* (2006) indicates that of 43 states who responded to the survey, only 27 (63%) of states acknowledged providing any mental health services to offenders under their correctional care. Despite efforts to assess and screen offenders at entry into the prison system for evidence of mental illness, people with mental illness are under-identified and remain an underserved, but increasingly high-risk, subset of the prison population who are ultimately released to the community (Lurigio, 2001).

Historical Context

The problems that face the criminal justice system with respect to mental illness have been a long time in the making and are the result of a series of events that significantly undercut the fiscal and resource capacity of the medical field to manage people with mental illness. The most damaging of these changes to mental health care policy and practice was the movement in the 1960s to deinstitutionalize the treatment and care of the mentally ill. To that time, most people who were diagnosed with a serious mental illness were institutionalized in psychiatric institutions (Baillargeon et al., 2010). Moreover, people with mental illness who were deemed to be harmful to themselves or others were routinely involuntarily hospitalized in psychiatric facilities for long periods of time (Lamb & Grant, 1982). Judges, family members, and others made decisions about whether mentally ill people could function in society and, if it was determined that the person could not do so, they were often hospitalized against their will. At their peak, psychiatric institutions were able to accommodate more than 550,000 inpatient psychiatric patients nationwide (Torrey et al., 2008).

By the 1960s, the concept of deinstitutionalization gained legitimacy. A set of recommendations from The Joint Commission on Mental Illness and Health (1961) suggested that people with mental illness could and most times probably should be treated in a community setting. Community-based treatment would reduce the need for hospitalization and by extension decrease costs associated with managing mental illness.

As part of its set of recommendations, the Joint Commission also concluded that management of the mentally ill would be best served by reducing the number of inpatient psychiatric hospital beds and by shuttering or converting existing psychiatric hospitals to acute treatment centers (Baillargeon et al., 2010). The Joint Commission's recommendations were supported through passage of the Mental Health Centers Construction Act of 1963, an act created to provide financial incentives to local communities to build and/or establish community-based mental health treatment centers (Baillargeon et al., 2010).

The idea of treating people with mental illness outside the walls of a mental institution was attractive for a variety of reasons. Certainly, cost was a primary concern. However, one reason that is often given for why deinstitutionalization was embraced is the development of chlorpromazine, also called Thorazine. Thorazine was the first psychotropic drug developed that made the management of major psychiatric disorders easier and possible outside a restricted institutionalized setting. The use of Thorazine reduced the reliance on other, more invasive techniques and treatments, such as electroshock therapy, and resulted in improved patient prognosis and outcomes (Grob, 1991; Grob & Goldman, 2006). This in turn allowed for the management of some conditions, customarily treated in hospital settings, to be treated in the community (Slate & Johnson, 2008). Moreover, the community-based psychiatry movement was influential in promoting community-based mental health treatment (Grob, 1991). This movement was fueled by attempts by former patients to fight restrictive, involuntary hospitalizations and others who believed that the least restrictive environment was the best mechanism for managing and treating mental illness (Hoge, 2007; Slate & Johnson, 2008).

Still other events responsible for increased support for deinstitutionalization included a series of court decisions and statutory changes that significantly limited the ability of others to involuntarily civilly commit people to inpatient psychiatric care. California's Lanterman-Petris-Short Act of 1967 was in large part responsible for limiting involuntary commitment without evidence that the person in question was a danger to themselves or others or severely disabled and incapable of caring for themselves. Moreover, this act limited the length of time of involuntary commitment and provided the mentally ill who were civilly committed with the same due process protections as afforded criminal defendants (Baillargeon et al., 2010).

By the 1980s, virtually every state had passed legislation similar to the Lanterman-Petris-Short Act. A series of court cases (e.g., *O'Connor v. Donaldson* [1975]; *Covington v. Harris* [1969]; and *Addington v. Texas* [1979]) further reinforced the foundation of the Lanterman-Petris-Short Act in their support for severely restricted requirements for civil commitment. Specifically, *O'Connor v. Donaldson* (1975) distinguished between those that are civilly committed for an indefinite term and those who are adjudicated guilty and who are imprisoned for a fixed term. Subsequent to this ruling, correctional institutions were not bound to provide rehabilitative treatment to offenders sentenced to a fixed term of incarceration but were required to provide treatment to individuals who were civilly committed.

In tandem with changes in the field of mental health came ideological changes in the function and practice of criminal justice. A shift occurred from the indeterminate sentencing model that encouraged rehabilitative correctional practices to a model that emphasized accountability and strict sentencing guidelines. More restrictive sentencing requirements, including mandatory minimum sentencing and other get-tough criminal justice practices, resulted in a decrease in the discretion of judges and others who might have considered mental illness as a mitigating factor in charging and sentencing offenders (Hoge, 2007).

There is also some suggestion that the rise of the War on Drugs and the attendant emphasis on drug crimes may have increased the number of mentally ill people who came into contact with the criminal justice system if only because studies suggest that the mentally ill tend to present with increased incidence of substance abuse (Kessler et al., 1996) and that substance abuse has been associated with violent offending in people with serious mental illness (Elbogen & Johnson, 2009). These changes in sentencing and criminal justice practice have been directly attributed to the criminalization of the mentally ill and are believed to be responsible for the increase in the number of mentally ill offenders in prison presently (Slate & Johnson, 2008).

The deinstitutionalization of the mental health system in the United States brought with it myriad consequences, most significant of which was the transfer of management of mentally ill offenders from psychiatric hospitals to the criminal justice system. The term trans-institutionalization soon replaced deinstitutionalization (Lurigio & Swartz, 2000; Talbott, 1975). The fundamental principle of deinstitutionalization was the belief that prolonged psychiatric hospitalizations could be reduced through releasing people with mental conditions to community-based psychiatric care, but a lack of capacity to serve these clients in a community setting resulted in people with mental illness being more likely to end up in jail or prison than in treatment. Unfortunately, the expectation that a significant number of community-based mental health treatment centers would be available by the mid-1970s as a result of the Joint Commission's recommendations was never realized (Lamb & Bachrach, 2001). As of 1980, only 768 of the 1,500–2,000 projected centers had received funding (General Accounting Office, 2000).

A series of studies beginning in the 1970s provide empirical support for the contention that as the deinstitutionalization movement gained momentum, more people with mental illness were processed through the criminal justice system than were hospitalized (Abramson, 1972; Swank & Winer, 1976). In their study of 102 jail inmates who were referred for psychiatric evaluation, Lamb and Grant (1982) found that more than 75% met the criteria for involuntary hospitalization and 90% had a history of hospitalization for a psychiatric disorder. Moreover, Teplin's 1984 study found that mentally ill people were more likely to be arrested at higher rates (15.8%) than those who did not present with a mental health condition (7.5%). Today, greater than three times more individuals with serious psychological disorders are admitted to prisons or jails than hospitals in the U.S. (Torrey et al., 2010).

In a study of U.S. police encounters during this time, Bonovitz and Bonovitz (1981) noted that police encounters with the mentally ill increased by 227% in just four years (1975–1979). Scholars argued that the deinstitutionalization movement thrust police into the role of triage service providers to the mentally ill (Patch & Arrigo, 1999). Police were now serving the role as gatekeeper for both the criminal justice and mental health care systems (Patch & Arrigo, 1999).

Research also indicates that psychiatric hospitals released large numbers of people to the community void of community-based treatment support (Lamb & Bachrach, 2001). Snook and Torrey (2018) indicate that between the peak in 1955 and 2016, the number of state psychiatric hospital beds decreased by 97%. To put this in perspective, there are fewer psychiatric beds per capita in the United States than there were in 1850 (Snook & Torrey, 2018). Unable to support the influx of large numbers of mentally ill people, communities found themselves with large numbers of people who were often homeless, poor, and without access to proper medication and treatment, a combination that put this group of people at increased risk for contact with the criminal justice system (Whitmer, 1980). As Baillargeon and colleagues (2010) so eloquently note,

> the end results have been a fragmented patchwork of mental health agencies struggling to provide care for the masses of formerly institutionalized patients and the shunting of large numbers of these individuals into the criminal justice system. (p. 364)

Current Trends

One of the limitations of relying on data of offenders with mental illness is that definitions of mental illness vary, and follow-up times and methods of reporting (i.e., self-reports versus official data) are often study dependent. Consequently, prevalence rates of offenders with mental illness vary significantly and are often very conservative estimates of the presence of illness or spectrum of illnesses in the offender population.

Bronson and Berzofsky (2017) note that 37% of prisoners and 44% of jail inmates have been identified by a mental health professional as having a mental illness. Nearly one-quarter (24%) of prisoners were told they had a major depressive disorder, 17.5% indicated a bipolar disorder, and close to 9% were told they had schizophrenia or other psychotic disorders (a history of mental disorders was measured through a series of self-reported questions as part of the 2011–12 National Inmate Survey). Bronson and Berzofsky (2017) further indicate 14% of prisoners and 26% of jail inmates meet the criteria for serious psychological distress (defined using a score from the Kessler 6 nonspecific psychological distress scale), a rate three to five times higher than adults in the general population. It is therefore unsurprising that other data suggests that jails and prisons hold three times more people with serious mental illness than do psychiatric hospitals (Fellner, 2006). Case in point, the three largest inpatient psychiatric facilities in the nation are county jails located in Los Angeles, Chicago, and New York (National Public Radio, 2011). Astoundingly, the criminal justice system is now the largest provider of mental health treatment in the United States (American Psychiatric Association (APA), 2004; Gelman, 2007). Overall, people with mental illness tend to be arrested for more minor crimes than offenders who are not mentally ill, and half of all people with mental illness have been arrested at least once in their lifetime (Cuellar et al., 2007). Moreover, offenders with mental health concerns tend to be "churners" or "frequent fliers": people who wind their way in and out of the system on a regular basis (Baillargeon et al., 2009). To that point, 47% of mentally ill prisoners have three or more prior incarcerations; seven percent have 11 or more (James & Glaze, 2006). These percentages are not unexpected given that the mentally ill are more likely to be homeless and are therefore more likely to come in contact with the police (James & Glaze, 2006).

Once imprisoned, the clinical condition of offenders with mental illness tends to worsen, and these offenders are often subject to victimization (Kondo, 2000). The rigid structure and policies of prison environments can be traumatic and exacerbate clinical symptoms (APA, 2004; Wexler, 2003). Furthermore, people in prison who have undiagnosed or untreated mental illness are at greater risk for committing suicide (Veysey & Bichler-Robertson, 2002) and being injured in altercations with other inmates (James & Glaze, 2006).

Once offenders with mental illness make contact with the system, they tend to serve more time in jail or prison than their counterparts who are not mentally ill (James & Glaze, 2006; McNiel & Binder, 2007; Solomon & Draine, 1995b). This is largely due to mentally ill offenders being at a higher risk for violating prison rules, reducing their likelihood of parole and causing the loss of earned good time credits for early release.

In their nationally representative sample of state prisoners, Houser and colleagues (2012) reported inmates with mental health disorders were almost three times more likely to be charged with a serious institutional infraction and almost twice as likely to be charged with a minor infraction compared to inmates with no disorders. In another nationally representative sample of female inmates over two waves, Steiner and Wooldredge (2009) noted that female inmates with a mental health disorder were significantly more likely to engage in both violent and non-violent prison infractions. For many mentally ill inmates, their infractions are symptomatic manifestations of their disorders (e.g., refusing to come out of their cell, poor hygiene); however, these are often responded to by correctional officers as intentional misbehaviors resulting in punitive sanctions (Adams, 1986). Some scholars suggest that the mentally ill are also treated more harshly for their infractions. In their study of incarcerated women, Houser and Belenko (2015) found women with co-occurring mental health and substance use disorders charged with minor rule infractions were more likely to receive severe disciplinary sanctions compared to women with singular (e.g., mental health disorder only or substance use disorder only) or no disorders.

Although the National Commission on Correctional Health Care provides standards for inmates in segregation, the mentally ill are also more likely to find themselves in segregated housing for their infractions (Anno, 2000; Cohen & Gerbasi, 2005). The isolating effects of segregation can be deleterious to their mental health status, worsening their clinical conditions (Cohen & Gerbasi, 2005; Fellner, 2007; Spencer & Fallon, 2012; Wexler, 2003). Moreover, segregated housing often precludes continued participation in programs, limiting the mentally ill to medication and brief mental health checks at their cells (Fellner, 2007). Limited access to programs has the additional consequence of reducing the opportunity to earn good time credits toward early release (Lovell et al., 2001). Kaba and colleagues (2014) further note that the seriously mentally ill are more likely to inflict self-harm (e.g., cut themselves, head banging) when placed in solitary confinement. On the heels of several class-action suits arguing that the mentally ill are not able to withstand the physical and psychological conditions of segregation, many states are now moving towards reducing the use of segregation for the seriously mentally ill (Orr, 2014).

While research is somewhat inconclusive on the influence of mental health in parole decision-making, a large body of research does suggest that mentally ill inmates are less likely to be paroled than non-mentally ill inmates (Houser et al., 2019a). Feder (1994) noted that inmates with histories of psychiatric hospitalizations were 30 times less likely to be paroled than inmates with no prior hospitalizations. Caplan's (2007) review of empirical research found mental health to be one of the most influential factors in parole decision-making. Why then, are findings mixed on the influence of mental health on parole? As discussed in chapter 2, some scholars argue that mental health may have an indirect influence on parole decision-making (Houser et al., 2019a). While it is no surprise that the mentally ill are more likely to have risk factors unique to mental illness, they also have significantly more general risk factors for criminal recidivism than their non-mentally ill counterparts (Skeem et al., 2014). Thus, the mentally ill tend to perform poorly on criminal justice risk assessments commonly used in parole decision-making, suggesting an indirect effect of mental health on release decisions.

In general, female offenders present with higher overall rates of mental health concerns than males (James & Glaze, 2006). These data are generally supported by more recent information that indicates that 35% of male and 66% of female inmates are likely to have a mental illness (Bronson & Berzofsky, 2017). Estimates further suggest that 21% of female offenders and 14% of male offenders meet the criteria for a serious psychological disorder (Bronson & Berzofsky, 2017). Female offenders are also more likely to present with co-occurring substance use disorders, further complicating their clinical picture (James & Glaze, 2006). Despite the often gender-specific pathway to the criminal justice system for woman, prison-based mental health and substance use treatment programs are typically based on the needs of male offenders (Shearer, 2003). These programs fail to address the prevalence of trauma and physical, sexual, and emotional victimization that are present in the lives of many incarcerated women and contributed to their involvement in criminal behavior (Traylor & Richie, 2012).

When a side-by-side comparison of offenders with and without documented mental health problems is made, the extent of problems that mentally ill offenders face becomes all the more apparent.

Table 8-1. Demographics of Mentally Ill Offenders

	State Prison Inmates	
Selected Characteristics	With Mental Health Problem (%)	Without Mental Health Problem (%)
Criminal Record	61	56
Current/past violent offense	25	19
3+ prior incarcerations	74	56
Mean sentence length (all offenses)	146 months	141 months
Substance abuse/dependence alcohol and/or drugs ever	74	56
Drugs used one month prior to arrest	63	49
Homeless one year prior to arrest	13	6
Employed one month prior to arrest	70	76
Physically abused prior to admission	27	11
Family member ever incarcerated	52	41
Charged with violating institutional rules	58	43
Injured in a fight since admission to prison	20	10

Adapted from James & Glaze, 2006.

As Table 8-1 indicates, in all principal domains, offenders with documented mental health problems demonstrate more serious criminal records, longer overall mean sentences, and higher rates of drug usage ever. Additionally, these individuals have higher rates of homelessness, decreased chances for employment prior to incarceration, an increased likelihood of being abused or having a family member who has been incarcerated, and are more likely to have institutional infractions or be injured in a fight in prison than offenders in state prison who did not report a mental health problem. These results are supported by data from Mallik-Kane and Visher (2008), who found similar dimensions of abuse and comorbidity in the offenders included in their sample.

While the differences between offenders in prison with and without mental health deficits is marked, data indicate that approximately 60% of offenders with mental health problems received treatment while in prison. The number of mentally ill offenders who accessed treatment decreased to 50% upon release from prison and up to approximately one year after release (Mallik-Kane & Visher, 2008). Unfortunately, the services accessed were primarily emergent in nature; within 2–3 months of release from prison to the community, 20% of men and 33% of women were likely to have accessed emergency room services (Mallik-Kane & Visher, 2008).

One reason why emergent mental health care is so often used by correctional facilities is because of inferior screening, assessment, and treatment of mentally ill offenders in the prison setting. In many instances, corrections personnel have had to make do with managing mentally ill offenders in prison through a patchwork of programs that are ill-equipped to meet these offenders' specific needs. The increase in the number of mentally ill offenders in prison has challenged corrections personnel to learn how to identify and manage this specialized population; something they do not know how to do or did not routinely do in the past. As a result, poor or nonexistent mental health screening is common (Steadman et al., 2005).

In addition, prisons often have inadequate funding to support treatment capacity, have untrained or poorly trained staff, and perpetuate an intolerance for people with mental health problems, making treatment and management of the mentally ill in the prison setting challenging, difficult, and mostly inadequate (Lurigio & Swartz, 2006; National Commission on Correctional Heath Care, 2002). Few states offer more than four hours of correctional officer training on how to respond to mentally ill prisoners (Slate et al., 2013). Sadly, most prisons do not meet the basic minimum standards for proper mental health treatment (National Commission on Correctional Heath Care, 2002), despite that fact that states are constitutionally mandated to provide minimal mental health care treatment as a result of *Estelle v. Gamble* (1976) and *Ruiz v. Estelle* (1980).

While very few studies assessing recidivism rates of offenders with mental illness exist, a study by Feder (1991) indicates that the rearrest rate for offenders with mental illness within 18 months of release was

64%, compared to 60% for people without mental illness. In addition, 48% of offenders with mental illness were hospitalized sometime after release, compared with 1% of offenders without mental illness. Lovell and colleagues (2002) noted a felony recidivism rate of 37% within two years of release for offenders leaving prison without mental illness compared with 4% for offenders released from prison who had been diagnosed with mental illness. Interestingly, technical violations and misdemeanors were the most common offense committed after release, accounting for nearly 72% of new incidents committed. This finding contradicts the notion (unproven as it is) that mentally ill offenders commit more violent offenses than others (Lovell et al., 2002).

A study of over 79,000 offenders in Texas prisons indicates that there is a strong association between serious mental illness and increased risk of recidivism (Baillargeon et al., 2009). Results indicate that offenders who presented with major depressive disorder, bipolar disorder, schizophrenia, or a non-schizophrenic psychotic disorder were more likely to have a history of previous incarcerations than inmates without serious mental illness (Baillargeon et al., 2009). Another study conducted in Utah found similar results. The median time to recidivate (i.e., return to prison) for offenders with serious mental illness was 385 days, compared with 743 days for offenders without serious mental illness (Cloyes et al., 2010).

A recent study of close to 5,000 parolees returning to the City of Philadelphia found mental health disorders and co-occurring mental health and substance use disorders significantly raised the probability of a parolee being reincarcerated for a new crime, controlling for the traits of the individual as well as the neighborhood characteristics of the parolee's residence (Houser et al., 2019b). Houser and McCord (2018) found women with mental health disorders were more likely to return to prison within three years of release than women with no disorders or women with substance use disorders. The findings further revealed women with mental health conditions returned to prison 471 days earlier than women with no disorders. The results of these studies suggest that offenders with serious mental illness are returning to prison more frequently and more quickly than others, but the reasons for their return are not straightforward.

Reentry Considerations

If the mental health profile of offenders in the system is this dire, the prospects for offenders with mental health concerns at reentry are grim. Recent reports as part of the *Going Home* initiative that specifically explore the mental health dynamics of offenders returning to the community indicate that in the month prior to release from prison, 15% of men and 35% of women reported having been diagnosed with some sort of mental health condition (Mallik-Kane & Visher, 2008). Navigating the challenges associated with reentry is daunting for any offender, but particularly difficult for offenders who are mentally ill and who are required to overcome not only the stigma of being an ex-offender, but the reality of being an ex-offender who is mentally ill (Hoge, 2007).

As James and Glaze (2006) note in their report, offenders who are mentally ill tend to present with multiple deficiencies in several reentry domains, including housing, employment, substance abuse, and criminal involvement. With regards to housing, offenders with mental health problems are less likely to have made solid arrangements for housing prior to release, less apt to live with family members after release, and display problems with maintaining stable housing in the long term compared with offenders without mental health problems (Mallik-Kane & Visher, 2008). As noted in an earlier chapter, access to housing is severely limited for all returning offenders. Unfortunately, mentally ill offenders are further restricted from accessing public housing. If an offender with mental illness has been convicted of a violent crime or drug offense, Section 8 housing is not a viable option (Hoge, 2007).

Given severely limited housing options, it appears that offenders with mental illness who leave prison without the benefit of a place to live (and the attendant intermittent access to community-based mental health services that comes with this) are often homeless. As a consequence, they tend to attract the attention of criminal justice personnel. Given that 33% to 50% of homeless people have a severe mental illness, it is not unreasonable to expect that odd or bizarre behavior perpetrated by homeless people might become the focus of criminal justice intervention in the community (McQuistion et al., 2003) and result in police and law enforcement tactics that might (purposefully or not) target the mentally ill.

Employment is another dimension of reentry exacerbated by mental illness. As with housing, offenders with mental illness are found to have problems getting and maintaining employment after release compared with offenders released from prison that are not mentally ill (Mallik-Kane & Visher, 2008). In many instances, mentally ill offenders are not able to work. Consequently, released offenders with mental illness are more likely to rely on other sources of income, including friends, family, and public assistance (Mallik-Kane & Visher, 2008).

Research suggests that people who suffer from mental illness (whether or not they are offenders) tend to rely more heavily on public assistance SSI or SSDI than others (Hoge, 2007). Unfortunately, at the time that offenders with mental illness enter prison, these benefits are discontinued. Upon release, it may take from 45–90 days for these benefits to be reinstated. Fiscal and resource support in the interim between release and receipt of benefits often occurs on an ad-hoc basis (Hoge, 2007).

Offenders with mental illness are also likely to have an attendant substance abuse disorder. For those with co-occurring substance use disorders, reentry may prove even more difficult. Comorbid disorders are particularly salient among the offender population, with 54% of female and 41% of male prisoners meeting the diagnostic criteria for a dual disorder (James & Glaze, 2006). However, these estimates are likely conservative due to the overlapping nature of the disorders and limited dual diagnosis screening tools in correctional settings (Hiller et al., 2011; Sacks et al., 2007). The interaction of having two or more disorders exacerbates the symptomatic nature of the individual disorders, reduces treatment compliance and completion, and has been found to increase the likelihood of recidivism (Substance Abuse and Mental Health Services Administration [SAMHSA], 2015). The MacArthur Violence Risk Assessment Study found a 25% increase in violent recidivism among individuals with a co-occurring substance use disorder compared to individuals with a mental health disorder only (Steadman et al., 1998). Further complicating their diagnostic picture, offenders with co-occurring disorders are more likely to experience deficiencies in psychosocial skills and have significant cognitive impairments, including deficiencies in concentration, planning skills, and verbal memory, further hindering their ability to meet the challenges of reentry (SAMHSA, 2015).

Oftentimes, criminal justice professionals are not able to recognize the signs and symptoms of mental illness or to differentiate between behaviors exhibited by the mentally ill or substance abusing offender due to the overlapping nature of the disorders, as addressed above. To the untrained eye, the criminal justice practitioner who observes someone using illegal drugs or who is intoxicated may miss an underlying problem of mental illness and may manage the disruptive behavior in a way that exacerbates the person's mental health problem. Conversely, practitioners may not recognize that an offender with mental illness is also actively using drugs. Lack of training of officers and others who interact with mentally ill offenders who use drugs or alcohol makes diagnosis and subsequent treatment elusive.

If appropriate diagnosis is not made, appropriate treatment is not possible. More often than not, inappropriate or misdiagnoses of offenders who present with both mental health and substance abuse concerns (co-occurring disorders) results in improper treatment placement (Slate & Johnson, 2008). Furthermore, offenders who present with both mental health and substance abuse disorders often are excluded from treatment programs due to their complex problems or may come in to contact with programs that have not been created to meet their specific co-occurring disorder needs. Co-occurring disorders necessitate integrated treatment programs that address both disorders simultaneously (Dennison, 2005; Peters & Hill, 1997). Integrated programs, however, are often unavailable in correctional facilities and are limited in the community setting (Houser & Welsh, 2014; Houser et al., 2012; James & Glaze, 2006; Peters & Hill, 1997; Wexler, 2003). Despite the need for services, lifetime treatment rates among offenders with co-occurring disorders is low (Hunt et al., 2015). Not surprisingly, the failure to adequately treat and manage this specific offender population generally leads to recidivism (Hartwell, 2004).

If the challenges associated with managing housing, employment, and co-occurring disorders was not enough for the mentally ill offender returning to the community, research indicates that this select offender population has more post-prison criminal justice system involvement than other offenders who reenter society. While men with mental health conditions are not arrested, convicted, or reincarcerated more than other men, women are more likely to be arrested than women without mental health difficulties (Mallik-Kane & Visher, 2008). Notably, mental illness does not necessarily result in a higher likelihood of committing crime. However, research indicates that the attendant factors surrounding one's mental condition, including homelessness, may contribute to more contact with the criminal justice system (Draine et al., 2002). Moreover, many offenders with mental illness do not benefit from community-based supervision (i.e., parole) due to the fact that they often do not qualify for parole release (Clear et al., 1993). If offenders with mental illness do qualify for parole, parole officers are often not equipped to manage them either because they don't have the skill set or training or because community capacity to handle mentally ill offenders is lacking (Lurigio, 2001).

The scarcity of treatment programs and services for parolees with mental illness makes continuity of care from prison to community difficult. Beck and Maruschak (2001) indicate that only 66% of prisons assist mentally ill offenders with accessing community mental health services upon release. Moreover, a survey of parole administrators notes that only 25% of paroling agencies provided special programming or opportunities for offenders with mental illness who were on parole (Watson et al., 2001). Lurigio (2001) notes that mental health services are often excluded from reentry case planning unless the offender is displaying overt symptoms. This may be particularly problematic as an offender's symptoms may be controlled while in prison due to compliance with prescribed medications; however, on release, the mentally ill are more likely to stop medication and needed treatment services, resulting in a deterioration of their clinical status.

The need for continuity of service between prison and community is particularly critical given that a significant number of mentally ill offenders released to the community are more likely to leave prison having completed their sentence than through parole. While one may argue the merits of parole supervision, offenders who are paroled at minimum have better access to information regarding reentry treatment programs and services than their counterparts who leave prison at completion of sentence. For the offender population who is mentally ill, this could be the difference between connecting with needed services or not.

Lack of access to services has significant consequences. Offenders who do not engage in community-based mental health services often over-utilize emergency room services as their principle means of treatment. Communities who are forced to refer offenders to hospital emergency rooms in lieu of being able to provide them with treatment programs further tax already limited hospital resources. Moreover, the care that mentally ill offenders receive in the emergency room is acute-based care rather than long-term illness management (Mallik-Kane & Visher, 2008).

Promising Practice

There are several new and promising practices that attempt to fill the significant void in community-based care for the returning mentally ill offender. Not surprisingly, these programs require significant collaboration between mental health professionals and the criminal justice system. One such program is mental health courts. These courts combine court supervision with community-based treatment and promote a collaborative case management approach to service. The intention of these courts is to intervene at the early stages of the justice system (e.g., pretrial) and divert mentally ill defendants into treatment instead of jail (Goldkamp & Irons-Guynn, 2000). While mental health courts are more typically geared toward diversion from the traditional criminal justice system, some mental health courts offer supervision and services to those released from prison, but who are still under the supervision of the Department of Corrections.

Mental health courts are predicated on the principle of therapeutic jurisprudence (McNiel & Binder, 2007). Therapeutic jurisprudence argues that law and justice can embrace therapeutic principles that include decision-making and treatment-driven interventions rather than a more formal focus on punishment and punitive legal concerns. In contrast to more traditional methods of jurisprudence, mental health courts require cooperation between criminal justice and mental health providers, a treatment-driven approach to case management, and legal advocacy for the mentally ill. This approach is unique in that it is sensitive to the specific needs of the mentally ill but is also one that holds people accountable for their actions. There are currently 46 states in the U.S. with operational mental health courts; over 450 state mental health courts and three federal mental health courts located in Pennsylvania, Utah, and Missouri (Lowder et al., 2018; National Drug Court Resource Center, 2021).

Results from studies that have evaluated the efficacy of mental health courts indicate that people who take part in mental health courts tend to do better (i.e., recidivate less) than those who do not (Redlich, 2005). Specifically, participants in a mental health court evaluated one year after enrollment were four times more likely to not be arrested compared with the year prior to their enrollment in the program (Steadman et al., 2005). Other more recent studies have also demonstrated the beneficial effects of participation in mental health courts in reducing rates of recidivism (Hiday & Ray, 2010; Hiday et al., 2013; Lowder et al., 2018; McNeil & Binder, 2007; Snedker et al., 2017; Steadman et al., 2011). Hiday and colleagues (2013) reported a significant reduction in rearrest among mental health court participants compared with a treatment as usual comparison group in the year following completion. A follow-up study found the effects remained two years following completion of the court (Hiday et al., 2016). Moreover, studies have also found participation influences time to rearrest, with court participants typically remaining in the community for longer periods of time than non-participants (Anestis & Carbonell, 2014; Costopulous & Wellman, 2017; Lowder et al., 2018; McNeil & Binder, 2007).

Other promising practices include specialized parole caseloads for offenders with mental illness. Specialized caseloads are a vast improvement from traditional case management approaches often utilized by parole officers. Traditional case management most often requires parole officers to broker services for mentally ill offenders by arranging needed services in the community. High caseloads and large numbers of referrals means that parole officers are often left to check in on their clients, perpetuating passive rather than active involvement in the reentry process. Specialized caseloads, on the other hand, are generally managed by officers who have (or should have) specific training and knowledge of mental health issues and who are able to provide continuity of service within the community to include counseling, crisis stabilization, and proper referrals (Lurigio, 2001).

Other improvements include more and better attempts by corrections departments to provide continuity of mental health services that begin in prison and follow the offender into the community upon release (Lurigio, 2001). In addition, cross training corrections and parole personnel on mental health issues and concerns increases knowledge and understanding of the issues that mentally ill offenders face in prison and the community (Lurigio, 2001). For mental health services to be most effective, the continuum of service must begin the moment a person is diagnosed with a mental health problem and continue indefinitely. Realistically, offenders who may be diagnosed or treated for mental health issues while in prison should receive continued care upon release to the community.

Continuity of service is predicated on a comprehensive discharge plan that clearly identifies offenders' needs and treatment and service requirements. This case management plan is of benefit to the supervising officer (if the offender is on parole) and to the community provider as it clearly outlines needs, a treatment plan, and specific goals.

Specifically, Draine and Herman advocate the use of critical time intervention (CTI), a nine-month intervention program that assists in the development of a series of individualized linkages (formal and informal) in a community setting that builds problem-solving skills through enhanced community support and engaged treatment (Draine & Herman, 2007). CTI is routinely used for mentally ill people who leave psychiatric institutions, but could be a useful addition to the discharge or transition planning mechanisms suggested for offenders with mental illness leaving prison (Draine & Herman, 2007). CTI attempts to strengthen people's ties to the community, family, and friends and to provide support during a critical period of transition. The intervention is meant to provide temporary support during transition and to build support for a more permanent network of community ties in the long term.

Another important development in the management of mentally ill offenders in the community is the development of assertive community treatment (ACT). Originally developed in the 1970s, ACT programs include treatment, rehabilitation, and support services in a multi-disciplinary team comprised of psychiatrists, nurses, and vocational rehabilitation counselors, among others (Lamberti et al., 2004). ACT teams were originally developed to cater to people who were at high risk for hospitalization and who presented with other co-morbid health disorders.

Forensic assertive community treatment (FACT) teams were specifically developed as an outgrowth of the criminalization of mental health and the significant increase in the number of offenders leaving prison and returning to the community who were diagnosed with mental illness. FACT teams are similar to the ACT teams in their composition, with the exception of the addition of criminal justice personnel from jails, prisons, and parole as necessary. Moreover, one of the primary goals of FACT teams is to prevent arrest and reincarceration of offenders with mental illness through comprehensive service provision from multiple disciplines (Morrissey et al., 2007).

Research on ACT teams has demonstrated more positive outcomes for patients who participated in ACT treatment than for patients who did not. Specifically, ACT was found to be effective in reducing hospital stays and in improving symptoms, but not in reducing jail stays or decreasing arrests (Mueser et al., 1998). A study evaluating the efficacy of case management alone, ACT alone and ACT with brokered case management yielded interesting results. Clients assigned to the ACT team with and without brokered case management had better outcomes (i.e., were hospitalized less and more satisfied with treatment) than clients who received brokered case management services only (Wolff et al., 1997), suggesting that clients with mental health deficits likely require more intensive services and treatment than case management alone can provide.

Research evaluating the efficacy of FACT programs or ACT programs that manage offenders is minimal. Project Link is a FACT program that has had some efficacy in managing offenders with severe mental illness who have been released from prison to the community. This program is an interdisciplinary program that brings together healthcare, criminal justice, and social service agencies with offenders who are severely mentally ill. Project Link incorporates three methods of service delivery: assertive community treatment (ACT), modified therapeutic community, and jail diversion (Weisman et al., 2004). Staff of Project Link work with the criminal justice system when mentally ill offenders are in jail/prison and collaborate with community-based services to provide a continuum of service from prison to the community (Weisman et al., 2004). A study evaluating changes in direct service and residential treatment costs as a result of Project Link indicate that nearly $40,000 in direct service and residential treatment costs were saved per patient comparing costs per patient incurred in the year prior to participation in Project Link compared with costs incurred during the first year of participation in the program (Weisman et al., 2004).

The extent to which mentally ill offenders are a challenge to identify and treat within and outside prison walls is not in question. What is questionable is the degree to which the system is able to manage this subset of the offender population. Research indicates that historically, practitioners have not done a very good job of doing so. Improved outcomes for mentally ill offenders will only become a reality when practitioners are better trained and when treatment and service provision takes priority over punitive punishment.

Part II

Contextualizing Offender Reentry

Chapter 9

Risk Factors, Risk Prediction, and Recidivism

Virtually all judgments and decisions about offenders are made in the context of risk. Bail is set (or not) depending on whether or not defendants are determined to be a flight risk. Sentences are often passed down based upon the type of offense committed and the risk that the judge feels a person may pose to the community. Parole decisions are often made based on the likelihood that an offender will commit a crime in the future. Risk is everywhere, and decisions based on risk are fundamental to the criminal justice (CJ) system. Understanding reentry in the context of risk requires that we understand what risk factors are, how risk predictions work, and when people recidivate and why.

Risk Factors

In the criminal justice system, risk is defined in terms of factors or characteristics that impact the likelihood of offending. By evaluating risk factors, predictions can be made about who may (or may not) offend. The ability to assess and understand risk is particularly relevant when we consider the reentering offender, as risk is the primary objective benchmark upon which offenders are measured in terms of their ability to be successful (or not) in the reentry process. Therefore, the ability to predict whether or not an offender may reoffend with some level of accuracy and precision is important and worthy of consideration.

There have been a variety of factors empirically proven to assess risk. Individual-level characteristics or predictors of risk include, but are not limited to, age (Andrews & Bonta, 1995), criminal history, prior institutional commitments (Gendreau et al., 1996), drug abuse, family relationships, delinquent peers (Haynie, 2001; Murray & Farrington, 2005), and gender (Holtfretter & Cupp, 2007). These predictors represent individual-level factors that have been shown to impact whether or not and to what extent offenders may reoffend. Additional research evaluating other individual-level factors by Andrews and Bonta (2003) suggests that social status, financial status, self-esteem, and social support for behavior are also significant predictors of criminal behavior. Overall, these risk factors have been firmly established in the literature as representing the best predictors of offending (Gendreau et al., 1996; Tillyer & Vose, 2011).

There are two categories of risk factors that predict offending: static and dynamic risk factors. Static factors (e.g., age, previous convictions) are those factors in an offender's life that are predictive of offending but cannot change. Conversely, dynamic factors (e.g., peer associations, behaviors, and attitudes) are commonly referred to as criminogenic needs or predictive factors that can be changed through participation in targeted programming and treatment (Andrews & Bonta, 1994). Empirical support for using both static and dynamic predictive factors when assessing risk is plentiful. Most risk/needs assessment instruments employ both types of risk factors when assessing risk and identifying offender needs, and are able to do so with a fair degree of accuracy (Gendreau et al., 1996).

In addition to individual- or micro-level factors associated with criminal behavior, some scholars argue that macro-level, or community-level, factors exist that may influence offending. Recent research suggests that in addition to the predictors mentioned above, characteristics such as where people live (Gottfredson & Taylor, 1988; Kubrin & Stewart, 2006) and social-structural issues such as access to substance abuse treatment, social problems, and lack of access to employment and job skills also impact reoffending (Garland et al., 2011; Phillips & Lindsay, 2011; Sung et al., 2001). Still other research supports the notion that the strength and quality of social networks, and the extent to which one is able to harness these resources effectively, can be a viable predictor of future offending as well (Kubrin & Stewart, 2006). Finally, others argue that the degree of racial segregation in communities can impact future offending (Mears et al., 2008).

Results from studies evaluating the role of macro-level factors in influencing reoffending are mixed. Hipp and colleagues (2010b) found that neighborhood-level predictors effect reoffending, while Tillyer and Vose

(2011) found limited support for these risk factors. Recent studies are also addressing the presence of non-residential land uses in neighborhoods for their influence on re-offending. Houser and colleagues (2018), for example, found limited support for the role of neighborhood context on reincarceration; however, they did note that parolees living within one-quarter mile of a bar or liquor outlet were more likely to return to prison, and their presence reduced a parolee's time in the community by 20 days. Contrary to these findings, Miller and colleagues' study on new arrest or parole revocation found no support for the presence of bars on recidivism (Miller et al., 2016). No doubt, further research evaluating the complex interplay between macro-level variables and reoffending is warranted, but their existence and impact cannot be ignored.

Recent research not only attempts to bridge the gap between micro- and macro-level analyses of predictors of reoffending, but also seeks to evaluate whether specific reentry concerns such as education, employment, housing, and treatment programming act as risk factors for offending. This research is unique because these variables can be evaluated as both individual-level predictors and neighborhood- or community-level factors that can inhibit offender reentry. Results from this scholarship support the contention that barriers to reentry are related to criminal behavior. Measures of education, employment, and residential mobility are associated with reoffending; once released from prison, offenders have difficulty adjusting to life in the community, and this impacts their ability to remain crime free (Makarios et al., 2010).

In addition to research that evaluates micro- and macro-level variables that may influence reoffending, research also considers whether risk factors vary by gender. While some studies have found that many of the risk factors for reoffending are the same for males as for females (Makarios et al., 2010; Manchak et al., 2009; Smith et al., 2009), some studies suggest otherwise.

Work by several scholars indicates that there may be similarities and differences in reoffending risk factors between men and women. While Van Voorhis (2008) found that the addition of gender-specific factors such as depression or anxiety, victimization, self-esteem, and relationship support enhanced prediction models, Uggen and Kruttschnitt (1998) found that substance abuse, prior record, education, and having children yielded stronger predictive results for women than for men. Recent research indicates that some predictors of reoffending vary by gender and the level of violence of the crime committed (Collins, 2010). Likely, there may be some predictive measures that are gender invariant and others that may be unique to women (Zahn et al., 2008).

Risk Prediction

Once risk factors for criminal offending were identified, so began the business of employing this knowledge to predict criminal behavior. Historically, there have been two distinct methods of risk prediction utilized in criminal justice: clinical (subjective) and mechanical (objective). Subjective prediction is grounded in clinical judgment, a process that encourages practitioners to make decisions using risk factors but is based on informal, subjective methods that are susceptible to bias. Conversely, mechanical prediction includes statistical and actuarial methods of predicting risk in an objective way.

Actuarial methods of prediction have manifested themselves in risk prediction instruments that combine risk factors and were originally developed and utilized by the insurance industry. These techniques are predicated on statistical analysis of past behavior to predict future probabilities of the same behavior. Insurance companies often employ actuarial risk techniques to establish car and health insurance rates based on the premise that people can be classified into groups based on their level of risk.

Insurance companies are able to determine car and health insurance premiums based on the likelihood that people in particular risk groups will have an automobile accident or require medical attention (Ericson & Haggerty, 1997; Reichman, 1986). Lower risk individuals are given more desirable auto and health insurance rates because there is a low probability that they will require service, while people deemed "high risk" are charged higher premiums for the same service because it has been statistically determined that they are more likely to utilize auto or healthcare resources. In the realm of criminal justice, actuarial risk assessments seek to divide the offender population into subgroups that vary by the level of risk offenders pose in a variety of settings and circumstances (e.g., on probation, in prison, on parole). Using this approach, offender populations are managed differently depending on their risk for reoffending.

Proponents of utilizing actuarial methods of prediction argue that the ability to predict criminal behavior using objective measures outweighs subjective decision-making. This argument is supported by a growing number of corrections and criminal justice practitioners who have adopted these types of prediction instruments as part of their system of offender classification and assessment.

Without question, actuarial or objective methods of predicting behavior have significantly improved the manner in which predictions of risk are made. Andrews and Bonta (2003) note that prediction methods that rely solely on clinical judgments often perform poorly compared with prediction methods that are objective. Work by Grove and Meehl (1996) also assesses the benefits and limitations of utilizing one method of prediction over another. Empirical comparisons of subjective or clinical and mechanical or objective methods of prediction support the objective method of prediction as almost invariably equal to or superior to clinical methods (Grove & Meehl, 1996).

One of the problems associated with attempting to predict offender behavior is that human behavior is—in and of itself—unpredictable. Consequently, it is unreasonable to believe that every prediction will be correct; sometimes errors will occur. There are two types of prediction errors that significantly impact prediction outcomes: false negatives and false positives. False negatives result when risk is erroneously predicted as not to exist when it actually does. False positives occur when risk is predicted to exist when, in fact, it does not.

Interestingly, the repercussions of not being able to consistently make correct predictions are not equal. False negatives and false positives impose different costs both to the offender, to the criminal justice system, and to the community at large in terms of how offenders are managed and the manner in which resources are allocated. Additionally, these errors often adversely impact public perception of the efficacy of criminal justice programs and the criminal justice system in general and can reinforce stigmatization.

False negative errors are far more visible than false positive errors. For example, a false negative error can result in someone who was originally thought not to be at risk, being released to the community and posing an actual risk. Understandably, these types of errors are very visible to criminal justice officials and the public and have a significant impact on how the system operates because these errors usually result in a new criminal event. Conversely, false positive errors are often called invisible errors. Rarely does the general public learn about the offender who was determined to be at risk and released to the community, but who did not actually pose a risk. An individual who was deemed at risk but successfully reintegrated into the community or completed parole without incident would rarely come under public scrutiny.

Given the fact that errors in scoring risk are bound to occur, practitioners must determine the extent and type of error they are willing to tolerate, as this directly impacts policy and procedure as well as the amount of resources allocated for programming and supervision. A determination of an acceptable level of false negative and false positive errors is critical to ensuring that resources are allocated as efficiently and effectively as possible. For example, jurisdictions that present with a high percentage of false positive errors (errors in which offenders are scored as being at risk when in fact they are not) usually end up spending too much money and time supervising and managing people that don't require the level of service they are receiving. On the other hand, organizations that have a high percentage of false negative errors (errors in which offenders are scored as not being at risk when in fact they are) are not allocating resources properly and are likely undermanaging offenders to the detriment of public safety. If practitioners wish to locate the majority of their decisions regarding offenders within the context of risk, then they must be prepared to address any error associated with attempts to predict offender behavior. Furthermore, criminal justice personnel must understand the impact that risk and the error associated with determining risk has on assessing offender outcome, particularly as it relates to recidivism.

Recidivism

Derived from the Latin *recidere*, meaning to fall back, recidivism is the act of committing a crime again after having committed one previously. Recidivism is generally considered to be the most important measure of criminal behavior, and one of the most common benchmarks used to measure the success or failure of the programs in which offenders participate because it illuminates the degree to which offenders were successful (or not) in remaining crime free.

While recidivism may be universally accepted as the gold standard for determining the degree to which offenders recommit crime, the act of actually measuring and understanding recidivism is difficult. Oftentimes, information required to determine whether or not someone has recidivated is incomplete or is inconsistent, and measures of recidivism are not always accurate primarily due to errors in the scoring of risk that can yield improper results that misidentify some offenders as recidivists when they are not.

While risk prediction would not be possible without the existence of predictors or risk factors, these predictors must be measured against some criterion or outcome variable to determine the extent to which the predictor is accurate. Nearly all methods of prediction utilize some form of official record of offending as the outcome variable or measure of recidivism: arrest, conviction, incarceration, or parole revocation (Baird, 1991; Farrington & Tarling, 1985).

Of course, it is never as simple as assigning an outcome variable and measuring it. Each measure of recidivism has both benefits and limitations. When considering arrest, Maltz (1984) suggests that while arrest charges are often a function of offender behavior, the type of arrest matters. In other words, people should not be assumed to be guilty just because they have been arrested; people are often arrested and later released without being charged. Consequently, arrests that are made and that result in prosecution are more viable manifestations of recidivism than merely an arrest followed by release.

Moreover, because the standard of proof for arrest is much lower than for conviction, it is likely that more arrests are made than actually meet the burden of proof required for prosecution. Where probable cause is sufficient to arrest someone, proof beyond a reasonable doubt is the requirement for conviction (Maltz, 1984). Furthermore, likelihood of arrest is much higher for ex- offenders than for people with no prior record. Police often arrest known offenders before they arrest others. As a result, if arrest is the only measure of recidivism considered, it is likely to result in an increase in the likelihood of false positive outcomes (e.g., people who are arrested but later found not to have committed a crime) and policies and practices that ultimately penalize people who actually did nothing wrong.

Convictions are often not reliable methods of prediction because of the time it takes for conviction data to be entered into databases. Significant lapses between conviction and data entry can result in researchers observing artificially low rates of conviction. Furthermore, prosecutorial discretion often drives prosecution and subsequent conviction—a measure of criminal justice system behavior, not offender behavior (Klienman & Lukoff, 1981). As the majority of cases result in plea bargains, the crimes for which people are convicted are not always true manifestations of actual crime committed. Consequently, using conviction as a measure of recidivism may actually minimize the reporting of the severity and type of crime actually perpetrated.

As a result, because the standard of proof for conviction is higher than for arrest, an arrest followed by conviction is usually a better indicator of recidivism than arrest alone (Maltz, 1994). Scholarship does indicate that both arrests and convictions represent most actual law-violating behavior and that the correlation between the two measures is often so high (r=.80 or higher), either can be used as the principal outcome measure (Baird, 1991).

Incarceration has also been used as a benchmark for recidivism, but it too is not a perfect indicator. In many cases, people who are arrested and convicted are not incarcerated. As incarceration is the most restrictive punishment one can receive, it makes sense that incarceration is reserved for the most serious cases and circumstances. In this way, those who are incarcerated represent only a small proportion of the total number of people arrested and only a slightly larger number of people who were convicted (Maltz, 1994). Therefore, using incarceration as the sole recidivistic measure also does not account for punishments that fall short of incarceration, like additional time on parole or probation. Consequently, incarceration may under-count the actual amount of recidivistic behavior that occurs.

Finally, parole revocation is also frequently used as a predictive outcome measure, but it too suffers from some of the limitations of the other measures mentioned above. Parole revocation is often more representative of the criminal justice system's response to parole violations than of the actual frequency or severity of offender behavior. Furthermore, there is significant variance among parole/probation officers in terms of revocations practice due to the extraordinary amount of discretion they are allowed to exercise. Officer preference and job orientation may influence whether or not revocations proceedings are initiated, thereby either artificially inflating (if job orientation is law and order-based) or deflating (if job orientation is more rehabilitation/social work-based) the actual number of documented parole revocations. In turn, this could significantly impact resource allocation and supervision management (Clear et al., 1992). In addition, the emphasis that paroling authorities place on whom to revoke and under what circumstances is greatly impacted by agency mission and vision. Organizations that promote a law enforcement-oriented approach to parole violations will be more likely to revoke than agencies that may support treatment and rehabilitative ideals.

Despite the limitations of arrest, conviction, incarceration, and parole revocation as predictors of outcome, these measures are the most widely accepted criterion variables used in prediction research (Baird, 1991; Maltz, 1984). In an effort to minimize the potential bias or shortcomings of one measure over another, most scholars contend that multiple criterion variables should be utilized in order to present the most complete picture of offender behavior possible.

Another factor to consider when predicting offender behavior is the follow-up period, or the interval during which offender behavior is observed. Follow-up periods of one year or less are generally not thought to be of sufficient duration because of the lag time between the commission of a recidivating event and when information is entered into a data management system (Maltz, 1984). In this situation, recidivating events are often under-reported due to the fact that information often does not appear in data management systems until long after the event has occurred and therefore the event is not counted as having happened.

Conversely, follow-up periods of one year or longer require researchers to wait significant periods of time before they are able to assess outcome information. Long-term recidivism studies require that years elapse before data on outcomes may be collected. Consequently, researchers often consider multiple follow-up periods. The Bureau of Justice Statistics (BJS) routinely looks at recidivism one, two, and three years post-release. Most recently the BJS conducted their longest follow-up period of nine years. BJS has found that multiple follow-up periods help control for data management and/or administrative lag times while providing short-, medium-, and long-term outcome results.

While criterion variables and time to follow-up impact our knowledge of recidivism, so too does the way in which data is collected. In only very limited instances is complete criminal justice data available. Where arrest data is the purview of local policing jurisdictions, prosecution and conviction data is under the governance of judiciary personnel, and incarceration and parole data are often under the auspices of departments of corrections and paroling authorities. Not surprisingly, data entry by a multitude of people from different agencies only increases the possibility of data entry errors and misinformation and makes verification of data between agencies extremely difficult (Maltz, 1994).

As is evident, the use of recidivism as a criterion measure for evaluating offender behavior is fraught with limitations. The fact that scholars have been unable to agree on a definition of recidivism that is comprehensive in scope leaves other important issues related to measurement, the length of time between offenses, the role that technical violations play in definitions of re-offending, and the criteria constituting a return to custody inadequately addressed (Chaiken et al., 1982; Petersilia, 1980).

With respect to measuring recidivism, many scholars have adopted the delinquent/non-delinquent or recidivist/non-recidivist dichotomy (Farrington & Tarling, 1985). While convenient and easy because this measure merely assesses the presence or absence of a recidivating event (a relatively easy piece of information to obtain), more complex measures that take into account issues of frequency and seriousness of offense, time to first offense, and rate of offending per unit time at risk are far more meaningful (Blumstein et al., 1986; Farrington & Tarling, 1985; Jones, 1996; Maltz, 1984; Schmidt & Witte, 1988). Researchers contend that these enhanced measures of recidivism are useful because of nuances associated with when recidivism occurs, to what degree, and under what circumstances (Farrington & Tarling, 1985). Knowledge about how long it takes someone to recidivate, what type of crime they commit at the time they recidivate, and how many times they recidivate is central to developing a more complex understanding of the characteristics associated with recidivism. Understandably, a more robust knowledge of recidivism could result in different and more effective approaches to managing it.

One of the most serious problems associated with understanding and addressing recidivism is the fact that it takes an exceedingly long time to obtain information about who recidivates. Remember that in order to collect data on recidivism, someone who left prison and who is out in the community must again engage in criminal activity that is officially recognized through one of the criterion variables: arrest, conviction, re-incarceration, and/or parole revocation. This means that time must pass and researchers essentially must "lie in wait" for a recidivating event to occur. Case in point: the most recent national data on recidivism was collected between 2005 and 2014 and released in 2018. Certainly, more timely recidivism data has been collected and evaluated by individual states and jurisdictions, but national recidivism data is often far older. It is difficult to rest any policy or programmatic decisions about how to address recidivism on data that is clearly stale and likely does not reflect current trends.

Longer follow-up periods, such as the most recent nine-year recidivism study by BJS, however, provide observations that cannot be gleaned through shorter periods (Alper et al., 2018). For example, in their comparison of observations at three years and nine years, the basic recidivism percentage (defined as the cumulative arrest percentage following release) was increased by 15 percentage points (Alper et al., 2018). Moreover, the nine-year study revealed the percentage of released prisoners arrested in states outside of the state that they were incarcerated was twice as high as observed in the three-year study. When we consider perceptions of desistance from criminal activity between the three-year and nine-year outcomes, 32% of offenders appeared to have desisted from crime at three -years post release; however, if we extend this out to nine years, the percentage of offenders with no new arrests declined to 17%—almost half (47%) of offenders with no arrest within three years of release were arrested in years four through nine (Alper et al., 2018, p. 5). Alper and colleagues (2018) note that while longer term recidivism studies provide greater insight into desistance measures and "enable researchers to understand more complex patterns of desistance," this is balanced with concerns of immediacy and availability of data for policymakers and practitioners (p. 14).

No discussion about recidivism can take place without an understanding of what the most recent recidivism data show. The most recent national study on recidivism evaluated over 67,000 randomly sampled prisoners representing the greater than 400,000 state prisoners released in 2005 among 30 states (Alper et al., 2018). The criterion variable used to measure recidivism was arrest for a new crime. Probation and parole violations were included as public order offenses. Arrests were further broken down by offense type (violent, property, drug, and public order).

As figure 9-1 indicates, rates of rearrest were not evenly distributed over time. Offenders who were rearrested were more likely to be rearrested earlier than later. Results from the study indicate that within three years of release, 68% of offenders were arrested, 79% within six years and 83% within nine years of release (Alper et al., 2018). Five percent of offenders arrested in the first year were not rearrested again over the nine-year period. Among offenders arrested for a new crime during the nine-year follow-up period, the majority (53%) were arrested for the first time during the first three years following release. Forty-four percent of offenders were arrested in the first year of release while 24% were arrested in year nine. Offenders had an average of five arrests over the nine-year period (Alper et al., 2018).

Figure 9-1. Percentage of Prisoners Arrested after Release by Year of First Arrest (2005–2014)

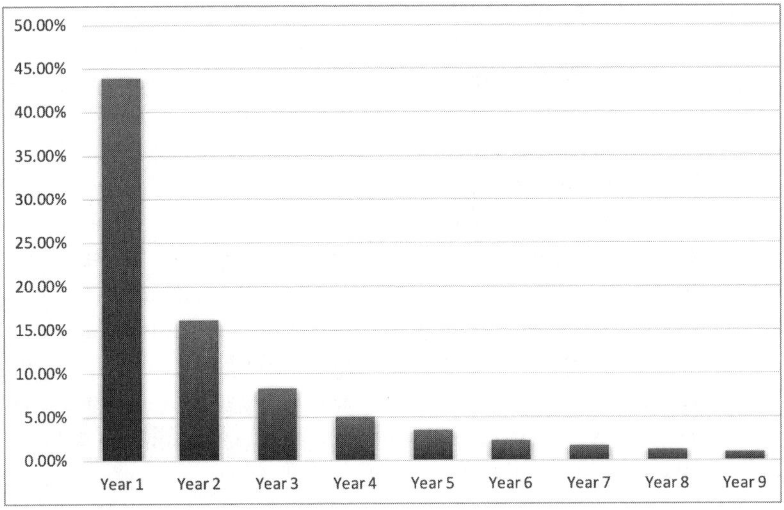

Adapted from Alper et al., 2018.

When considering recidivism by the most serious commitment offense type, in the first year of release 39% of violent offenders were arrested; 11% of those arrests were for violent crimes. The percentage of released property offenders who were arrested for a new crime in their first year of release (51%) was higher than the percentage of arrested drug or violent offenders. This pattern was maintained over the nine-year follow-up period. Forty-three percent of drug offenders were arrested in the first year of release, 22% were arrested for a drug offense and 7% for a violent offense (Alper et al., 2018. p. 10). Consistent with criminological literature, less than one quarter (23%) of released offenders were responsible for half of the nearly two million arrests during the nine-year follow-up. A similar percentage (23%) of offenders were responsible for half of the arrests during the three-year follow-up period (p. 7).

Looking at differences in recidivism by gender in the first year of release, the percentage of males arrested was 10% higher than for females (45% and 35% respectively). However, the percent difference between males and females narrowed by year nine, with 24% of male offenders arrested compared with 21% of female offenders (Alper et al., 2018). Overall, 84% of males and 77% of females were arrested within nine years of release. Offenders aged 24 and younger were more likely to be arrested in each of the nine consecutive years than any other age group, with a total of 90% arrested within nine years. Inmates aged 40 and older had the lowest overall arrest rates with 77% arrested in nine years. When considering recidivism by race, findings showed 87% of black prisoners were arrested within nine years of release compared with 81% of white and 81% of Hispanic prisoners.

The fact that significant numbers of people who were in prison continue to commit crime after their release suggests that conventional attempts to predict and measure risk have not been entirely successful. The failure of traditional methods of managing recidivism begs the question of whether new ways of viewing old problems can result in better (or at least different) outcomes. One alternative interpretation of recidivism is very relevant and useful to this conversation. In this worldview, Zamble and Quinsey (1997) refer to recidivism as a process rather than as a static event wherein offenders may recidivate or relapse, but are people who can go on to lead productive, crime-free lives. Using results of a study they conducted on substance abusing offenders, Zamble and Quinsey locate the recidivism process in the context of static and dynamic predictors of risk. They argue that dynamic risk factors are most important when attempting to mitigate recidivism (because these risk factors are changeable) and that researchers should be focused on the process through which offenders travel that leads them to recidivism, not merely the event itself (Zamble & Quinsey, 1997).

Specifically, Zamble and Quinsey (1997) suggest that recidivism is not only a criminal act committed after release from prison, but also a psychological process. The authors contend that

> new criminal offenses result from an interaction between internal dispositions and external events so that a variety of dynamic factors [are] included, among them measures of stress, social support, coping skills, substance abuse, supervisory and intervention variables, and affective states. (p. 9)

Clearly, dynamic risk factors significantly impact offenders' abilities to cope and manage stress. Further enhancing this view by contextualizing the discussion of recidivism in relapse theory (a theory generally applied to substance abusers) also provides an entirely different way of thinking about the problem.

By way of background, coping theory argues that people manage problems in different ways and that they develop coping mechanisms to deal with their problems. A study by Zamble and Porporino (1998) found that while the issues and problems that offenders face are principally no different in kind and severity from the ordinary challenges that most people encounter, their ways of coping were limited and ineffective. Further research found that recidivism could be predicted using several measures of coping and that the predictive validity of coping measures were in keeping with other traditionally used recidivistic outcomes such as rearrest and reconviction. These findings resulted in a "coping criminality" hypothesis that argues that inadequate coping responses to stressors and problems often result in offenders falling back on old, known behaviors such as criminal activity in an effort to cope with a problem (Zamble & Porporino, 1988).

Relapse theory is relevant to the discussion because it argues that relapse is a "failure to maintain behavior change, rather than a failure to initiate change" (Annis & Davis, 1991). Relapse is a natural process that occurs as people learn new ways to cope or manage damaging and high-risk behaviors. The premise is that people are taught coping skills that assist them with managing situations where relapse might be a concern (e.g., how to go out to dinner with others who are drinking alcohol when you are an alcoholic). These newly learned skills, however, must be practiced and exercised regularly, as this is the only way in which new skills and ways of thinking become routine and effortless.

However, if a person finds themselves in a particularly stressful situation in which their newly minted coping skills are not strong enough to ward off temptation, they may choose to fall back into old, comfortable behaviors in their efforts to manage the situation (Zamble & Quinsey, 1997). Relapse theory attempts to identify critical points where increased control and pro-social decision-making (e.g., the conscious decision that one must make to not take a drink just because other people are drinking) are necessary for positive outcomes (e.g., not getting drunk again). Put another way, people must learn ways of recognizing and anticipating behavioral landmines before they trigger poor decisions. The use of positive coping skills helps mitigate relapse. "Relapse prevention relies heavily on the client's ability to learn and to initiate appropriate coping behaviors at the earliest possible point in the relapse process" (Hall, 1989, p. 139). In their study, Zamble and Quinsey found that offenders generally present with poor coping skills, unstable emotions, and untraditional perceptions and cognitions, all of which can and often do result in recidivism. The effectiveness with which offenders are able to mitigate these problems through the use of pro-social coping mechanisms determines whether or not they will relapse and/or continue to engage in criminal behavior.

Without doubt, the idea that recidivism is a series of peaks and valleys mediated by learned coping skills and relapse prevention techniques is unique and likely has significant implications for offender management both inside prisons and out (Zamble & Quinsey, 1997). If policymakers and practitioners agreed to leave conventional perceptions of recidivism at the door and reframe recidivism to include notions of coping and relapse, offender case management, treatment, and supervision would undergo fundamental reform. A change in the way we interpret and react to recidivism might revolutionize how we perceive offenders and how we measure their success or failure in the community.

Chapter 10

Resilience and Desistance

If we visualize risk as a continuum, recidivism might dominate one end, resilience the other, and desistance might fall somewhere in the middle. Where recidivists are people at risk for committing crime who do so at least once and who do it again, resistors are people who, despite being at risk for engaging in criminal activity, never do so. Desistors, on the other hand, embody characteristics of both concepts. Desistors are people who are at risk for committing crime and who do so, but who do not do so again in the future. Given that upwards of 68% of offenders recidivate within three years from release from prison, it is of particular importance to consider the characteristics that differentiate a recidivist from a desistor or someone who never commits crime in the first place.

Resilience

Resistors are people who should do something wrong (people who possess all of the characteristics of people who do something wrong) but who do not. In criminal justice terms, resistors are a unique group because they possess some or all of the risk factors associated with criminal behavior but never actually engage in deviant acts. Of course, the $64,000 question is why? What factors compel certain people who possess risk factors associated with deviant behavior not to commit crime?

Historical Context

The study of resilience finds its basis in psychology, specifically in the area of schizophrenia research. Prior to the 1970s, much of the research on schizophrenia focused on understanding the set of characteristics or maladaptive behaviors with which patients of the disease presented (Luthar et al., 2000). Yet, a subset of schizophrenics possessed a set of factors that limited the impact of the disease on their quality of life. These atypical schizophrenic patients were able to work, engage in relatively normal social relationships, and marry (Zigler & Glick, 1986). While these patients were not found to be wholly resilient to schizophrenia, the study of these patients revealed the presence of some resilient qualities that limited the destructive nature of the disease.

Additional research on children of schizophrenic mothers further informed the resilience literature. In these studies, research indicated that despite the high-risk status and increased likelihood of children of schizophrenic mothers having the disease, many were able to adapt and remain disease free (Masten et al., 1990). These findings encouraged researchers to further evaluate how individual responses to adversity impact outcome.

Research on resilience expanded significantly after the publication of a seminal study of children in Hawaii. This study followed the lives of 505 people born in 1955 on the Island of Kauai (Werner & Smith, 1992). Results of this longitudinal study found that children who grow up in poverty experience a wide variety of health and other developmental problems. Furthermore, findings demonstrated that approximately two-thirds of the children who were followed in this study, and who grew up in poverty, presented with myriad problems as adults. However, the study also found that one-third of the children in the study that faced similar or same adverse conditions had no significant problems as adults (Werner & Smith, 2001). The question born from this study was, why did only some children present with developmental concerns as adults while others did not?

As a consequence of these findings, research on resilience has flourished. Current topics in resilience research include the impact of socioeconomic disadvantage, parental mental illness, maltreatment, urban poverty, community violence, chronic illness, and catastrophic life events on the ability to thrive (Luthar et al., 2000). Where initial studies on resilience primarily concerned themselves with identifying specific protective factors that shield or insulate people from harmful outcomes (Johnson & Wiechelt, 2004), other work evaluates risk factors or characteristics present in an individual that inhibit normal functioning and put someone at-risk for engaging in actions with expected negative outcomes (e.g., such as criminal behavior). Where risk factors represent identified deficits in individual characteristics, the existence of protective factors indicate strengths people possess that minimize or insulate them from being adversely impacted by negative or detrimental outcomes (Johnson & Wiechelt, 2004).

Protective factors can be intrinsic or extrinsic to an individual and are generally not one- size-fits-all. In other words, protective factors that work for one person may not work for another, or may not work again for the same person if that individual finds themselves in a similar situation at another point in time (Luthar & Zigler, 1991). Consequently, isolating specific protective factors is very difficult and not always useful. Despite this limitation, Werner and Smith (2001) identified shared protective factors that led to resilience in the Hawaiian study sample and that have been applied and validated in other contexts.

Werner and Smith (2001) found that children who developed one close personal relationship to a role model or caregiver were more likely to be resilient. They also determined that children with easy temperaments and who were affectionate, responsive, and good-natured, who had friends and interests including active participation in group activities, and who had better language and reasoning skills, were more likely to be resilient than their counterparts (Werner & Smith, 2001). Other studies evaluating protective factors have replicated these results in children (Long & Vaillant, 1984; Sameroff et al., 1984).

In a 1994 article, Masten reviewed a multitude of research from different disciplines and determined that there was a convergence of findings regarding protective factors and resilience. Specifically, she reviewed findings from work in the areas of parental mental illness, economic hardship, teenage parenting, foster care children, chronic illness, childhood maltreatment, and delinquency and criminality.

Masten (1994) identified ten protective factors that play a role in resilience, including effective parenting, connections with competent adults, appeal to adults, good intellectual skills, talents or accomplishments valued by self or others, self-efficacy, self-worth, and hopefulness, religious faith, socioeconomic advantage, good schools or other community assets, and good fortune. Unfortunately, little is known about how these protective characteristics operate because research in the area is still ongoing. Moreover, it is unknown if, to what extent, and how these protective factors apply to adults. Furthermore, upon second glance, it would appear that risk and protective factors could theoretically be mirror images of one another. The same characteristic that may promote at-risk behavior (e.g., socioeconomic disadvantage) could also be the same factor that inhibits law-breaking behavior (e.g., socioeconomic advantage).

Contemporary studies on protective factors have focused less on identifying specific factors of resilience and more on the underlying protective processes that are associated with successful adaptation to seemingly disastrous circumstances (Luthar, 1999; Masten, 1994). "Positive adaptation despite exposure to adversity involves a developmental progression such that new vulnerabilities and/or strengths often emerge with changing life circumstances" (Luthar et al., 2000, p. 544).

Current Trends

There are a variety of issues that surround the study and understanding of resilience. First, one is only resilient if they have experienced past trauma or other catastrophic life experience and weathered the storm. In other words, in order to be judged resilient, one must have been in a position to demonstrate characteristics ordinarily associated with resilience. Only when in the face of a significant negative threat to development (e.g., exposure to violence) a positive adaptive response occurs, can resilience be claimed (Masten, 2001).

Second, there is little consensus about the definition of resilience. Scholars have trouble agreeing on whether resilience is a trait, characteristic, or dynamic process and are unclear about what resilience is and what it is not, making a clear and concise definition and measurement of the concept elusive at best (Luthar et al., 2000). Third, the relationship between protective factors and resilience is unclear (Luthar & Cushing, 1999).

As researchers and practitioners continue to try to understand the human condition, they do so by seeking to evaluate what propels us to persevere in the face of extreme adversity. One-dimensional approaches to this task have been replaced with more complex notions of what it means to be resilient. Recent research argues that resilience is comprised of a set of psychological characteristics shaped through life experiences that result from the interplay between relational, social, cultural, and ecological contexts (Harvey, 1996, 2007). Resilience is also viewed as being a dynamic (as opposed to static) process that results from the interplay between the individual, the event, and the environment (Johnson & Wiechelt, 2004). Additional advances in resilience research suggest that there are multiple paths to achieving resilience and that its fluid nature means approaches that succeed in one instance will not always succeed in other instances. This explanation of resilience further supports the notion that resilience is a process rather than a static event (Johnson & Wiechelt, 2004).

Given the confusion associated with what resilience is and how it works, it is not surprising that some researchers have approached the study of resilience as if it were the exception to the rule. In fact, the bulk of scholarship on resilience argues that the majority of people have poor coping skills and adaptive capabilities and that people who are resilient are in fact outliers (Bonanno, 2004). However, more recent research suggests the opposite. Some scholars argue that resilience is commonplace and that it appears to be an ordinary phenomenon and the product of individual methods of adaptation. As long as adaptive behaviors or traits function well, resilience is the rule rather than the exception.

> Resilience does not come from rare or special qualities, but from the everyday magic of ordinary, normative human resources in the minds, brains, and bodies, of children, their families and relationships and in their communities. (Masten, 2001, p. 235)

Only if individual adaptive structures are impaired or damaged in some way is resilience negatively impacted (Masten, 2001). Once adaptive systems are compromised in some way, deleterious outcomes are more likely, especially for people exposed to extreme and sustained adversity (Masten, 2000).

Reentry Considerations

Work on resilience has not specifically focused on crime or offender-related concerns. However, it seems reasonable to conclude that people who experience the sustained effects of violence and abuse, the incarceration of family members, and the subsequent release of loved ones from prison to the community undergo significant adversity.

Moreover, it is then not a stretch to understand how violence, abuse and incarceration might trigger maladaptive coping techniques and potentially impact the likelihood that people might engage in at-risk behavior. So, extrapolating what we have learned about resilience, why do some people exposed to firmly established risk factors for criminal behavior (e.g., intergenerational histories of crime and violence, for instance) not engage in criminal activity while others do?

Resilience is likely a combination of both micro- and macro-level indicators. As Harvey and colleagues (2007) argue, we must consider the influence of the community, as well as the normative culture and subculture, on resilience. This is possible through approaching the discussion of resilience from a uniquely ecological perspective that requires that we evaluate the extent to which interpersonal and psychological processes facilitate adaptive, positive development and how this development varies within familial, social, and cultural contexts (Harvey et al., 2007).

> The widely held view of resiliency as an individual disposition, family trait, or community phenomenon is insufficient . . . resiliency cannot be understood or improved in significant ways by merely focusing on these individual-level factors. Instead, careful attention must be paid to the structural deficiencies in our society. (Seccombe, 2002, p. 385)

Harvey develops his theory of micro- and macro-level dynamics of resilience through adapting Bronfenbrenner's person-process-context model—a concept worth understanding in light of the application of resilience to offender reentry. Harvey suggests that psychological and developmental processes must be considered when assessing the presence or absence of resilience and that these processes are a function of reciprocal relationships that exist in different environments. These environments are nested in the sense that they expand outward from individual environments to more inclusive settings, including home, work, community, city, state, etc. Environments are "conceived of as a set of nested structures, each inside the next, like a set of Russian dolls" (Bronfenbrenner, 1979, p. 3).

Further empirical support for micro- and macro-level studies of resilience suggests that there are multiple domains that should be studied in an effort to understand how and to what extent resilience is present. These domains include evaluating individual relationships, the community, and culture (Ungar, 2006). The extent to which people belong to religious organizations, are tolerant of others' religious views, and possess a cultural and/or spiritual identity can drastically impact the degree to which resilience is present (Ungar, 2006).

If we are to consider what encourages people to persevere in the face of adversity despite having the deck stacked against them, we must critically evaluate what specific characteristics and processes encourage resilience for whom and under what circumstances (Harvey et al., 2007). This is particularly relevant when considering the potential impact that resilience and attendant protective factors could have on future generations of people who possess risk factors for crime and deviance. If we can understand just how and to what extent resilience interacts with the individual, family, community, and larger settings, we might be able to fashion a system that promotes those factors that enhance resilience while minimizing those that do not.

Desistance

Where resilience and recidivism represent opposite ends of the risk spectrum, desistance occupies a place somewhere in the middle. Where recidivism evaluates when and (sometimes) why offenders commit crime again, desistance asks the question, why and (sometimes) when do they stop? Perhaps fundamental differences between offenders who commit crime and continue and those who commit crime and desist from further criminal activity exist—differences that could be mitigated if we only understood what they were (Maruna, 2000).

Historical Context

As with resilience and recidivism, desistance is fraught with definitional, methodological, and theoretical issues, making the study of this important phenomenon challenging. While the study of desistance has gained momentum within the last decade, scholars are still struggling to establish the best way to analyze and evaluate what it means.

One of the reasons why desistance is so difficult to understand and study is because it is nearly impossible to define. No consensus on a definition of desistance exists (Laub & Sampson, 2001; Piquero et al., 2003). Definitions of desistance are vague, include arbitrary age-based cutoffs, or are very specific to the particular sample under study (Farrington & Hawkins, 1991; Shover, 1996; Warr, 1998). It is also unclear whether multiple definitions of desistance are necessary in order to distinguish between "temporary" desistance, or "lulls in offending" (Clarke & Cornish, 1985, p. 173), and permanent desistance from crime (Weitekamp & Kerner, 1994).

The confusion surrounding how to define desistance prompted Loeber and Le Blanc to develop a four-pronged definition of desistance (1990, p. 409). First, this definition accounts for deceleration in the frequency of offending over time through a tapering off of overall crime commission. The second aspect of the definition suggests that desistance includes reductions in crime specialization or a progression from very specific to more generalized criminal activity. The third component of Loeber and Le Blanc's definition argues that desistance includes a de-escalation in crime seriousness that presupposes a transition from very serious to less serious crime over time. Finally, Loeber and Le Blanc contend that people who desist from crime may reach a ceiling wherein they achieve saturation with respect to crime commission.

The absence of a clear definition of desistance clearly makes measurement of the concept challenging. While some scholars have chosen to measure desistance much like recidivism by creating a desistor/nondesistor dichotomy (LeBlanc, 1993), others have endeavored to measure desistance in time; the time between criminal events or the time until no further crime is committed (Laub et al., 1998). Furthermore, where some scholars view desistance as a static event (Bushway et al., 2001; Farrington & Hawkins, 1991; Warr, 1998), others view desistance as a dynamic process (Bottoms et al., 2004; Bushway et al., 2003; Maruna, 2001).

Still other research argues that desistance is unlikely to occur suddenly as a single event and that it is more likely that people zig-zag or move in and out of desistance over time (Laub & Sampson, 2003; Piquero, 2004). Viewing desistance in a dichotomous way likely minimizes the subtleties associated with it and likely obscures the length of time in which people actually desist from crime (Bushway et al., 2003).

Other concerns related to measuring desistance include when true desistance (actual cessation of crime) occurs and when false desistance exists (when offenders may take a break between criminal events). Scholars argue that mistaking a false desistance event for a true desistance event could result in erroneous conclusions about the desistance process. Moreover, assuming that desistance is intermittent, desistance is likely to change in rate and length over time, making the differentiation between true and false desistance important to understand but almost impossible to determine (Kazemian, 2007).

As Stall and Biernacki (1986) argue, spontaneous desistance is the cessation of crime that occurs without any external intervention, while Baskin and Sommers (1998) contend that cessation of crime over a two-year period is enough to claim "temporary" desistance (p. 143). However, as Farrington has noted, there are no guarantees that even a prolonged period of crime-free activity equates to a true cessation of crime, or true desistance (Farrington, 1986). Length and type of follow-up for measuring desistance is neither agreed upon nor firmly established (see Laub & Sampson, 2001; Mischkowitz, 1994; Uggen & Kruttschnitt, 1998).

While the study of desistance has been impeded due to definition and measurement problems, desistance has also had some difficulty finding a theoretical home. Most of the seminal work on the topic has been located within the realm of the criminal careers literature; research that looks at the career of a criminal over time as a way of longitudinally assessing when, where, and how often offenders commit crime. There is also further support for the notion of desistance in the rational choice and social learning theoretical camps.

It is well known that there is a direct relationship between age and crime. That is, the older an offender is the less likely they are to engage in crime (Gottfredson & Hirschi, 1990). While most scholars agree that the factors related to desistance vary by chronological age and that as offenders get older they are less likely to commit crime, there is no consensus about exactly when desistance will occur. Some researchers suggest that early desistance occurs before the age of 18 and that late desistance is likely to occur after age 30 (Weitekamp & Kerner, 1994). Other scholars contend that desistance is predicated on onset of criminal offending. Offenders who begin offending early are more likely to desist at a time different than late onset offenders (Tremblay, 1994).

The earliest work evaluating the relationship between age and crime over the life course was conducted by Sheldon and Eleanor Glueck. Results from this study, which compared both delinquent and non-delinquent boys from English, Irish and Italian families in poor urban areas, found that the proportion of boys arrested decreased from 71% in the first 5-year follow-up to 57% in the third five-year follow-up (Glueck & Glueck, 1943, p. 109). Other large-scale studies have further informed the discussion of criminal careers and the relationship between age and crime (McCord, 1980; Wolfgang et al., 1987). Overall, studies support the notion that juvenile delinquency is linked to adult crime and that onset of offending, level of participation in crime, crime type, and length of participation in crime all inform the criminal career (Laub & Sampson, 2001).

While the initial work on desistance has been located within the context of criminal careers research, other work on the subject has focused on specific characteristics that may positively (or negatively) impact desistance. Gibbens' work following a large-scale cohort indicated that marriage produced "increasing social stability" (1984, p. 61). A study by Rand (1987) found similar results. Marriage and other life events such as completing high school, vocational educational training, and joining the military were all related to reduced incidence of criminal involvement.

Perhaps the seminal work on this topic, however, was written by Sampson and Laub (1993), who contend that there are significant events in one's life that play a role in altering pathways seemingly developed early in life; events that can alter the initiation of criminal activity and its duration. Moreover, as adults these events can and do impact desistance from crime. Sampson and Laub (1993) argue that marriage and employment with inherent job stability are key ingredients to altering the landscape of type, length, and seriousness of adult criminal activity.

Yet, if getting married and having a job were the only requirements for reducing crime, the solution to the crime problem would be simple and likely implemented long ago. Research suggests that social bonds formed through relationships with friends, relatives, or religious or other organizations, and social relationships in general, take time to develop. Therefore, as gradual a process as the development of social relationships is, so too is the process of desistance (Laub et al., 1998). The quality of social bonds and social relationships (including marriage) can impact when and if desistance from crime will occur (Horney et al., 1995; Laub et al., 1998). Sampson and Laub note that it is not the mere presence or absence of marriage and employment that will determine whether or not someone desists from crime, it is the nature and degree to which these characteristics impact social bonds and social control that is key (Sampson & Laub, 1993).

Other theoretical constructs that have been used to explain desistance include rational choice and social learning theory. Rational choice theorists suggest that people make conscious decisions to engage in and therefore desist from crime based upon a risk/benefit analysis of the situation. If the risks associated with engaging in crime outweigh the benefits of doing so, a person will desist from engaging in criminal activity (Clarke & Cornish, 1985; Cornish & Clarke, 1986; Gartner & Piliavin, 1988; Paternoster, 1989).

Social learning theory argues that the same attributes that can influence the commission of crime can, in reverse, be responsible for desistance. As we know, social learning theory posits that people will come into contact with different people throughout the life course who have different attitudes and values. Some of these relationships will be positive and others not; some of the relationships that people will encounter will model criminal behavior. It is how an individual defines these attitudes and behaviors (i.e., good or bad, right or wrong) and whether or not the criminal behaviors are reinforced in a positive way that will, in large part, determine how an individual behaves (Akers, 1985). Akers (1988) argues that social learning theory can impact the ability of people to desist from crime by increasing relationships with non-criminal friends, lessening exposure to criminal activity, and improving attitudes and orientations that are pro-social in nature, including increased conformity to law-abiding behaviors.

Current Trends

Where the majority of work evaluating desistance has been quantitative in its approach, qualitative work that deconstructs offenders' personal accounts of desistance provides an added dimension through which to consider the issue. In his 2001 study, *Making Good*, Maruna interviewed 65 men and women. Through life-history narratives, Maruna sought to understand why and under what circumstances offenders were able to desist from crime. Maruna found consistencies among desistors; those who were able to desist from crime tended to be other-centered as opposed to self-centered. Desistors also felt greater control over their lives and saw themselves as agents of their own change (Maruna, 2001).

Furthermore, Maruna found that people who desist from crime "need to make sense of their lives" (2001, p. 7). Maruna argues that desistors' efforts to take control and make sense of their lives result in the creation of redemption scripts wherein a desistor will reframe their life story in such a way so that they see themselves as a good person who has overcome significant hurdles to the point that they are now able to understand and acknowledge and act upon their potential to engage in pro-social (e.g., non-criminal) behavior (Maruna, 2001).

Maruna's research is relevant not only because he took a qualitative approach to understanding desistance, but because of his focus on the individual desistor. Most prior research on desistance highlighted patterns in offending between offenders (comparing those who persist to those who desist) rather than evaluating what specific factors (external and internal) influence whether or not an offender desists (Bottoms et al., 2004; Kazemian, 2007).

Maruna and others are convinced that desistance cannot be properly assessed outside of the social context within which it occurs (Bottoms et al., 2004; Maruna, 2001). These scholars contend that offenders who desist from crime are shaped by external opportunities, cultural viewpoints, self-identity, peers, and the need to take control of their own destiny (Bottoms et al., 2004; Shover, 1983). If correct, it follows that a criminal justice system that provides opportunities for offenders to redeem themselves through engagement in resources designed to emphasize positive accomplishments and offender strengths, better positions them to desist from crime (Maruna, 2001).

That being said, desistance doesn't occur in a vacuum. Maruna (2001) notes that there is usually an event or catalyst for change (whether internal or external), something that triggers one's motivation to begin the desistance process. Rumgay (2004) furthers this line of inquiry by suggesting that there are a series of cognitive changes that occur in stages in people who wish to desist from crime. Rumgay argues that offenders must find themselves in a place wherein they are ready for reform in order for the reformation process to begin.

This notion of readiness to reform is predicated on work by Prochaska and DiClemente (1986). Primarily used in psychology, the trans-theoretical model is a theory that views behavioral change as a process that takes place over time and requires progression through five discrete stages of change (Callaghan, 2005). This theory has been particularly useful in mitigating a variety of problems including health concerns (e.g., weight loss) addictive behaviors (e.g., substance abuse), and psychological disorders such as anxiety and depression (DiClemente et al., 2004; Prochaska & DiClemente, 2002).

The trans-theoretical model is comprised of five stages of change (Norcross et al., 2011). The *precontemplation* stage is a time in which an individual has no intention of changing. In many cases an individual may be completely unaware that change should or can occur, but family and friends have acute knowledge that there is a problem that must be addressed. Next, the *contemplation* stage occurs when an individual is aware that a problem exists and begins the process of seriously thinking about how to manage the problem at hand. At this point, the individual has still not committed to taking action, but recognition of a problem has occurred. This stage is fraught with internal struggles to overcome poor, destructive behavior and awareness that it will take great effort to overcome it.

Stage 3, the *preparation* stage is the stage in which individuals have committed to take action. They may have already begun the process of "trying out" new behaviors or attitudes and may fail, but they are testing the waters and employing new skills. Subsequently, the *action* stage is a time when individuals are actively changing behaviors. Significant time, energy, and commitment is required in this stage in an effort for individuals to overcome desires to fall back on old behaviors that are easier and more familiar. It may take a significant period of time for individuals to successfully overcome their dysfunctional behavior. Finally, the *maintenance* stage is a time for encouraging continued commitment to new behavior patterns and requires effort to prevent relapse.

Rumgay integrates the stages of change into her evaluation of the role of desistance in offending. Specifically, she interweaves these stages of change into her assessment of three primary components of desistance: personal identity, opportunity, and behavioral scripts. While Rumgay's work specifically references female offenders, there is relevance to applying her ideas to male offenders as well.

Personal identity is the arena in which change first begins. Rumgay argues that various studies of desistance indicate that desistance from crime closely resembles accounts of withdrawal from drugs (Graham & Bowling, 1995; Maruna, 2001; Shover, 1985). In order for the identity change process to begin, the experience of engaging in crime must change from positive to negative. This aversion to crime may occur because of increased fear associated with getting caught, doubts about the morality of engaging in criminal behavior, stress, etc.

For personal identity changes to continue, an offender must have an increased interest in adopting a conventional lifestyle. What results is a conflict between an offender's deviant identity and the values that come with it, and a developing pro-social identity that requires the adoption of a new set of values (Rumgay, 2004). This identity transformation does not happen immediately and likely does not happen the first time it is attempted. More realistically, the magnetic pull of the status quo (the deviant identity) encourages offenders in transition to "fall off the wagon" (Prochaska et al., 1992; Rumgay, 1998).

What encourages an offender in transition to put forth continued effort toward reframing their personal identity is the opportunity for reform (Giordano et al., 2002). Offenders must not only see that an opportunity is available, they must believe that they can access it and by extension make something of it. In other words, offenders must believe that if they take the opportunity before them, that a positive outcome will result. Motivation to seize an opportunity for reform comes from the motivational state of the individual. If an offender encounters opposition early on in the stages of change, it is likely that they will not view certain situations as opportunities or may not put forth the effort required to modify their personal identity. Conversely, the more motivated an offender is to change, the more likely they will be to recognize and take advantage of any opportunities available to them (Rumgay, 2004). Finally, Rumgay argues that changing one's personal identity also requires changing the way in which one acts and how they are perceived in the world.

> Personal identities carry with them socially recognized behavioral routines, or "scripts" for their enactment which not only portray the actor as an individual who has a credible claim on that identity, but are accepted by onlookers as the hallmarks of its possession. (Rumgay, 2002, p. 409)

Therefore, reframing one's identity requires that offenders must engage in an alternate set of routines and behaviors that must ultimately replace old behaviors and habits if the offender is to fully desist from crime. One cannot hope to fully desist from crime by only partially adopting a new script or new way of behaving. The investment in desistance is all or nothing and must be complete if it is to have any hope of being sustainable in the long term.

Complete and total desistance from crime requires shedding old habits and lifestyles in exchange for pro-social ones on an ongoing basis (Rumgay, 2004). This is normally achieved through increased participation in conventional roles and relationships (Sommers et al., 1994). Moreover, the degree to which offenders in transition can fall back on pro-social social networks that encourage law-abiding instead of law-breaking behavior will in large part determine the extent to which they are successful (Rumgay, 2004).

Reentry Considerations

Why is desistance worth studying, and how is it relevant to a discussion of offender reentry? First, a more well-rounded understanding of why people do not commit further crime is just as important as a clear awareness of why they do. Second, if characteristics or predictors of desistance can be isolated, it seems only smart to consider these when developing criminal justice interventions. Third, a critical evaluation of differing viewpoints related to desistance can provide a more robust picture of the phenomenon; one that can influence who should be the target group for desistance intervention and when it is best to initiate such activity. For example, Ward and colleagues (1997) suggested that understanding the underlying cognitive process behind why people desist from crime may be relevant to developing cognitive behavioral programming.

Fourth, while studying between-offender change is useful and has yielded significant information about desistance (desistors v. persistors), evaluating within-offender or individual change may allow for a more nuanced understanding of how desistance works and under what circumstances, thereby influencing treatment and service provision in a community setting (Kazemian, 2007). Finally, viewing desistance as a process rather than as a finite, static event in time encourages an individual-level understanding of changes in behavior throughout the life course. As Kazemian (2007) suggests, this more detailed understanding of how desistance works could also impact the nature and type of treatment and service provision, depending on when in the life course the offender desists from crime.

Moreover, if desistance is a process and one that is intermittent in nature, additional theoretical constructs could assist scholars in studying and evaluating criminal careers and help account for the temporary nature of crime. For example, there is some support for the notion that offenders make choices to drift between law-breaking and law-abiding behavior (Piquero, 2004). If criminal careers are not linear or unidirectional, this opens up new avenues for researching the rather fluid interchange between crime cessation, instigation of criminal activity, and management of offenders in the community.

Of course, no discussion of desistance should take place without considering it from the perspective of the people who do it. Scholarship evaluating offender perceptions and thoughts about desistance reveals that people who desist from crime tend to consider some types of offending acceptable (e.g., taking drugs). Moreover, offenders who desist generally have negative attitudes about police and have friends and family members who have offended at some point (McIvor et al., 2004). Perhaps most interestingly, people who desist from crime seem to view desistance as a period of flux in which people drift into and out of crime (Piquero, 2004). Shover notes that many people who have committed crime but who wish to desist may "reduce the frequency of their offenses but continue committing crime for months or even years" (1996, p. 122).

Research further indicates that people who desist from crime agree that they grow up or grow out of the desire or need to offend, and that engaging in significant transitional events (e.g., marriage, work, having a baby, etc.) does often facilitate the desistance process (Byrne & Trew, 2008; McIvor et al., 2004). As Shover and Thompson indicate, "the probability of desistance from criminal participation increases as expectation for achieving friends, money, autonomy, and happiness via crime decrease" (1992, p. 97). Furthermore, the removal or mitigation of financial problems coupled with an increase in the number of pro-social relationships also increased the likelihood that desistance from crime would occur (Byrne & Trew, 2008).

There do seem to be some nuanced differences associated with how men and women desist from crime and how they view desistance. Overall, research suggests that women tend to desist from crime earlier than men (McIvor et al., 2004). Graham and Bowling (1995) also found that life transitions (particularly parenthood) seem to be more strongly related to desistance in women than in men. Furthermore, women seem more willing and able to disassociate themselves from anti-social peers and seek alternative, pro-social acquaintances and friends (McIvor et al., 2004). Where men and women agree that lifestyle changes are necessary in order for desistance to occur, women attribute some major life crisis to their decision to change their behavior (Sommers et al., 1994).

Interestingly, the notion of identity seems to significantly impact women's pathways away from and into crime. How women view themselves and the way in which the social world impacts them profoundly affects desistance (Byrne & Trew, 2008). The degree to which identities are changed or are changeable seems paramount to successful launch of the desistance process and positive reentry outcomes (Gadd & Farrall, 2004).

The similarities between resilience, recidivism, and desistance are hard to ignore. Each concept marries risk and outcome in its own unique way. On one end of the continuum are people who are resilient; people who often possess factors that put them at risk for committing crime, but who never do. On the opposite end of the spectrum are recidivists, or people who are at risk for committing crime, who do so, and then do so again. Desistors are those people who are at risk for committing crime, who do so, but who consciously choose not to do so again.

The research on resilience, recidivism, and desistance indicate one outcome is not predestined over another. Apparently, people possess characteristics that can and do make a difference in terms of whether and to what extent they will commit crime. Given this reality, we as scholars and practitioners are short sighted if we do not consider what those traits are and how best to manage them in ways that maximize the opportunity for a positive outcome (desistance) and mitigate the likelihood of a negative one (recidivism).

Chapter 11

Risk Management and Risk Reduction

Risk management and risk reduction are by-products of using risk factors to predict the likelihood of risk and the degree to which people may recidivate or desist from crime.

Independently, risk management and risk reduction each serve an important purpose in the offender reentry process in determining who should reenter the community (based upon an assessment of the risk offenders pose) and under what circumstances (what specific treatment and programming offenders should receive once they return). Implemented in tandem, risk management and risk reduction have the ability to change the landscape of the offender reentry process by integrating effective assessment with risk/needs-based case management and supervision, thereby resulting in reductions in recidivism.

Risk Management

The stark reality is that criminal justice practitioners have a finite number of resources whose allocation must be prioritized in some way. Unfortunately, a stagnant and/or shrinking pool of resources must be used to manage an increasing number of people under the auspices of the criminal justice system. As a result, one method of managing criminal justice resources that has gained legitimacy in recent years is risk assessment. Risk assessments are objective tools comprised of questions that determine the level of risk offenders pose based on those risk factors such as criminal history, education and employment status, attitudes about crime, etc.

Not surprisingly, practitioners have been and continue to be interested in developing and implementing the most efficient, effective, and accurate methods of assessing and determining offender risk. For example, risk assessment tools can be used in the courts to make pretrial bail and release decisions, in probation and by paroling agencies to determine levels of supervision and drive case management, in prison and jail systems to establish security levels, and by parole boards to guide release decisions. These instruments are valuable tools that can be used in the criminal justice process to affect significant results (Pew Center on the States, 2011).

Historical Context

Objective risk assessment has evolved over time. Bonta (1996) describes first-generation assessments as relying exclusively on clinical intuition and professional judgment. And while subjective judgment was once thought to be an effective method of predicting and evaluating criminal behavior, it lacks scientific validity (Grove et al., 2000; Meehl, 1954). Assessments of risk that rely solely on subjective or clinical judgments suffer from several limitations. First, human error or bias is always possible. Second, Grove and colleagues (2000) suggest that clinicians making judgments on risk have not routinely received feedback on the accuracy of their predictions, thus providing them with little opportunity to change or improve judgment habits.

First-generation methods of risk assessment have been found not only to lack validity but to be inferior to actuarial instruments (Bonta et al., 1998; Grove & Meehl, 1996; Grove et al., 2000; Mossman, 1994). In a meta-analysis (an analysis of multiple studies) conducted by Grove and colleagues in 2000, objective methods of assessment were found to be as accurate as or more accurate than clinical assessment. Despite these findings, clinical judgment and intuition have been, and in many cases continue to be, a widely accepted method to manage risk (Clear & Gallagher, 1985). Only very recently have corrections and criminal justice administrators begun to realize the efficacy, usefulness, and accuracy of objective risk assessment tools.

Where first-generation methods of assessment are subjective, second-generation methods of evaluating criminal behavior employ actuarial or objective techniques. Second-generation instruments include criteria that have been researched and validated, thus meeting the standards of scientific rigor. One such actuarial instrument is the Salient Factor Score (SFS), which was originally developed to assist in the federal parole selection process in the 1970s and 1980s and was actively utilized by the federal government until federal parole was abolished (Hoffman, 1982; 1994). The use of the SFS marked the first instance in which an objective risk assessment instrument was used in a way that resulted in a definitive, measurable impact on paroling decisions.

The SFS consists of seven items, including age at first commitment, employment, drug history, number of convictions, types of offenses, number of incarcerations, and parole history. When scoring the instrument, the higher the score, the less likely an offender is at risk for recidivism. Revisions to the SFS in the 1990s resulted in a reduction in the number of items contained in the instrument (specifically, a reduction in the number of non-criminal history or status items such as living arrangements). As a result, the SFS now weighs criminal history items most heavily (Hoffman, 1994). With the exception of drug history, the SFS includes primarily static predictors: predictors that do not change over time.

By 1994, the SFS had been administered in more than 200,000 cases, and research conducted on the validity of the assessment tool (the ability of the tool to accurately predict outcome) found empirical support for the use of the instrument. Hoffman (1994) found that SFS scores correlated with the likelihood of recidivism measured as the number of people who were rearrested or returned to prison for a parole violation. Moreover, Hoffman (1994) found that the SFS had not diminished in its predictive accuracy over time.

There are benefits and limitations to the SFS and other second-generation risk assessment instruments. The primary benefit of the SFS is that it represents a substantial improvement over clinical judgment. As one of the first objective risk instruments to be utilized by practitioners in any significant way, the SFS made clear the benefits of objective risk assessment over clinical judgment. However, a primary limitation of the SFS is that it does not adequately consider other important dynamic factors related to recidivism (Andrews & Bonta, 2003).

The hallmark of the SFS and other second-generation risk assessment instruments is that they include only static factors, something that Andrews and Bonta believe severely limits their functionality (Andrews & Bonta, 2003; Bonta, 2003). Yet despite this major limitation, second-generation assessments such as the SFS have been and continue to be useful, though not optimal, tools for classifying and managing prison and/or jail offender populations. In fact, in some instances, corrections practitioners have developed and utilized institutional and parole decision-making classification techniques predicated on the SFS model (Petersilia & Turner, 1987).

Third-generation risk prediction assessment instruments are considerably better than previous methods of assessment in a number of ways. Compared with other assessments, third-generation prediction instruments are unique because they assess static as well as dynamic risk factors. Remember that static predictors are risk factors such as age, gender, and criminal history; facts or events that cannot be changed (Andrews & Bonta, 2003). Conversely, dynamic risk factors are often discussed within the context of criminogenic needs, such as poor use of leisure time (Rogers, 1981) and companions (Thornton, 2002), which Andrews and Bonta (2006) theorize are needs that directly affect criminal behavior and are changeable over time. Scholars argue that if criminogenic needs or dynamic factors of risk are addressed, the chances of criminal involvement can be reduced. The use of both static and dynamic risk factors in the risk assessment process also allows practitioners to assess multiple confounding factors that may impact the likelihood of an offender committing a future crime while also identifying offender needs (Bonta, 1996).

One of the hallmarks of third-generation risk/needs assessment instruments is that they are grounded in theory. Specifically, Andrews and Bonta (2006) developed a psychology of criminal conduct (PCC) that seeks to understand variations in delinquency and in the criminal behavior of individuals. Andrews and Bonta's theory examines individual predictors of behavior in addition to other static correlates of crime using an amalgam of different theories from psychology, sociology, and criminology.

Psychodynamic theory suggests that criminal behavior reflects psychological immaturity, particularly weak self-control in specific situations. Grounded in the theory of Freud and research by the Gluecks (1950), the work of Hirschi (1969) and Gottfredson and Hirschi (1990) constitutes the equivalent of modern-day psychodynamic theory with a focus on weak self-control in specific situations and social control in general.

Strain theory rests on the idea that there is inequality in the distribution of societal wealth, power, and prestige. This concept has made class, level of success at school and work, feelings of alienation, and perceptions of limited opportunity, in combination with the desire for conventional success, routine considerations when attempting to address offender risk (Merton, 1938).

Differential association is yet another theory upon which third-generation assessments is based. Sutherland's differential association theory emphasizes the belief that ideas and behaviors that support and encourage law violation can be learned (Sutherland, 1939). Additional work by Burgess and Akers reformulated Sutherland's theory by introducing the idea that learning can also take place through direct interactions with the environment, independent of associations with other people (Akers, 1973; Burgess & Akers, 1966). Clearly, third-generation risk assessments improve upon past instruments by providing a more comprehensive evaluation of the factors that are associated theoretically and empirically with criminal behavior (Andrews & Bonta, 2006; Hanson & Bussiers, 1996).

Examples of third-generation risk/needs assessment tools include the Wisconsin Risk and Needs Assessment (Baird, 1981; Baird et al., 1979) and the Level of Service Inventory-Revised (Andrews, 1982). The Wisconsin Risk and Needs Assessment was created in the 1980s and consists of three components, including a risk and needs scale and a client management classification system (CMC). The CMC suggests specific types of treatment interventions depending upon offenders' needs.

The three components of the Wisconsin instrument operate independently of each other. However, some overlap does exist between the risk and needs scales in that an offender is assigned to a level of supervision depending upon the scale in which he/she receives the highest score. One limitation of the Wisconsin instrument is that the needs scale was developed without taking into account the fact that offender needs can also be potential risk factors. Consequently, dynamic factors such as peer relationships, education, and employment readiness are not adequately assessed (Andrews & Bonta, 2006).

Results from empirical studies evaluating the Wisconsin assessment found that the instrument predicted whether or not people recidivated (Baird, 1981; Bonta et al., 1994), although other results indicate that the instrument had only marginal predictive validity (Ashford & LeCroy, 1988; Bonta et al., 1994). Unfortunately, these studies were only conducted on the risk scale. There is no research linking the needs scale to outcome, suggesting that the relationship between static and dynamic factors and the risk and needs scale was not adequately considered when the instrument was developed.

The Level of Service Inventory-Revised (LSI-R) is perhaps the most well-known third-generation risk management tool. The LSI-R is comprised of 54 questions and 10 subcategories and has been utilized as a risk/needs management tool in a multitude of criminal justice populations (Multi-Health Systems, 1995, 1999). Each item in the LSI-R is scored using a score of "0" or "1," with the LSI-R total score equivalent to the sum of all of the scored items. The items in the LSI-R are sub-divided as follows (with the number of items scored within each subgroup identified in parentheses):

Criminal History (10)	Leisure/Recreation (2)
Education/Employment (10)	Companions (5)
Financial (2)	Alcohol/Drug Problems (9)
Family/Marital (4)	Emotional/Personal (5)
Accommodation (3)	Attitudes/Orientation (4)

Once LSI-R scores are tallied, the raw score is plotted on a risk scale ranging from 0–54. As the raw score increases so too does the likelihood of risk and the degree of offender need. In most cases, particular risk/need categories are developed that correlate with recidivism. Offenders with LSI-R scores who are least likely to recidivate are placed in a low-risk category. Offenders who recidivate most are placed in a high-risk category. From a risk management perspective, low risk/need offenders require minimal intervention while offenders in the high-risk/need category demand more intense supervision and management.

Research on the validity of the LSI-R is overwhelmingly consistent. A multitude of studies have found the instrument to be a valid predictor of recidivism. In fact, research on the LSI-R has demonstrated validity among specialized offender types (Girard & Wormith, 2004; Hollin & Palmer, 2003; Manchak et al., 2008; Simourd, 2004; Simourd & Malcom, 1998), ethnic and cultural offender sub-groups (Holsinger et al., 2006; Lowenkamp et al., 2001; Schlager & Simourd, 2007), and women (Fass et al., 2008; Holsinger et al., 2003; Vose et al., 2009).

Current Trends

Recently, scholars have intensified a simmering debate regarding the applicability of currently available risk/needs assessment instruments to female offender populations out of concern that the assessments currently in use have not been "normed" on a female offender population (Hardyman & Van Voorhis, 2004). Moreover, some scholars contend that current instruments may not be sensitive to gender-specific needs given that they were developed using male offender populations (McShane et al., 2002).

Truth be told, most risk assessments were developed using male offender populations because until relatively recently, the number of female offenders in prison or on probation or parole was relatively small. Most of the literature on women and their experiences in the criminal justice system traditionally suffered from small sample sizes and lack of generalizability (Braithwaite et al., 2005; Jiang & Winfree, 2006). The fact that the number of women under state or federal correctional control now approaches 7% and 13% of jail populations changes the research dynamic considerably (Carson, 2022; Zeng, 2020). Now more than ever there is an impetus (and data) to produce studies that are more representative of women and their experiences in the criminal justice system (Bloom et al., 2003).

It is only within the last 10 years or so that scholars have addressed the relevance of current risk/needs assessment instruments and gender. While some scholars argue that current risk assessment instruments outright ignore gender-specific components of female offending (Blanchette & Brown, 2006; Reisig et al., 2006) others insist that current assessment instruments account for variations in offending by gender (Andrews & Bonta, 2003). Still other scholars wonder whether men and women possess some criminogenic needs that are similar and some criminogenic needs that may be gender specific (Blanchette, 2002). While criminal history, antisocial peers, lack of employment, and the nature of family relationships have been determined to be important predictors of offending for both males and females, other factors such as prior victimization and drug abuse may be particularly relevant in predicting offending in women (Van Voorhis & Presser, 2001).

Ultimately, arguments about the efficacy of currently available risk/needs assessment instruments and gender are governed by a belief that male and female criminality cannot be explained in the same way (Belknap, 2001; Chesney-Lind, 1989). Researchers point to the fact that current risk assessment instruments do not adequately address issues related to relationships, depression, parental concerns, self-esteem, trauma, and victimization to bolster their position (Blanchette, 2004; Blanchette & Brown, 2006; Bloom et al., 2003; Hardyman & Van Voorhis, 2004; Reisig et al., 2006; Van Voorhis & Presser, 2001). And naturally, if risk/needs assessments are not sensitive to gender, these tools may not be useful in predicting and/or managing risk for women (Hollin & Palmer, 2006).

The existing risk/needs instrument upon which most gendered evaluation has been conducted is the LSI-R. This is primarily because this instrument is used in an overwhelming majority of correctional jurisdictions (Lowencamp et al., 2009). However, scholars challenge the use of the LSI-R on gendered populations for a multitude of reasons. Researchers question whether or not the theoretical underpinnings of the instrument (social learning theory and cognitive psychology) adequately take into account gendered behavior (Morash, 2009). Moreover, others are convinced that the LSI-R does not properly account for gendered pathways or the economic and societal factors that marginalize women (Taylor & Blanchette, 2009).

Despite these concerns, support for the use of the LSI-R in female offender populations does exist. The first study that assessed the validity of the LSI-R on a female offender population found that the instrument was predictive of recidivism for women one year after release from prison (Coulson et al., 1996). A meta-analysis of 11 studies on the LSI-R further indicates that the instrument predicts extreme recidivistic outcomes between men and women (Holtfreter & Cupp, 2007). A 2008 study comparing recidivism rates of men and women using the LSI-R in New Jersey found a significant "overlap" between the risks and needs of male and female offenders (Heilbrun et al., 2008). A meta-analysis of 25 published and unpublished studies indicates that the predictive validity of the LSI-R was similar for males and females (Smith et al., 2009).

While studies have supported the predictive validity of the LSI-R for males and females, Van Voorhis and colleagues reported the addition of a gender-responsive supplement, the Women's Risk Need Assessment (WRNA), improved its predictive validity, suggesting the instrument may be ignoring factors relevant to the classification of women (Van Voorhis et al., 2010). Moreover, the addition of specific variables recommended different treatment priorities for women. Follow-up studies confirmed the contribution of the WRNA among prison, probation, and pre-release populations (Van Voorhis et al., 2012, 2013a, 2013b).

Attempts to mediate the lack of gender-specificity in risk/needs assessment instruments have been addressed in three ways. In some cases, jurisdictions have done nothing. This inaction has resulted in the use of a single risk/needs assessment instrument to all offenders, regardless of gender. The second course of action has been for some jurisdictions to modify currently existing instruments to include gender-specific risk/need factors by adding and deleting items and developing different risk categories for men and women (Blanchette & Brown, 2006). The third method of addressing the issue of gender-specific risk/needs assessment instruments has involved the development of new gender-specific instruments using only samples of women.

In addition to advances in gendered risk assessment, within the last several years, fourth-generation risk/needs assessment instruments have been developed. These instruments combine the best attributes of third-generation instruments (a foundation in criminologic theory, an emphasis on static and dynamic factors, etc.) with case management tools that marry the principles of effective intervention (discussed later in this chapter) with risk and need (Andrews et al., 2006). These newest instruments also attempt to address the limitations of previous instruments, including the lack of gender sensitivity of third-generation instruments as well as the failure of third-generation instruments to assess offender strengths or protective factors (Brennan et al., 2009). These assessment tools also allow for seamless integration of the risk and needs information with criminal justice agency operations and data management systems (Brennan et al., 2009). Examples of fourth-generation risk/needs assessment tools include the Correctional Assessment and Intervention System (CAIS) and the Level of Service/Case Management Inventory LS/CMI (Brennan & Oliver, 2000; Andrews et al., 2004).

The CAIS is a broad-based actuarial tool that provides separate risk estimates for violence, recidivism, sentencing decisions, and community failure (Fass et al., 2008). In addition, the CAIS provides a needs profile of the offender that includes information regarding criminal history, criminal attitudes, and other factors such as criminal opportunity, criminal personality, and social support (Brennan & Oliver, 2000). Moreover, the CAIS includes information on offender strengths or resiliency—information that is often useful when developing individualized case plans and that has been empirically proven to reduce recidivism (Andrews et al., 2006). When reviewed in totality, the information obtained from the CAIS allows criminal justice personnel the ability to structure and manage supervision based on risk and need at a variety of points in the system.

The LS/CMI is a contemporary of the LS-R. This instrument is comprised of 43 items (rather than the 54 items from the LS-R) and assesses not only major predictors of recidivism (criminal history, education/employment, etc.), but also includes pro-criminal attitudes, integrates barriers to release, and contains a case management plan and a discharge summary (Andrews et al., 2004). This information is integrated into a case management and supervision plan that can be adjusted upwards or downwards depending on changing elements of offenders' risk and need.

As the CAIS is a relatively new instrument, data evaluating the reliability and validity of the instrument is not plentiful. However, the research that is available suggests that the instrument is able to predict general recidivism (Brennan et al., 2007; Fass et al., 2008). Data on the validity of the LS/CMI indicates that the assessment tool predicts recidivism well in men and women (Andrews et al., 2012) in addition to general and violent recidivism in women (Rettinger & Andrews, 2010). More research is needed before firm conclusions regarding the reliability and validity of these fourth-generation instruments can be drawn.

Reentry Considerations

Criminal justice practitioners deem risk management paramount because it enables them to "manage" their offender populations by triaging them into categories according to the potential risk they pose. This is done by taking the score from the risk/needs instrument and using it as a marker of possible recidivism and placement in a risk group. In theory, this makes infinite sense. An offender with a higher score poses a higher risk and therefore should be placed in a category with other offenders who present with similar scores. By extension, offenders who pose similar risks can be localized and managed in similar ways.

The more critical concern relates to how offenders are managed in the community once they are placed into specific risk categories. Theoretically, offenders who pose a high risk to the community should be managed differently than those who pose a low risk to the community. This only makes sense. Why would we provide the same level and intensity of service to everyone when assessments indicate that risk management should differ by risk category? This seems like an ineffective and inefficient allocation of resources. And it is. This is why risk management cannot work in a vacuum and why risk reduction is a necessary adjunct to any risk management technique employed.

Risk Reduction

As noted above, assessment tools are particularly valuable because these instruments not only allow practitioners to classify offenders into risk categories based upon potential risk (risk management), but they also highlight offender needs in a variety of substantive treatment and program areas that can, with mediation, result in reductions in risk and recidivism (risk reduction). Put another way, where risk management is the act of categorizing or classifying offenders according to the risk that they pose, risk reduction targets specific risk factors and uses treatment and programming to decrease the overall probability that offenders will commit a new offense in the future.

Targeting offender needs and addressing them is difficult. In prisons, there is no question that treatment and program constraints have often resulted in offenders not receiving the services they require. Specifically, the scarcity of correctional program resources makes appropriate treatment assignment difficult. Moreover, significant cuts to institutional and community corrections budgets make the prioritization of services even more problematic. However, arguably the most difficult barrier to overcome is the contention that offender programming and treatment—whether in the institution or in the community—does not work.

Historical Context

In the 1950s and 1960s, offender treatment and programming, especially in correctional institutions, consisted of one-on-one clinical intervention. Unfortunately, little research was conducted to quantify or evaluate treatment provision and program outcome (Bailey, 1966; Kirby, 1954). By the mid-1970s, questions regarding the efficacy of institutional treatment and programming began to increase. In an effort to address these concerns, Robert Martinson and colleagues (1974) conducted a meta-analysis that evaluated 231 studies on correctional programming—research that would forever change the way practitioners and researchers alike would view correctional treatment and programming. The analysis was stunning. The study concluded that the majority of correctional programs did not work. Martinson reported that treatment programs were not effective and that corrections agencies were better off focusing on other types of interventions (Lipton et al., 1975; Martinson, 1974, 1979).

Response to this research was swift and vocal. Critics of the research argued that the negative conclusions regarding the effectiveness of correctional treatment were accepted virtually without question and that Martinson and his colleagues had provided a biased review of studies that were supportive of treatment. Conversely, others suggested that no criticism was leveled against studies that were critical of treatment (Andrews & Bonta, 2006).

One of the most damaging aspects of the research study was that Martinson did not account for the lack of reliability of the measurement tools used to assess treatment outcomes. Martinson assumed *a priori* that poor instrument reliability led to the invalid finding of positive treatment effects rather than considering that poor measurement tools might be an underlying reason why positive effects of treatment were not observed (Andrews & Bonta, 2006; Lipton et al., 1975; Martinson, 1974).

Scholars quickly came to the defense of correctional programming, writing a flurry of reports that attempted to contradict Martinson and his conclusions (Palmer, 1975). Ultimately, in 1979, Martinson recanted much of his 1974 article and conceded that while some treatment programs did not work, others clearly did (Martinson, 1979). Unfortunately, the damage had already been done. By the time Martinson's retraction to the original research was issued, many had already come to embrace the idea that "nothing works." As a result, the winds shifted and practitioners became far more invested in tools that would help manage risk to the exclusion of programs and treatment that would help mitigate it.

Since Martinson's initial article in 1974, scholars have been on the defensive, feeling compelled to continually justify the need for and veracity of correctional treatment and programming (Cullen & Gilbert, 1982; Ross & Gendreau, 1980; Travis & Cullen, 1984). Those fighting this battle argue that "nothing works" scholarship is predicated on the idea of knowledge destruction: the premise that researchers have been taught to focus on what does not work in correctional programming as opposed to what does work (Cullen & Gendreau, 2001). Furthermore, Cullen and Gendreau (2001) contend that knowledge destruction has inhibited scholars and practitioners from developing correctional treatment and programs that move beyond basic risk management. As a consequence, this practice has resulted in the perpetuation of research that supports the "nothing works" position and programming that is not effective.

Current Trends

The most sustained attack against nothing works has come from outside the field of traditional criminology. Clinical psychologists primarily from Canada have led the charge in developing, implementing, and evaluating correctional treatment and programming causing some proponents of nothing works to reconsider their position on the efficacy of correctional treatment interventions. Much of the research that has served to turn the tide in support of correctional programs has focused on individual differences among offenders in prison or community correctional settings. As a result of this research, scholars have developed principles of effective intervention that when followed have resulted in meaningful reductions in recidivism (Cullen & Gendreau, 2001).

The principles for effective intervention include the principles of risk, need, and responsivity (RNR) and are derived from meta-analyses that evaluated the effectiveness of correctional treatment and assessed which specific aspects were effective (Andrews, Zinger, et al., 1990; Andrews, Bonta et al., 1990). These principles have been the mainstay of effective correctional intervention since the 1990s, and programs that have implemented these principles into their operation have yielded significant reductions in recidivism compared with those programs that have not included the principles of RNR (Andrews & Bonta, 2010; Andrews et al., 2011). Research indicates that programs that incorporate the principles of RNR in their content and function can realize between 26% to 30% reductions in recidivism (Andrews et al., 1990).

Risk Principle

There are two components of the risk principle. The first premise of the risk principle is that criminal behavior can be predicted. The second facet of the risk principle is that offenders who are matched to levels of treatment service by risk will derive maximum treatment effect. High-risk offenders require more intense service and will do better (i.e., recidivate less) if they receive services commensurate with their risk level than low-risk offenders. Consequently, low-risk offenders pose little or no risk and therefore require little or no intervention (Andrews & Bonta, 2006;

Andrews & Friesen, 1987; Andrews & Kiessling, 1980; Baird et al., 1979; O'Donnell et al., 1971).

Unfortunately, most practitioners do not subscribe to this method of program placement. Many practitioners provide the same level of service to low-risk as well as high-risk offenders because they believe that all offenders must receive the same level of service. Furthermore, some personnel believe that low-risk offenders are easier to manage and therefore should receive more services than high-risk offenders.

These misconceptions can have significant adverse treatment effects. Not only does the research contend that high-risk offenders do better (i.e., recidivate less) than low-risk offenders when they are provided access to treatment modalities, scholars have found that when treatment is matched to the risk level of the offender, reductions in recidivism are likely. High-risk offenders who receive a high level of service and low-risk offenders who receive little or no intervention will be more successful than offenders who receive services that are not in keeping with the risk that they pose. Moreover, research indicates that when intensive services were provided to low-risk offenders, these services either had a minimal or negative effects on recidivism (Andrews & Kiessling, 1980; Baird et al., 1979; Bonta et al., 2000; O'Donnell et al., 1971).

Need Principle

The need principle suggests that offenders, especially high-risk offenders, have a variety of criminogenic needs. Criminogenic needs such as education, employment training, and peer influences are important because they represent the subset of an offender's risk level that can be changed. Criminogenic needs are dynamic risk factors that, when addressed through treatment and programming, are associated with reductions in recidivism. Consequently, it only makes sense to target risk factors of offenders that can reduce recidivism through appropriate treatment and service provision.

One criminogenic need that is widely supported is criminal attitudes. Since criminal behavior cannot always be observed, the best surrogate for reducing criminal behavior is changing overall behavior as well as an offender's interpretation and reaction to issues or circumstances (Andrews & Bonta, 2006; Andrews & Wormith, 1984). Research on pro-criminal attitudes has repeatedly shown significant associations with criminal behavior among adult criminals (Andrews et al., 1985; Simourd, 1997;

Simourd & Oliver, 2002). That is, the more present criminal attitudes are, the more likely a person will be to offend. Therefore, if program and interventions can be designed to address the specific criminogenic needs of offenders, better program and recidivistic outcomes will result (Andrews et al., 2001).

Responsivity Principle

Finally, the responsivity principle emphasizes the need to develop and deliver programs that fit the specific needs, abilities, and learning styles of offenders. Offenders (like the rest of us) respond better to programming that caters to their learning style. Characteristics such as interpersonal sensitivity, anxiety, verbal intelligence, and cognitive maturity can significantly influence how well anyone performs in treatment and may affect the degree to which people are receptive to different treatment modalities and styles of service. In fact, by identifying personality and cognitive styles, treatment programs can be developed and provided to better match the needs of an individual client.

Despite broad-based support for the efficacy of RNR, some scholars dispute the notion that the principles of effective intervention equate to women as they do men. This argument is rooted in the idea that the risk principle is predicated on male-dominated notions of what risk is and the variables used to predict it (Bloom, 2000; Reisig et al., 2006). Therefore, if assessments of risk are superimposed on female offender populations, the outcome will be an increased number of misclassified female offenders, resulting in erroneous calculations of risk and assessments of need (Van Voorhis & Presser, 2001; Reisig et al., 2006). Yet, a study by Lovins and colleagues (2007) found that the risk principle did apply to a sample of female offenders in residential treatment. Women found to be high risk showed a lower probability of being rearrested compared with low-risk women who were exposed to the same treatment modality.

Disdain for application of the needs principle to women focuses on the belief that criminogenic needs for men and women differ and that the full panoply of needs of female offenders are not taken into consideration (Belknap & Holsinger, 2006; Blanchette, 2002; Blanchette & Brown, 2006). Not only are women's needs different but the way in which these needs are experienced impacts recidivistic outcomes for women (Hannah-Moffat, 2009). Perhaps, as several scholars suggest, gender is a responsivity issue only. That is, treatment and programs for men and women should be similar in their inclusion of traditional principles of risk and need but that treatment and program delivery should vary by gender (Andrews & Bonta, 2006; Smith et al., 2009; Blanchette & Brown, 2006).

Results from a number of studies show differential effects on outcome depending on the type of treatment provided and the characteristics of the client. Client characteristics have ranged from anxious to amenable (i.e., verbal, anxious, and motivated) and treatment styles have ranged from the psychodynamic to the medical (e.g., drug therapy) (Andrews & Bonta, 2006; Losel, 1995). In fact, treatment and programming that emphasizes behavioral/social learning/cognitive behavioral strategies are the most successful types of programs for male and female offenders alike (Andrews & Bonta, 2006; VanVoorhis, 1988).

Cognitive behavioral therapy (CBT) evolved from experimental psychology and is a combination of social learning theory, cognitive, and behavioral therapy. Practitioners who utilize CBT argue that problems are an outgrowth of erroneous learning, incorrect assumptions made from inadequate information, and the inability of some people to be able to distinguish between fact and fiction (Freeman & Dattilio, 1992). Proponents of CBT contend that when cognitive change (i.e., changes in the way people think through issues or situations) takes place, changes in behavior will follow. In turn, positive behavioral changes will reinforce and promote further changes in thought patterns and encourage pro-social decision-making (Hansen, 2008).

CBT has been found to be particularly useful in the field of corrections precisely because offenders tend to present with significant distortions in cognition—impairments that severely limit their ability to reason, accept blame, and interpret social cues (Hansen, 2008; Lipsey et al., 2007). In offender populations, CBT is useful in assisting offenders with learning techniques and strategies to alter their thinking patterns and behavior so that they are able to act and react to problems or issues in socially acceptable and law-abiding ways (Pearson et al., 2002).

Recent research indicates that while specific programs that utilize CBT are available, it is less a function of whether a particular program is effective than program implementation that matters. Programs that properly incorporated CBT into their program practice were most likely to have the greatest positive effect on reducing recidivism (Landenberger & Lipsey, 2005). Programs with low program integrity and that did not implement CBT fully were less likely to be effective than programs that had high program integrity. Moreover, CBT programs that target high-risk offenders tend to be more effective (Landenberger & Lipsey, 2005).

Researchers also have evidence to support the belief that programs that build their foundation on RNR are more effective than those that don't, but that the best programs will be ineffective if program implementation is not successful and program integrity is low (Andrews & Bonta, 2006; Dowden & Andrews, 2004). In fact, a meta-analysis found that poor staff acuity and low program integrity were in large part responsible for poor program outcomes (Andrews & Bonta, 2006; Dowden & Andrews, 2004).

Reentry Considerations

Despite the apparent usefulness of risk/needs instruments as catalysts for proper risk management and risk reduction, the adoption of these tools has not been wholly embraced (Boothby & Clements, 2000). In the context of offender reentry, these tools could provide critical information that maximize effective risk management and risk reduction. Not only could an assessment instrument evaluate the risk a reentering offender might pose and provide insight on how best to manage that offender in the community, the instrument could also identify specific offender needs that could be mediated through appropriate case management and supervision in an effort to enhance the likelihood of successful reintegration.

There are a multitude of reasons for the rather lukewarm acceptance of assessments as critical components in offender reentry. Some scholars have rebuffed the use of these instruments on structural and organizational grounds. Some practitioners continue to embrace the notion that subjective assessment is best or feel insulted that agency management does not trust their ability to make decisions regarding their caseload (Schlager, 2009; Schneider et al., 1996). Staff must believe in an instrument they are using and must demonstrate confidence in the risk assessment process if credible assessments are to take place (Austin, 2006). Lack of trust and belief in the instrument and the process will manifest itself in inaccurate assessment results and ultimately poor recidivistic outcomes (Austin, 2006).

Moreover, a reliance on traditional methods of classification and the tendency by personnel to reject out-of-hand something new simply because it contradicts the way they have always done it, may be responsible for an unwillingness to employ risk assessments in a comprehensive way. No doubt, the use of actuarial risk/needs assessments in offender reentry represents a significant paradigm shift. Merely telling officers that they have to use a new instrument and change the way they supervise will not make it happen and surely will not ensure that it happens correctly.

The practitioners using these instruments have relied on subjective clinical judgment or lesser-evolved instruments for some time. They may not be amenable to change and may actively attempt to thwart it (Schlager, 2009). Furthermore, fear of loss of control over caseload management and diminished discretion often drives the extent to which actuarial assessments are embraced by practitioners and may result in the sabotage of the results of the instrument in a desperate attempt to preserve the status quo (Austin, 2006).

Practitioners may also be reluctant to embrace the use of risk assessment instruments because they feel that the instruments have not been scientifically proven. The level of distrust among practitioners regarding evidence-based practice (i.e., practice that is grounded in research) is significant. Much of this distrust is driven by a lack of knowledge of the value of science as a means to guide practice, as well as unwillingness by practitioners to admit that they may not always be right. For example, despite research that indicates that clinical assessment is not as effective as actuarial assessment, practitioners still cling to the idea that they know best (Harris, 2006).

Still others that are concerned about the use of risk/needs assessment in offender reentry note that staff that utilizes these instruments is not always qualified and that assessor characteristics likely impact assessment process and practice (Austin, 2006; Byrne & Pattavina, 2006). Moreover, a majority of practitioners have indicated that they believe that the time required to complete these instruments is prohibitive and that the questions are often confusing for the correctional population (Farabee et al., 2011). Furthermore, because assessment instruments are often implemented without validation on the population on which it is being used, there is no way to know with any certainty whether the instrument is properly scoring people as at-risk or not (Byrne & Pattavina, 2006; Whiteacre, 2006).

Ultimately, it may be the implementation process that most severely restricts or co-opts the use of risk/needs instruments in the offender reentry process. Even best intentions may fall short if agencies are not fully invested in the idea that risk/needs assessment should be part of the case management and supervision of offenders leaving prison and returning to the community (Schlager, 2009). Lack of leadership, poor professionalism, a lack of commitment to evidence-based practice, and muddled communication are all issues that can spell the premature end of even the most well-intentioned assessment implementation plan. When one considers the public safety repercussions associated with improper or inadequate risk/needs assessment (e.g., mis-scoring an assessment and releasing the wrong person from prison), implementation becomes all the more concerning (Schlager, 2008, 2009).

Unfortunately, some practitioners have not recognized the full potential of the assessment instruments they so vociferously reject. They seem to appreciate the benefit of assigning risk but don't necessarily recognize how addressing risk factors through treatment and programming impacts recidivistic outcome. Sadly, efforts to marry risk management and risk reduction are not routine or well understood (Schlager & Pacheco, 2011). Practitioners seem unable (or unwilling) to implement policies and practices that tie risk scores (risk management) to case management and supervision plans (risk reduction) (Schlager, 2009; Taxman, 2006).

Yet for some time, scholars have been lobbying for risk/needs instruments to serve not only as assessors of risk but to be used to promote the principles of RNR by linking treatment and program placement to need and learning styles (Andrews & Bonta, 2006; Grove & Meehl, 1996; Hoge, 1999; Taxman et al., 2007). In fact, research has determined that

> the value of risk tools is that they assist program administrators to identify offenders that are likely to be prone to criminal conduct and have a greater need for treatment services, permitting—in the latter instance—the efficient use of scarce treatment resources. (Taxman et al., 2007, p. 1230)

Given the significant gap that exists between offender treatment and program need and treatment and program capacity, one would think that efficient and effective use of these resources to target those most at risk and most in need would take place. This practice is even supported by research that found that case plans that address dynamic factors or criminogenic needs have been empirically proven to reduce recidivism up to 10% (Andrews & Bonta, 2006; Lipsey, 1995; Losel, 1995). Still another study evaluating changes in risk/needs scores over time determined that criminogenic needs that were addressed through case planning resulted in reductions in risk scores (Schlager & Pacheco, 2011).

Interestingly, some scholars argue that the adoption of risk/needs assessment instruments has signaled a shift in jurisprudence away from ideologies that support individualized treatment and rehabilitation to support for policies and practices that encourage the categorization of people into groups based solely on the system's ability to manage offender populations in an efficient way (Feeley & Simon, 1992). Ironically, it appears that the quest to create assessment tools to better assist in risk management and risk reduction through the use of the principles of effective intervention has resulted in a mindset that supports reliance on efficient risk management to the exclusion and desire (not to mention need) for programming that emphasizes risk reduction. Assuredly, policy and practice that promotes the primacy of risk management over risk reduction will result in poor outcomes. The people who do the job of assessment, case management, and supervision must come to this understanding if offenders reentering the community from prison are to have a fighting chance at success.

Chapter 12

Stigma and Public Opinion

While practitioners may routinely contextualize offenders within the framework of risk, other constructs such as stigma and public opinion significantly impact how we view offender reentry. Stigma is of paramount concern when thinking about offender reentry if only because scholars are unsure about the role it plays in the reentry process and the ways in which offenders manage it. In fact, public opinion regarding offender reentry is responsible, to a large extent, for creating an environment in which stigmatization is encouraged. The public's attitudes and perceptions of offenders and crime and criminality often form the basis for thoughts, actions, and ideas that promote stigma. If minimizing barriers and impediments to offender reentry is a goal to which we aspire, we must consider the extent to which stigma can limit reentry opportunities and how public opinion may aid in reinforcing stereotypes that promote it.

Stigma

One's status as an offender is not immediately apparent. Unlike someone who may demonstrate visible signs of behavior or characteristics that outwardly stigmatize them (e.g., an amputee), there is no visible sign that someone is an offender. If we (society) are not told or if we do not find out in some other way, it is unlikely that we will be able to differentiate between who is an offender and who is not (Lee & Craft, 2002). It is only when one's status as an offender is officially acknowledged (e.g., sex offender notification laws, prison identification cards, background checks, etc.) that the proverbial cat is let out of the bag (Harding, 2003).

Once one's offender status is formally recognized by society, the label of "offender" is almost always applied. Not surprisingly, the resulting label carries with it significant meaning to society and mostly negative consequences for the person to whom it is attached. Often just hearing the word offender engenders negative feelings and preconceived notions—some accurate, most not. Assigning the label offender to an individual can be potentially crippling as it may trigger the placement of additional obstacles to reentry that can ultimately prove to be detrimental to both the offender and society (Harding, 2003; LeBel, 2008).

Stigma can take many shapes. It can present itself when an offender applies for a job, is qualified, but is not hired because he has a criminal record. Stigma can impact access to job skills training, occupational licensing, where offenders are allowed to live, with whom offenders are allowed to associate, and whether they are allowed to vote or hold public office. But it doesn't stop there. The stigma associated with being assigned the label offender impacts not only the individual offender, but close friends and family as well. Family and friends of offenders may find themselves ostracized from the community and estranged from each other (Clear et al., 2001; Pager, 2003; Petersilia, 2003; Travis, 2005). Ultimately, stigma can and does impact how offenders view themselves and how others view them.

Historical Context

Labeling theory, the theory that undergirds much of the work on stigma, finds its genesis in symbolic interactionism; a concept that suggests that words have meanings and that these meanings conjure up specific images. For example, the terms "nerd" or "bookworm" elicit images that influence our interpretation of what we think about and how we view the people to whom these labels are applied. Early labeling theory argues that acts of deviance are generally transitory in nature unless and until they are labeled as such. Only once an official label of deviant is applied to a behavior is the behavior officially recognized (Tannenbaum, 1938).

Tannenbaum (1938) suggests that labels are self-fulfilling prophecies. Once a person is labeled as deviant, changes to self-perception and identity occur. These changes result in a person acting out the role of criminal and continually engaging in deviant/criminal behavior. Over time, the person begins to organize his identities and self-concept around deviance/the criminal act labeled as deviant.

Lemert (1951) expanded Tannenbaum's concept of labeling to suggest that perceptions of self can change over time and do so based upon assigned labels. Lemert argues that the initial assignment of the label is of less importance than the reaction by society to the label. Stigmatization occurs, suggests Lemert (1951), when individuals try to defend themselves against negative social reactions to assigned labels. Importantly, labeling doesn't cause deviance in Lemert's view. Instead, deviant/criminal behavior that continues long after the assignment of the deviant label is a result of a decision by labeled individuals who determine that it is easier to be deviant than it is to fight society's perceptions of their behavior (Lemert, 1951). It is the reaction of other people to criminal acts and the subsequent effects of those reactions on the person who is labeled that encourage or perpetuate deviance.

Perhaps Erving Goffman's seminal work on stigma best sums up the relationship between labeling and stigma. Goffman (1963) notes that stigma often develops as part of a process by which the reactions of others create a "spoiled identity." So, where labeling is the act of attaching a word with symbolic meaning to an individual (e.g., offender), stigma is a resulting action (e.g., loss of right to vote).

Recently, labeling theory was modified to argue that stereotypes exist and that they are pervasive in everyday life. In essence, modified labeling theory (MLT) represents the gray area between primary deviance as defined by Tannenbaum and secondary deviance as promoted by Lemert. MLT suggests that in attempts to deal with being labeled, people adopt strategies to manage the label or stigma attached to the label they have been assigned (Link et al., 1989). As detailed by Winnick and Bodkin (2008), these strategies of stigma management include hiding (e.g., keeping the crime a secret), avoidance (e.g., withdrawing from social life so as not to draw attention to them or the crime), and education (e.g., telling people the truth about a conviction before they ask).

Not surprisingly, each of the above-mentioned methods of stigma management has limitations. For example, preventative telling or keeping a secret may ensure getting a job in the short term, but an offender will likely not keep the job in the long term; someone always finds out the secret. Likewise, avoidance or techniques of withdrawal can certainly help keep the secret but the offender gains no access to valuable relationships and opportunities that will help them successfully reintegrate in the long term. Finally, while proactively telling people about one's criminal record is a noble strategy, it is not likely to have the desired effect. Preconceived notions of who and what offenders are will likely seriously impede the public's ability to see past deviant acts to the point that they are willing to assist. Ironically, while these strategies attempt to mediate stigma, they often result in further deviance/criminal behavior on the part of the labeled precisely because, while well-intended, they have the opposite effect (Winnick & Bodkin, 2009).

Current Trends

The moniker offender or "ex-con" has serious consequences for those to whom it is assigned. In many cases, the negative connotations associated with these labels result in a self-fulfilling prophecy wherein many returning offenders are not able to successfully return to the community after having served time in prison. Unfortunately, while there is research to suggest that success may be fleeting for most offenders returning from prison to the community due to the application of negative labels, and that success is even more elusive for people of color (Hagan & Dinovitzer, 1999).

People of color and who are offenders are doubly labeled. They are at once offender and "black" or "Hispanic." Along with the label comes the stereotype. Preconceived notions or stereotypes usually drive the assignment of labels by some to others. These ideas come from the development of mental constructs that allow people to process new and different information by creating comparisons to ideas or things they already know; it allows a person to draw conclusions about new experiences based on experiences that are familiar (Hirschfield & Piquero, 2010). So, how we know what we know matters.

Information that the general public has about criminal justice is usually limited to what they hear on the 10 o'clock news or what they read in the local newspaper. The public tends to demonize offenders, viewing them as, "dangerous, dishonest, or otherwise disreputable" (Hirschfield & Piquero, 2010, p. 28). The internet has only increased the breadth and depth of information and the speed with which information is available. Information about criminal justice is generally reserved for talking about the bad; rape, murder, and mayhem. And who is usually broadcast as the bad guy? A person of color.

Most offenders are people of color because of the disproportionate number of minorities in the justice system. At last count, black and Hispanics represented 31.6% of the general population of the United States and 55% of men and women sentenced to state or federal prisons in 2019, 42% of probationers, and 53% of parolees in 2017. Black men are imprisoned at a rate approximately six times greater than white men and more than two times greater than Hispanic men (Carson, 2020; Kaeble & Alper, 2020; United States Census Bureau, 2019). Knowing nothing else, people might (and do) assume that because so many people of color are criminal justice involved that they must commit more crime than their white counterparts. Of course, this conclusion is erroneous and short-sighted because it does not take into consideration different policing, prosecutorial, or correctional practices that do not always provide people of color with the same benefits of social status as white people (Mauer, 2011; Thompson, 2008). Sadly, people tend to fall back on stereotypes perpetuated by half-truths and media hype because they are generally easier to believe than the alternative.

Reentry Considerations

How and to what extent offenders in the community are able to manage the stigma of being labeled an offender is the focus of much recent research. Work By Winnick and Bodkin (2008) indicates that offenders fully anticipate rejection as a primary reaction to their return to the community. They seem acutely aware that they will be viewed and treated differently than others, that their abilities and person will be devalued, and that they will be perceived as being failures and outcasts. Therefore, it is not surprising that offenders often utilize preventative telling (i.e., keeping the secret) as their primary means of managing stigma (Winnick & Bodkin, 2008).

Interestingly, while the label offender is applied often, negative stigma is not always the universal response. In some instances, the label offender is viewed as a badge of honor, rather than the scarlet letter. In neighborhoods where significant concentrations of people who have been incarcerated and who have returned home reside, perceptions of offenders are usually different. The normalization thesis contends that the stigma associated with incarceration is sometimes blunted in places where imprisonment is commonplace (Fagan & Meares, 2008; Nagin, 1998).

In these instances, offenders do not face rebuke or reproach from the community, but are often welcomed home. Some scholars have even determined that in severely impoverished and resource-deprived neighborhoods where the cycling of offenders in and out of the community to and from prison occurs routinely, incarceration is perceived as a normal and expected life experience; a rite of passage (Anderson, 1999; Shakur,

2004). It is not a stretch to conclude that in neighborhoods such as the ones described above, residents have a familiarity with the criminal justice system, incarceration, and reentry that members of other communities do not likely possess. Therefore, it is understandable that people with personal knowledge or understanding of the criminal justice system or individuals who have been incarcerated may refrain from or minimize the application of negative labels, stereotypes, and stigma to those with whom they may be able to identify (Hirschfield & Piquero, 2010).

Where the normalization thesis is often used to explain differences in tolerance for offenders in the community, so too is the legitimation thesis. This theory argues that minority groups and others who have developed a strong distrust in the function and operation of the criminal justice system often are more tolerant of law-breaking behavior and less likely to assign negative labels that promote stigma (Garfinkel, 1956). Results from a recent study indicate that this thesis has merit. In a study by Hirschfield and Piquero (2010) that studied the normalization and legitimation theses, data show that because African Americans often know more people who have offended and tend to have less confidence in the criminal justice system, they are less likely to negatively label and stigmatize offenders. This finding was apparent for both offenders who knew or were related to other offenders and victims of crime as well.

Work by Winnick and Bodkin (2009) further evaluates the credibility of these ideas by exploring whether race differences exist in perceptions of stigmatization and whether or not black individuals are less likely than white individuals to hide their status as ex-offenders upon release. Results of this study found that white individuals were more apt to identify with being labeled an offender and to view themselves as deviant (Winnick & Bodkin, 2009). Conversely, African Americans were less likely to attach formal labels to behavior, providing support for both the normalization and legitimation theses (Winnick & Bodkin, 2009).

Other scholarship contradicts these findings. This research indicates that not only do offenders anticipate positive reintegration rather than stigmatization, but they believe that they will be able to adjust well to the outside world and that there will be a support network to assist them (Benson et al., 2011). This finding is grounded in the notion that offenders do not reenter society in a vacuum; that they have informal supports available to them that are likely much more effective in helping them achieve positive reentry outcomes than formal agencies and organizations (Benson et al., 2011). Consequently, stigmatization may not necessarily preclude reintegration but may be dependent on a variety of factors including informal social supports, the willingness of offenders to take responsibility for their actions, and the offender's experience in the system and with the sanction or punishment they received (Benson et al., 2011).

While consensus regarding the impact of stigmatization on offenders is conflicting, the body of scholarship does suggest that offenders customarily rely on a variety of techniques to manage stigma. It may not matter whether offenders accept the label and internalize the stigma, develop coping mechanisms through which to mitigate it, or because of their social, racial, and/or ethnic status become normalized to it. At the end of the day, it is apparent that reentering offenders must be prepared to employ multiple strategies to manage and/or mitigate stigma while recognizing that use of these techniques will result in uncertain outcomes.

Public Opinion

Offender reentry occurs on a daily basis in towns and cities across the nation. Of this we can be certain. On any given day, people are released from prison and (in most cases) choose to return to the communities from whence they came. While some towns and cities may be the recipient of more returning offenders than others, offenders are released from prison daily and venture forth somewhere. Release from prison is a usual and customary event, even if it isn't at the forefront of our collective minds.

While offender reentry might not be a daily consideration for most of us, one would think that given the frequency with which it occurs that the American public would know something about it. Sadly, this is not the case for the majority of Americans. As research indicates, there is a "fundamental public ignorance of the central facts of political life" (Neuman, 1986, p. 14). Kinder (1998) argues that there is, "a depth of ignorance that is breathtaking" (p. 785). We may be fascinated by criminal justice and what we see on the 10 o'clock news and read in the paper, but we generally know and understand very little about what we are seeing, reading, or hearing (Chiricos et al., 2000; Roberts & Hugh, 2005).

Even more perplexing is that what we do know about crime and criminal justice is usually not accurate (Hutton, 2005; Ismaili, 2006). We tend to have misguided beliefs about who commits crime and why and what punishments are best. We often rush to judgment without considering all of the facts and routinely lambast defendants for defending themselves, conveniently forgetting that we have a Constitution that provides all citizens the legal protection to do so.

Of particular concern is the fact that civic ignorance and our singular lack of informed knowledge about crime and criminal justice issues often initiates and perpetuates unwarranted and unsubstantiated public reactions to crime and criminal justice. Ultimately, the bits and pieces of incomplete and inaccurate information upon which we often make judgments manifest themselves in unreasonable expectations for what the criminal justice system can accomplish, including irrational beliefs about what works to reduce crime. Furthermore, these uninformed views about crime and criminals perpetuate policies, practices, and perceptions that often have stigmatizing effects on the people to whom they are applied (Applegate et al., 2002).

Current Trends

The sad fact is that the public is generally uninformed about most relevant civic and social processes that occur in the United States (Galston, 2001). That said, the fact that the public understands virtually nothing regarding the depth and breadth of offender reentry should not be shocking. Interestingly, what paltry information we do have regarding public views about reentry comes from a hodge-podge of responses to questions that assess public attitudes regarding community corrections and alternatives to incarceration—relevant concerns but issues not expressly germane to offender reentry.

Research indicates that the public generally endorses a balanced response to people who break the law, blending punitive responses with rehabilitative ideals (Cullen et al., 2000). There is also evidence that the public embraces punishment that is not fixed but is more fluid and continuous and predicated on crime seriousness, agreeing that less serious crime sanctions can and should be provided in a community setting (Cook & Lane, 2009; Roberts & Hough, 2005).

Findings suggest that the public endorses a variety of interventions in a community setting, including restitution, community service, electronic monitoring, and probation, among others (DiMasco et al., 1997; Reichel & Gauthier, 1990; Roberts & Hough, 2005). Approximately 77% of adults agree that the most appropriate sentence for nonviolent, non-serious offenders is probation, restitution, community service, or some other community-based service. Only if these options fail should jail or prison time be considered (Hartney & Marchionna, 2009). Support for parole is also evident, even if the public doesn't always understand what parole is and what it accomplishes. A study by Beldon Russonello & Stewart (2001) indicates that 90% of respondents favored parole as an option for offenders who have committed nonviolent crimes.

Public support for community-based interventions is also driven by practicality. When the public was provided detailed information regarding the costs associated with incarceration versus community-based treatment and programming, they tended to support community-based interventions in lieu of more restrictive punitive sanctions (Doble et al., 1991; Farkas, 1993; Jacobs, 1993). However, the public is ambivalent about the use of non-custodial penalties when they are universally applied. There seems to be support for a graduated system of community-based punishment that is a function of crime type, crime seriousness, and individual evaluation (Roberts & Hough, 2005; Turner et al., 1997).

Somewhat surprisingly, there is ample public support for community-based restorative justice practices that seek to make the victim, offender, and the community whole by repairing the harm caused by the offender. The general public seems positively disposed to restorative justice practices because offenders are forced to earn their way back into the good graces of the victim and the community through hard work, taking responsibility for their actions, and expressing remorse for what they have done (Flanagan, 1996; Walther & Perry, 1997).

Overall, the public agrees that rehabilitation is a viable option for offenders and that an appropriate venue within which to effectuate rehabilitative treatment and programming is the community. While the general public tempers its support for community-based programs based on crime type, in principle it supports the idea that community-based interventions are better than institutional ones. Over 50% of respondents to the National Council on Crime and Delinquency survey indicated that they did not think that serving time in prison or jail reduces the likelihood that someone will commit a crime in the future (Hartney & Marchionna, 2009).

However, public support for community-based programming requires that treatment and programming exist in the community and that offenders be allowed to return to the community to partake (Benzvy-Miller, 1990). A problem arises when an increased number of offenders are located in the community and are in need of programming, a circumstance that promotes anxiety on the part of the public about where community-based treatment and programming facilities are located. This is otherwise known as the "not-in-my-backyard" or NIMBY principle.

Predicated on misinformed and preconceived notions of who offenders are, fear of crime, and concerns over the impact that community-based programs might have on property values, the NIMBY principle has been responsible for the demise of many a community corrections program (Benzvy-Miller, 1990). In addition, sensational cases that draw negative media attention also stoke communal fear and reinforce beliefs that rehabilitation and programs in the community are fine as long as they aren't located in my backyard (Krajick, 1980). NIMBY is a real problem with real consequences even if it is based on erroneous information. The public tends to like the idea of treating people in the community in the abstract. They just have not quite evolved to the point where they understand, let alone accept, the fact that this treatment must occur in some tangible place.

Reentry Considerations

The literature available specifically on public opinion and offender reentry is sparse. Recent work by the Urban Institute and the Reentry Roundtable has begun to shed light on this most interesting aspect of public opinion and criminal justice, but research in this area is still in its infancy. What we do know about public attitudes as they specifically relate to offender reentry is that they are complex and variable (Eagleton, 2001).

Public opinion survey results indicate a cursory understanding by the general public that reentry must be difficult but illustrate a fundamental lack of knowledge about what those specific difficulties are (Eagleton, 2001). As Immerwahr and Johnson (2002) found, "[the public] was surprised, even dumbfounded, to learn about some of the barriers and constraints [offenders face] in some states" (p. 9). A series of recent studies attempt to fill this gap in the literature through capturing opinions of residents and stakeholders in the community about how offender reentry impacts them and their environment.

In these studies, while most people did not routinely think about offender reentry, when asked directly about it, most understood what it was and how complex the process can be (Brooks et al., 2006; Immerwahr & Johnson, 2002). Most respondents had an almost instant recognition that offenders released from prison returning to the community would face hardships in getting and maintaining employment, accessing substance abuse and/or mental health treatment, obtaining housing, and improving education. Focus group respondents in greater Philadelphia and Cleveland agreed that offenders were not properly prepared for release from prison or for the challenges that would await them at release (Brazzell & LaVigne, 2009; Brooks et al., 2006; Immerwahr & Johnson, 2002).

In Houston, Texas, focus groups participants understood the need for providing housing, education, and other services to reentering offenders, but also reflected their understanding of how difficult personal challenges such as reuniting with family and avoiding negative influences would likely be on those offenders returning home (Brazzell & LaVigne, 2009). Focus groups in Cleveland specifically identified jobs and education, along with a felony record as being the most significant barriers that returning offenders must overcome (Brooks et al., 2006).

A majority of residents surveyed in South Carolina favored community-based programs and services for returning offenders, noting the importance of providing stable housing and employment for successful reentry (Ouellette et al., 2017). Support weakened, however, when respondents were told that a tax increase might be necessary to pay for the services. Moreover, less than 40% of those surveyed believed ex-offenders are as deserving of services as non-criminal justice-involved individuals. While the strongest support came in the form of access and assistance to housing, when asked how they would feel about an ex-offender living in their neighborhood, the majority of respondents noted that "it would bother them to live next to an ex-offender" (p. 778). Overall findings suggested modest support for broad reentry policy initiatives, but the support was dependent on the context of the assistance

National public opinion surveys suggest high levels of support for providing job training (88% strongly favor) and employment placement (58% strongly favor) to offenders reentering society. Moreover, there is support for mitigating current collateral consequences to incarceration by restoring voting rights (68% strongly favor) to people with felony convictions at the time that they are released from prison, but not while they are incarcerated (Eagleton, 2001; Immerwahr & Johnson, 2002). People of color are particularly opposed to taking away offenders' right to vote, especially for offenders on parole or living in the community after they have served their sentence.

Interestingly, many focus group respondents indicated that if offenders were "reformed" it was because of their individual will to do so and not the assistance of prison or community-based programs (Brooks et al., 2006; Immerwahr & Johnson, 2002). Personal motivation, focus, and determination were believed to be the deciding factors in whether or not a returning offender would be successful. Yet despite this belief, most focus group participants had no problem with the idea of allocating significant funds to post-release treatment and rehabilitation programs (Immerwahr & Johnson, 2002). Focus group respondents in Ohio felt strongly that the family dynamic was a critical and oftentimes deciding factor in determining how offender reentry would proceed. These participants found family support as both necessary and critical to reentry transition while sometimes a negative influence and difficult to manage for the offender coming home (Brooks et al., 2006).

Participants in the greater Philadelphia focus groups noted that they had very little respect for supervision in the community and the impact it can or would have on someone returning home (Immerwahr & Johnson, 2002); this finding was also supported by the Houston, Texas, focus groups. Post-release supervision (i.e., parole) was viewed as being insufficient and in need of improvement (Brazzell & LaVigne, 2009). Residents of Cleveland, however, had high expectations for what parole would accomplish and how parole officers would and should do their jobs. In the minds of Cleveland residents, parole was to serve as a clearinghouse of information on programs, services, and treatment in the community (Brooks et al., 2006). National focus groups support this contention and aptly recognized that in many cases offenders who were able to successfully reintegrate did so in spite of, not because of, official governmental intervention (Eagleton, 2001).

Focus group respondents were clear in their belief that offenders should not be provided with accessibility to resources to which law-abiding citizens cannot take advantage. Specifically, most participants felt that offenders should not have access to grants and other funds to access education that were not accessible to free citizens (Eagleton, 2001; Immerwahr & Johnson, 2002). Focus groups from Cleveland indicated that they understood what needs returning offenders had but felt that much of the problem regarding program and treatment access was a function of offenders not availing themselves of resources readily available in the community (Brooks et al., 2006). A lack of motivation to engage in treatment and programs or lack of knowledge about how to access these services was the reason why recently released offenders did not engage, not a lack of service capacity.

Taking this issue of service capacity and knowledge of available services to heart, many communities have put together reentry guides, pamphlets, and books that are provided directly to offenders that include important information for the offender just returning home. These guides have been compiled in an effort to provide some discharge planning information to those offenders who receive none in prison and to augment what little planning others do receive. These reentry guides contain a variety of information, from addresses, phone numbers, and websites of local, county, and state services, to details regarding available mental health and substance abuse treatment programs, homeless shelters, and food kitchens.

Unfortunately, the majority of these guides are not as helpful as they could and should be. Where some reentry guides are written at a level that is too difficult for many offenders to comprehend, other guides are not easily accessible and understandable (i.e., they don't include an index or table of contents [Mellow & Christian, 2008]). These guides, provided to offenders by departments of corrections and local community providers, are representative of the "disconnect" that exists between what residents of communities feel are ample programs and services and the offenders' knowledge of and/or ability to access these services (Mellow & Christian, 2008). In their study of parolees returning to Philadelphia, Houser and colleagues argue that the mere presence of treatment and/or social services in the community may not be sufficient to allow returning offenders access to them or the ability to navigate these services (Houser, McCord, & Nicholson, 2018).

While a reentry guidebook seems useful in theory, the inability of these guides to provide information in a format that is useable and meaningful underscores an interesting finding with respect to public opinion. While stakeholders and residents in focus groups understood and encouraged the need for the involvement of churches and other faith-based organizations and grassroots organizations in the reentry process, they did not always agree on the extent to which community-based organizations should be involved. Residents tended to view reentry as a governmental problem and not one that should be supported by local governments or non-profit organizations (Brazzell & LaVigne, 2009; Brooks et al., 2006). In Cleveland, very few focus group members saw the community having direct responsibility for the success or failure of offenders returning to the community from prison (Brooks et al., 2006).

While residents from Cleveland neighborhoods exhibited little confidence that offenders transitioning from prison to the community would not revert to criminal behavior and therefore did not encourage or promote significant community involvement in their reentry (Brazzell & LaVigne, 2009; Brooks et al., 2006), focus groups from Philadelphia, Cleveland, and Houston all seemed to distinguish between individual methods of support for returning offenders and community-based or local institutional methods of support (Brazzell & LaVigne, 2009; Brooks et al., 2006; Immerwahr & Johnson, 2002).

When evaluating the impact of returning offenders on changes that had taken place in the community, residents of Cleveland felt that any changes that had occurred in their communities had been gradual (over the last 20–30 years), and they attributed it directly to problems in the economy and the shift away from the manufacturing and service industry. They also felt as if community values had changed; communities had become more fractious, less unified, and less trusting of their neighbors. Residents attributed these changes to increases in drug use, violence, single parenting, a decline in spirituality, and less discipline of children (Brooks et al., 2006).

Interestingly, residents of Cleveland did not in any way attribute the decline of their communities to offenders returning from prison. In fact, most participants in the Cleveland focus group indicated that they viewed the return of offenders to their community in a positive light; they saw returning offenders as being able to serve as mentors to local youth who might choose the wrong path and to other offenders who might need assistance (Brooks et al., 2006). The only offender for whom the focus group exhibited the least bit of concern was the return of sex offenders. Furthermore, the Cleveland community members who took part in the focus group did not believe that there was an overwhelming number of offenders returning to their communities and did not see local politicians or community members as being outspoken or engaged in conversations relative to offender reentry. Moreover, in their minds, the stigma associated with having gone to prison was minimal for both the community and offenders (Brooks et al., 2006).

Ultimately, focus group participants expressed ideas and thoughts that were complex and often diametrically opposed to each other (Brazzell & LaVigne, 2009; Brooks et al., 2006; Immerwahr & Johnson, 2002). Participants had difficulty reconciling helping offenders with believing that offenders should be punished for their actions. They also struggled with the belief that people can change versus wishing to limit the risk that the community faces when offenders are released to the community. Other concerns included having an awareness of the significant difficulties offenders face upon release but displaying a low tolerance for failure once released. Moreover, many participants couldn't reconcile the understanding for the need for individual program and treatment decisions with a lack of confidence in criminal justice professionals to provide meaningful decisions (Brazzell & LaVigne, 2009; Brooks et al., 2006; Immerwahr & Johnson, 2002).

Results from these studies indicate that while the public understands (at least to some extent) the barriers and impediments to successful reentry that await offenders who leave prison and return to the community, this knowledge is incomplete. Citizens do not recognize that communities are sometimes responsible for obstacles in the reentry process that may contribute to the failure of both the offender and the community to thrive (Eagleton, 2001). Instead, the citizenry believes that any barriers to reentry that exist are of offenders' making. In this way, the public minimizes any responsibility it may collectively have for creating and perpetuating impediments that might adversely impact the reentry process. One can only be left to assume that this frame of reference likely influences community responses to and interactions with offenders and the extent to which a community embraces or stigmatizes offenders upon their release.

It is unclear from public opinion data whether and to what extent communities recognize the adverse impact that stigma has on the reentering offender. The data is silent on the extent to which the public is able to make the connection between their opinions about crime, criminal justice, and reentry and how those opinions dictate the treatment of offenders with whom they may come in to contact. What is evident from public opinion in Houston, Cleveland, and Philadelphia, is that the public believes that failure to thrive post-prison is more a consequence of offenders' inability or unwillingness to access services and programming than any barriers that may influence or bias communal responses to offenders and their needs.

Chapter 13

Gender and Reentry

Discussions regarding offender reentry are usually generalized to include both men and women. This is a common, although some would argue not very accurate, practice. As previous data and information indicate, the criminal justice system has been and continues to be primarily a man's world. This does not mean that women have not and do not commit crime and that they are not relevant to the reentry discussion. It does mean that until relatively recently, specific consideration was not given to women and the potentially unique circumstances under which they commit crime, endure incarceration, take part in treatment and programming, and transition to the community.

Historical Context

The female criminal, while relevant to the criminal justice landscape for some time, has often been overlooked. Moreover, research on women and crime indicates that women have largely been ignored in the discourse on why crime is committed. If they have been included, it has usually been in a traditionally gendered context. Put another way, most scholarship argues that explanations of female criminality are grounded in eighteenth-century notions that women were criminals because they exhibited behaviors that were not uniquely "feminine" and that they blurred the lines between traditional gender roles (Rafter, 1985a). Criminal women were often "fallen" women (i.e., prostitutes, unwed mothers, etc.) who either did not or could not conform to traditional turn-of-the-century feminine ideals.

A review of historical scholarship indicates that these differing perceptions of gender roles have resulted in inequities in punishment between men and women. In eighteenth-century America, women were often punished and imprisoned for crimes for which men were not. Specifically, women often received prison time for crimes related to sexual misconduct, drunkenness, and prostitution (Rafter, 1985b). Moreover, sentencing inequities were common; double judicial standards were the mainstay of the day. Women and men, all else being equal, were likely sentenced to significantly different terms of incarceration because judges often adjudicated women based on chivalry, resulting in shorter sentences for women compared with men (Rafter & Stanko, 1982).

Initially, women and men were housed in prisons together. However, it soon became obvious that other accommodations were necessary. Female prisons were created in an effort to localize female offender populations and as a means to try to inculcate female offenders with feminine ideals. Women's prisons focused on educational and vocational training in the areas of housework and domesticity and structured living arrangements that emphasized order and treatment for their ills (Rafter, 1985b). Furthermore, women's prisons were designed much like early juvenile facilities in that women lived in cottages on the grounds of a reformatory. The architectural differences between men's and women's prisons were intended. It was believed that women were in need of "gentle discipline" that could be best afforded to them in an environment that supported and promoted reform (Rafter, 1985a, p. 236).

Stereotypical assumptions about women have historically governed the processing, adjudication, treatment, and incarceration of women in the criminal justice system (Rafter & Stanko, 1982). Theories that argue that the feminine ideal was in large part responsible for gender-based treatment in the criminal justice system were replaced by decidedly feminist arguments in the 1970s. For example, Adler and Simons' work (1979) argues that social-structural explanations of crime and its application to women should be considered in lieu of the more traditional gender-based notions.

Generally speaking, the feminist perspective on crime supports the contention that gender discrimination exists in all areas of life, including crime. This discrimination is a function of inequality in the power structure between men and women and fosters patriarchy—culturally developed constructs wherein males dominate females physically and financially. Social constructs of what it means to be a man (i.e., the breadwinner) and a woman (i.e., docile, motherly) are preeminent. Consequently, women who do not fit in to these socially constructed notions of gender are viewed as outsiders. Women who commit crime shatter traditional beliefs about gender roles; women who commit crime engage in masculine behaviors when they steal, use drugs, etc.

For some time, the larger audience in criminal justice has not appropriately understood either the feminist arguments about crime or the seminal role that female offenders play in the criminal justice system. In an effort to reframe the discussion, work by Daly and Chesney-Lind (1988) contextualized the issue as the generalizability and gender-ratio problem. The generalizability problem argues that because most criminologists are male, most criminological theory may not be applicable to female offending. While it is only within the last 50 years that scholars have considered that theories about crime and criminality may apply to both males and females, feminists argue that traditional methods of explaining crime do not take special characteristics relevant to women into consideration. Support for this contention is mixed (Steffensmeier & Allan, 1998). Equivocal empirical support notwithstanding, feminists suggest that while traditional theories may account for some explanation of female offending, these theories do not provide a complete explanation (Chesney-Lind & Faith, 2001). Further support for the generalizability problem is found in the fact that the bulk of empirical testing on theory and programming has been conducted with male offender populations.

The gender-ratio problem argues that while males may account for the overwhelming majority of crime committed, women do commit crime, and it is important to explore gender differences as a means to try to explain why. Classic works by Adler (1975) and Simon (1975) argue that the rise of the women's movement provided greater opportunities for women to engage in activities traditionally believed to be male dominated, both legally and illegally. Other scholars have come to recognize that both men and women are exposed to criminogenic factors, some of which are similar and some of which are not. While exposure to delinquent peers and antisocial attitudes might occur for both males and females, other factors such as problems with school performance, victimization, and childhood abuse have been found to be more prevalent in females (Belknap, 2007). Different levels and types of exposure along with varying likelihoods of possessing certain criminogenic factors therefore suggests different trajectories or pathways to crime and criminality for men and women.

Ground-breaking work by Kathleen Daly (1994) resulted in a typology of female offenders that is frequently used to test the belief that there are gendered pathways to crime. In her study, Daly evaluated presentence investigation reports and other court records in an effort to determine what specific factors encourage women to engage in crime (Daly, 1994). As Table 13-1 on the next page indicates, Daly created five typologies to explain female criminal behavior.

Table 13-1. Typology of Female Offenders

Type of Offender	Description
Street women	These women live on the street because they have endured high levels of abuse at home. These women are most likely to be arrested for prostitution, theft, or drug-related offenses, generally have extensive arrest records, and have likely been previously incarcerated.
Harmed- and harming women	These women have usually experienced abuse or neglect as children, grew up in chaotic home environments, and may have had contact with the juvenile court system. These women are more likely to be addicted to drugs or alcohol, have mental health problems, and engage in violent behavior.
Battered women	These women are usually in an ongoing abusive relationship with a partner. These women are likely to commit crimes related to harming their partner.
Drug-connected women	These women often use, manufacture, and/or distribute drugs in networks that include partners or family.
'Other' women	These are women that do not fit into one of the categories listed above. These women are likely to commit crimes of greed (i.e., embezzlement or fraud), not committed for the purposes of satisfying basic needs.

Adapted from Daly (1994).

An evaluation of these typologies suggests that women engage in crime for a variety of reasons but that their motivations can be generally categorized to reveal certain influences.

More recent work uses Daly's typologies as a springboard to suggest that a woman's motivation for committing crime is different from a man's. Where men may commit crime for personal gain, independence, or a need to assert (or reassert) masculinity (Connell, 1995; Messerschmidt, 1993), women generally commit crime out of feelings that choices and resources are limited (Heidensohn, 1996; Naffine, 1997). Factors associated with crime commission seem to be more complex for women, include financial need, and are driven by complex relationship dynamics, mental health considerations, drug use and abuse, and prior victimization (Belknap, 2007; Byrne & Trew, 2008; Chesney-Lind, 1997; Greenfeld & Snell, 1999; Maidment, 2006; Owen & Bloom, 1995). Investigation of these complex issues has led to the rise of a gender-responsive literature that highlights female pathways to criminal behavior in some detail (Belknap, 2007; Chesney-Lind & Sheldon, 2004).

While theoretical advances in understanding women and crime have been made, other more practical considerations related to women and crime merit discussion. Most notably, a series of laws in the 1980s were developed to heavily penalize offenders for engaging in drug-related crimes. Where women had been previously arrested and adjudicated for gendered crimes (e.g., prostitution, theft, killing an abusive partner), 1980s drug legislation predicated on the War on Drugs brought an increasing number of women to the attention of the criminal justice system for the commission of low-level drug crimes (Schram et al., 2006). Case in point, the proportion of women convicted of drug offenses more than doubled between 1986 (12%) and 2019 (26%) (The Sentencing Project, 2022).

Specifically, the rise in the availability of cocaine was believed to be responsible for significant increases in drug use and addiction (Thompson, 2008). The subsequent marketing of crack cocaine (a less potent, but more affordable version of cocaine) only fueled fear associated with drug use and prompted politicians and others to act in an effort to attempt to gain control of what many believed to be a faltering social order (Thompson, 2008). Usual and customary law enforcement efforts that targeted drug manufacturing, distribution, and use were deemed ineffective.

Instead, police and law enforcement personnel were forced to change the way they did business by attempting to directly attack drug markets, usually located in large, urban, inner city neighborhoods (Thompson, 2008). As these intense police actions took place, an increasing number of low- and mid-level drug dealers became part of the formal criminal justice apparatus, of which a significant number were women.

Not only did increased police presence and seemingly progressive law enforcement strategies impact who was being arrested and adjudicated by the system, so too did sentencing practice. As previously noted, judges traditionally engaged in chivalrous and/or paternalistic sentencing practices for women, reinforcing the notion that women should not be imprisoned for as long as men, or should receive alternatives to incarceration because of family circumstances. Conversely, judges sometimes exercised more strenuous sentencing for women, punishing them more harshly for crimes that were determined to be unfeminine or non-maternal (i.e., child abandonment).

The War on Drugs changed all that. Sentencing practices during the 1980s were universally harsh, but particularly so for low-level drug dealers caught dealing small amounts of crack—primarily women. Women were routinely sent to prison for drug-related offenses for extended periods of time (Zingraff & Randall, 1984). In some instances, judges lost the ability to use their judgment in sentencing people convicted of drug offenses. The Sentencing Reform Act of 1984 restricted judicial discretion in the sentencing process, making sentences for women who were low-level drug dealers often as severe as for mid- or high-level male drug distributors (Thompson, 2008). The most extreme example of this practice occurred in New York, where a series of laws were passed by Nelson D. Rockefeller that required offenders convicted of selling, manufacturing, and distributing drugs to serve minimum prison sentences of 15 years or more. Known as the Rockefeller Drug Laws, these laws were some of the toughest laws in the country that, intended or not, targeted women (Partnership for Responsible Drug Information, 2012).

Current Trends

Since 2009, the prison population has steadily declined for both men and women. In the ten years between 2011 and 2021, women saw a 28% decline in imprisonment rates compared with a 29% decline for men (Carson, 2022). Year-end 2019 marked the fourth consecutive year imprisonment rates fell for women and the twelfth consecutive year for men. While these recent statistics may be encouraging from a crime reduction perspective, the number of incarcerated women increased by more than 475% between 1980 and 2020 (26,326 to 152,854 respectively): a growth rate twice that of men since 1980 (The Sentencing Project, 2022).

Community supervision (probation and parole) rates have also been declining (Kaeble & Alper, 2020). As of 2018, offenders on community supervision were at their lowest levels since 1998. Women on parole accounted for 13% of the total parole population; a slight increase from 12% in 2008. Also virtually unchanged, women accounted for 26% of the total probation population in 2018 compared with 23% in 2008 (Kaeble & Alper, 2020).

As a function of the system as a whole, women offenders account for 28% of all arrestees, 21% of all violent offender arrests, 38% of property offenders, and 25% of drug arrests as reported to the Uniform Crime Report for year-end 2019 (Federal Bureau of Investigations Uniform Crime Report [UCR], 2019). Women accounted for almost half (47%) of all persons arrested for larceny-theft and approximately one quarter (24%) of aggravated assaults. When considering arrest trends over the ten-year period between 2010 and 2019, the percentage of females arrested as a whole fell 15% compared with a 23% decline for males. Similarly, when looking at the decline of violent arrests by gender over this same period, there was a 0.2% decline in arrests of women compared with a 10% decrease in violent crime arrests for men. Overall arrests of females rose in six offense categories between 2010 and 2019, with the greatest being motor vehicle theft (56%) and drug abuse violations (26%) (UCR, 2019).

While women accounted for 7.5% of all prisoners sentenced in state courts in 2018, more than a third (38%) were sentenced for violent offenses compared with more than half (58%) of sentenced men (Carson, 2020). A larger percentage of women, however, are serving sentences for drug (26%) or property (24%) offenses than males (13% and 16% respectively). Among the 38% of women sentenced for violent crimes, 21% were for murder or aggravated/simple assaults. Larceny theft (7.6%), burglary (6.8%), and fraud (6.5%) were the most common property offenses among women (Carson, 2020).

Demographic characteristics of women in state prison between October 2003 and May 2004 are highlighted in Table 13-2.

Table 13-2. Demographic Characteristics of Women in State Prison, October 2003–May 2004

Characteristics	%
Race	
White non-Hispanic	44
Black non-Hispanic	34
Hispanic	15
Other	7
Age (average age: 35.6)	
16–30 years	33
31–40 years	38
41 years and above	29
Married at the time of incarceration	18
High school graduate/GED	62
Employed 30 days prior to arrest	58
Prior arrest history	75
Prior history of sexual victimization	42
Prior history of physical victimization	49
Current offense types	
Violent	50
Non-violent excluding drug offenses	28
Drug	22
Disorders	
Mental illness only	21
Substance use only	16
Co-occurring mental health and substance use	43
No disorders	20

Adapted from Houser and colleagues (2012) using data from the *Survey of Inmates in State Correctional Facilities*, 2004 collected by the Bureau of the Census for the Bureau of Justice Statistics.

When evaluated by race, white women in state prisons accounted for 44% of the total female inmate population while 34% and 15% of women in state prison were black or Hispanic, respectively. The median age of women in state prison in 2003/2004 was 36 years, with 33% of women between the ages of 16 and 30, 38% between 31 and 40, and 29% 41 or older. At time of admission to prison, 18% of the women reported being married and a little over half (58%) were employed in the 30 days prior to arrest. With respect to criminal history, three-quarters (75%) of women had at least one prior arrest at the time of incarceration. Close to half of the women (49%) reported being a victim of physical abuse and 42% had histories of sexual victimization. Evaluating by disorder types, more women met the diagnostic criteria for a co-occurring mental health and substance use disorder (43%) than the singular disorders of mental health (21%) or substance use disorder (16%) (Houser et al., 2012).

Overall, a typology of women in the criminal justice system emerges. Women who are criminal justice involved are generally poor, uneducated, unskilled, and disproportionately women of color and women who hail from primarily urban environments and who were raised by a single mother or were part of the foster care system (Covington, 2003). Women who are drug users generally choose crack/cocaine as their drug of choice and have more severe drug histories compared with their male counterparts. Women also report low self-esteem and more extensive histories of physical and sexual abuse than men (Messina et al., 2001). Research indicates that women have very real issues in several substantive areas that directly impact women's pathways to crime, adjudication, imprisonment, and release. These specific domains are financial need, relationships, mental health, self-esteem/self-efficacy, drug use, and victimization.

Financial Need/Educational Attainment

Poverty is a real and significant issue for female offenders. While 40% of women reported being employed full time prior to their arrest, nearly 30% reported receiving some type of public assistance during the same time interval. In an attempt to "stay afloat," many women function on the economic margins of society and struggle to survive, often through engaging in illegal activity (Covington, 2003).

According to data collected by the Survey of Inmates in State Correctional Facilities, between 2003 and 2004, less than three quarters (62%) of women in state prison had a high school diploma or GED at the time of incarceration (Houser et al., 2012). In a sample of more than 1,700 women sentenced to state prison in Pennsylvania, researchers found the average IQ score was 95, placing many of the women in an average intelligence category; however, their average level of educational attainment was eleventh grade with an eighth-grade reading level (Houser & Welsh, 2014). Because most women in prison present with lower average years of education compared with men, it is not difficult to understand how lack of education would translate into diminished or nonexistent opportunities for wage-earning upon release (Belknap, 2007).

If employment options are significantly reduced or nonexistent for the majority of women leaving prison and returning to the community, it is likely that these women are exposed to increased poverty and/or rely on public assistance, further complicating their ability to remain crime free. Holtfreter and colleagues (2004) found that poverty increased the likelihood of arrest for women by a factor of 4.6. In contrast, women who did live below the poverty level but who were provided access to public assistance (i.e., education, health care, housing, etc.) were 83% less likely to recidivate. Economically marginalized women often find themselves engaging in criminal behavior for survival (Giordano et al., 2002).

Relationships

The relationships that female offenders have are complex and often difficult to disentangle. Damaging and destructive relationships may occur because female offenders do not feel empowered and/or comfortable in their own identities and often identify themselves based on the relationships that they have with others (Gilligan, 1982; Kaplan, 1984; Langan & Pelissier, 2001). Reduced or damaged self-identity coupled with high rates of abuse, trauma, and neglect that these women may have experienced as children and adults decreases their ability to recognize damaging relationships and to seek out positive ones (Covington, 1998). Moreover, because of the dependent nature of the relationships that these women often have, they sometimes gravitate to relationships that are damaging and encourage their involvement in criminal behavior (Koons et al., 1997; Richie, 1996). Conversely, research also indicates that women may forgo involvement in criminal activity precisely because of their desire to hold on to pro-social, positive relationships (Benda, 2005; Blanchette & Brown, 2006).

The nature and type of relationships that women have has been found to be a factor in female offending with adults as well as children. As previously noted, an overwhelming number of women in prison or under the auspices of the criminal justice system are mothers. More than half (58%) of women in state and federal custody have at least one child under the age of 18; forty-seven percent have a child(ren) under the age of 10 (Maruschak et al., 2021a). Feelings of inadequacy, the inability to achieve or assume scripted gender expectations, economic hardship, and active substance abuse are just some of the aggravating factors that lead to stress and make it difficult, if not almost impossible, for female offenders to take care of their children prior to incarceration and after release (Ferraro & Moe, 2003; Greene et al., 2000; Ross et al., 2004). No doubt, issues related to child visitation and custody also exacerbate the situation (Bloom & Chesney-Lind, 2000; Bloom et al., 2003). Moreover, given that 31% of women were single parents living with their children prior to incarceration compared with 4% of men, the pressures and concerns facing female offenders with respect to making arrangements for their children while they are incarcerated are likely overwhelming (Van Voorhis et al., 2010).

Recent research has evaluated the role that self-esteem and self-efficacy play in gendered pathways to crime. Self-esteem is tied to feelings of empowerment, self-worth, and levels of perceived control over one's life. Research indicates that female offenders view self-worth as a significant factor associated with engaging in or desisting from crime (Carp & Schade, 1992; Case & Fasenfest, 2004; Schram & Morash, 2002). Self-efficacy is distinct from self-esteem. Self-efficacy is related to a person's confidence in their ability to achieve specific goals. While little is known about the impact that this variable has on gendered pathways to crime, there is research available that suggests that it is very important (Rumgay, 2004). Research indicates that many women become involved in criminal behavior at the prompting of family members or significant others (Chesney-Lind, 1997). Women are often introduced to drug use by their partners and often engage in crime because of feelings of inadequacy and low self-esteem and self-efficacy (Covington, 2003).

Mental Health

Female offenders are more likely to present with mental health deficits compared with their male offending counterparts. Women who come in to contact with the criminal justice system tend to suffer from depression, anxiety, and self-mutilating behaviors at higher rates than men (Belknap & Holsinger, 2006; Bloom et al., 2003). Specifically, DSM-V mood disorders such as depression, bipolar disorder, post-traumatic stress, eating disorders, and panic attacks plague female offenders, as do co-occurring mental health and substance abuse disorders (Bloom et al., 2003; Holtfreter & Morash, 2003; Owen & Bloom, 1995). Mental health diagnoses more common to women are often un- or underreported due to limited diagnostic assessments, further hindering access to needed treatment services while in prison (Houser & Welsh, 2014). Women are also more likely to experience serious psychological distress in the month prior to incarceration than men (Maruschak et al., 2021b).

Almost 17% of women with a mental health disorder in state prison reported being homeless in the year prior to admission, placing them in more direct contact with police and the criminal justice system (James & Glaze, 2006). Women also tend to experience trauma at very high rates compared with men—trauma that impacts their mental health and often manifests itself in post-traumatic stress disorder (Veysey, 1997). This trauma is often in the form of sexual or physical abuse that they experience or that they witness (Bloom et al., 1994). Indeed, women in state prison with mental health disorders are approximately three times more likely to report having been a victim of sexual or physical abuse (James & Glaze, 2006). Standard operating procedures in prison such as strip searches and restraints can serve to further traumatize women, particularly women experiencing post-traumatic stress disorders (Covington & Bloom, 2003).

Drug Use

Some scholarship supports the contention that while male and female offenders use drugs at high rates, the effects of this use on women is different for women than for men (McLellan et al., 1999). Almost half (49%) of women confined in state prisons have used alcohol, drugs, or both at the time of the offense for which they were committed to a term of incarceration (Bronson et al., 2017). Moreover, female offenders were more likely to meet the criteria for drug dependence or abuse than men;

69% for women compared with 57% for men (Bronson et al., 2017). More than men, women report regular use of methamphetamine and heroin/opiates. Overall, women who use drugs are more likely to be involved in crime (Merlo & Pollock, 1995). Furthermore, 47% of women in state prison indicated that they used drugs in the month before they committed their offense (Bronson et al., 2017). High rates of co-occurring disorders and the added dynamics of prior victimization may exacerbate drug use and result in women using drugs for different reasons than men (Covington & Bloom, 2007; Veysey, 1997). Pelissier and Jones (2005) suggest that the onset of substance use for women is often a means of self-medication to mask the pain of a life crisis (e.g., emotional loss, victimization, or family disruption).

Victimization

Women who come in to contact with the criminal justice system appear more likely to have experienced physical and sexual abuse as a child and, as adults, are abused at higher rates than male offenders and women in the general population (Greenfeld & Snell, 2000; McClellan et al., 1997). While official rates of abuse have been noted between 23% and 39%, other research indicates that these rates of abuse in female offenders have reached 75% (Browne et al., 1999; Greene et al., 2000; Owen & Bloom, 1995).

There also seems to be a link between childhood victimization and the likelihood of engaging in criminal behavior as an adult. Traylor and Richie (2012) assert "the linkage between women's victimization and their pathways to incarceration can best be described as a culmination of a host of traumatic life events" (p. 572). Widom (1989) and Siegel and Williams (2003) have found that girls who were abused (sexually or physically) and/or neglected were more likely to have been formally adjudicated delinquent and have adult criminal records compared with girls who were not abused or neglected. Women who are abused are more likely to abuse drugs or alcohol (Covington, 2003).

Moreover, adult victimization is believed to play a prominent role in perpetuating women's criminal behavior (Pollock, 1999, 2002; Benda, 2005). Using a matched comparison group of incarcerated and non-incarcerated women, researchers reported incarcerated women were at significantly greater risk of trauma exposure and multi-victimization (Grella et al., 2003). However, research that evaluates the relationship between childhood and adult victimization and crime is not airtight. Some studies have reported such relationships while other scholarship has not. Inconclusive findings are likely due to issues related to the reporting of these very personal crimes by female victims as well as fear of reprisal (Brown et al., 1999).

Recidivism

Women tend to recidivate less than men. A study comparing female parolees to male parolees indicates that female parolees were 12% more likely to succeed in their first year on parole compared with men during the same time period (McShane et al., 2002). A study comparing men and women's performance on probation yielded similar results. Women on probation were less likely to be rearrested compared with men from the same sample (Olson et al., 2003).

However, when considering recidivism only as it relates to women, the outcomes are sobering. Huebner and colleagues (2010) found that 47% of women were reconvicted or reincarcerated within eight years of release, with the majority of failures occurring within the first two years of release. Moreover, women who were identified as being dependent on drugs after release were the most likely to fail; one-third of women who recidivated were using drugs at the time of recidivism (Huebner et al., 2010). Furthermore, women on parole tend to be repeat offenders; over 66% were not first-time offenders and had been incarcerated for a nonviolent offense (Snell, 1994).

In the most recent recidivism outcome study by the Bureau of Justice Statistics, data of annual arrest percentages revealed that 45% of male prisoners were arrested in the first year post-release, compared with 35% of female prisoners; In year-9, 24% of males were arrested compared with 21% of females. Interestingly, the authors point out that while we see a narrowing in the percentages between males and females from year 1 to year 9, "the difference between male and female prisoners decreased proportionally. During year-1, the percentage of female prisoners who were arrested following release was 78% of that for male prisoners, while during year-9 the percentage of female prisoners was 87% of that for male prisoners" (pp. 8–9).

There are several characteristics of women that seem to impact when and to what extent women recidivate. A study by Kruttschnitt and Gartner (2003) indicates that age, offense type, drug history, and length of criminal history directly impact likelihood of recidivism. Younger women incarcerated for property offenses that present with a substance abuse history and significant prior criminal history are more likely to recidivate (Kruttschnitt & Gartner, 2003). Education is also a significant predictor of recidivism for women. In a more recent study, women with a high school degree were less likely to fail on parole (Huebner et al., 2010). LaVigne and colleagues (2009) found that women are almost twice as likely as men to recidivate within a year after release in large part due to drug-related or property offenses fueled by addiction. Houser and McCord (2018) found women with mental health disorders or co-occurring mental health and substance use disorders were more likely to return to prison and to have overall shorter periods of time in the community between release and return to prison.

Understanding the nuances of recidivism in women is particularly relevant given the increasing number of women who fall under the auspices of the criminal justice system. Not only is it important to be able to detect differences in time to recidivism between men and women, but there are also real practical concerns related to offender supervision, public safety, and allocation of treatment and program resources (Bonta et al., 1995).

Current Practice

Historically, female offenders were placed in co-Ed prisons. As female offending populations grew, gender-specific prisons were created. However, as the number of women's prisons has grown, so too have the criticisms regarding their form and function. First, women tend to be placed in facilities farther away from home than men. This taxes the ability of family and friends to be able to visit and maintain close family relationships (Arditti, 2003). Second, research on the nature, type, and capacity of institutional correctional programming for women has not yielded particularly favorable outcomes.

Generally, women's prisons have not been able to provide comprehensive program opportunities. Moreover, the programs that are available often reinforce stereotypical perceptions of women and "acceptable" occupations (Morash et al., 1998; Pollock-Byrne, 1990). Furthermore, in the past, women's access to reproductive healthcare has been restricted or nonexistent (Pollock-Byrne, 1990). The increase in the number of women-only prisons has made these issues less of a concern in recent years.

However, many current reentry services do not sufficiently meet the needs of women leaving prison and returning to the community, specifically in the areas of childcare, parenting skills, healthcare and counseling services, housing, transportation, and education (Scroggins & Malley, 2010). Reasons for this lack of service provision include program capacity, location of program, and restrictions on the amount of time the programs/services may be utilized (Scroggins & Malley, 2010). Moreover, current programming does not always target the specific gender-responsive criminogenic needs that women have (Holtfreter & Morash, 2003). Still other programs do not offer the necessary support for women returning to the community because they do not teach marketable skills, but only teach skills traditionally viewed as feminine or women's work, such as secretarial work and cleaning (Morash et al., 1994).

Reentry Considerations

Research suggests that the very pathways that lead women to crime are the same pathways that can impede their successful return to the community. Specifically, feelings of marginalization (Huebner et al., 2010; Sampson et al., 1997; Wilson, 1997) and poor or weak communal ties significantly limit employment opportunities (Reisig et al., 2002). Given that many women are not employed prior to incarceration, it is unlikely that gainful employment is a foregone conclusion after release. This is only complicated by the fact that at time of incarceration, many women don't have a high school diploma or a GED (Freudenberg et al., 2005).

As O'Brien notes in her study of women reentering the community from prison, the availability of vocational and educational programming opportunities for women are not equal to that of men and are generally limited to low- or no-skilled employment positions (O'Brien, 2001). Other factors attendant to employment eligibility, such as childcare and discrimination, have also been identified as impacting the likelihood of employment for female offenders released from prison to the community (Golden, 2005; Harm & Phillips, 2001).

Over 80% of women who are incarcerated have at least one child for whom they were the primary provider prior to imprisonment compared with 26% of fathers (Arditti & Few, 2006; Glaze & Maruschak, 2008). The physical separation of the mother from the child is stressful for both mother and child and is further exacerbated by the fact that most women's prisons are located far away from urban centers and the neighborhoods where these children often live (Berman, 2005). Children often provide high levels of social attachment and commitment and often assist these women in the development and maturation of positive self-images that assist them as they transition from prison to the community (Edin & Kefalas, 2005; Giordano et al., 2002).

Children have been found to provide women returning to the community with an incentive to desist from crime (Robbins et al., 2009), but reuniting with children can be difficult and stressful and can impact the reentry process (Dodge & Pogrebin, 2001). Fear of loss of parental rights (if these rights have not been revoked already) coupled with anxiety related to reunifying with their children can make the reentry process for female offenders particularly difficult (Kruttschnitt & Gartner, 2003). As Bloom and Brown (2009) argue, "[women] are viewed as having violated both the tenets of the law and the prescriptions for gendered behavior" (p. 314).

Scholars suggest that women use drugs to cope with the pain associated with abuse and present with high levels of drug use prior to incarceration (Chesney-Lind, 1997; Greenfeld & Snell, 1999). Moreover, women tend to present with more serious drug problems than men once they leave prison (Vito & Tewksbury, 2000). This is often the case because women attempt to self-medicate un- or under-treated mental health disorders (Covington, 2001). Depression and substance abuse have also been linked to maternal malaise, a condition that scholars argue is associated with negative parenting and social and economic outcomes for women leaving prison and reentering the community (Arditti & Few, 2008; Arendell, 2000). Maternal malaise is grounded in the notion that women suffer physiological symptoms (i.e., depression and unhappiness) in part because of increased victimization, drug abuse, and low self-esteem. However, this malaise is also attributed to internal struggles that female offenders have reconciling imprisonment with motherhood and the fears that they have about returning to the community and fulfilling not only their own expectations but those of others (Arditti & Few, 2008).

Work by Mallik-Kane and Visher (2008) indicates that women who presented with mental health and substance abuse diagnoses at entry to prison were less likely to gain employment, were less likely to receive assistance from family, were more likely to be homeless, and recidivated at higher rates upon release from prison compared with women who did not have these issues. Women who have suffered prior physical and mental abuse during childhood and adulthood are also more likely to offend again (Daly, 1998; Owen & Bloom, 1995). Interestingly, data suggest that women who return to the community tend to establish or seek out relationships with others like themselves; women who may be ex-offenders, prior drug users, or who have mental health concerns (Leverentz, 2006; Richie, 2001).

While a significant number of offenders suffer from homelessness prior to incarceration, women report being homeless at rates higher than men prior to incarceration and again at release (Richie, 2001). Women seem in a particularly difficult positions to establish secure, stable housing at the time of release from prison. The issue of housing is made more stressful for female offenders because lack of stable housing often impedes their ability to reunite with their children (Kruttschnitt & Gartner, 2003; Richie, 2001). As Scroggins and Malley (2010) note, "It is not enough, however, just to offer housing to women; in order for it to be an effective aid to successful reentry, housing must be safe, affordable, child-friendly, and supportive of a sober lifestyle" (p. 150).

Women who reenter society often do not have access to federal and state welfare benefits because of the crime for which they were incarcerated. As an increasing number of women have been incarcerated for drug-related crimes, they are ineligible to receive Temporary Assistance to Needy Families (TANF) because of a provision that denies benefits to anyone with a felony drug conviction. While this ban affects men as well as women, the impact on women is particularly significant because of women's reliance on these funds to help support their children (Greenfeld & Snell, 1999).

In addition to the dynamics mentioned above, women released from prison to the community on parole must contend with meeting and managing their parole conditions (Opsal, 2009). This can make compliance impossible for some and difficult for most. Recent qualitative work exploring female offender's perceptions of parole supports this position. Women on parole who were interviewed viewed parole as primarily a surveillance function; that officers were there to monitor their actions rather than to assist them with reentry (Opsal, 2009). While this fact was difficult for some women to deal with, most women were fearful of violating their conditions of parole and being sent back to prison—an event that would delay or even deter them from being with their children (Opsal, 2009).

Promising Practice

The panoply of issues that female offenders face makes for a very stressful and taxing return to the community and one that is not always successful (Severance, 2004). The recipe for increasing the likelihood of successful reintegration of women back to the community fuses supervision with services that address the specialized needs of female offenders, "in highly structured, safe environments where accountability is stressed" (Austin et al., 1992, p. 21). Successful reentry programs for women also emphasize learning coping abilities and problem-solving skills and include programs that stress empowerment (Austin et al., 1992). Programs that embody the empowerment model teach women how to gain control and a sense of independence over the various stressors and factors in their life that may impede their ability to succeed outside prison (Koons et al., 1997).

A study that evaluates what works in gender-specific reentry programming indicates that successful programs will employ staff that are dedicated and caring, and who may have had prior contact with the criminal justice system themselves. As discussed previously, programs that assist women in developing "real" skills are important, as are programs that involve peers and empower women to move past codependent relationships (Koons et al., 1997). Other recommendations for successful reentry of women to the community involve the community in the reentry process. Programs that can break down stereotypes and other barriers that impede women from being accepted into the communal fold are optimal (Covington, 2002). Wraparound service models which are holistic in their approach to helping women reintegrate are also encouraged, as they emphasize individual responsibility and comprehensive service provision. The foundation of these types of service plans is "wrapping necessary resources into an individualized support plan" (Malysiak, 1997, p. 12).

The push for gender-specific treatment and programming is grounded in the notion that there are gender-specific pathways to crime or criminogenic needs that must drive case management and treatment (Heilbrun et al., 2008). As discussed in detail in a subsequent chapter, gender-based risk/needs assessments can and do reveal gender-specific case management and supervision needs. It only follows that if one accepts that there are predictors of crime and criminality that are unique to women, success in mediating those factors must include gender-specific programming (Bloom et al., 2003; Salisbury et al., 2009).

If one accepts that risk and needs vary according to gender, then women and men would and should respond differently to gender-based treatment and programming. Given the research that indicates that women are more victimized as children and adults than men, it only makes sense that programming for women should address victimization. Furthermore, while the role that social relationships play in female criminality and treatment and programming is not fully understood, some research suggests that social relationships are a protective factor for women: that women with strong social relationships tend not to commit crime or not to do it again (Alarid et al., 2000). Therefore, a focus on treatment and programming that empowers women and provides them with a sense of self-efficacy would be beneficial (Benda, 2005; McLellan et al., 1997; Richie, 2001). When women themselves are asked to comment on what treatment and programs they think would be most beneficial, they agree that programs that are organized, multifaceted, and directly applicable to specific goals they set for themselves are most beneficial (Morash, 2009). "It's just like bakin' a cake. You can't leave out the flour. You need all the ingredients to make it come out right" (Richie, 2001, p. 294).

While the breadth and depth of understanding the role of women in the criminal justice system is just being realized, agreement exists regarding the fact that they consume considerable resources and impact the criminal justice system greatly. Women do have unique issues and problems that make gender-specific methods of treatment and programming driven by risk and need a necessity (Hannah-Moffat, 2009). This "co-occurrence of multiple demands" does significantly impact how and to what extent women are able to confront the challenges of reentry (Richie, 2001, p. 380).

Chapter 14

The Community

While offenders reenter society one person at a time, offender reentry is also a community-level process, especially when it occurs in high concentrations (Rose & Clear, 2002). Customarily, we attempt to understand the individual-level challenges associated with individual people leaving prison and returning to their individual places of residence (assuming they have one). This chapter attempts to take the micro-level approach to reentry and turn it on its head. Instead of thinking about the problem through the eyes of an offender, we will evaluate the problem of offender reentry from a macro- or community-level perspective. What is it like for towns and cities small, medium, and large when an offender is arrested and removed from the community and incarcerated; how is the city or town impacted by the offender's absence and subsequent return?

Historical Context

The etiology for much of the work on communities and crime may be found in social disorganization theory (Shaw & McKay, 1942). Social disorganization theory posits that individual characteristics matter less than geography when considering crime. As Ernest Burgess explained it, cities and towns grow in systematic ways, but outwardly in concentric rings with a central business district at the core (Park et al., 1925, 1967).

Cities grow in concentric circles predicated on economic growth driven by competition. Where the central business zone is the hub of commercial activity for any town, residential areas are often located far away from this hub in nicer areas void of pollution, noise, and traffic. However, Park and colleagues identified something called a zone of transition—a place just outside the central business zone that often includes businesses and residential living, a place that is always in flux (Park et al., 1925, 1967). The zone of transition is unstable because of a lack of social ties that help bind communities together. These scholars believe that this zone promotes social disorganization that brings with it a multitude of social problems, including crime and delinquency.

Using the concentric zone model, scholars Clifford Shaw and Henry McKay conducted a study wherein they divided Chicago, Illinois, into specific concentric zones including residential, factory and commuter zones, as well as transition zones, in an effort to evaluate rates of delinquency. Results from Shaw and McKay's study confirm what Park and Burgess suggested. Rates of delinquency differ by zone and are highest in the zone of transition; a place identified as being unstable and where communal ties were weakest (Park et al., 1925, 1967).

Shaw and McKay (1942) also suggest that towns and cities with specific characteristics can be identified as being susceptible to crime. These characteristics include: physical decay (neighborhoods with abandoned buildings and buildings in disrepair), heterogeneous populations (large numbers of ethnically diverse people located in one neighborhood), high levels of mobility (large numbers of people moving in and out of a neighborhood), and high rates of poverty. Shaw and McKay argue that these issues destabilize communities and interfere with community organization and cohesion, resulting in social disorganization and crime.

Contemporary study of social disorganization theory has expanded Shaw and McKay's findings and evaluates specific types of community disorder, such as economic disadvantage, residential stability, employment, mental illness, and disease (Austin & Hardyman, 2004; Massey & Denton, 1993; Wilson, 1997). Collectively, these studies further support Shaw and McKay's position that community-level variables significantly impact recidivism and public safety as much or more than characteristics of individual offenders released from prison (Austin & Hardyman, 2004).

A relatively recent addition to the literature on social disorganization is work that explores our understanding of the role and importance of the community in the offender reentry process. Researchers are now exploring the notion that neighborhood- or community-level indicators of social cohesion (e.g., social networks and volunteer associations) can and do impact crime rates and, by extension, the number of people who go to prison and the number of people who come home (Clear et al., 2005).

Despite the intense interest surrounding this issue, there are relatively few studies that actually evaluate the role of the community in the reentry process. A study by Gottfredson and Taylor (1988) found that depending on the neighborhood to which they return, offenders are more (or less) likely to succeed (i.e., recidivate less). In a unique natural experiment, Kirk (2009) reported offenders forcibly displaced from their communities due to Hurricane Katrina were less likely to return to prison, suggesting a criminogenic effect of returning to their core communities. Research has also found that offenders returning to communities with higher levels of socio-economic deprivation are more likely to be re-arrested and that the impact of the disadvantage extends beyond the immediate environs (Kubrin & Stewart, 2006; Hipp et al., 2010a). Other research by Lynch and Sabol (2001) that evaluates a series of community-level variables including voluntary associations and kin/family networks determined that as voluntary associations decrease, local crime and incarceration rates rise.

Additional work by Fagan and colleagues (2003) and Piquero and colleagues (2006) found that as incarceration rates for communities increased in one year, crime rates increased in the subsequent year. The author's attribute this rise in crime to reduced informal social control. While their research revealed similar findings, Clear and colleagues argue that the effects of incarceration are not linear (Clear et al., 2003). In a study evaluating the impact of incarceration on Tallahassee, Florida, neighborhoods, Clear and colleagues found that there is a "tipping point" at which the effect of incarcerating members from specific neighborhoods resulted in increased crime in those same neighborhoods in subsequent years (Clear et al., 2003, p. 36). From this work, the authors argue that a rise in crime rates may or may not correspond to a rise in incarceration rates. They posit that it is possible that the forced removal and return of large numbers of people from particularly impoverished neighborhoods may impact crime rates in different ways.

Current Trends

Increasingly, scholars agree that place matters and that neighborhood-level variables can be as important as individual-level concerns when seeking to understand social processes (Clear et al., 2005). Studies suggest that increased neighborhood cohesion can reduce burglary, auto theft, and robberies while reduced neighborhood cohesion is a predictor of higher crime rates and disorder (Bellair, 2000; Markowitz et al., 2001). Yet despite this recognition, little agreement among scholars exists about what community is and what community does. As Clear and colleagues (2005) indicate:

> There is a value in pondering the importance of community with regard to a problem such as reentry even if there is a certain fuzziness regarding just what is meant by the term. Communities are places where people live (or work) and where the nature of the places is such that the variance on certain measures *within* the community is less than the variance *between* that community and others nearby. (p. 182)

Given the lack of consensus among scholars about what community is, it is not surprising that researchers have only a scant understanding of what communities do, especially as they relate to offender reentry.

From a community context, offender reentry is the result of a sequence of events that begins with the removal of offenders from the community, continues with offenders' return, and often includes the additional removal of offenders from community to prison because of offenders' failure to thrive in the community environment. This process is called reentry cycling (Clear et al., 2005, p. 182). Yet research indicates that the process of offender reentry occurs neither randomly nor is it equally distributed across communities.

Instead, offenders who are removed from their communities to serve prison time almost always return to the same (or similar) neighborhood. Offenders often return to their neighborhood because of family, friends, and familiarity, including knowledge of the area and possible job prospects (Rose & Clear, 2001). Clear and colleagues (2003) suggest that because people who go to prison are disproportionately poor and of minority status, they come from and subsequently return to the same or similarly poor, ethnic neighborhoods.

Moreover, because the distribution of crime is not equal across communities, offenders who leave prison and return to the community do so in disproportionate ways. Lynch and Sabol (2001) found that prisoners are usually released to a small number of urban core counties, and that within these core counties, prison releases tend to be focused on a few, distinct neighborhoods, resulting in densely concentration pockets of offenders in a relatively few number of towns and cities. Work by Eric Cadora and colleagues confirms this phenomenon for neighborhoods in

Brooklyn, New York, and New Jersey (Travis et al., 2003) and other work by the Urban Institute indicates a similar phenomenon exists in Houston, Texas (Watson et al., 2004). In the Urban Institute study, of the 25% of offenders released to Harris County (the county in which Houston is located), 23% returned to five zip codes in Houston.

Significantly high concentrations of offenders returning to a few, targeted communities may have potentially serious ramifications for these communities. The "churning effect" of resident turnover through incarceration and re-entry serves to disrupt social networks needed to maintain informal social control in these communities (Rose & Clear, 1998). One study found that nearly 30% of male residents in specific neighborhoods were incarcerated on any given day (Bonczar & Beck, 1997). In keeping with prior findings, data indicate that incarceration is a phenomenon disproportionately located in specific minority neighborhoods and, when present in high concentrations, can result in the commission of more crime in the community, not less (CASES, 2000). Moreover, the geographic clustering of offenders returning to core communities further promotes reoffending behaviors; a phenomenon scholars refer to as a "spatial contagion effect" (Mennis & Harris, 2011). Chamberlain and Wallace (2016) found that high concentrations of parolees in neighborhoods differentially impacts individual recidivism; parolees clustered in concentrated neighborhoods were 67% more likely to reoffend.

As Gonnerman (2004) notes, select communities are comprised of million-dollar blocks; neighborhoods that are by all accounts poor until you consider the costs associated with incarcerating large numbers of its residents are upwards of $1,000,000.00. Antiquated and ineffective drug policies, a decrease in the number of viable community corrections options, and increased sentence lengths have encouraged and promoted incarceration—a situation wherein mass incarceration is responsible for creating more crime than it prevents (Clear, 2007). Resultant changes in crime rates along with the frequency with which people are removed and returned to poor communities ultimately disrupts the foundation of communal life, adversely impacting family structure, voting habits, political discourse, and community stability.

The disruption of the normal functions of a community due to the removal and return of people to neighborhoods as a result of incarceration is called coercive mobility (Clear et al., 2003). Where people may move in and out of neighborhoods and towns because they want to (voluntary mobility), coercive mobility involves the forcible relocation of citizens to and from their communities (Clear et al., 2003). Moreover, because coercive mobility takes place in primarily impoverished, urban areas, these communities have higher crime rates not only because they are comprised of large numbers of people who have committed crime, but also because the residents of these communities are often no longer self-supporting. In turn, communities where coercive mobility is greatest are communities where citizens are more likely to usurp communal resources (Clear, 2007).

Reentry Considerations

The aggregate impact of incarceration and reentry serves to significantly destabilize neighborhoods. Specifically, human capital, social networks, social capital, collective efficacy, and informal social control are disrupted in ways that have deleterious effects on the offender, the community, and society at-large.

Human Capital

Clear and colleagues (2005) define human capital as, "personal resources an individual brings to the social and economic marketplace" (p. 186). For example, the nature and type of education and job skills that employees possess determines to a great extent the value that an employer places on their employees. The more educated a person is, the more unique and defined skills a person possesses, the more desirable they are as an employee and as a contributor to the larger community. The degree of human capital that a community possesses does correlate with crime. Research indicates that while human capital is a uniquely individual attribute, towns and cities rich in this resource generally have low crime rates (Clear et al., 2005). Not surprisingly, offenders do not present with large amounts of human capital. As established elsewhere, offenders tend to be un- or under-educated and lacking in the minimal skills necessary to get and maintain employment. Therefore, it is easy to appreciate how reduced human capital results in increased financial hardship due to limited employment opportunities.

As research has demonstrated, ex-offenders leave prison and return to primarily large, urban communities with limited financial resources and extensive financial needs. Efforts by offenders to seek employment are often futile. Employment in large, urban centers is difficult for anyone to obtain, let alone an ex-offender. Job opportunities for ex-offenders are severely limited and, if available, do not pay well. Moreover, ex-offenders often have no incentive to work at a low-paying job when they can rely on family or friends for monetary support, even if it means unduly taxing families that are often already stretched thin (Rose & Clear, 2002). Unfortunately, an absence of individual human capital has detrimental effects on and consequences for the larger community.

Social Networks

Where human capital concerns itself with levels of education and specific skill sets that people do or do not possess, social networks are predicated on relationships between people where they live or work. Traditionally, social networks have consisted of friends and family and co-workers. The foundation of a social network is the strength of the link between an individual and the other members of the network. People who exhibit strong ties with others in their social network have small, but usually very tight networks. As Granovetter (1993) suggests, people with strong ties have close personal networks but are unable to extend their reach to others that may fall outside their group of intimates. Strong ties are relatively limited in scope. Conversely, people with weak ties are able to better manage themselves in a community environment because they tend to have more extensive social networks. Weak ties allow for more diverse relationships with more people (Granovetter, 1993).

Not surprisingly, offenders tend to have more strong ties than weak ones. This is because offenders customarily rely on family and close friends to assist them with the reentry process. The longer an offender has been out of circulation the more likely their network has reduced in scope. Family dynamics change significantly when offenders go to prison, as family members are forced to pick up the slack with regard to work and childcare. Moreover, relationships suffer not only while the offender is in prison, but also when he/she returns to the community (Rose & Clear, 2002). The limited social network most often available to offenders upon release makes it difficult for them to generate the support they need to help address any housing, treatment, or employment needs they may have. Moreover, the small social networks often compromised during incarceration are difficult if not impossible to sustain in the long term (Clear et al., 2005).

Social Capital

Social capital differs from social networks. Social networks are the relationships that people have with each other. Social capital is the "capacity of the networks to provide goods for people within these networks" (Clear et al., 2005, p. 191). This distinction is particularly relevant when we are talking about the degree to which offenders are able to use social networks to their advantage.

Ordinarily, offenders have social networks with strong ties that normally display low social capital. That is, the relationships that offenders have with others are usually very limited in scope and therefore do not provide the level of social capital necessary to meet their competing and demanding needs. The myriad needs that were once met either through employment, access to governmental assistance, or other means prior to incarceration are now not met. As is often the case, the people who comprise offenders' social networks distrust them and are not willing to provide the social capital or financial or other resources necessary to assist them.

Scholars argue that social capital is also, "a byproduct of social relationships that provides the capacity for collective understanding and action," and is a critical component necessary for the effective function of neighborhoods (Rose & Clear, 2001, p. 1). Because social capital promotes the sharing of resources among friends, it encourages like-minded people to join together. This sharing of resources brings the citizens of a community together to establish their collective values and goals (Rose & Clear, 2002). Consequently, people in the community who may not think like, act like, and/or support the similar goals of the majority are marginalized to the point of exclusion.

Collective Efficacy

Where social capital is the extent to which social networks are able to supply goods and services to those who reside within the network, collective efficacy is the ability of a group of people to come together to problem-solve or otherwise work together toward the collective good. Towns and cities with high levels of collective efficacy work together to solve problems and hold similar beliefs about cultural and societal norms. Communities with low levels of collective efficacy often do not agree on communal norms and are less able to work together to solve problems (Anderson, 1996).

Collective efficacy requires communal stability. Communities are unable to come together to work toward common goals if they are not stable in population, lifestyle, and normative beliefs. Therefore, it is understandable that neighborhoods that face high rates of mobility, lack a stable population, and have difficulty establishing norms are volatile and disorganized and have low levels of collective efficacy. These communities are also often comprised of people who form superficial interpersonal relationships and who withdraw from public participation because they do not feel engaged. As a consequence, social disorganization results, the outcome of which is often increased crime. People who live in high-crime areas may wish to move but are sometimes not able to do so (Wilson, 1997). The ability to voluntarily leave a community is difficult and made more challenging by coerced mobility or the cycling through of community members not because they are voluntarily coming and going, but because those that were removed from the community and incarcerated are also coming home (Clear et al., 2005).

Social Control

Informal social control is those relationships, networks, and other forces that maintain order and adherence to societal norms that are outside the formal authority of the state (Hunter, 1985). This is very different from formal social control that includes formal agents of control such as corrections departments, the courts, parole boards, etc.—organizations that have traditionally been responsible for offender reentry (Byrne et al., 2002). Where formal social control is important, it doesn't routinely change and is generally not as effective as informal social control in mediating behavior (Sampson, 1988; Gottfredson & Hirschi, 1990).

There are two specific types of informal social control: private and parochial. Private social control is comprised of the influence and authority of family and close friends who are able to encourage loved ones to conform to social norms and to engage in socially accepted behavior. Understandably, private social control relies on strong ties to encourage adherence to social expectations. Parochial social control is influence exercised by social relations that exist between individuals and local organizations, including churches, employers, etc. Weak ties are the foundation of this type of control (Clear et al., 2005)

The inability of a community to informally control the behavior of its citizens often results in changing community norms, thereby resulting in an increased incidence of disorder and crime (Markowitz et al., 2001; Sampson et al., 1997). Clear and colleagues (2003) argue that this often occurs as a result of coerced mobility. When coerced mobility takes place, collective efficacy, social capital, and parochial informal social control networks are jeopardized because families are often required to abandon (even if temporarily) their focus on weak ties in an effort to circle the wagons and exert strong ties as a means of assisting the returning offender.

Moreover, a focus on strong ties to the exclusion of weak ties upsets the balance of the community and causes them to become unstable in their ability to support their constituents (Clear et al., 2001). The movement of large numbers of people in and out of communities due to imprisonment reduces the ability of communities to effectively manage informal social control.

> When oversubscribed social networks are forced to accommodate a newly returning ex-prisoner, they become even less likely to shift attention to collective action at the community level. When locations absorb large numbers of ex-prisoners who do not return to welcoming family systems, the capacity for meaningful collectivity is even more burdened. (Clear et al., 2005, p. 193)

Reentry Cycling and Coercive Mobility

Incomplete or fractured informal social control creates feelings of distrust and alienation that results in more people abstaining from positive contributions to communal goals and norms. A community void of active civic participation creates reduced collective efficacy and social capital, and ultimately impacts public safety (Clear et al., 2005). Moreover, given that the act of cycling in and out of the community is coerced, it is not difficult to imagine how the constant tide of people moving in and out of the community against their will would destabilize the lives of those incarcerated as well as those who remain behind (Clear et al., 2003).

No doubt, some family and friends of incarcerated individuals benefit from their departure; they may feel safer, no longer be victims, etc. However, despite the benefits of this removal, families often feel great loss. As established elsewhere, family members often withdraw from social life when their loved one is incarcerated due to fear and judgment of others. These actions may result in changes in family members' attitudes about their loved one and the system itself. Poor attitudes about the police or the criminal justice system may further weaken already tenuous levels of informal social control (Clear et al., 2003). Moreover, while the neighborhood might be a safer place because a family member has been incarcerated, family stability is weakened and familial burdens often increase (Rose & Clear, 2001).

The result of people cycling in and out of impoverished communities is concentrated and overlapping and has a cumulative effect over time (Clear et al., 2005). Large numbers of people cycling through communities means they are transient rather than static participants in the community-building process, often resulting in breakdowns in social capital, collective efficacy, and informal social control. Moreover, the cumulative effect of this cycling process over time creates constant instability in the community due to a "homeostasis of missing people" (Clear et al., 2005, p. 202).

Removing criminally active residents assuredly reduces crime to some extent. Returning them undermines that effect. Having some proportion of residents in flux destabilizes social relationships in ways that undercut informal social control. "The net result is that, at high enough levels, reentry cycling can result in considerable social disruption and produce the very problems that incarceration is meant to ameliorate" (Clear et al., 2005, p. 202).

Promising Practice

The extent to which reentry cycling, coercive mobility, social capital, and collective efficacy can be mediated with current criminal justice practice is unclear. One could easily argue that traditional criminal justice practice has failed to definitively address criminal justice needs in the community, mostly because of the one-size-fits-all, universal approach to managing crime, incarceration, and ultimately, offender reentry. Moreover, despite public opinion that supports offender rehabilitation, public opinion indicates that by and large, residents of communities to where offenders return believe that the impetus for reform and rehabilitation lies in the individual. Apparently, communities have not made the link between community engagement and offender reentry outcome. How do scholars and practitioners reconcile community perceptions about who is responsible for achieving positive reentry outcomes with the knowledge that what residents think and what researchers know about what works is different?

Despite constituents' beliefs about who is responsible for reentry, communities are a necessary ingredient for successful offender reintegration. In fact, scholars generally agree that offender reentry must be a collective effort between the offender, official state entities (i.e., corrections authorities), and the community if any positive outcomes are to be achieved (Wilkinson, 2005). By way of example, community corrections entities (e.g., probation and parole) have been lobbying for some time for criminal justice policies and practices that expand the locus of community supervision through coordinating and developing community capacity to assist offenders in the areas of mental health, substance abuse, and employment. One way to accomplish this task is to put the "community" back in community corrections by having probation and paroling authorities address community as well as individual offender concerns and moving probation and parole officers out from behind the desk so that they are able to supervise in neighborhood settings (Byrne, 1989). By way of example, the neighborhood of Coronado in Phoenix, Arizona, established a neighborhood probation office. The officers work only with residents of Coronado in a space donated at the back of a church. Caseloads include the probationer, their family, their neighbors, and the community in which they live. Systematic efforts are made to incorporate the community and input of residents into case management planning and to improve the quality of life in the neighborhood. "The probation office promotes three key concepts: (1) awareness in the community, (2) partnerships in the community, and (3) the exchange of knowledge and ideas among community members and influential parties to create innovative techniques to guide offender supervision and community development" (Clear & Cannon, 2002, p. 44).

Of course, criminal justice practice that encourages participation from various stakeholders in the reentry process is fundamentally different than a community-centered approach to offender management. Community justice is a vision of a justice system that links its actions to the quality and safety of community life. It redefines justice objectives away from traditional, disinterested law enforcement toward an activist, involved system that treats crime as a community problem to be unraveled (Clear & Karp, 1999, p. 16).

The underlying assumption of community justice is that there are specific locations where crime occurs and where concentrated efforts to manage it must intersect. And while the laws that govern these neighborhoods and towns might be similar, the responses to these problems should be neighborhood-specific and driven by specific local needs (Clear & Cadora, 2003).

Several scholars advocate for an approach that puts the community squarely in the middle of the reentry process. They argue that community justice models not only support programs and treatment for offenders in a community setting, but also emphasize the role of the community as the heart of the reentry process (Corbett et al., 1999; Petersilia, 1999). A community-centric approach to offender reentry would provide services that are place dependent rather than offender dependent. Reorienting public views of offender management from the individual to the communal level might also encourage the public to rethink their stance on the role that the community plays in the reentry process (Rose & Clear, 2001). This method of service provision would likely also be more efficient and cost effective. Community-based service centers associated with specific neighborhoods would be neighborhood-specific and would be a reflection of the specific needs of the community in which they were located, thereby enhancing social capital and collective efficacy (Rose & Clear, 2001).

Clear suggests that there are three core principles to the community justice model: an emphasis on restoration, maintaining those who are convicted of crimes in community-based interventions, and a more balanced approach to managing offenders—one that includes pro-social or ameliorative interventions as well as punitive ones (Clear, 2007). Various permutations of Clear's suggestions have been implemented, most recently through the Reentry Partnership Initiatives.

These community-based and community-centric programs are geographically located in areas that demonstrate the most need (i.e., they target one or two zip codes or areas that have been determined to have significantly high numbers of people incarcerated and who are actively preparing for reentry from prison to the community). Furthermore, these partnership initiatives are proactive and emphasize problem-solving techniques that highlight community, not individual offender, problems and promote decentralized program authority and accountability (Young et al.,2002). Study sites are located across the United States in Maryland, Vermont, California, and Nevada. Other examples of community justice models of reentry include Manhattan's Community Court and Operation Night Light (Barajas, 1998).

One of the central criticisms of community justice is that it focuses on integrating current methods of criminal justice practice in the community but does not principally restructure how society views justice. That is, while community justice is a method of dealing with crime and criminality at the local or neighborhood level, it uses principles of justice that are retributive in nature and part of conventional methods of implementing criminal justice. Critics contend that in order for community justice to be effective, retributive justice must be replaced by restorative justice policy and practice.

Where the focus of retributive justice is to punish the offender in a way that approximates the amount of harm done to the victim, or punishment for punishment's sake, restorative justice seeks to restore and repair harm by rebuilding relationships (Van Ness & Strong, 2010). Restorative justice is predicated on the idea that social capital will improve and communal ties will strengthen when communities work together toward a common goal. It is a way of viewing justice that eschews traditional adversarial approaches to punishment in favor of a system that seeks to repair harm caused by crime in a non-adversarial process that invites offenders to take responsibility rather than simply to take their punishment (Bazemore & Maruna, 2009; Settles, 2009). Put another way, restorative justice seeks to strengthen community bonds, enable victims to regain control over their lives, and promote offender reintegration in an effort to reduce crime (Center for Restorative Justice and Mediation, 1996).

Restorative justice is comprised of three basic principles: the principles of repair, stakeholder involvement, and transformation in community and government roles and relationships. The principle of repair argues that the primary purpose of any restorative process is to repair the harm caused by the offender (and the crime) to the greatest extent possible. When a crime is committed, several victims are harmed. First, the individual victim of a crime is harmed. Second, the community in which the crime took place is harmed. While physical destruction of communal property might occur, more likely a communal sense of safety is jeopardized. Third, offenders harm themselves through engaging in criminal activity (Van Ness & Strong, 2010).

The principle of stakeholder involvement encourages active, rather than passive participation in the justice process. Currently, victims have relatively little say in how cases are managed. Victims often play a secondary or tertiary role in the adjudication process. Moreover, community participation is generally limited to serving on juries; something most community members make concerted efforts to avoid. Furthermore, offenders are generally passive participants in the justice process. Most often, justice is done to offenders (Van Ness & Strong, 2010).

The final principle of restorative justice requires communities and governments to rethink their roles and relationships with victims and offenders and each other. Reactive approaches to doing justice should be replaced with collaborative efforts to heal loss and repair harm (Bazemore & Maruna, 2009).

> By recognizing communities as being corollary victims to crime, communities become better positioned to coalesce around the goal of collective engagement and form reciprocal relationships with each other, victims, and offenders that ultimately serve the purpose of reintegration. (Settles, 2009, p. 294).

Restorative justice programs take a variety of forms, including circles of support and accountability (COSA), conferencing, mediation, and impact panels. Circles are a very popular form of restorative justice that promote discussion about the harm that crime causes the community and seeks to encourage offenders to understand the impact of their actions on the community (Van Ness & Strong, 2010). Circles were derived from aboriginal peacemaking practices and are meetings that include the community, victims, offenders, and members of the justice system. The facilitator is usually a community member whose primary responsibility is to keep order. Members of the circle are encouraged to speak openly and honestly about general issues related to crime; an offender's specific crime is less important to the discussion than the offender's willingness to understand their role in the community and the consequences their actions have on the community at large (Van Ness & Strong, 2010). By way of example, citizen circles in Ohio neighborhoods have expanded community support for offenders actively engaged in the reentry process since 2001 (Jenkins & Bazemore, 2006).

Conferencing attempts to bring together victims and the offender who harmed them. In some cases this is possible, and in other instances the victim and/or the offender do not wish to meet. For those victims and offenders who agree to meet, conferencing provides the opportunity to discuss issues related to specific harms. These meetings are facilitated and often also include family members (Van Ness & Strong, 2010).

Where conferencing encourages the victim, offender, and family to come together to talk, mediation brings the victim and offender together to talk about the crime and to agree on specific interventions. The victim and the offender are encouraged to resolve the dispute together and to agree on the steps necessary to make that happen. The goals of mediation are to empower participants, promote dialogue, and encourage mutual problem-solving (Van Ness & Strong, 2010).

Impact panels are a constructive way of emphasizing restorative principles when offenders and their victims would prefer not to meet or other logistical issues prevent a one-on-one meeting from occurring. Victim impact panels bring together groups of victims and offenders who are matched by crime type. These panels provide victims with the opportunity to inform offenders about how their behavior caused damage to others and provide victims with an opportunity to voice their frustrations (Van Ness & Strong, 2010).

The extent to which restorative justice is utilized as an adjunct to already existing criminal justice policy and practice or as a method of bringing the victim, the community, and the offender into the crime control process, is not known. Most restorative justice programming has been implemented in New Zealand and in Western Europe because of perceptions of crime and punishment that are more amenable to embracing restorative justice principles (Bazemore & Maruna, 2009). Moreover, outcomes-based evaluations of restorative justice programs are not prevalent.

However, the promise of implementing restorative justice techniques is great. First, the community-centric nature of restorative reentry makes it a unique criminal justice practice. Communities that are invested partners in the process associated with people leaving prison and returning to the community, turn communal liabilities into assets and become the primary facilitators (and owners) of the reentry process (Maloney et al., 2001; Maruna, 2001). Second, a reparations-based justice model promotes offender accountability. Through giving back to victims and communities through community service or restitution, the offender earns redemption and actively attempts to make good (Bazemore & Erbe, 2004; Bazemore & Maruna, 2009; Maruna, 2001).

Third, offender reentry that is restorative in nature seeks to reduce or minimize the stigma and degradation associated with having been removed from the community and with being an ex-offender by encouraging a process of reentry that is transparent, understandable, and acceptable to victims and the community alike. A model of jurisprudence that changes the way offenders see themselves and how the public views offending can only work to strengthen ties between offenders and the community (Bazemore & Maruna, 2009; Maruna, 2001). Moreover, modified perceptions of offenders and offending could and likely would result in increased tolerance for offenders in the community setting and a greater willingness on the part of the community to provide social capital and informal support and assistance (Bazemore & Stinchcomb, 2004).

Some scholars argue that restorative justice will not be embraced or implemented in any wholesale way because its aims and goals will be co-opted. Research indicates that even though the premise of restorative justice is restoration, offenders may feel coerced into participating in restorative justice programming (Brown, 1994). Some scholars argue that use of restorative justice principles will extend the reach of the criminal justice system to minor offenders: people that would not have been included in traditional criminal justice interdictions (Bazemore & Umbreit, 1995). Still others contend that restorative justice practices may expand the number of community-based supervision requirements (conditions of probation and parole) that some offenders must follow (Bazemore & Umbreit, 1995).

Other detractors suggest that restorative justice ignores the principles of effective intervention in the sense that it does not take into account how offender risk and need impact treatment and program provision (Levrant et al., 1999). These naysayers contend that restorative justice is only concerned with matching interventions to the extent of the harm caused by the crime or the seriousness of the offense (Gendreau et al., 1996; Levrant et al., 1999).

Disagreements regarding restorative justice aside, the impact of a community-level approach to understanding offender reentry cannot be ignored. Consideration of individual-level reentry hurdles associated with housing, education, and employment is not enough. Community-level factors must also be recognized as catalysts to the reentry process. Where high levels of social capital and collective efficacy can significantly positively impact the reentry experience, communities in which social networks are poor and where low levels of informal social control exist can make the reentry process futile.

Part III

Blueprint for Change

Chapter 15

A Strengths-Based Approach to Offender Reentry

By now, it should be evident that usual and customary management of offenders reentering the community is deficit driven. The fact is that efforts to manage and mitigate offender reentry are traditionally grounded in deconstructing, assessing, and evaluating problems. Whether the individual-based issue is homelessness, lack of education, unemployment, substance abuse, physical health problems, mental health deficits, or family concerns, problems are the genesis of current reentry ideology, policy, and practice. Contextual factors of reentry are also generally problem centered. Whether one views reentry through the risk assessment, risk management, or risk reduction lens, one is more concerned with what's wrong with offenders than what is not. Even consideration of reentry in the context of stigma, public opinion, gender, and community presupposes that offenders lack identity, have minimal support from the public, differ by gender, and adversely impact not only themselves and their families, but the larger community as well.

At base, a deficit-based approach to viewing the world significantly limits our collective ability to think more broadly, and therefore differently, about social issues in general and the offender reentry problem in particular. Unfortunately, the criminal justice system's reliance on a problem-based approach to offender reentry suggests that problems are much easier to identify than to solve. However, if we introduce a different dialogue—a narrative that promotes positive offender engagement and perspective—perhaps the Reentry conversation can change and reentry policy and practice can improve in meaningful ways.

The Deficit-Based Approach

Since its inception as a recognized discipline, social work has used methods specifically designed to determine problems, including the adoption of a deficit-based approach to managing social issues. This practice began as part of a larger movement in American social history wherein social problems were treated as any illness might be treated in medicine. This evolution in thought is also an outgrowth of the professionalization movement in social work.

The medical model was grounded in terminology borrowed from the medical and psychology fields. In social work terms, the medical model manifested itself in the medicalization of social problems that required the diagnosis of problems and assignment of treatments based on symptoms or pathology (Rapp et al., 2005). Of course, framing social problems in a medical context encouraged a focus on disorders, problems, weaknesses, and deficits. If a problem can be identified (i.e., diagnosis), then a solution (i.e., treatment) can be developed (Kaminer, 1993). The medical model provided a means by which social workers were able to diagnose a problem and then choose from an available array of interventions that would minimize or eradicate the issue altogether. Interestingly, what the medical model does is to reinforce the notion that people with problems are different. This problem-centric method argues that people need help because they have problems that set them apart from the mainstream. Consequently, in order to overcome problems, people require assistance from professionals who are qualified to help manage problems and facilitate solutions—professionals such as social workers.

Unfortunately, the medical model is a self-fulfilling prophecy. An individual who is viewed by self or others as having problems enlists someone to play the role of problem-solver (Weick et al., 1989). The problem becomes the focus of the relationship between the helper and the helped to the point that people are labeled (i.e., alcoholic, offender) and the helper/helped relationship is perpetuated to the point that people are unable to identify their own strengths and abilities, let alone understand how to use them properly (Staudt et al., 2001). This creates a dynamic wherein the helper (i.e., social worker) is placed in a position of authority or primacy over the clients they serve, essentially wresting any control or agency away from the client and placing it in the hands of the person who knows best. Once this relationship is established, it is difficult to move beyond this paradigm. Clients are forever tied to seeking assistance for problems that professionals deem legitimate and to accepting solutions they had little or no hand in developing (Weick et al., 1989).

What problem-based approaches to client management fail to consider is that people may have deficits, but they also possess strengths; qualities, characteristics, and points of view that can positively impact their quality of life. Where an emphasis on deficits showcases individual weakness, concern for strengths encourages people to address problems using their own abilities, skills, and talents, thereby providing them with some semblance of control over their problems and their lives. Moreover, investment in the process (i.e., active participation in identifying the problem and helping to develop a solution) often results in greater commitment to the outcome (Weick et al., 1989).

The Strengths-Based Approach

It is overly simplistic to assume that the shift from a problem-based to strengths-based approach to managing client problems occurs overnight. Instead, it is more likely that the issue has always been one of emphasis wherein social work has, "focused on problems and problem reversal coupled with helping people move forward to realize their dreams and potential" (McMillen et al., 2004, p. 321).

Naturally, when a paradigm shift occurs, it is easiest to understand the change by viewing it as a dichotomy. In this way, a compare/contrast approach is able to highlight differences between the old and new modes of thinking. As Table 15-1 illustrates, problem-oriented approaches to managing social problems often result in an emphasis on hierarchical relationships rather than collegial ones.

Table 15-1. Comparison/Contrast of Problem-Oriented and Strengths-Based Approaches to Client Management

Problem-Oriented Approach	Strengths-Based Approach
Hierarchical relationships	Collaborative relationships
Assignment of blame that results in guilt and shame	Encourage accountability, responsibility through positive action
Elicits defensive response	Promotes positive engagement
Minimizes capabilities, emphasizes problems	Maximizes capabilities, minimizes problems
Focuses on individual-level problems	Focuses on problems at the individual and community level

Adapted from McMillen et al., 2004.

Moreover, clients addressed from a deficit standpoint are often labeled and feel shame and guilt and, as a result, may become defensive when they feel that they constantly have to justify themselves and their actions. Furthermore, a deficit-based approach to managing social issues often results in assignment of minimal goal expectations because a person's positive qualities and capabilities are constantly obscured by an emphasis on problems.

As the social work discipline has moved away from deficit-driven approaches to problems, it has embraced "strengths-based, solution-focused, capacity building, asset creating, motivation enhancing" empowerment models that accentuate the positive (McMillen et al., 2004, p. 317). Saleebey (1992) best defines the strengths-based perspective as an orientation that asserts:

- All people possess strengths that can be identified and used to improve the quality of people's lives
- People are motivated to achieve goals based upon strengths they possess or believe they possess
- Discovering one's strengths is not easy but is possible with the assistance of professionals
- Attention to people's strengths to the exclusion of a focus on deficits encourages a forward-looking approach
- All environments contain resources

Put another way, a strengths-based perspective is a goal-oriented approach to problem solving that encourages people to take control of their lives and to work proactively to locate and employ solutions to increase their capacity for well-being (Blundo, 2001). A strengths-based approach emphasizes positive attributes and highlights individual capabilities. This paradigm is predicated on the belief that everyone has redeeming qualities or characteristics that can assist them in moving forward. In essence, people have untapped resources or, "undetermined reservoirs of mental, physical, emotional, social, and spiritual abilities that can be expressed" (Wieck et al., 1989, p. 352). For offenders to desist from crime, Maruna argues that they must "develop a coherent, prosocial identity for themselves" (2001, p. 7). Desisters from crime have described themselves as having a "good brain, good heart or some other positive attribute" that was able to be re-established with the help of others who believed in them (Maruna, 2001, p. 91). When these qualities are expressed positively, personal growth is possible. Ronel and Segey (2014) suggest that "reducing negative causes and managing risk will not automatically prompt positive human development and elements that are associated with desistance" (p. 1389). An emphasis on positive attributes encourages positive personal growth compared with problem-oriented approaches that accentuate the negative. People do not grow by concentrating on their problems. "Treatment is not just fixing what is broken; it is nurturing what is best within ourselves" (Seligman, 1998, p. 1). In fact, a focus on the negative only serves to undermine confidence and weaken self-esteem (Wieck et al., 1989). In most instances, people know what is best for them. One need only ask.

Unfortunately, not everyone is able or knows how to harness the positive attributes they possess. In this instance, they may require the assistance of others who are able to guide and assist them in doing so. The social worker's job becomes one where they encourage people to evaluate and assess their options and to increase their consciousness and self-realization about what is best (Weick & Pope, 1988). In this paradigm, the professional works collaboratively with the client to identify desires and resources, rather than acting in the capacity of expert (Staudt et al., 2001).

In essence, a strengths-based approach requires people to set goals for themselves and to determine the steps they need to achieve them by focusing on their strengths rather than their weaknesses (Rapp et al., 2005). Goal setting can be overwhelming, and most people do not know where to begin. Therefore, a strengths-based approach emphasizes goal setting that utilizes existing strengths with an eye toward cultivating and developing these strengths in the long-term. In this way, short- as well as long-term goals can be set with specific tasks, roles, and responsibilities identified so that people have a clear sense of what will be required of them in order to progress. Strengths-based problem management also places an emphasis on those qualities that people possess that enable them to persevere and move forward in the face of adversity. In the context of our discussion here, a strengths-based approach to problem-solving harnesses protective factors so that people learn how to manage problems and adapt to change in often negative or difficult situations (Rapp et al., 2005).

Efforts to assess client strengths mirror those used to identify client deficits. Clients are interviewed/evaluated in some way and an assessment of their strengths and their ability to employ them takes place (Cowger, 1994). This approach to assessment is extremely beneficial because it promotes personal empowerment rather than the unequal power dynamic that is emphasized in a deficit-based assessment approach (Cowger, 1992). How a client defines situations and circumstances in their lives and the approach they take toward personal improvement will determine to a large extent the degree to which the client is able to achieve their goals. A strengths-based approach to assessment emphasizes an equal power relationship between the professional and the client, making people feel valued in the decision-making process and worthy and in control of their own destiny (Kisthardt, 2009).

When strengths-based assessment is utilized, the professional must respect clients' understanding of the facts. While there are multiple constructions of reality for all situations, professionals must be willing to assign relevance to the client's view of a situation or circumstance (Cowger, 1994). Perception can dictate to a large degree whether, and to what extent, clients will address and manage their problems. Clients will be less likely to manage problems they do not believe exist just as they will be more likely to acknowledge problems that they do believe exist. "A client's understandings of reality are no less real than the social constructions of reality of the professionals assisting them" (Cowger, 1994, p. 265). A practitioner who is judgmental of clients' decisions and actions fosters untrustworthiness and diminishes the likelihood that clients will divulge information that could be useful to their progress.

An understanding of client goals should be paramount to any strengths-based approach to client management. Of course, goal setting must be done as a collaborative exercise using language that the client understands and does not feel threatened by. Professionals should use interviewing techniques that encourage clients to express their strengths and plans for goal attainment (De Jong & Miller, 1995). Goals that are developed should be reasonable and specific and should impact behavior, but do not always have to be finite in scope (De Jong & Miller, 1995). Goals should be developed based on an understanding of the resources necessary to assist in goal attainment: resources that are located within the client's local neighborhood/community (Kisthardt, 2009). The more invested a client is in setting their goals, the more motivated they will likely be to attempt to achieve them. Mutually agreed upon goals forged between client and practitioner are more likely to stand the test of time and are goals that clients are motivated to achieve. If clients are not motivated, the best-intended goals will remain unrealized (Cowger, 1994).

Strengths-based case management focuses exclusively on the capabilities of the client. The development of a mutually agreed upon case management plan usually requires that the practitioner obtain information from the client on a variety of different issues. Research indicates that case management plans that are developed in concert between the practitioner and the client, and that engage clients in the intervention process promote successful outcomes (Sousa et al., 2006). One way to engage the client using a strengths-based interview perspective is to focus on questions that promote the positive and are forward looking, rather than the more customary deficit-focused questions. For example, instead of asking a client what is wrong with their lives, practitioners might ask the client to imagine what their future will look like when their problem or issue is solved. A focus on what can be different moves clients away from thoughts about what will never change (De Jong & Miller, 1995).

Effective strengths-based interviewing strategies use a variety of questioning techniques. Exception-finding questions encourage the interviewer to probe the client for information regarding occasions in a client's life when the problem in question could have occurred, but did not. These questions enable the practitioner to determine clients' prior successes and to use these in an effort to help the client frame goals for the future (De Jong & Miller, 1995). Questions that require clients to frame their issues on a sliding scale are also often useful to practitioners developing strengths-based case management plans. For example, interviewers might ask clients to rank the issue in question on a scale from one to ten. In this way, clients are able to make their own assessments about where they think they are in managing a problem and where they think they can be in the future (De Jong & Miller, 1995).

The way in which practitioners frame interview questions directly influences how clients view their problems and the degree to which they believe these problems can be solved. As a result, the relationship between the practitioner and client is an essential component of the strengths-based case management process. As practitioners interact with clients, their words and actions can significantly impact client actions and behavior. Practitioners' word choice and demeanor can serve to empower or alienate clients (Madsen, 1999). What practitioners say and how they say it can influence client outcome.

Another critical component of the case management process is to inform clients that goal attainment is a process: one that requires hard work, dedication, and perseverance. Clients should have (and professionals should provide) realistic expectations of what they will achieve and also recognize that change is difficult and does not come easily. Moreover, clients should recognize that failure is possible. Not surprisingly, clients may become disheartened if they do not achieve one or more of their goals. However, if clients are coached on how to view failure (as an opportunity to work harder rather than as a moral failing), they are more likely to be motivated to continue (De Jong & Miller, 1995).

Research and Evaluation of Strengths-Based Practice

In theory, strengths-based client management has merit, but how well does it work in practice? Research in this area is generally limited to the area of substance abuse treatment. A meta-analysis that evaluated the benefit of strengths-based case management over traditional case management models determined that clients who received strengths-based case management showed improvement over those who did not (Staudt et al., 2001). Other studies indicate that strengths-based case management is associated with increased retention in aftercare for drug-using clients (Siegal et al., 1997), improved retention and less severe substance use (Rapp et al., 1998), and enhanced functioning on the job (Siegal et al., 1996).

A study by Siegal and colleagues (1995) evaluated the benefit of strengths-based case management in an inpatient substance abuse program. Specific strengths-based case management techniques were employed, including not reading the client's substance abuse assessment or medical record prior to the first meeting so as to remain objective and asking the client to rate their level of functioning in nine principal domains (i.e., life skills, finance, leisure, relationships, living arrangements, occupation, education, health, internal resources, and recovery). These progress evaluation scales (PES) were not assessments of deficit, but evaluations of strengths. Clients were asked questions intended to determine when and to what extent they were able to accomplish a task, use a skill, or fulfill a goal in a particular domain (Siegal et al., 1995).

Ratings by both the case manager and client were then translated into specific goals in the case management plan. Only concrete strategies for attaining goals that were also reasonable and measurable were developed. For example, if a client goal was to improve their opportunity for professional advancement, two specific objectives for achieving that goal might include taking and passing the GED and completing a course on identifying job interests. Examples of strategies employed to meet those objectives might include studying for the GED ten hours per week and scheduling an appointment to take the GED (Siegal et al., 1995). Regular review of goals, objectives, and strategies encouraged clients to move forward, and goals were adjusted as necessary. Results from this study indicate that fully two-thirds of the total number of client objectives (n=868) were completed. Specifically, goals set to address tangible needs including the life domain (the ability to get along with others), living arrangements, education/employment, and recovery were most often and most successfully achieved (Siegal et al., 1995).

Qualitative work assessing the efficacy of strengths-based case management has also been conducted. The purpose of this research was to understand how clients interpreted the strengths-based interventions they received so that their needs could be more effectively met (Brun & Rapp, 2001). As in prior quantitative studies, client strengths assessments were conducted in the nine primary life domains. Clients were then asked to recount specific instances when they successfully demonstrated skills and abilities relative to a particular life domain. Case managers then worked with clients to develop structured goals with tangible, measurable, and attainable objectives and strategies (Brun & Rapp, 2001).

Results from this study are grouped into two thematic areas: individuals' responses to the strengths-based focus and individuals' responses to the professional relationship (Brun & Rapp, 2001). Data from the first theme, individuals' responses to the strengths-based focus, indicates that study participants felt positive and hopeful about their recovery, but recognized that there would be significant work involved in the process. Results from the second theme, individuals' responses to the professional relationship, reveal that clients felt that the relationships they developed with their case managers helped prepare them for reentering the community after they completed inpatient substance abuse treatment. Clients also expressed wonder at the fact that "[somebody would] care that much" and a sense of obligation toward the case manager when they felt they may have "let them down" (Brun & Rapp, 2001, p. 284).

One practical implication of the strengths-based approach to case management is the belief that clients would be uncomfortable sharing intimate details of their life or not "buy in" to the idea that they have strengths. Results from the Brun and Rapp (2001) study illustrate how an emphasis on strengths can stimulate enlightened and truthful discussion about wishes, goals, and desires. Furthermore, this study further underscores the importance of the relationship between the client and case manager.

Criticisms of Strengths-Based Practice

It would be short sighted to assume that the strengths-based approach has been universally embraced. On the contrary, this practice is not without its critics. One primary concern is that the strengths perspective is Pollyanna in its orientation. Some argue that the strengths approach ignores the fact that people can be manipulative, dangerous, and destructive, not only to themselves but to others (Saleebey, 1996). Another criticism is that the strengths perspective ignores or significantly downplays real problems and minimizes reality. A third concern is that the strengths perspective merely reframes misery to the extent that clients are not expected to do the work needed for life transformation (Saleebey, 1996).

In response to these criticisms, Saleebey offers the following. A strengths-based perspective asks only that practitioners agree that everyone has some useful skills and aspirations that can be used to address needs and resolve conflicts. Nowhere does this method of practice suggest that people will not be deceptive or manipulate situations or circumstances to get what they want. Instead, the challenge is for practitioners to identify useful skill sets and positive qualities in the clients they serve and to determine how to harness these characteristics in pro-social ways. While there may be some people for whom redemption is not possible, it is unreasonable (and unethical) to make such an assumption outright (Saleebey, 1996).

The second major criticism of strengths-based practice is that it ignores real problems. On the contrary, strengths-based practice recognizes problems (i.e., unemployment, homelessness) but does so by forcing clients to think about how they have managed the problems in the past and what they have learned from past experiences. If deficits are the focus of treatment and case management, the "diagnosis become[s] a cornerstone of identity" (Saleebey, 1996, p. 303). Addressing one's problems is a necessity; it is the way in which one does so that matters most. As Cousins (1989) argues, one may not be able to deny the verdict (a diagnosis or outcomes of an assessment), but one does not have to accept the sentence.

The third major concern regarding strengths-based practice contends that problems are reframed in such a way that people are not held accountable for their behaviors and actions. In actuality, problems will always persist; a strengths-based perspective just requires that clients are held accountable in a less punitive way to more constructive outcomes. What a strengths-based perspective does require is that we seek a new language or way of thinking about problem solving—one that focuses on possibility and opportunity, rather than negativity. Instead of articulating all that is wrong, strengths-based practice encourages clients to identify what is right and to develop skills, hopes, and aspirations so as to maximize the possibility that positive life change will occur (Saleebey, 1996).

Strengths-Based Practice in Criminal Justice

The paradigm shift from deficit-based to strengths-based practice has remained relatively localized. That is, other disciplines that might benefit from the strengths-based approach to case management—particularly criminal justice—have not adopted this method in any wholesale way. In fact, there is relatively little research on the strengths-based paradigm as it directly relates to offending populations. The scholarship that is available primarily addresses juvenile and substance-abusing offenders.

While there is scant research on the efficacy of strengths-based criminal justice practice, the principles do have merit. The first principle of strengths-based criminal justice practice is that punishment without treatment does not reduce recidivism. While significant empirical support for this statement exists (Gendreau et al., 2002; Gibbs, 1986; Taxman, 1999; Walters et al., 2007), minimal application of this principle occurs in practice. Criminal justice practitioners are loathe to accept that punishment alone will not motivate people to change. They struggle with the notion that people change because they think they can, because they are encouraged to do so, and because they believe that once they change, life will be better (Clark, 2009a).

There is no reason to believe that offenders respond to fundamentally different principles of learning, thinking, and motivation than the rest of humankind. Confrontational approaches become a self-fulfilling prophecy, engendering evasiveness and resentment while doing nothing to decrease the likelihood of repeat offenses (Viets et al., 2002, p. 27).

Criminal justice practitioners are highly skilled at telling offenders what to do, and much less familiar with the practice of engaging people in conversations about their skills and assets and what they think they may be able to achieve in the future (Clark, 2009a). If practitioners only listened to what offenders had to say, they might be better informed, more effective in their jobs, and actually learn something.

The criminal justice system claims (and current get-tough policies reinforce) that the purpose of punishment is to hold people accountable and to ensure that offenders take responsibility for their law-breaking behavior. However, the irony is that if accountability and responsibility are the foundations of our system, the foundation is on the verge of collapse. Why? Because a system that honestly promotes accountability and responsibility among its citizens would demand that any citizen who violates social norms be allowed the opportunity to seek corrective action through actively engaging in change. Strengths-based practice contends that the ability to change one's future behavior is the ultimate act of accepting responsibility for one's prior actions (Clark, 1997).

As this book has outlined in great detail, law-breaking behaviors impact a variety of different stakeholders in a variety of different ways. The offender commits a crime and a victim is harmed as a result, but there are other casualties of the offense, including victims' and offenders' families and children who are forever altered, community cohesion that is disrupted, punitive criminal justice policy that is reinforced, and stereotypes and perceptions about offenders that is perpetuated by citizenry. What separates strengths-based practice from traditional deficit-driven approaches to offender management is a focus on maximizing community support so that resources and opportunities for redemption and rehabilitation are available (Nissen, 2006). Whether the offender avails themselves of these opportunities is quite another matter.

The key to maximizing offender success lies in motivation. Without motivation, change will not occur. Consequently, it behooves criminal justice practitioners to understand how motivation works and what outcomes can result when a person is motivated to change. This, of course, requires that practitioners take an interest in the offenders on their caseload. Unfortunately, practitioners do not fully recognize the important role they play in the case management and supervision process. They are very powerful beings in the practitioner–offender dyad, leaving little question of who is in control and who holds the balance of power.

The issue lies in practitioners' needs to express this power, most often in ineffective ways. Problem-only approaches to case management provide the practitioner with the opportunity to inform the offender about all that is wrong and offer a prime opportunity to remind the offender who is boss. When practitioners exercise their power in this way, offenders feel dominated, persecuted, and are not likely to make efforts to do what practitioners tell them to do. However, when officers engage offenders in a discussion about goals, the offender is more likely to be agreeable. To that end, one of the greatest expressions of power that officers can exhibit is not their ability to wag their finger and tell people what is wrong, but their ability to motivate.

Motivation has several characteristics that make it particularly challenging. First, motivation is changeable. People can be encouraged or discouraged to complete tasks/meet goals. A good practitioner will know what motivates the offender on their caseload and will use that knowledge to encourage the offender to complete tasks/achieve goals. Second, while a motivated person does not guarantee positive action, it does increase the likelihood that the person will change. An unmotivated person will most likely not complete a task or achieve a goal where a motivated individual is at least more likely to do so (Clark, 2009a).

Third, everyone is motivated by something. The challenge is to determine what the motivating factor for each individual is and to use that information to move the offender forward. Fourth, internal and external factors impact motivation. However, people who are internally motivated are more likely to meet their goals than those whose sole motivation is extrinsically based (Clark, 2009a). For example, an offender may be motivated to complete parole because they are afraid of going back to prison (external motivation) and because they believe that being home will provide emotional and financial stability for their child (internal motivation). The child will serve as a more effective and sustainable motivator for the offender than fear of returning to prison (Viets et al., 2002).

Implementation of a strengths-based approach to criminal justice practice obviously requires the offender to change, but these changes will not be sustainable unless the system changes first. Case in point: the mechanism by which most (but not all) offenders leave prison and return to the community (parole) is predominantly deficit and problem based. Parole officers routinely identify offender problems (read as risks) and dictate the terms under which they will behave. When offenders do not behave as they are expected to, officers often sanction them through enhanced supervision techniques such as electronic monitoring, increased urine testing, more frequent office reports, and the like. Unfortunately, research has concluded that this enhanced punitive approach to supervision has little overall influence on offender behavior (Petersilia & Turner, 1991).

More startling is the fact that traditional parole practice may not pose any enhanced effect on offender outcome than if it did not exist. A study by MacKenzie and colleagues (1999) examined what factors influenced probation outcome. Results indicate that level of supervision and the degree of social control exhibited over offenders on probation did not significantly impact probation outcomes. The authors concluded that "although probation itself may reduce criminal activity, there is little evidence that what happens during probation has any additional effect on either criminal activities or violations of conditions" (Mackenzie et al., 1999, p. 446).

Given these findings, it would seem prudent to regroup and rethink customary parole practice. This idea requires pressing the reset button on how officers interact and engage with offenders. Closed off, domineering approaches to client management must be replaced with open, respectful communication. How officers behave and how they interact with others and with offenders, in addition to the words and body language they use (i.e., officer deportment), is central to offender management, particularly during the reentry process (Irwin, 1970). Recent work that explores the use of strengths-based practice in probation found that the probation officer–offender relationship is critical to successful community supervision for juveniles. Study results suggest that juvenile offenders were more responsive to officers who used a strengths-based approach and less responsive to officers who used deficit-based management (Page & Schaefer, 2011).

Current community supervision practice dictates that officers employ risk-based approaches to offender management. Risk/needs assessments are often used to identify specific areas of risk and need after which the information is used to develop a risk/needs-based case management plan. At the time that the plan is created, the officer informs the offender about their deficiencies and tells them what they need to do to correct these problems. Efforts to assist offenders with this process often include providing offenders with referrals for services in the community. Should offenders falter along the way, officers are most likely to use threats and sanctions as motivational techniques.

Where deficit-based caseload management risks alienating offenders along with increasing distrust and resentment, the strengths-based approach encourages the opposite. Officers who employ strengths-based practice engage the offender and seek to collaborate with them to develop a case plan that has meaning. This requires that offenders listen to the offender, validate their concerns, provide affirmation, praise success (however small), and assist the offender with locating resources that will directly assist them in meeting their goals (Page & Schaefer, 2011). By focusing on offender strengths, providing support and praise, and making offenders feel as if they have some modicum of control over their lives, officers build trust, gain respect, and ultimately have offenders on their caseload who are more willing to listen to their advice and council as well as to adhere to conditions of parole that directly impact public safety (Page & Schaefer, 2011).

Reentry Considerations

Clearly, for strengths-based practice to be effective in criminal justice, criminal justice practitioners must reorient their thinking about crime, punishment, and redemption (Clark, 1997). This requires that criminal justice personnel move past the status quo to embrace new (or at least different) ideas. Practitioners must themselves be willing to change if they hope to exact change among their charges. The challenge lies in the degree to which criminal justice personnel are able to put aside cynicism and despairing views of humanity and to express compassion (Van Wormer & Boes, 1999). This paradigm shift requires that practitioners accept the fundamental notion that offenders are human beings—a daunting task for many who are cynical about the people they supervise and the jobs they perform and have little faith in their own collective ability to help even one offender. At the heart of this change must be a belief in the basic goodness of mankind and the notion that even hardened criminals have strengths within themselves that have never been realized (Van Wormer & Boes, 1999).

On the heels of accepting the basic humanity in all, practitioners must also buy in to the idea that people must be empowered to change. Let's face it. The current purpose of a parole officer or other criminal justice practitioner is to facilitate change, but not in the way we might like or expect. Their directive is to convince the offender that law-breaking behavior is not beneficial and that only adhering to social norms and laws will keep them out of trouble. The message is laudable; the tactics are not. Practitioners operationalize their message through the use of enhanced surveillance techniques and more stringent police practices, the implementation of harsh sentences, and the provision of minimal treatment and programming inside prison and in the community. What if instead of only using coercive techniques, the system also sought to empower the very people they want to change, to change?

Modest efforts to integrate strengths-based practice into the criminal justice system have occurred. The juvenile justice system has recognized the benefits of this approach and has made some inroads in integrating strengths-based principles into policy and practice, but the reality is that a wholesale paradigm shift in the management of juvenile offenders has not taken place (Clark, 2009a). Strengths-based efforts for adults have been no better received.

Recent research contends that motivational interviewing (MI), an oft-used practice in criminal justice, is actually a strengths-based approach to offender management (Chung et al., 2010; Clark, 2006; Corcoran, 2005; Manthey et al., 2011). MI is a method of engaging the offender that seeks to specifically address offenders' motivation to take part in treatment and programming. Originally developed by Miller and Rollnick (1991) as a means to encourage substance abusers to change their behavior, MI has become a useful tool for probation and parole officers who seek to motivate offenders to work toward meaningful behavior change. Traditionally, MI has been associated with the responsivity principle: the belief that techniques that motivate rather than persuade should be used by practitioners to encourage offender program participation and behavior change (Andrews & Bonta, 2006).

More recently, Manthey and colleagues (2011) suggested that MI is comprised of three principal strengths-based components: collaboration, evocation, and autonomy. The authors further argue that MI encourages a collaborative environment between clients and practitioners, fosters a respect for the client's perspective and outlook, and creates an environment conducive to change. Evocation suggests that resources for change are driven by intrinsic motivation and are therefore located within the client. Finally, MI promotes autonomy as practitioners encourage the offender's ability to guide and direct change through choice (Manthey et al., 2011).

MI also alters the practitioner–offender dynamic by placing the responsibility for behavior change squarely in the hands of the offender (Clark, 2006). The premise of MI is that people who make an active effort to talk about change are more likely to change and sustain it in the long term. This change occurs through prompting people to make change statements that encourage them to express empathy for others, avoid arguing or justifying why change is not possible, and support a commitment to change (McMurran, 2009). "A person who argues in support of change is more likely to make that change, whereas a person who defends the status quo is more likely to persist in current behaviors" (Walters et al., 2010, p. 310). Furthermore, MI takes into account the fact that offenders may be ambivalent about change or may not understand or recognize how best to go about it. MI asks practitioners to meet the offender where the offender is with respect to Prochaska and DiClemente's stages of change and to serve as a guide as they move through the process (Clark, 2006).

In the context of offender populations, MI has three specific purposes: to increase program and treatment engagement and retention, to improve or enhance motivation for change, and to change behavior (McMurran, 2009). However, the extent to which MI is able to achieve these goals is mixed, primarily because program integrity varies significantly. While meta-analyses do show generally strong support for the use of this technique in offender populations (Burk et al., 2003; Hettema et al., 2005; McMurran, 2009), a recent study comparing probationers randomized to an MI and non-MI caseload indicated that outcome did not vary by caseload type (Walters et al., 2010). Unfortunately, very little is known about the specific mechanisms of action of MI and how it mediates change (Apodaca & Longabaugh, 2009; McMurran, 2009). Yet, despite these limitations, MI has been found to be more effective that traditional advice-giving 80% of the time (Hettema et al., 2005; Rubak et al., 2005) and to improve treatment engagement and retention (McMurran, 2009).

Another strengths-based approach to criminal justice management are reentry courts. Reentry courts are modeled after drug courts in the sense that judges and a collaborative team work together to take an active interest in the offender. The difference between drug and reentry courts is that reentry courts become "sentence management" entities wherein they oversee an offender from the time they are convicted to the time they return to the community (Maruna & LeBel, 2003; Travis, 2000, p. 8). Drug courts are often used on the front end in lieu of prison. The courts are able to fulfill their reentry court mission by using their authority to provide interventions and positive reinforcement to an offender once they return to the community. Particular aspects of the drug court model that have been integrated into reentry courts include assessment and strategic reentry planning, routine status update meetings, coordination of multiple support services, accountability to the community through citizen advisory boards, the application of graduated interventions when needed, and the allocation of rewards when applicable (Office of Justice Programs, 1999).

Maruna and LeBel (2003) argue that strengths-based principles may be particularly well suited to reentry courts. These authors suggest that reentry courts can work to destigmatize the reentry process by providing opportunities for offenders to make amends for what they have done. These courts can lead the way in emphasizing positive accomplishments, while also holding offenders accountable for their actions. These courts can emphasize monitoring, recording, and recognizing what offenders have done to redeem themselves through victim reparation, community service, volunteer work, mentoring, and parenting (Maruna & LeBel, 2003). Ultimately, reentry courts can publicly recognize offenders for their positive contributions, further reinforcing empowerment principles.

Still other strengths-based criminal justice practice includes the use of boundary spanners. A term originally developed for organizational management, boundary spanners are people who are tasked with interacting with people from a variety of different agencies who, because of contrasting goals, training, and skills, do not always communicate (Kerson, 2001). In the context of reentry, boundary spanners can serve as excellent resources for offenders attempting to navigate the uncertain waters of service acquisition.

A study by Pettus and Severson (2006) evaluated the role of the boundary spanner in the offender reentry process. These authors contend that a boundary spanner is a particularly useful entity in a system that often creates barriers to success, does not always support information sharing, and includes multiple agencies who present with different and sometimes competing goals (Pettus & Severson, 2006). A principal role of the boundary spanners is to evaluate for "fit." They look for congruence between organizations and agency missions, visions, goals, and objectives. They further identify who is currently providing services and assess what further services are required (Pettus & Severson, 2006).

Steadman (1992) has conceptualized boundary spanning as the process of moving between and within correctional agencies and treatment and service providers, while Bartel (2001) explains boundary spanning as a means to link organizations and agencies with key constituents in the external environment. Ultimately, boundary spanners promote system-wide coordination of individual needs across traditional system boundaries (Byrne et al., 2002; Castellano, 2011), while seeking to minimize breakdowns in communication that often lead to frustration and isolation among offenders leaving prison and returning to the community (Pettus & Severson, 2002). Boundary spanners achieve these goals by simultaneously playing the role of strategic planner, resource leverager, evaluator, and policymaker (Menefee, 1998).

Whether through motivational interviewing, reentry courts, or boundary spanners, strengths-based practice in criminal justice does exist. The degree to which these programs are embraced by practitioners and become central to reentry practice is quite another matter. Strengths-based criminal justice practice requires a revolution in role orientation for offenders, officers, and organizations alike—a challenge almost as difficult as the one offenders face when they return home from prison.

Chapter 16

A Narrative for Offender Reentry

Reentry is on our radar if only because high rates of incarceration have resulted in more offenders incarcerated, and thus, more offenders released. Where reentry has always occurred, it has generally taken place without notice. Every day since the first prison was built, people walked in the front door and left out the back. Apparently, it has taken large numbers of people engaging in the process to turn a rather private affair into a very public concern.

Now that reentry is on the radar, people are taking notice, and no one likes what they see. People leaving prison and returning to the community have problems aplenty. Deficits in education, employment skills, health concerns, and housing, and the need for legal assistance, financial assistance, public assistance, health insurance, transportation, a driver's license, clothes, and food represent just the tip of the iceberg. Where problems abound, solutions evade.

Realistically, problems of this depth and breadth do not suddenly appear. With few exceptions, these myriad issues exist at the time offenders arrive to prison, are not adequately addressed while the offender is incarcerated, and remain unmanaged at the time an offender is released from prison to the community. Of course, societal perceptions of crime, criminality, and offenders do not help matters. Grounded in an us-versus-them liturgy, politicians and practitioners alike perpetuate fear and trepidation among the masses regarding the criminal justice system's management of crime and by extension the reentry process. This results in overwhelming support for and wholesale implementation of a variety of get-tough strategies, including mandatory minimum sentencing and sentence enhancements such as three-strikes legislation that have only served to magnify problems exponentially. In addition, staunch opposition to treatment and programming along with support for collateral consequences of incarceration that extend the period of punishment long after people have left prison, have only fueled public ire and reinforced societal beliefs that these problems are theirs, not ours.

Of course, they are us. They work in the stores and businesses we frequent daily. We just do not realize it. Given that there are no outwardly distinguishing marks that identify someone as being an offender, we never know unless they (or someone) tell us. Absent a scarlet letter, all we can do is guess. Yet from these assumptions come generalizations and perceptions that are often misguided. We know what the newspapers and television tell us about what offenders do and who offenders are, but we are fundamentally uneducated regarding the law and how the criminal justice system operates. As a result, we often form opinions about offenders grounded in hearsay and belief, and we seem oblivious to the consequences of these actions. We fail to recognize how uninformed views about crime and criminals perpetuate policies, practices, and perceptions that have stigmatizing effects on the people to whom they are applied and how damaging this can be to society as a whole. We collectively abrogate our responsibilities as engaged citizens to the point that we tacitly agree with our politicians and practitioners that criminals should pay, without ever giving a second thought to what that means or who that impacts.

Because we are generally uneducated about the system, we fail to recognize that they who go to prison almost always leave and that, like it or not, they live amongst us, making their problems ours. The reality we choose to ignore is that we are them and they are us. Offender reentry is not just their problem, it is ours, too. While the crimes they commit are actions for which they must take responsibility, these crimes have far-reaching implications. Obviously, individual citizens are the victims that pay the most immediate (and sometimes ultimate) price for an offender's violation of social norms. But crime also impacts the community by inflicting significant damage to the social psyche and disrupting social cohesion both in the short and long term. The cycling of offenders from the community to prison and back fundamentally destabilizes communities to the point that they become even more vulnerable to criminal attack.

If we hope to make any progress in fighting crime, we cannot ignore offender reentry. We must take steps to move past a superficial understanding of the dimensions of the offender reentry problem to embrace a narrative that reorients the context within which we view it. This is a tall order for citizens and communities alike that may recognize that a problem exists, but who are unwilling to own it and who invoke and promote labels and stigma to widen the chasm between us and them as a means of shirking their responsibility to do so.

Identity Management through Civic Engagement

The idea that the community is a principal actor in the offender reentry process is not new. Scholars clearly elucidate the role of the community in crime (Shaw & McKay, 1942) and in mass incarceration and the impact that incarceration has on those who remain in the community and those who are removed and who ultimately return (Clear et al., 2001). What is less well understood is the degree to which the community is a conduit for helping offenders, practitioners, and policymakers alike achieve the coveted prize: successful offender reintegration.

Research regarding the civic engagement model forms the basis for this claim. The civic engagement model is predicated on the notion that decreased involvement in communal activities defined as a lack of civic commitment (e.g., the desire and/or ability to vote) impact social cohesion by weakening social bonds and reducing social capital (Bazemore & Stinchcomb, 2004). Societies that customarily deny some of their constituents access to opportunities that traditionally bind a society together, such as voting, access to occupational licenses, employment opportunities, the ability to serve in public office or participate on a jury, etc., decrease the likelihood that these members of society will engage in pro-social community life (Bazemore & Stinchcomb, 2004). As a consequence, citizens who are not fully engaged in pro-social activities in a community setting will be more likely to engage in criminal behavior.

Personal Identity

As Figure 16-1 indicates, the lynchpin to active civic engagement is personal identity. Because personal and civic identities are, at least in part, developed and maintained relative to the nature and type of relationships that people develop with others and with the social institutions with which they come into contact, significant restrictions on one's ability to take part in activities that foster civic cohesiveness and community participation result in diminished opportunities for people to promote positive identities and to exercise social capital. For example, the argument against the use of collateral consequences is that support for and exercise of policies and practices of this type exclude offenders from civic engagement, thereby negatively impacting personal identity and degrading social cohesion. As a result of these exclusionary practices, offenders are more likely to eschew traditional social norms in favor of less socially desirable behaviors (Wheelock, 2005).

Figure 16-1. Identity Management through Civic Engagement

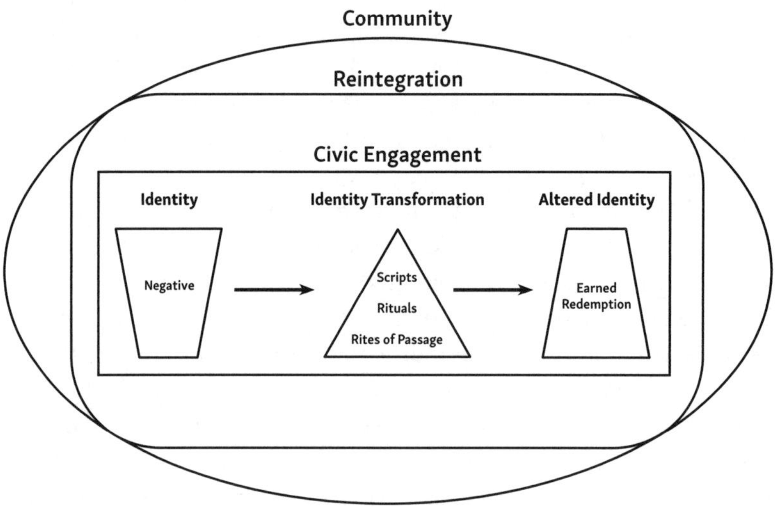

Personal identity is the product of internal and external forces. One avenue of research argues that people develop identities by being labeled by a system and those around them and through a self-fulfilling prophecy that says, "if you tell me I am it must be so" (Lemert, 1951). As a consequence, personal identities are shaped by labels society may place on us and that we may place on ourselves. It should not be shocking to anyone that people who are criminal justice-involved have negative personal identities. For example, the official labeling by society of a person as offender through adjudication of guilt or assignment to probation, prison, or parole impacts personal identity, just as an individual may come to believe that they are an offender precisely because they have been repeatedly told that they are by others. In either instance, a negative identity is easily perpetuated through the application of stigmatizing words and resulting practices that only serve to further separate them from us.

Not surprisingly, negative personal identities are difficult to overcome. In many situations, efforts to combat negative personal identities require that people employ coping practices to minimize the stigma that results from the application of derogatory labels (Link et al., 1989). Specifically, offenders often try to mitigate the stigma associated with having committed a crime or having been incarcerated through keeping the crime a secret (e.g., hiding) and withdrawing from social life so as not to draw attention to them or the crime (e.g., avoidance). In situations where they feel particularly emboldened, offenders may decide to educate or tell people the truth about their conviction before they are asked, but they often do so at significant social cost (Winnick & Bodkin, 2008).

Personal identities also impact the relationships people have with the community. People with positive personal identities are more likely to be socially engaged, invested in communal beliefs, and have a wide network of personal relationships. People with negative personal identities often find themselves on the margins with few attachments to the community. The degree to which people possess strong or weak ties in a communal environment impact the extent to which they are connected to others. As Granovetter (1993) notes, strong ties connote close personal relationships, but weak connections with people outside the inner circle. Conversely, weak ties suggest relationships with a broad spectrum of people. Where strong ties imply low social capital (people know fewer people who can help them obtain the goods and services they need), weak ties result in increased social capital because of the extensive networks people are able to rely on to assist them. Weak ties promote strong social capital and active community engagement: elements that perpetuate a positive personal identity, while strong ties result in decreased social capital and fractured civic engagement, thereby reinforcing negative personal identities. If negative personal identities are not addressed, social cohesion is jeopardized, and the possibility of active civic engagement is diminished.

Identity Transformation

The way in which negative personal identities are altered is through identity transformation. Identity transformation occurs primarily through the rewriting of scripts and a series of rituals that result in a rite of passage to earned redemption. In his qualitative work on returning prisoners, Maruna (2001) found that offenders who were most able and likely to transform their personal identities were those who felt greater control over their lives and who saw themselves as agents of their own change. Maruna argues that people, "need to make sense of their lives" (2001, p. 7). In an effort to do so, they create scripts that portray how they view themselves and their lives. Scripts are socially prescribed behavioral routines that often develop from the assignment of labels. For example, conventional scripts may dictate that "good" citizens are those that go to work each day and pay their taxes, while deviant scripts might promote rule-breaking and disregard for authority (Harré, 1981).

Maruna's research found that offenders who are likely to retain negative personal identities create condemnation scripts—narratives that are fatalistic and that blame others for their behavior. Conversely, offenders who are in the best position to transform their identities develop redemption scripts. Offenders who write these scripts reframe their lives so that they see themselves as good people who have overcome adversity and who wish to act on their potential to engage in pro-social (i.e., non-criminal) behavior (Maruna, 2001).

Of course, identity transformation is not as simple as merely rewriting one's script. There are challenges and temptations that make the transformation difficult and that may result in relapse to prior negative identities. Efforts to mediate negative identities require offenders to manage conflicts between the strong (and much more comfortable) offender identity and the desire to engage in pro-social activities that reinforce the new and desired positive identity (Rumgay, 2004). Motivation to transform comes from the desire to change, but requires constant positive reinforcement and support (Sommers et al., 1994).

As Sampson and Laub (1993) note, the strength of commitments to conventional activities such as marriage, having children, and getting a job can serve as motivation to help transition an offender from a life of crime to one that is law abiding. In this construct, identity transformation requires actions, not words. By adopting roles in the family, workplace, and in the community, offenders are able to "practice" their new identities and the other pro-social behaviors that often accompany these roles (Bazemore & Stinchcomb, 2004).

The way in which identity transformation is formalized is through rituals. Rituals are actions that are created to provide a sense of social order to the larger community (Durkheim, 1964). Society usually engages in ritualistic practice because it provides a catharsis. "Effective ritual is the solution to a seemingly insoluble problem, the management of collectively held, otherwise unmanageable distress" (Scheff, 1979, p. 133). An example of a criminal justice ritual is punishment (Maruna, 2011). Maruna (2011) contends that punishment is a ritual because it takes threats to the social order (crime and the offender) and transforms them through an act of social solidarity such as a trial.

The problem, Maruna (2011) argues, is that offender reentry has no such ritual. Where the process of turning citizens into prisoners is front-page news lauded by all, the act of turning prisoners back into citizens is little recognized and often ignored. To that end, Maruna and others suggest that reentry must be much more than the physical transition of offenders from prison to community. For reentry to truly be successful, it must include symbolic elements of "moral inclusion" such as atonement, forgiveness, and redemption (Braithwaite, 1989; Maruna, 2001, p. 4).

In order for these acts to have any societal meaning, atonement, forgiveness, and redemption must be formalized in some way. This is generally achieved through rites of passage. A rite of passage is the process wherein a person changes from one status to another. Common examples of rites of passage include baptisms, confirmations, and Bar/Bat Mitzvahs. In each instance, people possess one status that is, through ritual, replaced with another. In the context of criminal justice, punishment is a ritual that results in the degradation in one's status from citizen to offender (Garfinkel, 1956). The process of appearing in court, being adjudicated guilty, and being sentenced to incarceration is the rite of passage that propels an individual from one status to another.

As Maruna notes, no similar rituals exist for reentry as they do for punishment. Therefore, it follows that if we hope to establish atonement, forgiveness, and redemption as rituals, rites of passage must take place. However, where punishment involves what Garfinkel (1956) calls status degradation ceremonies, reentry must elevate one's status from offender back to citizen. Status elevation ceremonies that support forgiveness and redemption and that encourage offenders to atone for their actions would achieve these goals.

Rites of passage are only meaningful if they take place in the public eye. It makes no sense to atone for actions or seek forgiveness and redemption if no one knows about it. The hallmark of a ritual and the ensuing rite of passage is that it is a public display of social solidarity. Punishment is a prime example. Early punishments included public displays such as hanging and the stockade. These rituals were meant to not only dissuade individuals from committing crime (it is difficult to commit crime when one is dead), but also as methods of public deterrence. The very public nature of these punishments made them particularly impactful. Had these practices occurred in private, their influence would have been negligible.

To be successful, reentry rites of passage must occur in a community setting and employ restorative justice practices. Circles of support and accountability and victim/offender mediation are examples of restorative-based practices that can work to strengthen social cohesion and communal ties by bringing citizens together in pro-social ways. Predicated on the foundation of repairing harm, making amends, and taking responsibility, restorative justice emphasizes victim, offender, and communal involvement in the reentry process. Reentry rituals that encourage restorative justice practices through public rites of passage are fundamental to offenders' abilities to ultimately transform their identities.

For identity transformation to be complete, an ultimate rite of passage must take place. This status elevation ceremony would include a de-labeling process wherein established negative personal identities are replaced with positive ones and where "some recognized member(s) of the conventional community must publicly announce and certify that the offender has changed and that he is now to be considered essentially non-criminal" (Meisenhelder, 1977, p. 329). Examples of present-day status elevation ceremonies do exist and include specialty court graduations and certificates of rehabilitation. These ceremonies are tangible representations of earned redemption that can occur as a result of taking part in successful rites of passage (Maruna, 2001; Meisenhelder, 1997). Ultimately, earned redemption results in an altered personal identity that forms the foundation for community acceptance, renewed civic engagement, increased social cohesion, and successful offender reintegration.

Figure 16-2. A Strengths-Based Focus to Identity Transformation

A Strengths-Based Focus to Identity Transformation

Scripts, rituals, and rites of passage are important components of the identity transformation process, but they do not occur in a vacuum. Much behind-the-scenes work must occur in order for the identity transformation process to occur and for earned redemption to take place. The contention here is that positive identity transformation in offenders will have the best chance for success when it encompasses strengths-based criminal justice practice. This practice is predicated on the following principles as illustrated in Figure 16-2:

- Officer–offender relationships that emphasize collaboration will promote law-abiding, pro-social behavior
- Offenders who are empowered will be more likely to seek to change
- Cooperation from the community is key to successful offender reentry

Officer–Offender Relationships That Emphasize Collaboration Will Promote Law-Abiding, Pro-Social Behavior

The way to achieve law-abiding behavior (and ultimately reduce recidivism) is to highlight the strengths of an offender, not their problems. This is a particularly difficult notion for community-based practitioners to entertain given that current models emphasize problem- or deficit-based offender management. Consequently, practitioner emphasis of offender strengths over problems requires a fundamental reframing of professional purpose.

A reorientation of professional function supposes that current purpose is fully understood. Unfortunately, this is not the case. Much division exists within the criminal justice discipline about what community corrections is and what it is supposed to achieve. Scholars have several explanations for this confusion. Paparozzi (2003) contends that constantly changing correctional philosophies have made it difficult for community corrections to find its niche. Similarly, Cullen and Gendreau (2001) argue that correctional ideology has most often emphasized knowledge destruction; the belief that nothing works in correctional intervention, to the point that evidence-based efforts to critically assess what does work have been undermined. Still other scholars locate discrepant explanations for professional purpose within the context of professionalism (Latessa et al., 2002).

Latessa and colleagues (2002) argue that the community corrections profession is in crisis because it promotes correctional quackery wherein policy decisions are made in an unprofessional way based on what people think will work as opposed to what has been empirically proven to work. The authors contend that quackery is further perpetuated by staunch support for and defense of the status quo and an unwillingness to promote employee knowledge acquisition and advancement through education and training (Latessa et al., 2002).

A lack of professionalism translates into policy and practice that is generally one-dimensional and stagnant. Case in point, the status quo in community corrections presupposes deficit-based approaches to offender management that customarily emphasize risk-based supervision and case management in lieu of promoting factors that influence offenders to desist from crime. There is some tacit belief that if you address offender's problems, they will resolve themselves and result in reduced recidivism. There is little active effort to determine what other factors might play a role in the process. Recent research proposes an alternative.

Where traditional risk/needs assessment instruments reinforce the principles of risk (identifying factors predictive of recidivism and matching the level of treatment and program intervention to the predetermined level of risk), need (ensuring that therapy only targets those factors empirically linked to offending-criminogenic needs), and responsivity (matching interventions to offenders' level of motivation and learning style), the Good Lives Model is a strengths-based approach to assessment that targets offenders' interests and abilities through interventions that can assist offenders with acquiring the skills and capabilities to achieve their goals (Andrews & Bonta, 2006; Ward & Stewart, 2003).

The foundation of the Good Lives Model (GLM) is a core principle of strengths-based theory: that humans should be empowered to help themselves (Ward & Syversen, 2009) and that people wish to live acceptable and meaningful lives (Laws & Ward, 2011). A related premise of GLM is that offenders possess beliefs and characteristics called primary goods (e.g., life, knowledge, autonomy, etc.) that reflect their priorities (Purvis et al., 2011). Secondary goods are the means by which primary goods are attained. For example, an offender might begin taking GED courses (secondary good) in order to further the desire to improve their education/knowledge (primary good).

Where criminogenic needs as defined in the risk, needs, and responsivity (RNR) model are generally thought to be needs that (if addressed) can mitigate recidivism, GLM argues that criminogenic needs represent internal and external barriers toward attaining a good life (Ward et al., 2012). The GLM presumes that people organize their lives based on the core values they have prioritized for themselves and that the ability to uphold these values will lead to a good life. Offending results when flaws exist in a person's life plan (e.g., criminogenic needs) that directly or indirectly relate to the pursuit of primary goods (Ward & Maruna, 2007).

Similar to existing risk/needs instruments, the GLM uses assessment to determine how and to what degree offenders are able to demonstrate possession of primary goods. These assessments are conducted by asking offenders detailed questions about their core commitments to life and to articulate what activities in their life they value and what goals they hope to achieve (Ward et al., 2012). Based on results from these evaluations, case plans and goals are developed. A recent study supports the use of GLM in offender populations (Purvis et al., 2011; Ward & Maruna, 2007).

There is heated debate among scholars from the RNR (Andrews et al., 2011, 2012) and GLM camps (Ward et al., 2012) regarding the feasibility of one assessment modality over another. Here we operate from the premise that risk/needs-based assessments predicated on RNR have been empirically proven to reduce recidivism and are instruments worthy of implementation (Hollin, 1999), but that real case management and supervision gains may be derived through the use of the GLM as an enhancement to current assessment practice (Ward et al., 2012).

In fact, a combined approach to offender assessment could be extremely beneficial. Addressing offenders' immediate criminogenic needs (i.e., problems) by linking them with treatment and programming would obviously address short-term, acute concerns. Working with offenders to improve their overall situation and to help them reclaim control of their lives by emphasizing the positive qualities they possess (i.e., strengths) allows for a more long-term focus on behavior modification and goal achievement (McMillen et al., 2004). In this way, assessment utilizing a problem- and strengths-based approach might allow for reentry case management and supervision to take on a more fluid and dynamic character that might, in turn, encourage continuous goal reevaluation. Of course, assessments of any type are only valuable if the information derived from them is utilized for some meaningful purpose. In the context of offender reentry, the information gleaned from an assessment is only relevant if it is integrated into offender management practice. For reentry-based case management to be effective, it must embrace the foundational strengths-based precept of collaboration.

Officer–offender collaboration is easier said than done. It requires that community corrections officers reorient their current position of practitioner-as-all-knowing to one of practitioner-as-collaborator. Fundamental shifts in how one sees and does one's job do not happen immediately and usually require significant investment by employees and employer alike. Individual adjustments to officer role orientation, while laudable, will not prompt agency-wide role transformation. Changes in job orientation must be organizationally supported through agency mission, vision, and goal statements and strong leadership that promotes this ideology as well as training that reinforces it.

On a micro level, the practitioner-as-collaborator relationship can be best promoted through reframing officer–offender interactions. This is achieved most easily through recognizing that officer deportment can impact offender outcome (Schlager, 2008). Officers who adopt an antagonistic, us-versus-them approach to offender management, do not engender the trust of the people on their caseload and likely never achieve buy in to case plan goals and parole requirements. Officers that introduce themselves, shake hands, and address the offender with respect likely have more fruitful interactions and better outcomes. There is empirical support for this position. Confrontational case management styles show limited efficacy (Hubble et al., 1999; Miller & Rollnick, 2001). Research indicates that these types of management styles produce twice the resistance and only half as many positive client behaviors as do supportive, offender-centered approaches (Miller et al., 1993).

Offender management that occurs through confrontation is most often used because officers continue to believe that if you tell people what they must do, they will do it. Furthermore, officers justify their actions by saying that people who break the law are not worthy of respect. Officers will place officer–offender interactions within an either/or construct, claiming that offenders must be told what to do so that the officer may assert their authority (Clark, 2009b). These same officers will also argue that "hug a thug" approaches (in their minds, the diametrically opposed approach to confrontation) coddle the offender and absolve them of any responsibility that they must take for their crimes.

The strengths-based perspective supports a middle ground approach to deportment that neither condones criminal behavior nor is overly antagonistic, but one that is inherently collaborative in its focus. This partnership in no way obviates the requirement that offenders should take responsibility for their actions. However, this collaborative approach to deportment does encourage positive identity transformation by creating an environment that is conducive to change—one that focuses on offenders' activities that can influence future behavior, not one that seeks to dwell upon offenders' past actions. A case plan that includes the wishes of the officer over the needs and desires of the offender is a case plan that is little used, ineffectual, and one that results in inappropriate supervision recommendations.

The hallmark of strengths-based case management is a case plan that considers offender strengths and desired goals in concert with offender needs. These case plans should contain specific steps that offenders will take to achieve their goals. For example, if assessments that evaluate an offender's strengths and needs determine that he is "good at fixing things" and he wishes to attend school to obtain a vocational HVAC license, the offender should be encouraged to take the steps necessary to achieve this goal (e.g., obtain a GED, apply and be accepted to an HVAC vocational program, take and pass all necessary classes, obtain an HVAC license, get a job fixing HVAC systems).

Of course, the process required to achieve these goals can be overwhelming for even the most well-adjusted person. Therefore, in an effort to promote forward progress and to encourage reaching set goals, officers and offenders should develop case plans that are comprised of short- and long-term goals that are precise and measurable. A series of smaller goals that can be more easily realized will have a more positive effect on the offender and will motivate them to continue working, rather than larger goals that are amorphous and difficult to visualize.

Moreover, goals should be fluid, not static. Once an offender has met a goal (e.g., passed the GED), that goal should be replaced (e.g., apply and be accepted into an HVAC vocational program). In this way, the offender maintains momentum and gains a sense of accomplishment. Obviously, offenders will not always reach their goals but when they do, they should be praised for doing so and rewarded in some way either through a certificate of completion or some other ritual that connotes progress and achievement (Clark, 2009b). When offenders are not able to achieve their goals or when they veer off track, officers should utilize appropriate interventions to help the offender readjust. If the officer and offender have a good working relationship, this task will be much easier than if they do not because the offender will recognize that change is difficult and sometimes requires readjustment.

Finally, the case plan can and should function as an agreement between the officer and offender; a contract that outlines the expectations for achievement that the officer and offender have developed in collaboration (Taxman, 1999). Both the officer and offender should sign the contract, and both should be held accountable for meeting the goals as set forth in the document. In this way, both the officer and the offender feel a sense of obligation to uphold the contract and both clearly understand the consequences for not doing so. Of course, in theory this works, but the reality is that while case plans reflect the hopes and aspirations of offenders, they also contain legal requirements as set forth by the parole board or releasing authority that offenders must follow. How do we reconcile this reality with a strengths-focused approach to case management?

There is no question that conditions of parole are predetermined expectations for offender behavior that if violated, can result in an offender being returned to prison. The large number of offenders returned to prison for technical violations of parole as opposed to new crimes is case in point (Justice Policy Institute, 2010). Obviously, these are conditions to which offenders acquiesce in exchange for being released on parole, but it is likely that these conditions are not stipulations that the offender would have agreed to otherwise. Given that it is unlikely that conditions of parole will disappear anytime soon, in order to reconcile conditions of parole with strengths-based case planning, officers must educate and engage offenders regarding why compliance with conditions is necessary and how being compliant can assist them in moving forward with the goals they wish to achieve.

Offenders Who Are Empowered Will Be More Likely to Seek to Change

The secret ingredient to motivating offenders to adhere to the case plan is empowerment. Empowerment presupposes authority. People who are empowered are generally assigned authority to make decisions. People who are not empowered are generally marginalized from mainstream society. These people are viewed as being irrelevant and are therefore not routinely listened to or respected. There may be no population of people less empowered than offenders. Statutes that constrain liberty while in prison and once released (e.g., collateral consequences) serve to reinforce to society and to offenders that they are not valued and that what they think does not matter. However, for strengths-based reentry practice to be effective, this must change. If offenders are empowered to make decisions and to actively engage in the rehabilitation process, they are more likely to take it seriously and work toward achieving their goals. Officers who empower offenders to change by emphasizing strengths rather than weaknesses are officers who understand that offenders will respond more readily and agreeably to change when it is positioned in a positive light, than when it is held as a specter over their heads (Clark, 2009b).

While offenders must be empowered in order to maximize the likelihood that they will change, they must also be motivated to change. Motivation is driven by several factors. First, motivation is not static. It is a dynamic trait that can wax and wane over time. Therefore, officers must look for ways to keep motivation strong (Clark, 2009b). Effective officers determine what an offender's primary motivating factor is and use that to move the offender forward. For some, this primary motivator may be children, for others it may be reconnecting with family and friends. Regardless, officers who do not have solid knowledge of or who do not pay attention to the factors that motivate an offender to aspire to reach pro-social goals will have offenders on their caseload for whom identity transformation will be unrealized.

Understanding where an offender is in the change process is also central to successful identity transformation. Prochaska and DiClemente's (1986) stages of change are an excellent tool for officers to use when attempting to determine how amenable offenders are to change. Whether an offender is in the precontemplation (have no intention of changing), contemplation (problem awareness), preparation (committed to take action), action (actively engaging in changing behavior), or maintenance (continued commitment to changing and relapse prevention) stage of change will determine how the officer approaches case plan preparation and what motivating factors he/she will use to inch the offender forward.

Motivation is also behavior-specific and interactive. Offenders may be unmotivated to stop drinking but wish to work on their anger issues, not recognizing the relationship between the two. Officers must learn to harness offender strengths to help them achieve one goal for which they possess motivation (working on their anger) so that they have the opportunity to accomplish the other (stop drinking). Motivation is interactive in the sense that offenders will often take their cue from officers. How an officer interacts with an offender impacts what the offender thinks and talks about and can subsequently impact how the offender behaves (Clark, 2009b).

Finally, while motivation is influenced by internal and external factors, change that results from internal motivation is likely to last longer (Clark, 2009b). External motivators (e.g., I will take part in the substance-abuse assessment to avoid jail) may produce short-term positive outcomes, but are less likely to be maintained than outcomes that occur as a result of internal motivation (e.g., I wish to take part in the substance abuse assessment because I think drugs are impacting my relationship with my child). Put another way, offenders most likely to desist from crime are those who create redemption scripts that help them reshape their personal narratives in an effort to try to make good (Maruna, 2001). The redemption script that highlights the reunion between a mother and daughter after the mother has been released from in-patient substance abuse programming is a far more meaningful script than the one that merely describes a mother's exit from jail as a result of taking part in a substance-abuse assessment.

As we know, offenders who desist from crime often also possess protective factors or qualities that, when present, contribute to creating environments that foster resilience and protect individuals from making bad choices (e.g., engaging in criminal behavior). Several protective factors such as pro-social relationships, good intellectual skills, talents or accomplishments valued by self or others, self-efficacy, self-worth, and hopefulness have all been empirically proven to bolster one's ability to persevere in the face of adversity (Masten, 1994). The extent to which offenders are able to mobilize protective factors in an effort to move the change process forward is representative of the degree to which they will be successful.

A widely used method available to officers to facilitate the change process is motivational interviewing. Motivational interviewing (MI) specifically addresses offenders' motivation to take part in treatment and programming. MI complements the strengths-based approach to case management because it empowers offenders to make change (Clark, 2006). Offenders who feel empowered to change will be more successful than those who are told they must change.

Cooperation from the Community Is Key to Successful Offender Reentry

The "theater of change" for offenders is the world around them (Clark, 2009b, p. 143). The symbiotic relationship that exists between the offender and the community in which they live is mutually beneficial. The offender who is able to access services and take part in programming is the person who is better able to negotiate the stressors of reentry and the one who is less likely to commit crime. The offender who garners increased social capital and is able to obtain employment as a result is the person who is more invested in the health and welfare of the community and who seeks to take an active role in its existence.

The offender and the community must marshal their resources in order for this relationship to succeed. Informal resources at an individual level are called human capital; strengths and characteristics that make individuals marketable (e.g., tenacious, artistic, dedicated). In the context of the community, informal resources take the form of social capital or the ability of individuals to leverage relationships with family and friends in a community setting to achieve a goal. Draine and colleagues (2005) argue that it is an offender's ability to leverage their human capital in a social setting through the strength and type of relationships that they have with family and friends that best facilitates the change process. Consequently, reentry planning that involves case management that takes into consideration the needs of the offender, how those needs can be met in the community, and the degree to which the community is willing and able to provide services, is reentry planning that is most likely to be successful (Draine et al., 2005). In this context, case planning and case management "depends upon the individual's willingness and ability to act in accordance with specific social norms as well as the community's willingness and capacity to support the individual's pro-social efforts" (Draine et al., 2005, p. 691).

As this discussion has well pointed out, offenders have many problems that inhibit their ability to successfully reintegrate into society after they have been released from prison. Offenders may have no place to live, they have no job, may have mental or physical health constraints that limit their ability to find work, and may need additional education in order to find work. If these problems are not addressed in a coordinated and comprehensive way, both human and social capital is reduced to the point that reentry becomes illusory. Certainly, services to address issues in each of the principal domains (employment, physical and mental health, and education) are available, although they tend to be fragmented in nature and vary in availability from one jurisdiction to another. In most instances, these service entities operate with a "silo" mentality and usually without the benefit of understanding or communicating with the other. As a consequence, offenders who may require assistance may feel overwhelmed and unsure of how to access the services needed to assist them with reentry. An offender may well be motivated to obtain his GED, but he may be unfamiliar with how to go about the process of doing it at the same time that he requires outpatient mental health treatment.

A strengths-focused approach to positive identity transformation promotes the coordination of community-based resources in order to optimize reentry success. One method of achieving this goal is to use a boundary spanner. In this capacity, a boundary spanner assists in coordinating services for offenders among multiple agencies. In the context of offender reentry, the boundary spanner may be the parole officer who assists offenders with accessing formal and informal services in a community setting.

Of course, boundary spanning presupposes that community service providers want to come together to assist reentering offenders and, generally speaking, we know this to not be the case. In many instances, providers have to be brought kicking and screaming into any dialogue that concerns offenders, further reinforcing distinctions between us and them. However, for an offender to have even a marginal chance at reentry success, the community to which they return must first recognize their existence and then be willing to provide assistance. Cooperation among and between formal and informal service providers must be encouraged as must the empowerment of offenders be supported and legitimized (Maruna & King, 2004).

A cooperative communal environment that encourages offenders to change would signal a move from current, passive reentry practice where officers target offenders for programs and services to one where offenders play active roles in owning the reentry process and reframing communal identities (Bazemore, 1998; Maruna & LeBel, 2002). Communal identities could be strengthened in a multitude of ways by projects that fill community needs (e.g., cleaning up the local park), build community capacity (e.g., assist in building homes), and begin the process to repair harm caused by the offender to the victim and the community (Bazemore & Erbe, 2003; Bazemore & Maloney, 1994).

Strengths-Based Principles as the Catalyst for Offender Reentry

Reentry policy and practice that embodies strengths-based principles will result in successful identity transformation, increased civic engagement, and better reentry outcomes. However, this transformation will only occur if it is a collaborative effort and one that promotes empowerment and seeks the cooperation not only of the individual offenders who must be motivated to take part in the transformation process, but the communities to which they ultimately return.

Figure 16-3. A Community-Centric Model of Offender Reentry

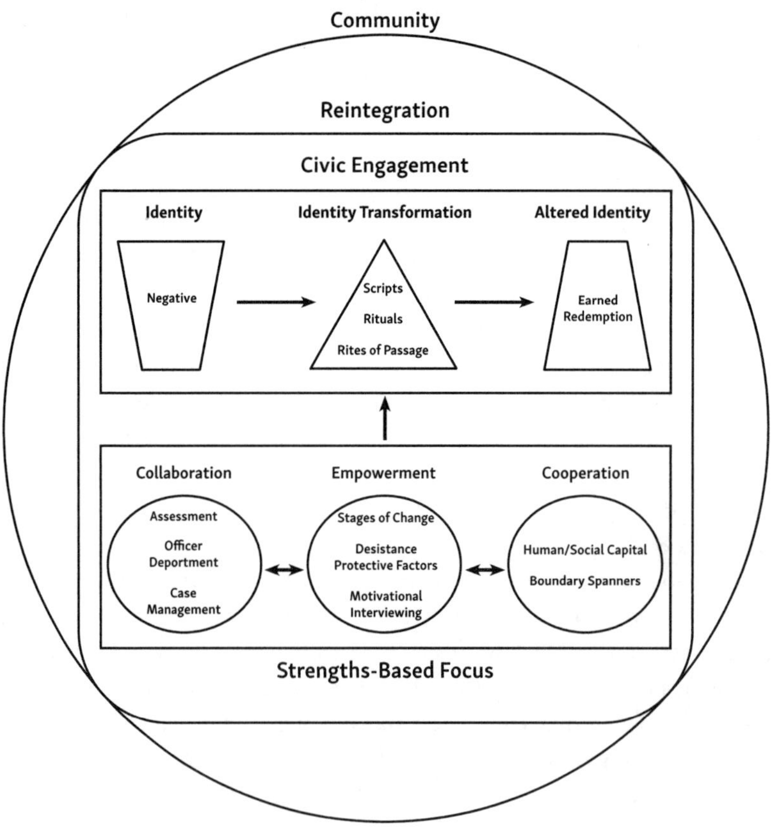

One example of a strengths-based activity that can promote identity transformation and earned redemption and that emphasizes relationship building, developing trust, and an understanding of collective responsibility is community service (Coleman, 1990; Rose & Clear, 1998). This idea is not new. Current parole plans routinely include community service as a condition of supervision. However, many people eschew community service as a correctional intervention because they do not believe it is effective or meaningful, despite evidence to the contrary (Jastrzab et al., 1999; McDonald, 1986; Pease, 1982). In fact, community service embodies the strengths-based principles of collaboration, empowerment, and cooperation in that it encourages offenders to make amends to victims, repair harm caused to the victim and the community, develop pro-social relationships, and work toward redemption all while building collective efficacy and increasing social capital (Bazemore & Boba, 2007; Braithwaite, 1989; Werner & Smith, 1992). Community service is a strengths-based practice that enhances civic engagement precisely because it allows people to give back with no reward or benefit to themselves (Bazemore & Boba, 2007).

Communities must recognize that strengths-based approaches to offender management make fiscal, political, and common sense. For example, community infrastructure can suffer irreparable fiscal damage when large numbers of people are removed or displaced from the workforce due to incarceration. As a result, the paucity of a stable and skilled workforce often prompts employers to relocate to other communities in search of willing and able employees (Western, 2007). Moreover, communities without sound financial footing cannot provide the goods and services that the citizens of the community expect and require, the product of which is an unstable community that is not invested in the lives of its citizens and residents who are not engaged in the civic process.

Strengths-based approaches to offender management also make political sense. For example, if significant numbers of people are removed from communities and are imprisoned only to return years later without the benefit of being able to vote, the offender is living "in" but not "of" the community. Jurisdictions' zeal to restrict or otherwise abolish offenders' right to vote results in communities that are elected by the few and that are not representative of the many (Uggen & Manza, 2002). In turn, laws are passed that do not necessarily reflect the needs or desires of the community at large. As a result, social capital and collective efficacy erode, and the constituents who are unable to take an active role in the civic process feel disconnected and unwelcome (Uggen & Manza, 2002).

Moreover, strengths-based approaches to offender reentry make common sense. Reentry policies and practices that promote inclusion and redemption make offenders feel worthy. People who feel valued want to contribute and are more likely to be motivated to change in an effort to do so. People who are able to positively transform themselves engage in behaviors that promote pro-social beliefs and support for activities such as education, employment, and community engagement. A person actively involved in the health and well-being of their community is one who is not likely committing crime.

Ultimately, strengths-based approaches to offender reentry make moral sense. We know that offender reentry is a problem of large proportions and one that comes at significant cost to the offenders who do time and come home, but also to victims, families, and communities. We also know that extraordinary resources have been leveled at the issue, but to this point, no compelling narrative that identifies the dimensions of reentry while placing them in context has been offered. A hodge-podge of programs, policies, and practices that do little to ameliorate the problem and sometimes much to exacerbate it, mark the exception rather than the rule. What we cannot seem to fathom is that offender reentry damages our social fiber in considerable ways and that for any gains to be achieved, we must upend the status quo and accept that we have a collective moral obligation to address a problem, the consequences of which are damaging to us all.

References

Court Cases

Addington v. Texas, 441 U.S. 418 (1979)

Board of Pardons v. Allen 482 U.S. 369 (1987)

Covington v. Harris, 419 F.2d 617 (D.C. Cir. 1969)

Estelle v. Gamble, 429 U.S. 97 (1976)

Farmer v. Brennan, 511 U.S. 825 (1994)

Greenholtz v. Nebraska 442 U.S. 1 (1979)

HUD v. Rucker 535 U.S. 125 (2002)

Morrissey v. Brewer, 408 US 471 (1972)

Newman v. Alabama, 349 F. Supp. 285 (M.D. Ala. 1972), *aff'd*, 503 F.2d 1320 (5th Cir. 1974); *cert. denied*, 421 U.S. 948 (1975)

O'Connor v. Donaldson, 422 US 563 (1975)

Ruiz v. Estelle, 503 F. Supp. 1265 (S.D. Tex. 1980). *aff'd in part and rev'd in part*, 679 F.2d 266 (5th Cir. 1982), *cert denied*, 460 U.S. 1042 (1983)

Statutes

Community Mental Health Centers Construction Act, Mental Retardation Facilities and Construction Act, Public Law 88–164

Housing Program Extension Act of 1996, 110 STAT. 834 Public Law 104–120

Lanterman-Petris-Short (LPS) Act (Cal. Welf & Inst. Code, sec. 5000 et seq.)

Sentencing Reform Act of 1984

Publications

Abadinsky, H. (1997). *Probation and parole*. New York: Prentice Hall.

Abeling-Judge, D. (2019). Stopping out and going back: The impact of educational attainment on criminal desistance among stopped-out offenders. *Crime & Delinquency, 65*(4), 527–554.

Abramsky, S. (2002). *Hard times.* New York: St. Martins Press.

Abramson, M.F. (1972). The criminalization of mentally disordered behavior: Possible side-effect of a new mental health law. *Hospital & Community Psychiatry,* 23, 101–105.

Adalist-Estrin, A. (1994). Family support and criminal justice. In S.L. Kagan & B. Weissbourg (Eds.), *Putting families first: America's family support movement and the challenge of change* (pp. 161–185). San Francisco: Jossey-Bass Inc.

Adams, K. (1986). The disciplinary experiences of mentally disordered inmates. *Criminal Justice and Behavior,* 13, 297–316.

Aday, R.H. (2003). *Aging prisoners: Crisis in American corrections.* New York: Praeger.

Adler, F. (1975). *Sisters in crime: The rise of the new female criminal.* New York: McGraw-Hill.

Adler, F. & Simon, R.J. (Eds.) (1979). *The criminology of deviant women.* Boston: Houghton Mifflin.

Akers, R.L. (1973). *Deviant behavior: A social learning approach.* Belmont, CA: Wadsworth.

Akers, R.L. (1985). Social Learning Theory and Adolescent Cigarette Smoking. *Social Problems,* 32, 455–73.

Alarid, L., Burton,V., & Cullen, F. (2000). Gender and crime among felony offenders: Assessing the generality of social control and differential association theories. *Journal of Research in Crime and Delinquency,* 37, 171–199.

Alarid, L., Cromwell, P.F., & DelCarmen, R.V. (2008). *Community based corrections.* 7th ed. Belmont, CA: Thomson Wadsworth.

Alper, M., Durose, M.R., & Markman, J. (2018). *2018 update on prisoner recidivism: A 9-year follow up period (2005–2014).* (NCJ 250975). Bureau of Justice Statistics.

American Correctional Association. (2000). *Vital statistics in corrections.* Lanham, MD: American Correctional Association.

American Correctional Association. (2006). Inmate health care and communicable diseases. *Corrections Compendium.* Alexandria, VA: American Correctional Association.

American Psychiatric Association. (2004). *Mental illness and the criminal justice system: Redirecting resources toward treatment, not containment.* Resource Document.

American Public Health Association. (1976). Retrieved from http://www.apha.org/.

Anderson, E. (1996). *Code of the street. Decency, violence and the moral life of the inner city.* New York: W.W. Norton.

Andrews, D. (1982). *The Level of Supervision Inventory (LSI): The first follow-up.* Ottowa, Canada: Carleton University.

Andrews, D.A., & Bonta, J. (2003). *The psychology of criminal conduct* (3rd ed.). Cincinnati, OH: Anderson Publishing.

Andrews, D.A., & Bonta, J. (1995). *LSI-R: The level of service inventory-revised user's manual.* Toronto: Multi-Health Systems, Inc.

Andrews, D.A., & Bonta, J. (2003). *Level of Service Inventory-Revised US norms manual supplement.* Tonawanda, NY: Multi-Health Systems.

Andrews, D.A., & Bonta, J. (2006). *The psychology of criminal conduct* (4th ed.). Newark, NJ: LexisNexis.

Andrews, D.A., & Bonta, J. (2010). Rehabilitating criminal justice policy and practice. *Psychology, Public Policy and Law, 16*, 39–55.

Andrews, D.A., Bonta, J., & Hoge, R. (1990). *Classification for effective rehabilitation: Rediscovering psychology. Criminal Justice and Behavior, 17*, 19–52.

Andrews, D.A., Bonta, J., & Wormith, S.J. (2004). *The Level of Service/Case Management Inventory (LS/CMI).* Toronto, Canada: Multi-Health Systems.

Andrews, D.A., Bonta, J., & Wormith, S.J. (2006). The recent past and near future of risk/need assessment. *Crime & Delinquency, 52*, 7–27.

Andrews, D.A., Bonta, J., & Wormith, J.S. (2011). The Risk-Need-Responsivity (RNR) model: Does adding the Good Lives Model contribute to effective crime prevention? *Criminal Justice and Behavior, 38*(1), 735–755.

Andrews, D.A., Bonta, J., & Wormith, J.S. (2012). Deferring to clarity, parsimony, and evidence in reply to Ward, Yates, and Willis. *Criminal Justice and Behavior, 39*(1), 111–120.

Andrews, D.A., Dowden, C., & Rettinger, J. (2001). Special populations within corrections. In J. Winterdyk (Ed.), *Corrections in Canada: Social reactions to crime* (pp. 170–212). Toronto, Canada: Prentice Hall.

Andrews, D.A., & Friesen, W. (1987). Assessments of anticriminal plans and the prediction of criminal futures: A research note. *Criminal Justice and Behavior, 14*, 33–37.

Andrews, D.A., Guzzo, L., Raynor, P., Rowe, R.C., Rettinger, L.J., Brews, A. & Wormith, S. (2012). Are the major risk/need factors predictive of both female and male reoffending? A test with the eight domains of the Level of Service/Case Management Inventory. *International Journal of Offender Therapy and Comparative Criminology, 56*(1), 113–133.

Andrews, D.A., & Kiessling, J. (1980). Program structure and effective correctional practices: A summary of the CaVIC research. In R.R. Ross & P. Gendreau (Eds.), *Effective correctional treatment* (pp. 439–463). Toronto, Canada: Butterworth.

Andrews, D.A., & Wormith, J. (1984). *Criminal sentiments and criminal behavior*. Ottawa, Canada: Solicitor General Canada.

Andrews, D.S., Wormith, J., & Kiessling, J. (1985). Self reported criminality propensity and criminal behaviour: Threats to the validity of assessment and personality. (Programs Branch User Report). Ottawa, ON: Solicitor General Canada, Service Canada. Retrieved from http://www.cscscc.gc .ca/text/rsrch/compendium/2000/index -eng.shtml.

Andrews, D.A., Zinger, I., Hoge, R., Bonta, J., Gendreau, P., & Cullen, F. (1990). Does correctional treatment work? A psychologically informed meta-analysis. *Criminology, 28*, 369–404.

Anestis, J.C., & Carbonell, J.L. (2014). Stopping the revolving door: Effectiveness of mental health court in reducing recidivism by mentally ill offenders. *Psychiatric Services, 65*(9), 1105–1112.

Angiello, E. (2005). Prerelease programs. In M. Bosworth (Ed.), *Encyclopedia of prisons and correctional facilities*. Thousand Oaks, CA: Sage Publications.

Annis, H., & Davis, C. (1991). Relapse prevention. *Alcohol Health & Research World, 15*(3), 204–213.

Anno, B.J. (2000). National correctional health standards. In J.B. Ashford, B.D. Sales, & W.H. Reid (Eds.), *Treating adult and juvenile offenders with special needs* (pp. 81–96). American Psychological Association.

Anno, B.J., Graham, C., Lawrence, J.E., & Shansky, R. (2004). *Correctional health care: Addressing the needs of elderly, chronically ill, and terminally ill inmates*. Middletown, CT: Criminal Justice Institute.

Anwar, S., & Fang, H. (2015). Testing for racial prejudice in the parole board release process: Theory and evidence. *Journal of Legal Studies, 44*, 1–37.

Aos, S., Miller, M., & Drake, E. (2006). *Evidence-based public policy options to reduce future prison construction, criminal justice costs, and crime rates*. Olympia, WA: Washington State Institute for Public Policy.

Apel, R., & Horney, J. (2017). How and why does work matter? Employment conditions, routine activities, and crime among adult male offenders. *Criminology, 55*(2), 307–343.

Apodaca, T.R., & Longabaugh, R. (2009). Mechanisms of change in motivational interviewing: A review and preliminary evaluation of the evidence. *Addiction, 104*, 705–715.

Applegate B., Cullen, F., & Fisher, B. (2002). Public views toward crime and correctional policies: Is there a gender gap? *Journal of Criminal Justice, 30*, 89–100.

Arditti, J.A. (2003). Locked doors and glass walls: Family visiting at a local jail. *Journal of Loss & Trauma, 8*(2), 115–138.

Arditti, J. (2012). *Parental incarceration and the family: Psychological and social effects of imprisonment on children, parents, and caregivers*. New York University Press.

Arditti, J.A., & Few, A. (2006). Mothers' reentry into family life following incarceration. *Criminal Justice Policy Review, 17*, 103–123.

Arditti, J.A., & Few, A. (2008). Maternal distress and women's reentry into family and community life. *Family Progress, 47*(3), 303–321.

Arditti, J.A., Lambert-Shute, J. & Joest, K. (2003). Saturday morning at the jail: Implications of incarceration for families and children. *Family Relations, 52*, 195–204.

Arditti, J.A., Smock, S., & Parkman, T. (2005). It's been hard to be a father: A qualitative exploration of incarcerated fatherhood. *Fathering, 3*, 267–283.

Arendell, T. (2000). Conceiving and investigating motherhood: The decade's scholarship. *Journal of Marriage and Family, 62*(4), 1192–1207.

Ashford, J.B., & LeCroy, C.W. (1998). Juvenile parole policy in the United States: Determinate versus indeterminate models. In B.W. Hancock, & P. Sharp (Eds.), *Juvenile delinquency: Historical, theoretical, and societal reactions to youth*. Englewood Cliffs, NJ: Prentice-Hall.

Atkinson, R., & Rostad K.A. (2003). *Employment dimensions of reentry: Understanding the nexus between prisoner reentry and work — Can inmates become an integral part of the U.S. workforce?* Retrieved from http://www.urban.org/publications/410854.html.

Austin, J. (2006). How much risk can we take? The misuse of risk assessment in corrections. *Federal Probation, 70*, 58–63.

Austin, J., Bloom, B., & Donahue, T. (1992). *Female offenders in the community: An analysis of innovative strategies and programs*. Washington, D.C.: National Institute of Corrections.

Austin, J., & Hardyman, P. (2004). *Objective prison classification: a guide for correctional agencies*. Washington D.C: National Institute of Corrections.

Bailey, W. (1966). Correctional outcome: An evaluation of 100 reports. *Journal of Criminal Law, Criminology, and Police Science, 57*, 153–160.

Baillargeon, J., Binswanger, I.A., Penn, J.V., Williams, B.A. & Murray, O.J. (2009). Psychiatric disorders and repeat incarcerations: The revolving prison door. *The American Journal of Psychiatry, 166*(1), 103–109.

Baillargeon, J., Hoge, S., & Penn, J. (2010). Addressing the challenge of community reentry among released inmates with serious mental illness. *American Journal of Community Psychology, 46*(3), 361–375.

Baird, C. (1981). Model classification systems in correctional field services. *Corrections Magazine, 43*, 36–41.

Baird, C. (1991). *Validating risk assessment instruments used in community corrections*. Madison, WI: National Council on Crime and Delinquency.

Baird, C., Heinz, R., & Bemus, B. (1979). *The Wisconsin case classification/staff deployment project: A two-year follow-up report*. Madison, WI: Wisconsin Health and Social Services Department.

Bales, W.D., & Mears, D.P. (2008). Inmate social ties and the transition to society: Does visitation reduce recidivism? *Journal of Research in Crime and Delinquency, 45*(3), 287–321.

Barajas, E. (1998). Community justice: An emerging concept and practice. In *Community justice: Concept and strategies* (pp. 11–26). K. Dunlap, (Ed.), Lexington, KY: American Probation and Parole Association and Council of State Governments.

Barklage, H., Miller, D., & Bonham, G. (2006). Probation conditions versus probation officer directives: Where the twain shall meet. *Federal Probation, 70*(3), 37–41.

Barrick, K., Lattimore, P.K., & Visher, C.A. (2014). Reentering women: The impact of social ties on long-term recidivism. *The Prison Journal, 94*(3), 279–304.

Barrow, S., Soto, G., & Cordova, P. (2004). *Final report on the evaluation of the Closer to Home initiative.* New York: Corporation for Supportive Housing.

Bartel, C.A. (2001). Social comparisons in boundary spanning work: Effects of community outreach on members' organizational identity and identification. *Administrative Science Quarterly, 46*, 379–413.

Baskin, D., & Sommers, I. (1998). *Casualties of community disorder: Women's careers in violent crime*. Boulder, CO: Westview Press.

Batiuk, M.E., Moke, P., & Roundtree, P.W. (1997). Crime and rehabilitation: Correctional education as an agent for change. *Justice Quarterly, 14*, 167–180.

Bauhofer, V. (1987). Prison parenting: A challenge for children's advocates. *Children Today, 15*(1), 15–16.

Baunach, P.J. (1985). *Mothers in prison.* New Brunswick, NJ: Transaction Books.

Bazemore, G. (1998). Restorative justice and earned redemption: Communities, victims & offender reintegration. *American Behavioral Scientist, 41*(6), 768–813.

Bazemore, G., & Boba, R. (2007). "Doing good" to "make good": Community theory for practice in a restorative justice civic engagement reentry model. *Journal of Offender Rehabilitation. 46*(1/2), 25–56.

Bazemore, G. & Erbe, C. (2003). Operationalizing the community variable in offender reintegration: Theory and practice for developing intervention social capital." *Youth Violence and Juvenile Justice, 1*(3), 246–275.

Bazemore, G., & Erbe, C. (2004). Reintegration and restorative justice: Towards a theory and practice of informal social control and support. In S. Maruna & R. Immarigeon (Eds.), *After crime and punishment: Pathways to offender reintegration* (pp. 27–56). Portland, OR: Willan Publishing.

Bazemore, G., & Maloney, D. (1994). Rehabilitating community service: Toward restorative service in a balanced justice system. *Federal Probation, 58*, 24–35.

Bazemore, G., & Maruna, S. (2009). Restorative justice in the reentry context: Building new theory and expanding the evidence base. *Victims and Offenders 4*(4), 375–384.

Bazemore, G., & Stinchcomb, J. (2004). A civic engagement model of reentry: Involving community through service and restorative justice. *Federal Probation, 68*(2), 14–24.

Bazemore, G., & Unbreit, M.S. (1995). Rethinking the sanctioning function in juvenile court: Retributive or restorative responses to youth crime. *Crime & Delinquency, 41*(3), 296–316.

Beck, A.J., & Hughes, T., & Wilson, J. (2001). *Trends in state parole, 1990–2000* (NCJ 184735). Washington, DC: Bureau of Justice Statistics.

Beck, A.J., & Maruschak, L.M. (2001). *Mental health treatment in state prisons, 2000* (NCJ 188215). Washington, DC: Bureau of Justice Statistics.

Beldon Russonello & Stewart. (2001). *Optimism, pessimism, and jailhouse redemption: American attitudes on crime, punishment, and over-incarceration: Findings from a national survey conducted for the ACLU.* Washington, D.C.: Beldon Russonello & Stewart. Retrieved from www.prisonpolicy.org/scans/overincarceration_survey.pdf.

Belenko, S., Houser, K.A., & Welsh, W. (2012). Understanding the impact of drug treatment in correctional settings. In J. Petersilia & K.R. Reitz (Eds.), *The Oxford handbook of sentencing and corrections* (pp. 463–491). Oxford University Press.

Belknap, J. (2007). *The invisible woman: Gender, crime, and justice* (3rd ed.). Belmont, CA: Thompson Wadsworth.

Belknap, J., & Holsinger, K. (2006). The gendered nature of risk factors for delinquency. *Feminist Criminology, 1*, 48–71.

Bellair, P.E. (2000). Informal surveillance and street crime. *Criminology, 38*, 137–170.

Bellair, P.E., & Kowalski, B.R. (2011). Low-skill employment opportunity and African-American-White difference in recidivism. *Journal of Research in Crime and Delinquency, 48*(2), 176–208.

Benda, B. (2005). Gender differences in life-course theory of recidivism: A survival analysis. *International Journal of Offender Therapy and Comparative Criminology, 49*(3), 325–342.

Benson, M., Alarid, L., Burton, V., & Cullen, F. (2011). Reintegration or stigmatization? Offenders' expectations of community reentry. *Journal of Criminal Justice, 39*, 385–393.

Benzvy-Miller, S. (1990). Community corrections and the NIMBY syndrome. *Forum on Corrections Research, 2*(2), 1–18.

Berg, M.T., & Huebner, B.M. (2011). Reentry and the ties that bind: An examination of social ties, employment, and recidivism. *Justice Quarterly, 28*(2), 382–410.

Berman, J. (2005). *Women offender transition and reentry: Gender responsive approaches to transitioning women offenders from prison to the community*. Washington, D.C.: Center for Effective Public Policy and National Institute of Corrections.

Beto, D.R., Corbett, R.P., & DiIulio, J.J. (2000). Getting serious about probation and the crime problem. *Corrections Management Quarterly* (4)2, 1–8.

Biddle, B.J. (1986). Recent developments in role theory. *Annual Review of Sociology 12*, 67–92.

Bixby, F.L. (1970). A new role for parole boards. *Federal Probation, 34*, 24–28.

Black, K., & Cho, R. (2004). *New beginnings. The need for supportive housing for previously incarcerated people*. New York: Common Ground Community and Corporation for Supportive Housing.

Blanchette, K. (2002). Classifying female offenders for effective intervention: Application of the case-based principles of risk and need. *Forum on Correctional Research, 14*, 31–35.

Blanchette, K. (2004). Revisiting effective classification strategies for women offenders in Canada. *Feminism and Psychology, 14*, 231–236.

Blanchette, K., & Brown, S. (2006). Assessment for classification of women offenders. In K. Blanchette & S. Brown (Eds.), *The assessment and treatment of adult female offenders* (pp. 41–52). Hoboken, NJ: John Wiley & Sons Ltd.

Blinn, C.L. (Ed.). (1997). *Maternal ties: A selection of programs for women offenders*. Lanham, MD: American Correctional Association.

Bloom, B. (2000). Beyond recidivism: Perspectives on evaluation programs for female offenders in community corrections. In M, McMahon (ed), *Assessment to Assistance: Programs for Women in Community Corrections* (pp. 107–138). Lanham, MD: American Correctional Association.

Bloom, B., & Brown, M. (2009). Reentry and renegotiating motherhood: Maternal identity and success on parole. *Crime Delinquency, 55*, 313–336.

Bloom, B., & Chesney-Lind, M. (2000). Women in prison: Vengeful equity. In R. Muraskin (Ed.), *It's a crime: Women and justice* (pp. 183–204). Upper Saddle River, NJ: Prentice Hall.

Bloom, B., Chesney-Lind, M., & Owen, B. (1994). *Women in California prisons: Hidden victims of the war on drugs*. San Francisco: Center on Juvenile and Criminal Justice.

Bloom, B., Owen, B., & Covington, S. (2003). *Gender responsive strategies: Research, practice, and guiding principles for women offenders*. Washington, D.C.: National Institute of Corrections.

Bloom, B., & Steinhart, D. (1993). *Why punish the children? A reappraisal of the children of incarcerated mothers in America*. San Francisco: National Council on Crime and Delinquency.

Blumer, H. (1969). *Symbolic interactionism: Perspective and method*. Englewood Cliffs, NJ: Prentice-Hall.

Blumstein, A., Cohen, J., Roth, J., & Visher, C.A. (1986). *Criminal careers and "career criminals"*. (Vol. 1). Washington, DC: National Academy Press.

Blundo, R. (2001). Learning strengths-based practice: Challenging our personal and professional frames. *Families in Society: The Journal of Contemporary Human Services, 82*(3), 296–303.

Bobbitt, M., & Nelson, M. (2004). The front line: Building programs that recognize Families' role in reentry. New York: Vera Institute of Justice. Retrieved from http://www.vera.org/publication_pdf/249_476.pdf.

Bonczar, T.P., & Beck, A.J. (1997). *Lifetime likelihood of going to state or federal prison* (NCJ 160092). Washington DC: Bureau of Justice Statistics.

Bonham, G., Janeksela, G.M., & Bardo, J. (1986). Predicting parole decision in Kansas via discriminate analysis. *Journal of Criminal Justice, 14*(2), 123–133.

Bonanno, G.A. (2004). Loss, trauma, and human resilience: Have we underestimated the human capacity to thrive after extremely aversive events? *American Psychologist, 59*, 20–28.

Bonovitz, J.C., & Bonovitz, J.S. (1981). Diversion of the mentally ill into the criminal justice system: The police intervention perspective. *American Journal of Psychiatry, 138*, 973–976.

Bonta, J. (1996). Risk needs assessment and treatment. In A.T. Harland (Ed.), *Choosing correctional options that work: Defining demand and evaluating supply* (pp. 18–32). Thousand Oaks, CA: Sage Publication.

Bonta, J., Law, M., & Hanson, R. (1998). The prediction of criminal and violent recidivism among mentally disordered offenders: A meta-analysis. *Psychological Bulletin, 123*, 333–352.

Bonta, J., Pang, B. & Wallace-Capretta, S. (1995). Predictors of recidivism among incarcerated female offenders. *The Prison Journal, 75*(3), 277–294.

Bonta, J., Parkinson, R., Pang, B., Barkwell, L., & Wallace-Capretta, S. (1994). *The revised Manitoba classification system for probationers.* Ottawa, Canada: Public Safety Canada.

Bonta, J., Wallace-Capretta, S., & Rooney, J. (2000). A quasi-experimental evaluation of an intensive rehabilitation supervision program. *Criminal Justice and Behavior, 27*, 312–329.

Boothby, J.L., & Clements, C.B. (2000). A national survey of correctional psychologists. *Criminal Justice and Behavior, 27*, 716–732.

Boswell, G. (2002). Incarcerated fathers: The children's view. *The Howard Journal of Criminal Justice, 41*(1), 14–26.

Bottomley, K. (1990). Parole in transition: A comparative study of origins, developments and prospects for the 1990s. In M. Tonry & N. Morris (Eds.), *Crime and justice: A review of research* (Vol. 12., pp. 319–374). Chicago: University of Chicago Press.

Bottoms, A., Shapland, J., Costello, A., Holmes, D., & Muir, G. (2004). Towards desistance: Theoretical underpinnings for an empirical study. *The Howard Journal of Criminal Justice, 43*(4), 368–389.

Boudin, C. (2011). Children of incarcerated parents: The child's constitutional right to the family relationship. *The Journal of Criminal Law & Criminology, 101*(1), 77–118.

Bradley, K.H., Oliver, R.M., Richardson, N.C., & Slayter, E.M. (2001). *No place like home: Housing and the ex-prisoner*. Boston, MA: Community Resources for Justice.

Bova, M. (2009, October). The collateral consequences of our drug laws. Retrieved from http://www.notabene.gwsba.com/story/364-collateral-consequences-our-drug-laws.

Braithwaite, J. (1989). *Crime, shame and reintegration*. Cambridge, UK: Cambridge University Press.

Braithwaite, R., Treadwell, M., & Arriola, K. (2005). Health disparities and incarcerated women: A population ignored. *American Journal of Public Health, 95*, 1679–1681.

Braman, D. (2002). *Families and incarceration* (NCJRA 202981). Washington, D.C.: U.S. Department of Justice. Retrieved from www.ncjrs.gov/pdffiles1/nij/grants/202981.pdf.

Braman, D. (2004). *Doing time on the outside: Incarceration and family life in urban America*. University of Michigan Press.

Brazzell, D., Crayton. A., Mukamal D.A., Solomon A.L., & Lindahl N. (2009). *From the classroom to the community: Exploring the role of education during incarceration and reentry*. Retrieved from Urban Institute website: http://www.urban.org/publications/411963.html.

Brazzell, D., & LaVigne, N. (2009). *Prisoner reentry in Houston: Community perspectives*. Washington, D.C.: The Urban Institute.

Breese, J.R., Ra'el, K., & Grant, G.K. (2000). No place like home: A qualitative investigation of social support and its effects on recidivism. *Sociological Practice: A Journal of Clinical and Applied Sociology, 2*(1), 1–21.

Brennan, T., Dieterich, W., & Ehret, B. (2009). Evaluating the predictive validity of the COMPAS risk and needs assessment system. *Criminal Justice and Behavior, 36*, 21–40.

Brennan, T., & Oliver, W.L. (2000). *Evaluation of reliability and validity of COMPAS scales: National sample*. Traverse City, MI: Northpointe Institute for Public Management.

Bronfenbrenner, U. (1979). *The ecology of human development: Experiments by nature and design*. Cambridge: Harvard University Press.

Bronson, J., & Berzofsky, M. (2017). *Special report: Indicators of mental health problems reported by prisoners and jail inmates, 2011–12* (NCJ 250612). Bureau of Justice Statistics.

Bronson, J., & Carson, E.A. (2019). *Prisoners in 2017*. (NCJ 252156). Bureau of Justice Statistics.

Bronson, J., Maruschak, L.M., & Berzofsky, M. (2015). *Disabilities among prison and jail inmates, 2011–12*. (NCJ 249151). Bureau of Justice Statistics.

Bronson, J., Stroop, J., Zimmer, S., & Berzofsky, M. *(2017). Drug use, dependence, and abuse among state prisoners and jail inmates, 2007–2009*. (NCJ 250546). Bureau of Justice Statistics.

Brooks, L., Visher, C., & Naser, R. (2006). *Community residents' perceptions of prisoner reentry in selected Cleveland neighborhoods. Washington*, D.C.: The Urban Institute.

Brown, J.G. (1994). Evaluating restorative justice programs. Humanity and Society, 22, 23–37.

Brown, M., & Bloom, B. (2009). Reentry and renegotiating motherhood: Maternal identity and success on parole. *Crime & Delinquency, 55*(2), 313–336.

Browne, A., Miller, B., & Maguin, E. (1999). Prevalence and severity of lifetime physical and sexual victimization among incarcerated women. *International Journal of Law & Psychiatry, 22*, 301–322.

Brun, C., & Rapp, R.C. (2001). Strengths-based case management: Individuals' perspectives on strengths and the case manager relationship. *Social Work, 46*, 278–288.

Bucklen, K.B., & Zajac, G. (2009). But some of them don't come back (to prison): Resource deprivation and thinking errors as determinants of parole success and failure. *The Prison Journal, 89*(3), 239–264.

Bureau of Justice Statistics (2000). *Characteristics of correctional populations, 1997* (NCJ177613). Washington, D.C.: Bureau of Justice Statistics.

Bureau of Justice Statistics. (2002). *Reentry trends in the U.S.: Characteristics of releases*. Washington, D.C.: Bureau of Justice Statistics. Retrieved from bjs.ojp.usdoj.gov/content/pub/pdf/reentry.pdf.

Bureau of Justice Statistics. (2002). *Reentry trends in the U.S.: Recidivism*. Washington, D.C.: Bureau of Justice Statistics. Retrieved from bjs.ojp.usdoj.gov/content/pub/pdf/reentry.pdf.

Bureau of Justice Statistics. (2002). *Reentry trends in the U.S.: Releases from state prison*. Washington, D.C.: Bureau of Justice Statistics. Retrieved from bjs.ojp.usdoj.gov/content/pub/pdf/reentry.pdf.

Burgess, R., & Akers, R. (1966). A differential association-reinforcement theory of criminal behavior. *Social Problems, 14*, 128–147.

Burke, B.L., Arkowitz, H., & Menchola,M. (2003). The efficacy of motivational interviewing: A meta-analysis of controlled clinical trials. *Journal of Consulting and Clinical Psychology, 71*, 843–861.

Burke, P.B. (1995). *Abolishing parole: Why the emperor has no clothes*. Lexington, KY: American Probation and Parole Association.

Burrell, W.D. (2005). Trends in probation and parole in the states. In *The book of the states, 2005* (Vol. 37, pp. 595–600). Council of State Governments.

Bush-Basketi, S. (2000). The war on drugs and the incarceration of mothers. *Journal of Drug Issues, 30*(4), 919–928.

Bushway, S.D. (1998). The impact of an arrest on the job stability of young white American men. *Journal of Research in Crime and Delinquency 35*(4), 454–479.

Bushway, S.D. (2004). Labor market effects of permitting employer access to criminal history records. *Journal of Contemporary Criminal Justice, 20*(3), 276–291.

Bushway, S.D., Piquero, A., Briody, L., Cauffman, E., & Mazerolle, P. (2001). An empirical framework for studying desistance as a process. *Criminology, 39*(2), 491–516.

Bushway, S.D., & Reuter, P. (2002). Labor markets and crime. In J.Q. Wilson & J. Peterselia (Eds.), *Crime: Public policies for crime control* (pp. 191–224). San Francisco, CA: ICS Press.

Bushway, S.D., Thornberry, T.P., & Krohn, M.D. (2003). Desistance as a developmental process: A comparison of static and dynamic approaches. *Journal of Quantitative Criminology, 19*(2), 129.

Byrne, C., & Trew, K. (2008). Pathways through crime: The development of crime and desistance in the accounts of men and women offenders. *The Howard Journal, 47*(3), 238–258.

Byrne, J.M. (1989). Re-integrating the concept of community into community-based corrections. *Crime and Delinquency 35*, 471–499.

Byrne, J.M., & Pattavina, A. (2006). Assessing the role of clinical and actuarial risk assessment in an evidence-based community corrections system: Issues to consider. *Federal Probation, 70*, 64–67.

Byrne, J.M., Taxman, F.S., & Young, D. (2002). *Emerging roles and responsibilities in the reentry partnership initiative: New ways of doing business.* Washington, D.C.: U.S. Department of Justice. Retrieved from www.ncjrs.gov/pdffiles1/nij/grants/196441.pdf.

Byrne, M.W., Goshin, L.S., & Joestl, S.S.,(2010). Intergenerational transmission of attachment for infants raised in a prison nursery. *Attachment & Human Development, 12*(4), 375–393.

Cahn, E. (1961). *The predicament of modern man.* New York: MacMillan.

Callaghan, R.C. (2005). A closer look at the work of Brogan, Prochaska, and Prochaska (1999): Comment. *Psychotherapy: Theory, Research, Practice, Training, 42*(2), 244–246.

Cammett, A. (2005). *Making work pay: Promoting employment and better child support outcomes for low-income and incarcerated parents.* Newark: New Jersey Institute for Social Justice. Retrieved from http://www.njisj.org/reports/makingworkpay.pdf.

Cann, D., & Isom Scott, D.A. (2020). Sex offender residence restrictions and homelessness: A critical look at South Carolina. *Criminal Justice Policy Review, 31*(8), 1119–1135.

Caplan, J.M. (2006). Parole system anomie: Conflicting models of casework and surveillance. *Federal Probation, 70*(3), 32–36.

Caplan, J.M. (2007). What factors affect parole: A review of empirical literature. *Federal Probation, 71*(3), 16–19.

Caplan, J.M. (2010). Parole release decisions: Impact of victim input on a representative sample of inmates. *Journal of Criminal Justice, 38*, 291–300.

Cardinale, M. (2004). *Triple decker disenfranchisement: First person accounts of losing the right to vote among poor, homeless Americans with a felony conviction.* Washington, D.C.: The Sentencing Project. Retrieved from www.sentencingproject.org.

Carlson, M.J., & McLanahan, S.S. (2002). Fragile families, father involvement and public policy. In C. Tamis-LeMonda & N. Cabrera, (Eds.), *Handbook of Father Involvement: Multidisciplinary Perspectives* (pp. 461–488). Mahwah, NJ: Lawrence Erlbaum Associates.

Carp, S., & Schade, L. (1992, August). Tailoring facility programming to suit female offender's needs. *Corrections Today*, 154–158.

Carroll, J.S., & Burke, P.A. (1990). Evaluation and prediction in expert parole decisions. *Criminal Justice and Behavior, 17*(3), 315–332.

Carroll, J.S., Wiener, R.L, Coates, D., Galegher, J., & Alibrio, J.J. (1982). Evaluation, diagnosis, and prediction in parole decision making. *Law and Society Review, 17*(1), 199–228.

Carson, E.A. (2014). *Prisoners in 2013* (NCJ247282). Washington, DC: Bureau of Justice Statistics.

Carson, E.A. (2015). *Prisoners in 2014.* (NCJ 248955). Bureau of Justice Statistics.

Carson, E.A. (2018). *Prisoners in 2016.* (NCJ 251149). Bureau of Justice Statistics.

Carson, E.A. (2020). *Prisoners in 2019.* (NCJ 255115). Bureau of Justice Statistics.

Carson, E.A. (2022). *Prisoners in 2021—Statistical tables.* (NCJ305125). Washington, D.C.: Bureau of Justice Statistics.

Carson, E.A., & Anderson, E. (2016). *Prisoners in 2015.* (NCJ 250229). Bureau of Justice Statistics.

Carson, E.A., & Cowhig, M.P. (2020). *Mortality in state and federal prisons, 2001–2016—Statistical tables.* (NCJ 251920). Bureau of Justice Statistics.

Carson, E.A., & Golinelli, D. (2013). *Prisoners in 2012: Trends in admissions and releases, 1991–2012.* (NCJ 243920). Bureau of Justice Statistics.

Carson, E.A., & Sabol, W.J. (2012). *Prisoners in 2011.* (NCJ 239808). Bureau of Justice Statistics.

Carson, E.A., & Sabol, W.J. (2016). *Aging of the state prison population, 1993–2013.* (NCJ 248766). Bureau of Justice Statistics.

Case, P., & Fasenfest, D. (2004). Expectations for opportunities following prison education: A discussion of race and gender. *Journal of Correctional Education, 55*, 24–39.

CASES. 2000. The community justice project: Report to the Open Society Institute. New York: Center for Alternative Sentencing and Employment Services.

Castellano, U. (2011). Courting compliance: Case managers as 'double agents' in the mental health court. *Law & Social Inquiry, 36*(2), 484–514.

Cecil, D.K., Drapkin, D.A., Layton Mackenzie, D., & Hickman, L.J. (2000). The effectiveness of adult basic education and life-skills programs in reducing recidivism: A review and assessment of the research. *Journal of Correctional Education, 51*(2), 207–226.

Cecil, D.K., McHale, J., Strozier, A. & Pietsch, J. (2008). Female inmates, family caregivers, and young children's adjustment: A research agenda and implications for corrections programming. *Journal of Criminal Justice, 36*(6), 513–521.

Celinska, K., & Siegel, J.A. (2010). Mothers in trouble: Coping with actual or pending separation from children due to incarceration. *Prison Journal, 90*(4), 447–474.

Center for Restorative Justice and Mediation. (1996). *Restorative justice: For victims, communities and offenders.* St. Paul, MN: University of Minnesota, School of Social Work.

Centers for Disease Control and Prevention (2003). *Prevention and control of infections with Hepatitis viruses in correctional settings.* (No. RR-1). Atlanta, GA: Centers for Disease Control and Prevention.

Centers for Disease Control and Prevention (2006). *Prevention and control of Tuberculosis in correctional and detention facilities: Recommendations from the CDC.* (No. RR-9). Atlanta, GA: Centers for Disease Control and Prevention.

Centers for Disease Control and Prevention. (2020a). *COVID-19 in correctional and detention facilities — United States, February–April 2020.* https://www.cdc.gov/mmwr/volumes/69/wr/mm6919e1.htm.

Centers for Disease Control and Prevention. (2020b). COVID data tracker. https://covid.cdc.gov/covid-data-tracker/#correctional-facilities.

Chaiken, J., Chaiken, M., & Peterson, J.E. (1982). *Varieties of criminal behavior: Summary and policy implications.* Santa Monica, CA: RAND Corporation. Retrieved from http://www.rand.org/pubs/reports/R2814z1.html.

Chamberlain, A.W., & Wallace, D. (2016). Mass reentry, neighborhood context and recidivism: Examining how the distribution of parolees within and across neighborhoods impact recidivism. *Justice Quarterly, 33*, 912–941.

Chappell, C.A. (2004). Post-secondary correctional education and recidivism: A meta-analysis of research conducted 1990–1999. *Journal of Correctional Education, 55*(2), 148–169.

Chase, J., & Dickover, R. (1983). University education at Folsom prison: An evaluation. *Journal of Correctional Education, 34*(3), 92–96.

Chatterji, P., & Markowitz, S. (2001). The impact of maternal alcohol and drug use on children's behavior problems: evidence from the children from the national longitudinal survey of health. *Journal of Health Economics, 20*(5), 703–731.

Cheng G.J., & Balter, L. (1997). Culturally sensitive education: A critical review of quantitative research. *Review of Educational Research, 67*(3), 339–369.

Chesney-Lind, M. (1997). *The female offender: Girls, women, and crime.* Thousand Oaks, CA: Sage Publications.

Chesney-Lind, M., & Faith, K. (2001). What about feminism? Engendering theory-making in criminology. In R. Paternoster & R. Bachman (Eds.), *Explaining crime and criminals* (pp. 287–302). Los Angeles: Roxbury.

Chesney-Lind, M., & Sheldon, R. (2004). *Girls, delinquency, and juvenile justice* (3rd ed.). Belmont, CA: Thompson Wadsworth.

Chipman, R., Wells, S.J., & Johnson, M.A. (2002). The meaning of quality in kinship foster care: Caregiver, child and worker perspectives. *Families in Society: The Journal of Contemporary Human Services, 83*(5/6), 508–520.

Chiricos, T., Padgett, K., & Gertz, M. (2000). Fear, TV news, and the reality of crime. *Criminology, 38*, 755–786.

Cho, R., & Tyler J. (2008). *Prison-based adult basic education (ABE) and post-release labor market outcomes.* Washington, D.C.: The Urban institute. Retrieved from http://www.urban.org/projects/reentry-roundtable/roundtable10.cfm.

Christ, J., & Bitler, B. (2010). Family engagement + professional compassion = successful reentry. *Corrections Today*, 72(6), 22–24.

Christian, J. (2005). Riding the bus: Barriers to prison visitation and family management strategies. *Journal of Contemporary Criminal Justice, 21*(1), 31–48.

Chung, R.J., Burke, P.J., & Goodman, E. (2010). Firm foundations: Strengths-based approaches to adolescent chronic disease. *Current Opinion in Pediatrics, 22*, 389–397.

Clark, L.M. (2007). Landlord attitudes toward renting to released offenders. *Federal Probation, 71*(1), 20–30.

Clark, M.D. (1997). Strength-based practice: The new paradigm. *Corrections Today, 59*(2), 110–112.

Clark, M.D. (2006). Motivational interviewing for probation officers: Tippin the balance toward change. *Federal Probation, 70*(1), 38–44.

Clark, M.D. (2009a). Juvenile justice and a strengths perspective: Complement or clash? *Reclaiming Children and Youth, 18(2)*, 21–26).

Clark, M.D. (2009b). The strengths perspective in criminal justice. In D. Saleebey (Ed.), *The strengths perspective in social work practice* (5th. Ed., pp. 122–145). New York: Pearson.

Clarke, R.V. & Cornish, D.B. (1985). Modeling offenders' decisions: a framework for research and policy. In M. Tonry & N. Morris (Eds.), *Crime and justice: An annual review of research* (Vol. 6., pp. 147–85). Chicago: University of Chicago Press.

Clear, T.R. (2007). *Imprisoning communities: How mass incarceration makes disadvantaged places worse*. NY: Oxford.

Clear, T.R., Byrne, J.M., & Dvoskin, J.A. (1993). The transition from being an inmate. In H.J Steadman, & J.J. Cocozza, (Eds.), *Mental illness in America's prisons* (pp. 131–158). Seattle, WA: National Coalition for the Mentally Ill in the Criminal Justice System.

Clear, T.R. & Cadora, E. (2003). *Community justice*. Belmont, CA.: Wadsworth Press.

Clear, T.R., & Cannon, J.B. (2012). Neighborhood probation offices in Maricopa County, Arizona. In D.R. Karp & T.R. Clear (Eds.), *What is community justice: Case studies in restorative justice and community supervision* (pp. 37–58). Sage Publications, Inc.

Clear, T.R., & Cole, G. (2000). *American corrections*. 6th ed. Belmont, CA: Wadsworth Publishing.

Clear, T.R., & Gallagher, K. (1985). Probation and parole supervision: A review of current classification practices. *Crime & Delinquency, 31*, 423–444.

Clear, T.R. & Hardyman, P.L. (1990). The new intensive supervision movement. *Crime and Delinquency, 36*(1), 42–60.

Clear,T.R., Harris, P., & Baird, C. (1992). Probationer violations and officer response. *Journal of Criminal Justice, 20*, 1–12.

Clear, T.R., & Karp, D.R. (1999). *The community justice ideal*. Boulder, CO: Westview.

Clear, T.R., & Latessa, E. (1993). Probation officer roles in intensive supervision: Surveillance versus treatment. *Justice Quarterly, 10*, 441–462.

Clear, T.R., Rose, D., & Ryder, J. (2001). Incarceration and the community: The problem of removing and returning offenders. *Crime and Delinquency, 47*, 335–351.

Clear, T.R., Rose, D.R., Waring, E., & Scully, K. (2003). Coercive mobility and crime: A preliminary examination of concentrated incarceration and social disorganization. *Justice Quarterly, 20*(1), 33–64.

Clear, T.R., Waring, E., & Scully, K. (2005). Communities and reentry: Concentrated reentry cycling. In J. Travis & C. Visher, (Eds.), *Prisoner reentry and crime in America* (pp. 179–208). Cambridge: Cambridge University Press.

Cleveland Clinic. (2020). Cirrhosis of the liver. https://my.clevelandclinic.org/health/diseases/15572-cirrhosis-of-the-liver.

Cloward, R., & Ohlin, L. (1960). *Delinquency and opportunity*. NY: Free Press.

Cloyes, K.G., Wong, B., Latimer, S., & Abarca, J. (2010). Women, serious mental illness and recidivism: A gender-based analysis of recidivism risk for women with SMI released from prison. *Journal of Forensic Nursing, 6*(1), 3–14.

Coalition for the Homeless. (2018). *2018 state of the homeless. Fate of a generation: How the city and state can tackle homelessness by bringing housing investment to scale*. https://www.coalitionforthehomeless.org/press/state-homeless-2018/.

Cochran, J.C. (2012). The ties that bind or the ties that break: Examining the relationship between visitation and prisoner misconduct. *Journal of Criminal Justice, 40*(5), 433–440.

Cochran, J.C., Mears, D.P., & Bales, W.D. (2017). Who gets visited in prison? Individual-and community-level disparities in inmate visitation experiences. *Crime & Delinquency, 65*(3), 545–568.

Cochran, J.C., Siennik, S.E., & Mears, D.P. (2018). Social exclusion and parental incarceration impacts on adolescent's networks and school engagement. *Journal of Marriage and Family, 80*, 478–498.

Codd, H. (2007). Prisoners' families and resettlement: A critical analysis. *The Howard Journal of Criminal Justice, 46*(3), 255–263.

Cohen, F., & Gerbasi, J.B. (2005). Legal issues regarding the provision of mental health care in correctional settings. In C.L. Scott & J.B. Gerbasi (Eds.), *Handbook of correctional mental health* (pp. 259 –283). American Psychiatric Publishing.

Cohn, A.W. (1997). Weapons and probation and parole officers: do they mix? *Journal of Offender Monitoring, 10*(3), 1–9.

Cole, G. & Logan, C. (1977). Parole: The consumer's perspective. *Criminal Justice Review, 2*, 71–80.

Coleman, J. (1990). *Foundations of social theory*. Cambridge, MA: Harvard University Press.

Coley, R., & Barton, P. (2006). *Locked up and locked out: An education perspective on the U.S. prison population*. Princeton, NJ: Educational Testing Service. Retrieved from http://www.ets.org/Media/Research/pdf/PIC-LOCKEDUP.pdf.

Comfort, M. (2002). Papa's house: The prison as domestic and social satellite. *Ethnography, 3*(4), 467–499.

Connell, R.W. (1995). *Masculinities*. Berkeley, CA: University of California Press.

Connerley, M., Arvey, R., & Bernardy, C. (2001). Criminal background checks for prospective and current employees: Current practices among municipal agencies. *Public Personnel Management, 30*(2), 173–184.

Contardo, J., & Tolbert, M. (2008, April). Prison postsecondary education: Bridging learning from incarceration to the community. In The Prisoner Reentry Institute and The Urban Institute, *Reentry Roundtable on Education*. Symposia conducted at the John Jay College of Criminal Justice. Retrieved from http://www.jjay.cuny.edu/ContardoTolbert_Paper.pdf.

Cook, C., & Lane, J. (2009). The place of public fear in sentencing and correctional policy. *Journal of Criminal Justice, 37*, 586–595.

Corbett, R., Beto, D., Coen, B., DiIulio, J., Faulkner, R. Fitzgerald, B., Gregg, I. (1999). *Broken windows' probation: The next step in fighting crime*. New York: Manhattan Institute. Retrieved from www.manhattan-institute.org/html/cr_7.htm.

Corcoran, J. (2005). *Building strengths and skills: A collaborative approach to working with clients*. New York: Oxford University Press.

CoreCivic (n.d.). *About CoreCivic*. Retrieved from https://www.corecivic.com/aboutCoreCivic. (2018).

CoreCivic 2018 annual report. http://ir.corecivic.com/static-files/60371436-e930-40bc-8cfa-830d12b4edd0.

Cornish, D., & Clarke, R.V. (Eds.). (1986). *The reasoning criminal*. New York: Springer-Verlag.

Corrections to College California. (2018). Don't stop now: California leads the nation in using public higher education to address mass incarceration. Will we continue? https://risingscholarsnetwork.org/wp-content/uploads/assets/general/dont-stop-now-report_v2.pdf.

Costopoulos, J.S., & Wellman, B.L. (2017). The effectiveness of one mental health court: Overcoming criminal history. *Psychological Injury and Law, 10*(3), 254–263.

Couloute, L. (2018). *Nowhere to go: Homelessness among formerly incarcerated people*. Prison Policy Initiative. https://www.prisonpolicy.org/reports/housing.html.

Coulson, G., Ilacqua, G., Nutbrown, V., Giulekas, D. & Cudjoe, F. (1996). Predictive validity of the LSI for incarcerated female offenders. *Criminal Justice and Behavior, 23*, 427–439.

Cousins, N. (1989). *Head first: The biology of hope.* New York: E.P. Dutton.

Covington, S. (1998). The relational theory of women's psychological development: Implications for the criminal justice system. In R.T. Zaplin (Ed.), *Female offenders: Critical perspectives and effective interventions* (pp. 113–128). Gaithersburg, MD: Aspen.

Covington, S. (2001). Creating gender-responsive programs: The next step for women's services. *Corrections Today, 63*(1), 85–87.

Covington, S. (2002, January). A women's journey home: Challenges for female offenders and their children. Presented at *From Prison to Home*, U.S. Department of Health and Human Services and the Urban Institute, Washington, D.C.

Covington, S. (2003). A woman's journey home: Challenges for female offenders. In J. Travis & M. Waul (Eds.), *Prisoners once removed: The impact of incarceration and reentry on children, families, and communities* (pp. 67–103). Washington, D.C.: The Urban Institute.

Covington, S.S., & Bloom, B.E. (2003). Gendered justice: Women in the criminal justice system. In B.E. Bloom (Ed.), *Gendered justice: Addressing female offenders* (pp. 1–20). Carolina Academic Press.

Covington, S., & Bloom, B. (2007). Gender-responsive treatment and services in correctional settings. In E. Leeder, (Ed.), *Inside and out: Women, prison, and therapy*. Binghamton, NY: Haworth Press. 29(3/4).

Cowger, C.D. (1992). Assessment of client strengths. In D. Saleebey (Ed.), *The strengths perspective in social work practice: Power in the people* (pp. 139–147). New York: Springer.

Cowger, C.D. (1994). Assessing client strengths: Clinical assessment for client empowerment. *Social Work, 39*(3), 262–268.

Crawley, E., & Sparkes, R. (2006). Is there life after imprisonment? How elderly men talk about imprisonment and release. *Criminology and Criminal Justice, 6*, 63–82.

Crayton, A., & Lindahl, A. (2007). *Back to school: A guide to continuing your education after prison*. New York: John Jay College of Criminal Justice. Retrieved from http://www.jjay.cuny.edu/Back_to_School_Final_5.28.08.pdf.

Crayton, A., & Neusteter, S.R. (2008, March). *The current state of correctional education*. Paper presented at the Reentry Roundtable on Education, John Jay College of Criminal Justice, New York. Retrieved from www.jjay.cuny.edu/CraytonNeusteter_FinalPaper.pdf.

Cuellar, A., Snowden, L.M., & Ewing, T. (2007). Criminal records of persons served in the public mental health system. *Psychiatric Services, 58*(1), 114–120.

Cullen, F., & Gendreau, P. (2001). From nothing works to what works: Changing professional ideology in the 21st century. *The Prison Journal, 81*, 313–338.

Cullen, F., Fisher, B., & Applegate, B. (2000). Public opinion about punishment and corrections. In M. Tonry (Ed.), *Crime and justice: Review of research* (Vol. 27, pp. 1–79). Chicago: University of Chicago Press.

Cullen, F. & Gilbert, N. (Eds.). (1982). *Reaffirming rehabilitation*. Cincinnati, OH: Anderson Publishing.

Dallaire, D.H. (2007a). Incarcerated mothers and fathers: A comparison of risks for children and families. *Family Relations, 56*(5), 440–453.

Dallaire, D.H. (2007b). Children with incarcerated mothers: Developmental outcomes, special challenges, and recommendations. *Journal of Applied Developmental Psychology, 28*, 447–492.

Dallaire D.H., Ciccone, A., & Wilson, L.C. (2010). Teachers' experiences with and expectations of children with incarcerated parents. *Journal of Applied Developmental Psychology, 31*, 281–290.

Daly, K. (1994). *Gender, crime, and punishment*. New Haven, CT: Yale University Press.

Daly, K. (1998). Gender, crime and criminology. In M. Tonry (Ed.), *The handbook of crime and punishment* (pp. 85–108). New York: Oxford University Press.

Daly, K., & Chesney-Lind, M. (1988). Feminism and criminology. *Justice Quarterly, 5*, 497–538.

Daniel, R., & Sawyer, W. (2020). *What you should know about halfway houses*. Retrieved from https://www.prisonpolicy.org/blog/2020/09/03/halfway/.

Davies, R.P. (1980). Stigmatization of prisoners' families. *Prison Service Journal, 40*, 12–14.

Davis, A. (1992). Men's imprisonment: the financial cost to women and children. In R. Shaw (Ed.), *Prisoners' children: What are the issues?* (pp. 74–85). London: Routledge.

Davis, L.M., Bozick, R., Steele, J.L., Saunders, J., & Miles, J.N.V. (2013). *Evaluating the effectiveness of correctional education*. RAND Corporation. https://www.rand.org/pubs/research_reports/RR266.html.

Day, R.D., Lewis, C., O'Brien, M., & Lamb, M.E. (2005). Fatherhood and father involvement: Emerging constructs and theoretical orientations. In V. Bengtson, A. Acock, K. Allen, P. Dilworth-Anderson, & D.Klein (Eds.), *Sourcebook of family theories* (pp. 341–351). London: Sage.

DEA history. (n.d.). Retrieved from http://www.justice.gov/dea/history.htm.

Dear, M. (1992). Understanding and overcoming the NIMBY syndrome. *Journal of the American Planning Association, 58*(3), 288–300.

DeGostin, L.K., & Hoffman, P.B. (1974). Administrative review of parole decisions. *Federal Probation, 38*(2), 24–28.

DeHart, D.D., & Altshuler, S.J. (2009). Violence exposure among children of incarcerated mothers. *Child and Adolescent Social Work, 26*(5), 467–479.

DeLisi, M. (2000). Who is more dangerous? Comparing the criminality of adult homeless and domiciled jail inmates: A research note. *Journal of Offender Therapy and Comparative Criminology, 44*(1), 59–69.

De Jong, P. & Miller, S.D. (1995). How to interview for client strengths. *Social Work, 40*(6), 729–736).

Del Carmen, R.V., & Louis, P.T. (1988). *Civil liabilities of parole personnel for release, non-release, supervision, and revocation.* Rockville, MD: National Institute of Corrections.

Dembo, R. (1972). Orientation and activities of the parole officer. *Criminology, 10*, 193–215.

DeMichele, M.T., & Payne, B. (2007). Probation and parole officers speak out — Caseload and workload allocation. *Federal Probation, 71*(3), 30–37.

Dennison, S.J. (2005). Substance use disorders in individuals with co-occurring psychiatric disorders. In J.H. Lowinson, P. Ruiz, R.B. Millman, & J.G. Langrod (Eds.), *Substance abuse: A comprehensive textbook* (4th ed., pp. 904–912). Lippincott Williams & Wilkins.

Derkzen, D., Gobeil, R., & Gileno, J. (2009). *Visitation and post-release outcome among federally sentenced offenders.* Correctional Service Canada.

DiClemente, C.C., Schlundt, D., & Gemmell, L. (2004). Readiness and stages of change in addiction treatment. *American Journal of Addiction, 13*(2), 103–119.

DiMascio,W., Mauer, M., DiJulia, K., & Davidson, K. (1997). *Seeking justice: Crime and punishment in America.* New York: Edna McConnell Clark Foundation.

DiZerega, M., & Shapiro, C. (2007). Asking about family can enhance reentry. *Corrections Today, 69*(6), 58–61.

Ditton, P.M. (1999). *Mental health and treatment of inmates and probationers* (NCJ 174463). Washington, DC: Bureau of Justice Statistics.

Ditton, P.M. & Wilson, D.J. (1999). *Truth in Sentencing in State Prisons.* (NCJ 170032). Washington, D.C.: Bureau of Justice Statistics. Retrieved from bjsdata.ojp.usdoj.gov/content/pub/pdf/tssp.pdf.

Dixey, R., & Woodall, J. (2012). The significance of "the visit" in an English category-B prison: Views from prisoners, prisoners' families and prison staff. *Community, Work & Family, 15*(1), 29–47.

Doble, J., Immerwahr, S., & Richardson, A. (1991). *Punishing criminals: The people of Delaware consider the options.* New York: Public Agenda Foundation.

Doble, J. Lindsay, M. (2003). *Is NIMBY inevitable?* Retrieved from http://centerforcommunitycorrections.org/?page_id=29.

Dodge, M., & Pogrebin, M. (2001). Collateral costs of imprisonment for women: Complications of reintegration. *The Prison Journal, 81*, 42–44.

Doherty, W.J., Kouneski, E.F., & Erickson, M.F. (1998). Responsible fathering: An overview and conceptual framework. *Journal of Marriage and Family, 60*, 277–292.

Donnellan, M.C., & Moore, H.A. (1979). Rehabilitation and protection: The goals and orientations of probation and parole workers. *Journal of Offender Rehabilitation, 3*(3), 207–218.

Dowden, C. & Andrews, D. (1999). What works for female offenders: A meta-analytic review. *Crime and Delinquency, 45*, 438–452.

Dowden, C. & Andrews, D. (2004). The importance of staff practice in delivering effective correctional treatment: a meta-analytic review of core correctional practice. *International Journal of Offender Therapy and Comparative Criminology, 48*(2), 203–214.

Dowdy, E., Lacy, M. & Unnithan, P. (2002). Correctional prediction and the Level of Supervision Inventory. *Journal of Criminal Justice, 30*, 29–39.

Draine, J. & Herman, D.B. (2007). Critical time intervention for reentry from prison for persons with mental illness. *Psychiatric Services, 58*(12), 1577–1581.

Draine, J., Salzer M.S., Culhane D.P., & Hadley T.R. (2002). Putting social problems among persons with mental illness in perspective: Crime, unemployment and homelessness. *Psychiatric Services, 53*(5), 565–572.

Draine, J., Wolff, N., Jacoby, J.E., Hartwell, S., & Duclos, C. (2005). Understanding community re-entry of former prisoners with mental illness: a conceptual model to guide new research. *Behavioral Sciences & the Law, 23*(5), 689–707.

Drug Policy Alliance. (n.d.). *A brief history of the drug war*. https://drugpolicy.org/issues/brief-history-drug-war.

Duguid, S. (1981). Prison education and criminal choice: The context of decision-making. In L. Morin (Ed.), *On prison education* (pp. 135–157). Ottawa: Canadian Government Publishing Centre.

Duguid, S. (1982). Rehabilitation through education: A Canadian model. *Journal of Offender Rehabilitation, 6*(2), 53–67.

Duwe, G., & Clark, V. (2011). Blessed be the social tie that binds: The effects of prison visitation on offender recidivism. *Criminal Justice Policy Review, 24*(3), 271–296.

Dyer, W.M. (2005). Prison, fathers, and identity: A theory of how incarceration affects men's paternal identity. *Fathering: A Journal of Theory, Research and Practice about Men as Fathers, 3*(3), 201–219.

Eagleton Institute of Politics Center for Public Interest. (2001, January). *Prisoner reentry: The state of public opinion*. Retrieved from http://njisj.org/reports/eagleton_report.html.

Edin, K., & Kefalas, M. (2005). *Promises I can keep: Why poor women put motherhood before marriage*. Berkeley: University of California Press.

Ehrenreich, B. (2001). *Nickel and dimed: On (not) getting by in America*. New York: Metropolitan Books.

Ekland-Olson, S., Supanic, M., Campbell, J., & Lenihan, K.J. (1983). Post-release depression and the importance of familial support. *Criminology, 21*(2), 253–275.

Elbogen, E.B., & Johnson, S.C. (2009). The intricate link between violence and mental disorder: Results from the National Epidemiologic Survey on Alcohol and Related Conditions. *Archives of General Psychiatry, 66,* 152–161.

Elder, G.H. (1985). Perspectives on the life course. In G.H. Elder (Ed.), *Life course dynamics* (pp. 23–49). Ithaca, NY: Cornell University Press.

Enos, S. (2001). *Mothering from the inside: Parenting in a women's prison.* Albany, NY: State University of New York Press.

Erickson, R.A. & Friedman, S.W. (1991). Comparative dimensions of state enterprise zone policies. In R.E. Green (Ed.), *Enterprise zones: New directions in economic development* (pp. 155–176). Newbury Park: Sage Publications.

Ericson, R. & Haggerty, K. (1997). *Policing the risk society.* Toronto, CA: University of Toronto Press.

Erisman, W., & Contardo, J.B. (2005). *Learning to reduce recidivism: A 50-state analysis of postsecondary correctional education policy.* Washington, DC: Institute for Higher Education Policy. Retrieved from www.ihep.org/Publications/publications-detail.cfm?id=47.

Esperian, J.H. (2010). The effect of prison education programs on recidivism. *The Journal of Correctional Education, 61*(4), 316–334.

Ewald, A.C. (2002). Civil death: The ideological paradox of criminal disenfranchisement law in the United States. *Wisconsin Law Review, 5,* 1045–1132.

Fagan, J., & Meares, T. (2008). Punishment, deterrence and social control: The paradox of punishment in minority communities. *Ohio State Journal of Criminal Law, 6,* 173–229.

Fagan, J., West, V., & Holland, J. (2003). Reciprocal effects of crime and incarceration in New York City neighborhoods. *Fordham Urban Law Journal, 30*(5), 1551–1602.

Fantuzzo, J.W., & Mohr, W.K. (1999). Prevalence and effects of child exposure to domestic violence. *Domestic Violence and Children, 9*(3), 21–32.

Farabee, D., Zhang, S., & Yang, J. (2011). A preliminary examination of offender needs assessment: Are all those questions really necessary? *Journal of Psychoactive Drugs, 7,* 51–57.

Farkas, S. (1993). Pennsylvanians prefer alternatives to prison. *Overcrowded Times, 4*(2), 13–15.

Farley, C., & McClanahan W.S. (2007). *Ready4Work: In Brief.* Philadelphia: Public/Private Ventures. Retrieved from http://www.ppv.org/ppv/publications/assets/216_publication.pdf.

Farrington, D.P (1986). Age and crime. In M. Tonry & N. Morris (Eds.), Crime and justice: An annual review of research (Vol. 7., pp. 189–250). Chicago: University of Chicago Press.

Farrington, D.P., & Hawkins, J.D. (1991). Predicting Participation, Early Onset, and Later Persistence in Officially Recorded Offending. *Criminal Behaviour and Mental Health, 1*, 1–33.

Farrington, D.P., & Tarling, R. (Eds.). (1985). *Prediction in Criminology.* Albany: State University of New York Press.

Fass, T.L., Heibrun, K., DeMatteo, D., & Fretz, R. (2008). The LSI-R and the COMPAS: Validation data on two risk-needs tools. *Criminal Justice and Behavior, 35*, 1095–1108.

Feder, L. (1994). Psychiatric hospitalization history and parole decisions. *Law and Human Behavior, 18*, 395–410.

Feder, L. (1991). A comparison of the community adjustment of mentally ill offenders with those from the general prison population: An 18-month followup. *Law and Human Behavior, 15*, 477–493.

Federal Bureau of Investigations. (2019). *Uniform Crime Report: Estimated number of arrests.*

Federal Bureau of Prisons. (n.d.). *Education programs.* https://www.bop.gov/inmates/custody_and_care/education.jsp.

Federal Bureau of Prisons. (2017). Management of HIV infection. https://www.bop.gov/resources/pdfs/mgmt_hiv.pdf.

Feeley, M., & Simon, J. (1992). The new penology: Notes on the emerging strategy of corrections and its implications. *Criminology, 30*, 449–474.

Fellner, J. (2006). A corrections quandary: Mental illness and prison rules. *Harvard Civil Rights-Civil Liberties Law Review, 41*, 391–412.

Fellner, J. (2007, July). Keep mentally ill out of solitary confinement. *Huffington Post.* https://www.huffpost.com/entry/keep-mentally-ill-out-of_b_56948.

Ferraro, K., & Moe, A. (2003). Mothering, crime, and incarceration. *Journal of Contemporary Ethnography, 32*(1), 9–40.

Finn, P., & Kuck, S. (2003). *Addressing probation and parole officer stress.* Washington, D.C.: National Institute of Justice. Retrieved from www.ncjrs.gov/pdffiles1/nij/grants/207012.pdf.

Fishman, L.T. (1988). Stigmatization and prisoners' wives: feelings of shame. *Deviant Behavior, 9*, 169–192.

Fishman, L.T. (1990). *Women at the wall: A study of prisoners' wives doing time on the outside.* Albany, NY: State University of New York Press.

Flanagan, N.A. & Bue-Estes, C.L. (2005). Health care needs of inmates leaving U.S. prisons and recommendations for improving transitional health care. *International Journal of Comparative & Applied Criminal Justice, 29*(1), 19–32.

Flanagan, T.J. (1996). Community corrections in the public mind. *Federal Probation, 60*(3), 3–9.

Flanagan, T.J., & Longmire, D.R. (1996). *Americans view crime and justice: A national public opinion survey.* Thousand Oaks, CA: Sage Publications.

Fleisher, W., Dressner, J., Herzog, N., & Hong, A. (2001). *Keeping the door open to people with drug problems: Volume III for programs in public housing.* New York: Corporation for Supportive Housing.

Fontaine, J., & Biess, J. (2012). *Housing as a platform for formerly incarcerated persons.* Washington, D.C.: The Urban Institute.

Foster, H., & Hagan, J. (2009). The mass incarceration of parents in America: Issues of race/ethnicity, collateral damage to children, and prisoner reentry. *The Annals of the American Academy of Political and Social Science, 62*(3), 179–194.

Fox, L.G., & Bruce, C. (2001). Conditional fatherhood: Identity theory and paternal investment theory as alternative sources of explanation of fathering. *Journal of Marriage and Family, 63*, 394–403.

Franz, J. (1999). *The wise listener: implementing consistent strength-based planning throughout the gateways of a community's human services system.* Madison, WI: Wisconsin Council on Children and Families.

Freeman, A., & Dattilio, F.M. (1992). *Comprehensive casebook of cognitive therapy.* New York: Plenum Press.

Freudenberg, N., Daniels, J., Crum, M., Perkins, T., & Richie, B.E. (2005). Coming home from jail: The social and health consequences of community reentry for women, male adolescents, and their families and communities. *American Journal of Public Health, 95*(10), 1725–1736.

Friedman, L.M. (1993). *Crime and punishment in American history.* New York: Basic Books.

Frye, S., & Sawe, S. (2008). Interventions for women prisoners and their children in the post-release period, *Clinical Psychologist, 12*(3), 99–108.

Fulton, B., Stichman, A., Travis, L., & Latessa, E. (1997). Moderating officer attitudes to achieve desired outcomes. *Prison Journal, 77*(3), 295–312.

Gabel, K., & Johnston, D. (Eds.). (1995). *Children of incarcerated parents.* New York: Lexington Books.

Gable, S. & Shindledecker, R. (1993). Parental substance abuse and its relationship to severe aggression and antisocial behavior in youth. *American Journal on Addictions, 2*(1), 48–58.

Gadd, D., & Farrall, S. (2004) Criminal careers, desistance and subjectivity: Interpreting men's narratives of change. *Theoretical Criminology 8,* 123–56.

Gadsden, V.L., & Rethemeyer, R.K. (2003). Heading home: Offender reintegration in the home. In V.L. Gadsden, (Ed.), *Linking father involvement and parental incarceration: Conceptual issues in research and practice* (pp. 39–88). Lathan, MD: American Correctional Association.

Gaes, G. (2008). The impact of prison education programs on post-release outcomes. *Reentry Roundtable on Education.* New York: John Jay College of Criminal Justice. Retrieved from http://www.dllr.maryland.gov/adulted/aeimpactprisoned.pdf.

Galston, W. (2001). Political knowledge, political engagement, and civic education. *Annual Review of Political Science, 4,* 217–234.

Garfinkel, H. (1956). Conditions of successful degradation ceremonies. *American Journal of Sociology, 61,* 420–424.

Garland, D. (2001). *The culture of control: Crime and social order in contemporary society.* Chicago: University of Chicago Press.

Garland, B., Wodahl, E., & Mayfield, J. (2011). Prisoner reentry in a small metropolitan community: Obstacles and policy recommendations. *Criminal Justice Policy Review, 22*(1): 90–110.

Gartner, R., & Piliavin, I. (1988) The aging offender and the aged offender. In P.B. Baltes, D.L. Featherman, & R.M. Lerner (Eds.), *Life-span development and behaviour* (Vol. 9, pp. 287–315). Hillsdale, NJ: Lawrence Erlbaum Associates.

Garvey, S.P. (1998). Freeing prisoners' labor. Cornell Law Faculty Publications. Paper 293. Retrieved from http://scholarship.law.cornell.edu/facpub/293.

Gehring, T. (1997). Post-secondary education for inmates: An historical inquiry. *Journal of Correctional Education, 48*(2), 46–55.

Geller, A., & Curtis, M.A. (2011). A sort of homecoming: Incarceration and the housing security of urban men. *Social Science Research, 40,* 1196–1213.

Gelman, D. (2007). Managing inmates with mental health disorders. *Corrections Today,* 22–23.

General Accounting Office. (2000). *Mental health: Community-based care increases for people with serious mental illness.* (Publication No. GAO-01 -224). Washington, D.C.: Government Printing Office.

Gendreau, P., Goggin, C., Cullen, F.T., & Paparozzi, M. (2002). The common-sense revolution and correctional policy. In J. McGuire (Ed.), *Offender rehabilitation and treatment: Effective programmes and policies to reduce re-offending* (pp. 358–386). Chichester, UK: John Wiley & Sons.

Gendreau, P., Little, T., & Goggin, C. (1996). A meta-analysis of the predictors of adult offender recidivism: what works! *Criminology, 34,* 575–607.

Gendreau, P. & Ross, R. (1987). Revivication of rehabilitation. Evidence from the 1980s. *Justice Quarterly, 4,* 349–407.

Genty, P.M. (2002). Damage to family relationships as a collateral consequence of parental incarceration, *Fordham Urban Law Journal, 30*(5), 1671–1684.

George Washington School of Law. (2012). *Program for Older Inmates.* Retrieved from http://www.law.gwu.edu/Academics/EL/clinics/Pages /POPS.aspx.

Gerber, J., & Fritsch, E.J. (1995). Adult academic and vocational correctional education programs: A review of recent research. *Journal of Offender Rehabilitation, 22*(1/2), 119–192.

Giancola, P.R. (2000). Neuropsychological functioning and antisocial behavior: Implications for etiology and prevention. In D.H. Fishbein (Ed.), *The science, treatment, and prevention of antisocial behaviors: Application to the criminal justice system* (pp. 11.1–11.16). Kingston, NJ: Civic Research Institute.

Gibbs, J.P. (1986). Deterrence theory and research. In G.B. Melton (Ed.), *The law as a behavioral instrument: Nebraska symposium on motivation* (pp. 87–130). Lincoln: University of Nebraska Press.

Gibbens, T.C.N. (1984). Borstal boys after 25 years. *British Journal of Criminology, 24,* 49–62.

Gilligan, C. (1982). *In a different voice: Psychological theory and women's development.* Cambridge, MA: Harvard University Press.

Giordano, P., Cernkovich, S., & Rudolph, J. (2002). Gender, crime, and desistance: Toward a theory of cognitive transformation. *American Journal of Sociology, 107*(4), 990–1064.

Girard, L., & Wormith, J. (2004). The predictive validity of the Level of Service Inventory — Ontario version on general and violent recidivism among various offender groups. *Criminal Justice and Behavior, 31*, 150–181.

Glaser, D. (1969). *The effectiveness of a prison and parole system.* Indianapolis: Bobbs-Merrill.

Glaze, L.E. (2011). *Correctional populations in the United States,* 2010. (NCJ236319). Washington, DC: Bureau of Justice Statistics.

Glaze, L.E., & Maruschak, I. (2008). *Parents in prison and their minor children.* (NCJ-222984). Washington, D.C.: Bureau of Justice Statistics.

Glaze, L.E., & Maruschak, I. (2010). *Parents in prison and their minor children.* (NCJ-222984). Washington, D.C.: Bureau of Justice Statistics.

Glaze, L. E., & Kaeble, D. (2014). *Correctional populations in the United States, 2013.* (NCJ 248479). Bureau of Justice Statistics.

Glueck, S., & Glueck, E. (1943). *Criminal careers in retrospect.* New York: Commonwealth Fund.

Glueck, S., & Glueck, E. (1950). *Unraveling juvenile delinquency.* New York: Commonwealth Fund.

Goffman, E. (1963). *Stigma: Notes on the management of spoiled identity.* New York: Prentice-Hall.

Golden, R. (2005). *War on the family: Mothers in prison and the families they leave behind.* New York: Routledge.

Goldkamp, J.S., & Irons-Guynn, C. (2000). *Emerging judicial strategies for the mentally ill in the criminal caseload: Mental health courts in Fort Lauderdale, Seattle, San Bernardino, and Anchorage.* U.S. Department of Justice, Office of Programs. http://www.ncjrs.gov/pdffiles1/bja/182504.pdf.

Gonnerman, J. (2004, November 9). Million dollar blocks. *Village Voice.*

Gonzalez, J.R., Jetelina, K.K., Roberts, M., Reitzel, L.R., Kendzor, D., Walters, S., & Businelle, M.S. (2018). Criminal justice system involvement among homeless adults. *American Journal of Criminal Justice, 43*, 158–166.

Goozh, J.L., & Jeweler, S. (2011). Explaining why mommy or daddy is in jail. *American Jails, 25*(1), 49–54.

Gotsch, K., & Basti, V. (2018). *Capitalizing on mass incarceration: U.S. growth in private prisons.* The Sentencing Project.

Gottfredson, G.D., & Gottfredson, D.C. (1985). *Victimization in schools.* New York: Plenum.

Gottfredson, M.R., & Gottfredson, D.M. (1988). *Decision making in criminal justice: Toward the rational exercise of discretion.* New York: Springer.

Gottfredson, M.R., & Hirschi, T. (1990). *A general theory of crime.* Stanford, CA: Stanford University Press.

Gottfredson, S.D., & Taylor, R.B. (1988). Community contexts and criminal offenders. In T. Hope and M. Shaw (Eds.), *Communities and crime reduction* (pp. 62–80). London: Her Majesty's Stationery Office.

Gough, E., Kempf, M.C., Graham, L., Manzanero, M., Hook, E.W., Bartolucci, A., & Chamot, E. (2010). HIV and hepatitis B and C incidence rates in US correctional populations and high-risk groups: A systematic review and meta-analysis. *BMC Public Health, 10*, 777–790.

Gover, A.R., Perez, D.M., & Jennings, W.G. (2008). Gender differences in factors contributing to institutional misconducts. *The Prison Journal, 88*(3), 378–403.

Graham, J., & Bowling, B. (1995). *Young people and crime.* London: Home Office.

Gramilich, J. (2018). *America's incarceration rate is at a two-decade low.* Pew Research Center. https://www.pewresearch.org/fact-tank/2018/05/02/americas-incarceration-rate-is-at-a-two-decade-low/.

Granovetter, M. (1993). Strength of weak ties. *American Journal of Sociology, 78*, 1360–80.

Green, J., & Doble, J. (2000) *Attitudes toward crime and punishment in Vermont: Public opinion about an experiment with restorative justice.* Englewood Cliffs, NJ: John Doble Research Associates.

Greenberg, E., Dunleavy, E., & Kutner, M. (2007). Literacy behind bars: Results from the 2003 national assessment of adult literacy prison survey. Washington, D.C.: U.S. Department of Education. Retrieved from http://nces.ed.gov/pubs2007/2007473.pdf.

Greenberg, G.A., & Rosenheck, R. (2008a). Jail incarceration, homelessness, and mental illness: A national study. *Psychiatric Services, 59*, 170–177.

Greenberg, G.A., & Rosenheck, R. (2008b). Homelessness in the state and federal prison population. *Criminal Behavior and Mental Health, 18*, 88–103.

Greene, J.A., & Schiraldi, V. (2002). *Cutting correctly: New prison policies for times of fiscal crisis*. San Francisco, CA: Center on Juvenile and Criminal Justice.

Greene, S., Haney, C., & Hurtado, A. (2000). Cycles of pain: Risk factors in the lives of incarcerated mothers and their children. *The Prison Journal, 80*(1), 3–23.

Greenfeld, L.A., & Snell, T.L. (1999). *Women offenders: Special report*. (NCJ 175688). Washington, D.C.: Bureau of Justice Statistics.

Greenfeld, L.A., & Snell, T.L. (2000). *Women offenders*. (NCJ 175688). Washington, D.C.: Bureau of Justice Statistics.

Grella, C., Lovinger, K., & Warda, U.S. (2013). Relationships among trauma exposure, familial characteristics, and PTSD: A case-control study of women in prison and in the general population. *Women & Criminal Justice, 23*, 63–79.

Griset, P. (1991). *Determinate sentencing: The promise and the reality of retributive justice*. Albany, NY: State University of New York Press.

Grob, G.N. (1991). *From asylum to community: Mental health policy in modern America*. Princeton, NJ: Princeton University Press.

Grob, G.N., & Goldman, H.H. (2006). *The dilemma of federal mental health policy: Radical reform or incremental change?* New Brunswick, NJ: Rutgers University Press.

Grove, W., & Meehl, P. (1996). Comparative efficiency of informal (subjective, impressionistic) and formal (mechanical, algorithmic) prediction procedures: The clinical-statistical controversy. *Psychology, Public Policy, and Law, 2*, 293–323.

Grove, W., Zald, D., Lebow, B., Snitz, B., & Nelson, C. (2000). Clinical versus mechanical prediction: A meta-analysis. *Psychological Assessment, 12*, 19–30.

Guerino, P.M., Harrison, P.M., & Sabol, W. (2011). Prisoners in 2010. (NCJ 236096). Washington, D.C.: Bureau of Justice Statistics.

Hagan, J., & Dinovitzer, R. (1999). Collateral consequences of imprisonment for children, communities, and prisoners. *Crime and Justice, 26*, 121–162.

Hagan, J., & McCarthy, M. (1997). *Mean streets: Youth crime and homelessness*. New York: Cambridge University Press.

Hahn, J.M. (1991). Pre-employment information services: *Employers beware. Employee Relations Law Journal, 17*, 45–69.

Hairston, C.F. (1989). Men in prison: Family characteristics and parenting views. *Journal of Offender Counseling, Services and Rehabilitation, 14*, 3–30.

Hairston, C.F. (1991a). Mothers in jail: Parent-child separation and jail visitation. *Women and Social Work, 69*(2), 9–27.

Hairston, C.F. (1991b). Family ties during imprisonment: Important to whom and for what? *Journal of Sociology and Social Welfare, 18*(1), 87–104.

Hairston, C.F. (1995). Fathers in prison. In D. Johnson & K. Gables (Eds.), *Children of incarcerated parents* (pp. 31–40). Lexington, MA: Lexington Books.

Hairston, C.F. (1998). The forgotten parent: Understanding the forces that influence incarcerated fathers' relationships with their children. *Child Welfare, 77*(5), 618–639.

Hairston, C.F. (2001a, January). *Prisoners and families: Parenting issues during incarceration*. Paper presented at the National Policy Conference, Washington, D.C.

Hairston, C.F. (2001b). Fathers in prison: Responsible fatherhood and responsible public policies. *Marriage & Family Review, 32*(3/4), 111–135.

Hairston, C.F. (2002a, April). The importance of families in prisoners' community reentry. *The ICCA Journal on Community Corrections*, 11–14.

Hairston, C.F. (2002b, January). *Prisoners and families: Parenting issues during incarceration*. From Prison to Home: The Effects of Incarceration and Reentry on Children, Families and Communities Conference, Washington, D.C. Retrieved from http://aspe.hhs.gov/hsp/prison-2home02/index.htm.

Hairston, C.F. (2003). Prisoners and the families: parenting issues during incarceration. In J. Travis & M. Waul (Eds.), *Prisoners once removed: The impact of incarceration and reentry on children, families, and communities* (pp. 233–258). Washington, D.C.: The Urban Institute Press.

Hairston, C.F. (2007). Focus on children with incarcerated parents: An overview of the research literature. Baltimore, MD: Annie E. Casey Foundation.

Hairston, C.F. (2008). *Children with parents in prison: Child welfare matters.* St. Paul, MN: University of Minnesota, Center for Advanced Studies in Child Welfare.

Hairston. C.F. (2009). Kinship care when parents are incarcerated: What we know, what we can do. Baltimore, MD: Annie E. Casey Foundation. Retrieved from www.aecf.org/.../Child%20Welfare%20Permanence/Foster%20Care/...

Hairston, C.F., & Lockett, P. (1987). Parents in prison: New directions for social services. Social Work, 32(2), 162–164.

Hall, R. (1989). Self-efficacy ratings. In D. Laws, (Ed.), *Relapse prevention with sex offenders* (pp. 137–146). New York: Guilford Press.

Halperin, R., & Harris, J.L. (2004). Parental rights of incarcerated mothers and children in foster care: A policy vacuum. *Feminist Studies, 30*(2), 339–352.

Hammett, T.M. (2006). HIV/AIDS and other infectious diseases among correctional inmates: Transmission, burden, and appropriate response. *American Journal of Public Health, 96*, 974–978.

Hammett, T.M., Kennedy, S., & Kuck, S. (2007). *National survey of infectious diseases in correctional facilities: HIV and sexually transmitted diseases.* Washington, D.C.: U.S. Department of Justice, Retrieved from www.ncjrs.gov/pdffiles1/nij/grants/217736.pdf.

Hammett, T., Roberts, C., & Kennedy, S. (2001). Health-related issues in prisoner reentry. *Crime & Delinquency 47*(3), 390–409.

Hanlon, T.E., Carswell, S.B., & Rose, M. (2005). Research on the caretaking of children of incarcerated parents: Findings and their service delivery implications. *Child Youth Services Review, 29*(3), 384–362.

Hannah-Moffat, K. (2004). Gendering risk: At what cost? Negotiations of gender and risk in Canadian women's prisons. *Feminism & Psychology, 14*, 243–249.

Hannah-Moffat, K. (2009). Gridlock or mutability: Reconsidering gender and risk assessment. *Criminology and Public Policy, 8*, 209–219.

Hanneken, D., & Dannerbeck, A. (2007) Practical solutions: Addressing offenders' educational opportunities and challenges. *Corrections Compendium, 32*(2), 1–4, 37.

Hansen, C. (2008). Cognitive-behavioral interventions: Where they came from and what they do. *Federal Probation 72*(2).

Hanson, R.K., & Bussière, M.T. (1996). *Predictors of sexual offender recidivism: A metaanalysis* (User Report 96-04). Ottawa, Canada: Department of the Solicitor General of Canada.

Harding, D. (2003). Jean Valjean's dilemma: The management of ex-convict identity in the search for employment. *Deviant Behavior, 24*, 571–595.

Harding, R.W., Rynne, J., & Thomsen, L. (2019). History of privatized corrections. *Criminology and Public Policy, 18*(2), 241–267.

Hardyman, P., & Van Voorhis, P. (2004). *Developing gender-specific classification systems for women offenders*. Washington, DC: National Institute of Corrections. Retrieved from static.nicic.gov/Library/018931.pdf.

Harer, M.D. (1995). *Prison education program participation and recidivism: A test of the normalization hypothesis*. Washington, D.C.: Federal Bureau of Prisons, Office of Research and Evaluation. Retrieved from www.bop.gov/news/research_projects/ . . . /recidivism/orepredprg.pdf.

Harer, M.D., & Langan, N. (2001). Gender differences in predictors of prison violence: Assessing the predictive validity of a risk classification system. *Crime and Delinquency, 47*, 513–536.

Harlow, C.W. (2003). *Education and correctional populations*. (NCJ 195670). Washington, D.C.: Bureau of Justice Statistics.

Harm, N., & Phillips, S. (2001). You can't go home again: Women and criminal recidivism. *Journal of Offender Rehabilitation, 32*, 3–21.

Harré, R. (1981). Rituals, rhetoric and social cognition. In J.P. Forgas (Ed.), *Social cognition: Perspectives on everyday understanding* (pp. 21, 1–24). London: Academic Press.

Harris, P.M. (2006). What community supervision officers need to know about actuarial risk assessment and clinical judgment. *Federal Probation, 70*(2), 8–14.

Hartman, J., Turner, M., Daigle, L., Exum, M., & Cullen, F. (2008). Exploring gender differences in protective factors: Implications for understanding resiliency. *International Journal of Offender Therapy and Comparative Criminology, 53*(3), 249–277.

Hartney, C., & Marchionna, S. (2009). *Attitudes of US voters toward nonserious offenders and alternatives to incarceration*. Oakland, CA: National Council on Crime and Delinquency.

Hartwell, S.W. (2004). Comparison of offenders with mental illness only and offenders with dual diagnosis. *Psychiatric Services, 55*, 145–150.

Harvey, M.R. (1996). An ecological view of psychological trauma and trauma recovery. *Journal of Traumatic Stress, 9*, 3–23.

Harvey, M.R. (2007). Towards an ecological understanding of resilience in trauma survivors: Implications for theory, research and practice. In M.R. Harvey & P. Tummala-Narra (Eds.), *Sources and expressions of resiliency in trauma survivors: Ecological theory and practice* (pp. 9–32). New York: The Haworth Maltreatment & Trauma Press.

Harvey, M.S., Mondesir, A., & Aldrich, H. (2007). Fostering resilience in traumatized communities: A community empowerment model of intervention. *Journal of Aggression, Maltreatment, and Trauma, 1*, 265–285.

Hawkins, K. (1972). Some consequences of a parole system for prison management. In D.J. West (Ed.), *The future of parole*. London: Duckworth.

Haynie, D.L. (2001). Delinquent peers revisited: Does network structure matter? *American Journal of Sociology, 106*(4), 1013–1057.

Healey, K. (1999, February). Case management in the criminal justice system. *National Institute of Justice: Research in action*. Washington DC: U.S. Department of Justice. Retrieved from https://www.ncjrs.gov/txtfiles1/173409.txt.

Heidensohn, F. (2006) Gender and justice: New concepts and approaches. Cullompton: Willan Publishing. Basingstoke: Macmillan.

Heilbrun, K., Dematteo, D., Fretz, R., Erickson, J., Yasuhara, K., & Anumba, N. (2008). How specific are gender-specific rehabilitation needs?: An empirical analysis. *Criminal Justice and Behavior, 35*, 1382–1397.

Heimberger T.S., Chang H.G., Birkhead G.S., DiFerdinando G.D., Greenberg A.J., Gunn R.,& Morse, D.L. (1993). High prevalence of syphilis detected through a jail screening program. A potential public health measure to address the syphilis epidemic. *Archives of Internal Medicine, 153*, 1799–804.

Heimer, C.A. (1996). Gender differences in the distribution of responsibility. In J. Baron, D. Grusky, & D. Trieman, (Eds.), *Social differentiation and social inequality* (pp. 241–273). Boulder, CO: Westview Press.

Helfgott, J. (1997). Ex-offender needs versus community opportunity in Seattle. *Federal Probation, 61*(2), 12–24.

Herrschaft, B.A., Veysey, B.V., Tubman-Carbone, H., & Christian, J. (2009). Gender differences in the transformation narrative: Implications for revised reentry strategies for female offenders. *Journal of Offender Rehabilitation, 48*(6), 463–482.

Hettema, J., Steele, J., & Miller, W.R. (2005). Motivational interviewing. *Annual Review of Clinical Psychology, 1*, 91–111.

Heuman, M., Pinaire, B., & Clark, T. (2005). Beyond the sentence: Public perceptions of collateral consequences for felony offenders. *Criminal Law Bulletin, 41*(1), 24–46.

Heyman, R.E., & Slep, A.M. (2002). Do child abuse and interparental violence lead to adulthood family violence? *Journal of Marriage and Family, 64*(4), 864–870.

Hickert, A., Tahamont, S., & Bushway, S. (2018). A tale of two margins: Exploring the probabilistic processes that generate prison visits in the first two years of incarceration. *Journal of Quantitative Criminology, 34*, 691–716.

Hiday, V.A., & Ray, B. (2010). Arrests two years after exiting a well-established mental health court. *Psychiatric Services, 61*(5), 463–468.

Hiday, V.A., Ray, B., & Wales, H. (2016). Longer-term impacts of mental health courts: Recidivism two years after court exit. *Psychiatric Services, 67*(4), 378–383.

Hiday, V.A., Wales, H.W., & Ray, B. (2013). Effectiveness of a short-term mental health court: Criminal recidivism one year postexit. *Law and Human Behavior, 37*(6), 401–411.

Hill, T., Williams, B.A., Cobe, G., & Lindquist, K.J. (2006). *Aging inmates: Challenges for healthcare and custody. A report for the California Department of Corrections and Rehabilitation*. San Francisco, CA: California Department of Corrections and Rehabilitation.

Hiller, M.L., Belenko, S., Welsh, W., Zajac, G. & Peters, R.H. (2011). Screening and assessment: An evidence-based process for the management and care of adult drug-involved offenders. In C.G. Leukefeld, J. Gregrich, & T. Gullotta (Eds.), *Handbook on evidence-based substance abuse treatment practice in criminal justice settings* (pp. 45–62). Springer.

Hipp, J.R., Turner, S., & Jannetta, J. (2010). Are sex offender moving into social disorganization? Analyzing the residential mobility of California parolees. *Journal of Research in Crime and Delinquency, 47*(4), 558–590.

Hipp, J.R., Petersilia, J., & Turner, S. (2010). Parolee recidivism in California: The effect of neighborhood context and social service agency characteristics. *Criminology, 48*, 947–979.

Hirschi, T. (1969). *Causes of delinquency*. Berkeley: University of California Press.

Hirschfield, P., & Piquero, A. (2010). Normalization and legitimation: Modeling stigmatizing attitudes toward ex-offenders. *Criminology, 48*(1), 27–55.

Hoffman, P. (1982). Females, recidivism, and Salient Factor Score: A research note. *Criminal Justice and Behavior, 9*, 121–125.

Hoffman, P. (1994). Twenty years of operational use of a risk prediction instrument: The United States parole commission's Salient Factor Score. *Journal of Criminal Justice, 22*, 477–494.

Hoffman, P. (2003). *History of the federal parole system. Washington, D.C.*: U.S. Parole Commission. Retrieved from www.fedcure.org/… /TheHistoryOfTheFederalParoleSystem-2003.pdf.

Hoffman, P.B., & DeGostin, L.K. (1974). *Parole decision-making: Structuring discretion*. Washington, D.C.: United States Board of Parole.

Hoge, R.D. (1999). An expanded role for psychological assessments in juvenile justice systems. *Criminal Justice and Behavior, 26*, 251–266.

Hoge, S.K. (2007). Providing transition and outpatient services to the mentally ill released from correctional institutions. In R.B. Greiginger (Ed.), *Public health behind bars: From prisons to communities* (pp. 461–477). New York: Springer.

Hollin, C.R. (1999). Treatment programmes for offenders: Meta- analysis, "what works," and beyond. *International Journal of Psychiatry and Law, 22*, 361–372.

Hollin, C.R., & Palmer, E. (2006). Criminogenic need and women offenders: A critique of the literature. *Legal and Criminological Psychology, 11*, 179–195.

Holsinger, A.M., Lowencamp, C.T., & Latessa, E. (2003). Ethnicity, gender, and the Level of Service Inventory-Revised. *Journal of Criminal Justice, 31*, 309–320.

Holsinger, A.M., Lowencamp, C.T., & Latessa, E. (2006). Predicting institutional misconduct using the Youth Level of Service/Case Management Inventory. *American Journal of Criminal Justice, 30*(2), 267–286.

Holtfreter, K., & Cupp, R. (2007). Gender and risk assessment: The empirical status of the LSI-R for women. *Journal of Contemporary Criminal Justice, 23*, 363–382.

Holtfreter, K., & Morash, M. (2003). The needs of women offenders: Implications for correctional programming. *Women & Criminal Justice, 14*, 137–160.

Holtfreter, K., Reisig, M., & Morash, M. (2004). Poverty, state capital, and recidivism among women offenders. *Criminology and Public Policy, 3*, 185–208.

Holzer, H. (1996). *What employers want: Job prospects for less-educated workers*. New York: Russell Sage Foundation.

Holzer, H., Raphael, S., & Stoll, M. (2001). *Will employers hire ex-offenders?: Employer preferences, background checks, and their determinants*. JCPR Working Paper 238. Chicago: Joint Center for Poverty Research, Northwestern University and University of Chicago. Retrieved from http://www.northwestern.edu/ipr/jcpr/workingpapers/wpfiles/holzer_raphael_stoll.pdf.

Holzer, H., Raphael, S., & Stoll, M. (2002). *Prisoner reentry and the institutions of civil society: Bridges and barriers to successful reintegration — Can employers play a more positive role in prisoner reentry?* Washington, D.C.: The Urban Institute. Retrieved from http://www.urban.org/publications/410803.html.

Holzer, H., Raphael, S., & Stoll, M. (2003a). *Employment dimensions of reentry: Understanding the nexus between prisoner reentry and work — Employment barriers facing ex-offenders*. Washington, D.C.: The Urban institute. Retrieved from http://www.urban.org/publications/410855.html.

Holzer, H., Raphael, S., & Stoll, M. (2003b). *Employer demand for ex-offenders: Recent evidence from Los Angeles*. Washington, D.C.: The Urban institute. Retrieved from http://www.urban.org/publications/410779.html.

Holzer, H., Raphael, S., & Stoll, M. (2006). Perceived criminality, criminal background checks, and the racial hiring practices among employers. *The Journal of Law and Economics, 49*, 451–480.

Horney, J., Osgood, D.W., & Marshall, I.H. (1995). Criminal careers in the short-term: Intra-individual variability in crime and its relation to local life circumstances. *American Sociological Review, 60*(5), 655–673.

Hornung, C.A., Anno, B.J., Greifinger, R.B. & Gadre, S. (2002). Health care for soon-to-be-released inmates: A survey of state prison systems. In *Health status of soon-to-be-released inmates.* A Report to Congress: Vol. 2. (pp. 1–11).

Houser, K.A., Belenko, S., & Brennan, P.K. (2012). The effects of mental health and substance abuse disorders on institutional misconduct among female inmates. *Justice Quarterly, 29*(6), 799–828.

Houser, K.A., & McCord, E.S. (2018). An examination of mental illness and substance use disorders among a sample of female parolees released to the City of Philadelphia. In L.M. Carter & C.D. Marcum (Eds.), *Female offenders and reentry: Pathways and barriers to returning to society* (pp. 62–75). Routledge.

Houser, K., McCord, E.S., & Nicholson, J. (2018). The influence of neighborhood risk factors on parolee recidivism in Philadelphia, Pennsylvania. *The Prison Journal, 98*(3), 255–276.

Houser, K.A., Saum, C.A., & Hiller, M.L. (2019b). Mental health, substance abuse, co-occurring disorders, and 3-year recidivism of felony parolees. *Criminal Justice and Behavior, 46*(9), 1237–1254.

Houser, K.A., Vilcica, R., Saum, C.A., & Hiller, M.L. (2019a). Mental health risk factors and parole decisions: Does inmate mental health status affect who gets released? *International Journal of Environmental Research and Public Health, 16*, 2950–2970.

Housing and Urban Development. (2020). *HUD 2019 Continuum of Care homeless assistance programs homeless populations and subpopulations.* Maguire, M., & Singer, J.K. (2011). A false sense of security: Moral panic drives sex offender legislation. *Critical Criminology, 19*, 301–312.

Hrabowski, F.A., & Robbie, J. (2002). The benefits of correctional education. *Journal of Correctional Education, 53*(3), 96–100.

Hu, A., Van Ryzin, M.J., Schweer-Colins, M.L., & Leve, L.D. (2020). Peer relations and delinquency among girls in foster care following a skill-building preventative intervention. *Child Maltreatment.* https://doi.org/10.1177/1077559520923033.

Hubble, M.A., Duncan, B.L., & Miller, S.D. (1999). Directing attention to what works. In M.A. Hubble, B.L. Duncan & S.D. Miller (Eds.), *The heart & soul of change. What works in therapy* (pp. 407–447). Washington, DC: American Psychological Association.

Huebner, B., DeJong, C., & Cobbina, J. (2010). Women coming home: Long-term patterns of recidivism. *Justice Quarterly, 27*(2), 225–254.

Hughes, T., Wilson, D., & Beck, A. (2001). *Trends in state parole, 1990–2000.* (NCJ 184735). Washington, D.C.: Bureau of Justice Statistics.

Human Rights Watch. (2012). *Old behind bars: The aging prison population in the United States.* New York: Human Rights Watch, Retrieved from: http://www.hrw.org/reports/2012/01/27/old-behind-bars-0.

Hume, K., Jones, N., Ramirez, R. (2011, March). *Overview of Race and Hispanic Origin: 2010.* (C2010BR-02). Washington, D.C.: U.S. Census Bureau.

Hunt, E., Peters, R. H., & Kremling, J. (2015). Behavioral health treatment history among persons in the justice system: Findings from the Arrestee Drug Abuse Monitoring II Program. *Psychiatric Rehabilitation Journal, 38*(1), 7–15.

Hunt, P., Smart, R., Jonsson, L., & Tsang, F. (2018). *Incentivizing employers to hire ex-offenders: What policies are most effective?* Rand Corporation.

Hunter, A.J. (1985). Private, parochial and public social orders: The problem of crime and incivility in urban communities. In G.D. Suttles & M.N. Zald (Eds.), *The challenge of social control: Citizenship and institution building in modern society* (pp. 230–242). Norwood, NJ: Ablex Publishing.

Hutton, N. (2005). Beyond populist punitiveness? *Punishment and Society, 7*(3), 243–258.

Idaho Department of Corrections. (2011). *Treatment pathways by site.* Retrieved from http://www.idoc.idaho.gov/content/document /treatment_pathways_by_site.

Immerwahr, J., & Johnson, J. (2002, March). *The revolving door: Exploring public attitudes toward prisoner reentry.* Washington, D.C.: The Urban Institute. Retrieved from www.urban.org/uploadedpdf/410804 _revolvingdoor.pdf.

Internal Revenue Service. (2020). *Work opportunity tax credit.* https:// www.irs.gov/businesses/small-businesses-self-employed/work-opportunity-tax-credit .

Ireland, C., & Prause, J. (2005). Discretionary parole release: Length of imprisonment, percent of sentence served and recidivism. *Journal of Crime and Justice, 28*, 27–50.

Irwin, J. (1970). *The felon.* Berkeley, CA: University of California Press.

Irwin, J., & Austin, J. (1994). It's about time: America's imprisonment binge. Belmont, CA: Wadsworth.

Isaacman, D.J., Purvis, K., Gyuro, J., Anderson, Y., & Smith, D. (1992). Standardized instructions: Do they improve communication of discharge information from the emergency department? *Pediatrics, 89*, 1204–1208.

Ismaili, K. (2006). Contextualizing the criminal justice policy-making process. *Criminal Justice Policy Review, 17*, 255–269.

Jacobs, G. (1993). *Punishing criminals: Pennsylvanians consider the options.* New York: Public Agenda Foundation.

James, D.J., & Glaze, L.E. (2006). *Mental health problems of prison and jail inmates: Special Report.* (NCJ 213600). Washington, DC: Bureau of Justice Statistics.

Jancic, M. (1998). Does correctional education have an effect on recidivism? *Journal of Correctional Education, 49*(4), 152–161.

Jason, L.A., & Ferrari, J.R. (2010). Oxford house recovery homes: Characteristics and effectiveness. *Psychological Services, 7*, 92–102.

Jastrzab, J.A., Blomquist, J., Masker, J., & Orr, L. (1997). *Youth corps: Promising strategies for young people and their communities.* Cambridge, MA: Abt Associates, Inc.

Jenkins, H.D. (2002). *Mandatory education: A status report.* Washington, D.C.: U.S. Department of Education.

Jenkins, H.D., Steurer, S.J., & Pendry, J. (1995). A post-release follow-up of correctional education program completers released in 1990–1991. *Journal of Correctional Education, 46*(1), 20–24.

Jenkins, M., & Bazemore, G. (2006). *State of Ohio citizens circle formative evaluation.* Columbus, OH: Ohio Department of Rehabilitation and Corrections.

Jensen, E.L., & Reed, G.E. (2006). Adult correctional education programs: An update on current status based on recent studies. *Journal of Offender Rehabilitation, 44*(1), 81–98.

Jiang, S., & Winfree, T. (2006). Social support, gender, and inmate adjustment to prison life: Insights from a national sample. *The Prison Journal, 86*, 32–55.

Johnson, J.L., & Wiechelt, S.A. (2004). The special issue of resilience. *Journal of Substance Use and Misuse, 39*(5), 657–670.

Johnston, D. (1995). Effects of parental incarceration. In K. Gabel & D. Johnston (Eds.), *Children of incarcerated parents* (pp. 59–88). New York: Lexington Books.

Joint Commission on Mental Illness and Health. (1961). *Action for mental health: Final report of the Joint Commission on Mental Illness and Health.* New York: Basic Books.

Jones, P. (1996). Risk prediction in criminal justice. In A.T. Harland (Ed.), *Choosing correctional options that work* (pp. 33–68). Thousand Oaks, CA: Sage Publications.

Jones, M., & Kerbs, J.J. (2007). Probation and parole officers and discretionary decision-making: Responses to technical and criminal violations. *Perspectives, 31*(1), 35–42.

Jucovy, L. (2003). *Amachi: Mentoring children of prisoners in Philadelphia.* Philadelphia, PA: Public/Private Ventures. Retrieved from www.ppv.org /ppv/publications/assets/21_publication.pdf.

Justice Policy Institute (2010, June). *How to safely reduce prison populations and support people returning to their communities.* Washington, D.C.: The Justice Policy Institute, Retrieved from http://www.google.com/search?q=Justice+Policy+Institute%2C+2010&ie =utf-8&oe=utf-8&aq=t&rls=org.mozilla:en-US:official&client=firefox-a.

Kaba, F., Lewis, A., Glowa-Kollisch, S., Hadler, J., Lee, D., Alper, H., Selling, D., MacDonald, R., Solimo, A., Parsons, A., & Venters, H. (2014). Solitary confinement and risk of self-harm among jail inmates. *American Journal of Public Health, 104*, 442–447.

Kachnowski, V. (2005). *Returning home Illinois policy brief: Employment and prisoner reentry*. Washington, D.C.: The Urban Institute. Retrieved from http://www.urban.org/publications/311215.html.

Kaminer, W. (1993). *I'm dysfunctional, you're dysfunctional: The recovery movement and other self-help fashions.* New York: Vintage Books.

Kaminski, J.W., Valle, L.A., & Filene, J.H., & Boyle, C.L. (2008). A meta-analytic review of components associated with parent training program effectiveness. *Journal of Abnormal Child Psychology, 36*, 567–589.

Kaeble, D. (2021). *Time served in state prison, 2018.* (NCJ 255662). Bureau of Justice Statistics Kaplan, A. (1984). *The "self in relation": Implications for depression in women* (Publication No.14), Wellesley, MA: Stone Center.

Kaeble, D., & Alper, M. (2020). *Probation and parole in the United States, 2017–2018*. (NCJ 252072). Bureau of Justice Statistics.

Kaeble, D., & Cowhig, M. (2018). *Correctional populations in the United States, 2016*. (NCJ 251211). Bureau of Justice Statistics.

Kazemian, L. (2007). Desistance from crime. *Journal of Contemporary Criminal Justice, 23*(1), 5–27.

Kelly, C.E., & Fader, J.J. (2012). Computer-based employment applications: Implications for offenders and supervising officers. *Federal Probation, 76*(1), 24–29.

Kerson, T.S. (2001). *Boundary spanning: An ecological reinterpretation of social work practice in health and mental health systems*. New York: Columbia University Press.

Kessler, R.C., Nelson, C.B., McGonagle, K.A., Edlund, M.J., Frank, R.G., & Leaf, P.J. (1996). The epidemiology of co-occurring addictive and mental disorders: Implications for prevention and service utilization. *American Journal of Orthopsychiatry, 66*, 17–31.

Keve, P. (1979). No farewell to arms. *Crime & Delinquency 25*, 425–435.

Kim, R.H., & Clark, D. (2013). The effect of prison-based college education programs on recidivism: Propensity score matching approach. *Journal of Criminal Justice, 41*(3), 196–204.

Kinder, D. (1998). Opinion and action in the realm of politics. In D.T. Gilbert, S.T. Fiske, & G. Lindzey (Eds.), *The handbook of social psychology* (Vol. 2., 4th ed., pp. 778–867). Boston: McGraw-Hill.

Kirby, B. (1954). Measuring effects of treatment of criminals and delinquents. *Sociology and Social Research, 38*, 368–374.

Kirby, L.D., & Fraser, M.W. (1997). Risk and resiliency in childhood. In Fraser, M.W. (Ed.), *Risk and resiliency* (pp. 10–33). Washington, DC: NASW Press.

Kirk, D.S. (2009). A natural experiment on residential change and recidivism: Lessons from Hurricane Katrina. *American Sociological Review, 74*, 484–505.

Kisthardt, W.E. (2009). The opportunities and challenges of strengths-based person-centered practice: Purpose, principles, and applications in a climate of systems integration. In D. Saleebey, (Ed.), *The strengths perspective in social work* (5th ed., pp. 47–71). New York: Pearson.

Klein, S., Tolbert, M., Burgarin, R., Cataldi, E.F., & Tauschek, G. (2004). *Correctional education: Assessing the status of prison programs and information needs*. Berkeley, CAA: MPR Associates, Inc. Berkeley, CA. Retrieved from http://www.mpinc.com/products_and_publications /pdf/corred_report.pdf.

Klienman, P., & Lukoff, I. (1981). Official crime data. *Criminology, 19*, 449–454.

Kluckow, R., & Zeng, Z. (2022). *Correctional populations in the United States, 2020—Statistical Tables*. (NCJ303184). Washington, D.C.: Bureau of Justice Statistics.

Knight, D.K., & Simpson, D.D. (1996). Influences of family and friends on client progress during drug abuse treatment. *Journal of Substance Abuse, 8*(4), 417–429.

Kondo, L.L. (2000). Therapeutic jurisprudence: Issues, analysis and applications: Advocacy of the establishment of mental health specialty courts in the provision of therapeutic justice for mentally ill offenders. *Seattle University Law Review, 24*, 373, 377.

Koons, B., Burrow, J., Morash, M., & Bynum, T. (1997). Expert and offender perceptions of program elements linked to successful outcomes for incarcerated women. *Crime & Delinquency, 43*(4), 512–532.

Krajick, K. (1980). Not on My Block: Local Opposition Impedes the Search for Alternatives. *Correctional Magazine, 5*, 15–29.

Kraut, J.R., & Haddix, A. (2008). *Health status of soon-to-be-released-inmates*. Chicago: National Commission on Correctional Health Care. Retrieved from www.ncchc.org/stbr/Volume2/Report5_Kraut.pdf.

Kraut-Becher J.R., Gift, T., Haddix, A., Irwin, K., & Greifinger, R. (2004). The cost-effectiveness of universal screening for chlamydia and gonorrhea in United States jails. *Journal of Urban Health, 81*, 453–471.

Kruttschnitt, C., & Gartner, R. (2003). Women's imprisonment. In M. Tonry (Ed.), *Crime and justice: A review of research* (Vol. 30, pp. 1–81). Chicago: University of Chicago Press.

Kubrin, C.E., & Stewart, E.A. (2006). Predicting who reoffends: The neglected role of neighborhood context in recidivism studies. *Criminology, 44*(1), 165–197.

Kumpfer, K.L., & Alvarado, R. (1998). *Effective family strengthening interventions. Juvenile Justice Bulletin Family Strengthening Series*. Washington, DC: Office of Juvenile Justice and Delinquency Prevention.

Kushel, M.B., Hahn, J.A., Evans, J.L., Bangsberg, D.R., & Moss, A.R. (2005). Revolving doors: Imprisonment amongst the homeless and marginally housed population. *American Journal of Public Health, 95*(10), 1747–1752.

Kuziemko, I. (2007). *Going off parole: How the elimination of discretionary prison release affects the social cost of crime.* Cambridge, MA: National Bureau of Economic Research. Retrieved from http://www.nber.org/papers/w13380.

LaFollette, H. (2005). Collateral consequences of punishment: Civil penalties accompanying formal punishment. *Journal of Applied Philosophy, 22*(3), 241–261.

Lahm, K.F. (2009). Educational participation and inmate misconduct. *Journal of Offender Rehabilitation, 48*, 37–52.

Lake, R.W. (1996). Volunteers, NIMBYs, and environmental justice: Dilemmas of democratic practice. *Antipode, 28*(2), 160–174.

Lamb, H.R., & Bachrach, L.L. (2001). Some perspectives on deinstitutionalization. *Psychiatric Services, 52*, 1039–1045.

Lamb, H.R., & Grant, R.W. (1982). The mentally ill in an urban county jail. *Archives of General Psychiatry, 39*, 17–22.

Lamberti, J.S., Weisman, R., & Faden, D.I. (2004). Forensic assertive community treatment: Preventing incarceration of adults with severe mental illness. *Psychiatric Services, 55*, 1285–1293.

Landefeld, C.S., Palmer, R.M., Johnson, M.A., Johnston, C.B., & Lyons, W.L. (2004). *Current geriatric diagnosis and treatment.* New York: McGraw-Hill.

Landenberger, N.A., & Lipsey. M.W. (2005). The positive effects of cognitive-behavioral programs for offenders: A meta-analysis of factors associated with effective treatment. *Journal of Experimental Criminology, 1*(4), 451–476.

Langan, N., & Pelissier, B. (2001). Gender differences among prisoners in drug treatment. *Journal of Substance Abuse, 13*, 291–301.

Langan, P., & Levin, D. (2002). *Recidivism of released prisoners in 1994.* (NCJ 193427). Washington, DC: Bureau of Justice Statistics.

Lanier, C.S. (1993). Affective states of fathers in prison. *Justice Quarterly, 10*, 49–65.

Laquale, M.G., Coppola, G., Cassibba, R., Pasceri, M., Pietralunga, S., Taurino, A., Senerraro, C., & Grattagliano, I. (2018). Confidence in attachment relationships and marital status as protective factors for self-perceived parental role and in-person visitation with children among incarcerated fathers. *Journal of Forensic Sciences, 63*(6), 1761–1768.

Lartey, J (2020). *Think private prison companies are going away under Biden? They have other plans.* Retrieved from https://www.themarshallproject.org/2020/11/17/think-private-prison-companies-are-going-away-under-biden-they-have-other-plans.

Latessa, E., Cullen, F.T., & Gendreau, P. (2002). Beyond correctional quackery: Professionalism and the possibility of effective treatment. *Federal Probation, 66*(2), 43–49.

Latessa, E.J., Travis,L., Fulton, B., & Stichman, A. (1998). *Evaluating the prototypical ISP: Final report.* Cincinnati, Ohio: University of Cincinnati and American Probation and Parole Assoc.

Lattimore, P., Steffey, D., & Visher, C. (2010). Prisoner reentry in the first decade of the twenty-first century. *Victims and Offenders, 5*, 253–267.

Laub, J.H., Nagin, D.S., & Sampson, R.J. (1998). Trajectories of change in criminal offending: Good marriages and the desistance process. *American Sociological Review, 63*(2), 225–238.

Laub, J.H., & Sampson, R.J. (2001). Understanding desistance from crime. *Crime and Justice, 28*, 1–69.

Laub, J.H., & Sampson, R.J. (2003). *Shared beginnings, divergent lives: Delinquent boys to age 70.* Cambridge: Harvard University Press.

LaVigne, N., & Parthasarathy, B. (2005). *Returning home Illinois policy brief: Prisoner reentry and residential mobility.* Washington, D.C.: Urban Institute. Retrieved from www.urban.org/url.cfm?id=311214.

LaVigne, N., Shollenberger, T., & Debus, S. (2009). *One year out: The experiences of male returning prisoners to Houston, Texas.* Washington, DC: The Urban Institute. Retrieved from www.urban.org/url.cfm?ID=411911.

LaVigne, N., & Thomson, G.L. (2003). *A portrait of prisoner reentry in Ohio.* Washington, D.C.: Urban Institute. Retrieved from www.urban.org/uploadedpdf/410891_ohio_reentry.pdf.

LaVigne, N., Visher, C., & Castro, J. (2004). *Chicago prisoners' experiences returning home.* Washington, D.C.: The Urban Institute. Retrieved from www.urban.org/url.cfm?id=311115.

Lawrence, S., & Travis, J. (2004). *The new landscape of imprisonment: Mapping America's prison expansion.* Washington, DC: The Urban Institute.

Retrieved from www.urban.org/uploadedPDF/410994_mapping_prisons.pdf.

Laws, D.R., & Ward, T. (2011). *Desistance and sexual offending: Alternatives to throwing away the keys*. New York: Guilford.

Layton-MacKenzie, D. (2012). The effectiveness of corrections-based work and academic and vocational education programs. In J. Petersilia & K.R. Reitz (Eds.) *The Oxford handbook of sentencing and corrections* (pp. 492–518). Oxford University Press.

Lazarus, R.S., & Folkman, S. (1984). *Stress, appraisal, and coping*. New York: Springer.

LeBel, T. (2008). Perception of and responses to stigma. *Sociology Compass, 2*, 409–432.

LeBlanc, A. (2003). *Random family: Love, drugs, trouble, and coming of age in the Bronx*. New York: Scribner.

Lee, J., & Craft, E. (2002). Protecting one's self from a stigmatized disease ...Once one has it. *Deviant Behavior, 23*, 267–299.

Lee, J.D., Fordyce, M.W., & Rich, J.D. (2007). Screening for public purpose. In R.B. Greifinger (Ed.), *Public health behind bars: From prisons to communities* (pp. 249–264). New York: Springer Verlag.

Legal Action Center. (2004). *After prison: Roadblocks to reentry: A report on state legal barriers facing people with criminal records*. Retrieved from lac.org/roadblocks-to-reentry/.

Lemert, E.M. (1951). *Social pathology: A systematic approach to the theory of sociopathic behavior*. New York: McGraw-Hill.

Level-of Service Inventory-Revised. (1995:1999). Tonawanda, NY: Multi-Health Systems.

Levenson, J.S. (2005). Collateral consequences of sex offender residence restrictions. *Criminal Justice Studies, 21*(2), 153–166.

Levenson, J.S., & Cotter, L.P. (2005). The impact of sex offender residence restrictions: 1,000 feet from danger or one step from absurd? *International Journal of Offender Therapy and Comparative Criminology, 49*(2), 168–178.

Leverentz, A. (2006.) The love of a good man? Romantic relationships as a source of support or hindrance for female ex-offenders. *Journal of Research in Crime and Delinquency, 43*(4), 459–488.

Levingston, K.D., & Turetsky, V. (2007). Debtor's prison. Prisoners' accumulation of debt as a barrier to reentry. *Clearinghouse review: Journal of Poverty Law and Policy*, July/August.

Levrant, S., Cullen, F., Fulton, B., & Wozniak, J. (1999). Reconsidering restorative justice: The corruption of benevolence revisited? *Crime and Delinquency, 45*(1), 3–27.

Lichtenberger, E.J., & Onyewu, N. (2005). *Virginia Department of Correctional Education's Incarcerated Youth Offender Program: A historical analysis* (Vol. 9). Department of Correctional Education.

Lillis, J. (1994). Prison education programs reduced. *Corrections Compendium, 19*, 1–4.

Lincoln T., Miles J., & Scheibel S. (2007). Public and community health collaborations with corrections. In R. Greifinger (Ed.), *Public health behind bars: From prisons to communities* (pp. 508–534). New York: Springer Verlag.

Lindquist, C., McKay, T., McDonald, H.S., Herman-Stahl, M., & Bir, A. (2009). Easing reentry by supporting fathers and families. *Corrections Today, 71*(6), 76–79.

Link, B.G., & Phelan, J.C. (2001). Conceptualizing stigma. *Annual Review of Sociology, 27*, 363–385.

Link, B., Cullen, F., Struening, E., Shrout, P., & Dohrenwend, B. (1989). A modified labeling theory approach to mental disorders: An empirical assessment. *American Sociological Review, 54*, 400–423.

Link, N.W., Ward, J.T., & Stansfield, R. (2019). Consequences of mental and physical health for reentry and recidivism: Toward a health-based model of desistance. *Criminology, 57*, 544–573.

Lipsey, M.A., Landenberger, N.A., & Wilson, S.J. (2007). Effects of cognitive-behavioral programs for criminal offenders. Nashville: Center for Evaluation Research and Methodology Vanderbilt Institute for Public Policy.

Lipton, D., Martinson, R., & Wilks, J. (1975). *The effectiveness of correctional treatment: A survey of treatment evaluation studies*. New York: Praeger.

Lochner, L. (1999). *Education, work, and crime: Theory and evidence* (Working Paper No. 465). Rochester Center for Economic Research.

Loeber, R., & LeBlanc, M. (1990). Toward a developmental criminology. In M. Tonry & N. Morris (Eds.), *Crime and justice: A review of research* (Vol. 12., pp. 375–437). Chicago: University of Chicago Press.

Long, J.V.F., & Vaillant, G.E. (1984). Natural history of male psychological health, XI: Escape from the underclass. *American Journal of Psychiatry, 141*, 341–346.

Looney, A., & Turner, N. (2018). Work and opportunity before and after incarceration. The Brookings Institute.

Lopoo, L.M., & Western, B. (2005). Incarceration and the formation and stability of marital unions. *Journal of Marriage and Family, 67*, 721–734.

Los Angeles Homeless Services Authority (2022). *FY2022–23 budget*. Retrieved from https://www.lahsa.org/documents?id=6887-fy-2022-2023-budget.pdf.

Losel, F. (1995). The efficacy of correctional treatment: A review and synthesis of meta-evaluations. In J. McGuire (Ed.), *What works: Reducing reoffending: Guidelines from research and practice* (pp. 79–111). West Sussex, England: John Wiley & Sons.

Lovell, D., Allen, D., Johnson, C., & Jemelka, R. (2001). Evaluating the effectiveness of residential treatment for prisoners with mental illness. *Criminal Justice and Behavior, 28*, 83–104.

Lovell, D., Gagliardi, G.J., & Peterson, P.D. (2002). Recidivism and use of services among persons with mental illness after release from prison. *Psychiatric Services, 53*(10), 1290–1296.

Lovins, L., Lowenkamp, C., Latessa, E., & Smith, P. (2007). Application of the risk principle to female offenders. *Journal of Contemporary Criminal Justice, 23*, 383–398.

Lowenkamp, C., Holsinger, A., & Latessa, E. (2001). Risk/Need assessment, offender classification, and the role of childhood abuse. *Criminal Justice and Behavior, 28*, 543–563.

Lowder, E.M., Rade, C.B., & Desmarais, S.L. (2018). Effectiveness of mental health courts in reducing recidivism: A meta-analysis. *Psychiatric Services, 69*(1), 15–22.

Lowenkamp, C., Lovins, B., & Latessa, E. (2009). Validating the Level of Service Inventory-Revised and the Level of Service Inventory: Screening Version with a sample of probationers. *The Prison Journal, 89*, 192–204.

Loza, W., & Simourd, D. (1994). Psychometric evaluation of the Level of Supervision Inventory among male Canadian federal offenders. *Criminal Justice and Behavior, 21*, 468–480.

Lucken, K. (1997). Dynamics of penal reform. *Crime, Law, and Social Change, 26*(4), 367–384.

Luna, E. (2005). The overcriminalization phenomenon. *American University Law Review, 54*, 703–743.

Lurigio, A.J. (2001). Effective services for parolees with mental illnesses. *Crime & Delinquency, 47*(3), 446–461.

Lurigio, A.J., Eppeson, M.W., Canada, K.E., & Babchuk, L.C. (2012). Specialized probation programs for people with mental illnesses: A review of practices and research. *Journal of Crime and Justice, 35*(2), 317–326.

Lurigio, A.J., & Swartz, J.A. (2000). *Changing the contours of the criminal justice system to meet the needs of persons with serious mental illness.* National Institute of Justice.

Lurigio, A.J., & Swartz, J.A. (2006). Mental illness in correctional populations: The use of standardized screening tools for further evaluation or treatment. *Federal Probation, 70*(2), 29–35.

Luthar, S.S. (1999). *Poverty and children's adjustment.* Thousand Oaks, CA: Sage Publications.

Luthar, S., Cicchetti, D., & Becker, B. (2000). The construct of resilience: A critical evaluation and guidelines for future work. *Child Development, 71*, 543–562.

Luthar, S.S., & Cushing, G. (1999). Measurement issues in the empirical study of resilience: An overview. In M. Glantz, J.L. Johnson (Eds.), *Resilience and development: Positive life adaptations* (pp. 129–160). New York: Plenum.

Luthar, S.S., & Zigler, E. (1991). Vulnerability and competence: A review of research on resilience in childhood. *American Journal of Orthopsychiatry, 61*, 6–22.

Lynch, J., & Sabol, W. (2001). *Prisoner reentry in perspective.* Washington, D.C.: Urban Institute. Retrieved from www.urban.org/uploadedpdf/410213_reentry.PDF.

Lynch, M. (1998). Waste managers? The new penology, crime fighting, and parole agent identity. *Law and Society Review, 32*, 839–869.

Machin, S., Marie, O., & Vujic, S. (2011). The crime reducing effect of education. *The Economic Journal, 121*, 463–484.

MacKenzie, D.L. (2000). Evidenced-based corrections: Identifying what works. *Crime and Delinquency, 46*, 457–471.

MacKenzie, D.L. (2006). *What works in corrections: Reducing the criminal activities of offenders and delinquents.* New York: Cambridge.

MacKenzie, D.L. (2008, March/April). Structure and components of successful educational programs. *Reentry Roundtable on Education.* Conducted at John Jay College of Criminal Justice. Retrieved from http://www.jjay.cuny.edu/DorisMackenzie_Final.pdf.

MacKenzie, D.L., Browning, K., Skroban, S.B., & Smith, D.A. (1999). The impact of probation on the criminal activities of offenders. *Journal of Research in Crime and Delinquency 36*(4), 423–453.

Madsen, W. (1999). *Collaborative therapy and multi-stressed families.* London: Guilford Press.

Mai, C., & Subramanian, R. (2017). *The price of prisons: Examining state spending trends, 2010–2015.* Vera Institute of Justice.

Maidment, M. (2006). *Doing time on the outside: Deconstructing the benevolent community.* Toronto, Canada: University of Toronto Press.

Makarios, M., Steiner, B., &Travis, L. (2010). Examining the predictors of recidivism among men and women released from prison in Ohio. *Criminal Justice and Behavior, 37*, 1377–1391.

Makaryus, A.G., & Friedman, E.A. (2005). Patients' understanding of their treatment plans and diagnosis at discharge. *Mayo Clinic Proceedings, 80*, 991–994.

Mallik-Kane, K., & Visher, C. (2008). *Health and prisoner reentry: How physical, mental, and substance abuse conditions shape the process of reintegration.* Washington, DC: The Urban Institute. Retrieved from www.urban.org/UploadedPDF/411617_health_prisoner_reentry.pd.

Maloney, D., Bazemore, G., & Hudson, J. (2001). The end of probation and the beginning of community justice. Perspectives, 25(3), 22–30.

Maltz, M. (1984). *Recidivism.* Orlando, FL: Academic Press.

Maltz, M. (1994). Deviating from the mean: The declining significance of significance. *Journal of research in crime and delinquency, 31*(4), 434–463.

Malysiak, R. (1997). Exploring the theory and paradigm base for wraparound fidelity. *Journal of Child and Family Studies, 7*(1), 11–25.

Manchak, S., Skeem, J.L., Douglas, K., & Siranosian, M. (2009). Does gender moderate the predictive utility of the Level of Service Inventory-Revised (LSI-R) for serious violent offenders? *Criminal Justice and Behavior, 36*, 425–442.

Manthey, T.J., Knowles, B., Asher, D., & Wahab, S. (2011). Strengths-based practice and motivational interviewing. *Advances in Social Work, 12*(2), 126–151.

Manza, J., Brooks, C., & Uggen, C. (2004). Public attitudes toward felon disenfranchisement in the United States. *Public Opinion Quarterly, 68*(2), 275–286.

Marcil, T., Lin, H., Riley, C.A., & Julien, P. (2016, January/February). Homeless inmates statistics for Orange County Corrections in Florida. *Corrections Today*, 16–19.

Markowitz, F., Bellair, P., Liska, A., & Liu, J. (2001). Extending social disorganization theory: Modeling the relationship between cohesion, disorder and fear. *Criminology, 39*, 293–320.

Marks, A. (1997). One inmate's push to restore education funds for prisoners. *Christian Science Monitor, 89*, 3.

Martin, E. (2017). Hidden consequences: The impact of incarceration on dependent children. (Journal 278). National Institute of Justice. https://www.ojp.gov/pdffiles1/nij/250349.pdf.

Martin, J.S. (2001). *Inside looking out: Jailed fathers' perceptions about separation from their children.* New York: LFB Scholarly Publishing LLC.

Martinez, D.J. (2006). Informal helping mechanisms: Conceptual issues in family support of reentry of former prisoners. *Journal of Offender Rehabilitation, 44*(1), 23–37.

Martinson, R. (1974). What works? Questions and answers about prison reform. *The Public Interest, 35*, 22–54.

Martinson, R. (1979). New Findings, new views: A note of caution regarding prison reform. *Hoffstra Law Review, 7*, 243–258.

Maruna, S. (2000). Desistance and Rehabilitation: A tale of two literatures. *Offender Programs Report, 4*,(1), 1–13.

Maruna, S. (2001). *Making good: How ex-convicts reform and rebuild their lives.* Washington, D.C.: American Psychological Association.

Maruna, S. (2006). Who owns resettlement? Towards restorative reintegration. *British Journal of Community Justice, 4*(2), 23–33.

Maruna, S. (2011). Reentry as a rite of passage. *Punishment & Society, 13*(1), 3–28.

Maruna, S. & LeBel, T. (2002). Revisiting ex-prisoner re-entry: A new buzzword in search of a narrative. In S. Rex & M. Tonry (Eds.), *Reform and punishment: The future of sentencing.* Devon, UK: Willan.

Maruna S., & LeBel, T.P. (2003). Welcome home? Examining the "reentry court" concept from a strengths-based perspective. *Western Criminology Review, 4*(2), 91–107.

Maruna, S., & King, A. (2004). Public opinion and community penalties. In T. Bottoms, S. Rex & G. Robinson (Eds.), *Alternatives to Prison: Options for an Insecure Society* (pp. 83–112). Cullompton: Willan.

Maruschak, L.M. (2008). *HIV in Prisons, 2007–08.* (NCJ 228307).Washington, D.C.: Bureau of Justice Statistics.

Maruschak, L.M. (2010). *HIV in Prisons, 2007–08.* (NCJ 228307).Washington, D.C.: Bureau of Justice Statistics.

Maruschak, L.M. & Beck, A.J. (2001). *Medical Problems of Inmates, 1997.* (NCJ 181644). Washington, D.C.: Bureau of Justice Statistics.

Maruschak, L.M., Berzofsky, M., & Unangst, J. (2015). *Medical problems of state and federal prisoners and jail inmates, 2011–12.* (NCJ 248491). Bureau of Justice Statistics.

Maruschak, L.M., & Bronson, J. (2017). *HIV in prisons, 2015—statistical tables.* (NCJ 250641). Bureau of Justice Statistics.

Maruschak, L.M., Bronson, J., & Alper, M. (2021a). *Survey of prison inmates, 2016 in prison and their minor children.* (NCJ 252645). Bureau of Justice Statistics.

Maruschak, L.M., Bronson, J., & Alper, M. (2021b). *Survey of prison inmates, 2016: Indicators of mental health problems reported by prisoners* (NCJ 252643). Bureau of Justice Statistics.

Maruschak, L.M., & Minton, T.D. (2020) *Correctional populations in the United States, 2017–2018.* (NCJ 252157). Bureau of Justice Statistics.

Maslach, C., & Jackson, S.E. (1981). The measurement of experienced burnout. *Journal of Occupational Behavior, 2*, 99–113.

Maslow, A.H. (1943). A theory of human motivation. *Psychological Review, 50*(4), 370–96.

Massey, D.S., & Denton, N.A. (1993). *American apartheid.* Cambridge: Harvard University Press.

Masten, A.S. (1994). Resilience in individual development: Successful adaptation despite risk and adversity. In M.C. Wang, E.W. Gordon, (Eds.), *Educational resilience in inner-city America: Challenges and prospects* (pp. 3–25). Hillsdale, NJ: Erlbaum.

Masten, A.S. (2000). *Children who overcome adversity to succeed in life.* Minneapolis, MN: University of Minnesota. Retrieved from http://www.extension.umn.edu/distribution/familydevelopment/components/7565_06.html.

Masten, A.S. (2001). Ordinary magic: Resilience processes in development. *American Psychologist, 56,* 227–238.

Masten A.S., Best K., & Garmezy, N. (1990). Resilience and development: Contributions from the study of children who overcome adversity. *Development and Psychopathology, 2,* 425–444.

Matejkowski, J., Drain, J., Solomon, P., & Salzer, M.S. (2011). Mental illness, criminal risk factors and parole release decisions. *Behavioral Sciences and the Law, 29,* 528–553.

Matejkowski, J., Severson, M.E., & Manthey, T.J. (2015). Strategies for post-release supervision of individuals with serious mental illness: Comparing specialized community corrections officers to those not serving on a specialized team. *Journal of Offender Rehabilitation, 54,* 520–537.

Mauer, M. (1999). *The race to incarcerate.* New York: The New Press.

Mauer, M. (2011). Addressing racial disparities in incarceration. *The Prison Journal, 91*(3), 875–1015.

Maurutto, P. & Hannah-Moffat, K. (2007). Response to commentary: Cross-examining risk knowledge. *Canadian Journal of Criminology and Criminal Justice, 49,* 543–550.

Mazza, C. (2002). And then their world fell apart: The children of incarcerated families. *Families in Society: The Journal of Contemporary Social Services, 83*(5), 521–529.

McCarthy, B., & Hagen, J. (1991). Homelessness: A criminogenic situation? *British Journal of Criminology, 31*(4), 393–410.

McCleary, R. (1975). How structural variables constrain the parole officers use of discretionary power. *Social Problems, 23,* 209–225.

McClellan, D., Farabee, D., & Crouch, B. (1997). Early victimization, drug use, and criminality: A comparison of male and female prisoners. *Criminal Justice and Behavior, 24*, 455–476.

McCord, J. (1980). Patterns of deviance. In S.B. Sells, R. Crandall, M. Roff, J.S. Strauss, & W. Pollin (Eds.), *Human functioning in longitudinal perspective* (pp. 157–162). Baltimore: Williams & Wilkins.

McDonald, D.C. (1986). *Punishment without walls: Community service sentences in New York City*. New Brunswick, NJ: Rutgers University Press.

McDonald, D.C. (1999). Medical care in prisons. In M. Tonry & J. Petersilia, (Eds.), *Prisons: Crime and justice: A review of research* (Vol. 26, pp. 427–478). Chicago: University of Chicago Press.

McGlone, J. (2002, September). *Status of mandatory education in state correctional institutions*. Washington, D.C.: Office of Vocational and Adult Education.

McHale J., Khazan I., Erera P., Rotman T., DeCourcey W., & McConnell M. (2002). Coparenting in diverse family systems. In M. Bornstein (Ed.), *Handbook of parenting*. (2nd Ed., pp. 75–107). New Jersey: Erlbaum.

McIvor, G., Murray, C., & Jamieson, J. (2004). Desistance from crime: Is it different for women and girls? In S. Maruna & R. Immariegeon (Eds), *After crime and punishment: Pathways to offender reintegration* (pp. 181–197). London: Willan.

McKelvey, B. (1977). *American prisons: A history of good intentions*. Montclair, NJ: Patterson Smith.

McLellan, A.T., Hagan, T.A., Levine, M., Meyers, K., Gould, F., Bencivengo, M., Durell, J., & Jaffe, J. (1999). Does clinical case management improve outpatient addiction treatment. *Drug and Alcohol Dependence, 55*, 91–103.

McMahon, M. (1995). *Engendering motherhood: Identity and self-transformation in women's lives*. New York: Guilford.

McMillen, J.C., Morris, L., & Sherraden, M. (2004). Ending social work's grudge match: Problems versus strengths. *Families in Society: The Journal of Contemporary Social Services, 85*(3), 317–325.

McMullan, E.C. (2011). Seeking medical and psychiatric attention. In L. Gideon & H. Sung, (Eds.), *Rethinking corrections* (pp. 253–277). Thousand Oaks, CA: Sage Publications.

McMurran, M. (2009). Motivational interviewing with offenders: A systematic review. *Legal and Criminological Psychology, 14*, 83–100.

McNiel, D.E., & Binder, R.L. (2007). Effectiveness of a mental health court in reducing criminal recidivism and violence. *American Journal of Psychiatry, 164*, 1395–1403.

McNiel, D.E., Binder, R.L., & Robinson, J.C. (2005). Incarceration associated with homelessness, mental disorder, and co-occurring substance abuse. *Psychiatric Services, 56*(6), 699–704.

McQuistion, H.L., Finnerty, M., Hirschowitz, J., & Susser, E.S. (2003). Challenges for psychiatry in serving homeless people with psychiatric disorders. *Psychiatric Services, 54*(5), 905–908.

McShane, M., Williams, F & H. Dolny, M. (2002). Do standard risk prediction instruments apply to female parolees? *Women and Criminal Justice, 13*, 163–182.

Mead, G.H. (1934). *Mind, self, and society*. Chicago: University of Chicago Press.

Mears, D.P., Wang, X., Hay, C., & Bales, W.D. (2008). Social ecology and recidivism: Implications for prisoner reentry. *Criminology 46*(2), 301–340.

Mechoulan, S., & Sahuguet, N. (2015). Assessing racial disparities in parole release. *The Journal of Legal Studies, 44*, 39–74.

Meehl, P. (1954). *Clinical versus statistical prediction*. Minneapolis: University of Minnesota Press.

Meisenhelder, T. (1977). An exploratory study of exiting from criminal careers. *Criminology, 15*(3), 319–334.

Mellow, J. (2007). Written health informational needs for reentry. In R.B. Greifinger (Ed.), *Public health behind bars: From prisons to communities*. New York: Springer.

Mellow, J., & Christian, J. (2008) Transitioning offenders to the community: A content analysis of reentry guides. *Journal of Offender Rehabilitation, 47*(4), 339–355.

Mennis, J., & Harris, P. (2011). Contagion and repeat offending among urban juvenile delinquents. *Journal of Adolescence, 34*, 951–963.

Menefee, D. (1998). Identifying and comparing competencies for social work management II: A replication study. *Administration in Social Work, 22*(4), 53–73.

Meredith, T., Speir, J., Johnson, S., & Hull, H. (2003). *Enhancing parole decision-making through the automation of risk assessment*. Atlanta: Applied Research Services, Inc.

Merlo, A., & Pollock, J. (1995). *Women, law, and social control.* Boston, MA: Allyn & Bacon.

Merton, R. (1938). Social structure and anomie. *American Sociological Review, 3*, 672–682.

Messerschmidt, J.W. (1993). *Masculinities and crime: Critique and reconceptualization of theory*. New York: Rowan & Littlefield Publishers.

Messina, N., Burdon, W., & Prendergast, M. (2003). Assessing the needs of women in institutional therapeutic communities. *Journal of Offender Rehabilitation, 37*(2), 89–106.

Messinger, S., Berecochea, J., Rauma, J., & Berk, R. (1985). The foundations of parole in California. *Law and Society Review, 19*, 69–106.

Metraux, S., & Culhane, D.P. (2004). Homeless shelter use and reincarceration following prison release. *Criminology & Public Policy, 3*(2), 139–160.

Metraux, S., & Culhane, D.P. (2006). Recent incarceration history among a sheltered homeless population. *Crime & Delinquency, 52*(3), 504–517.

Meyers, T.J., Wright, K.A., Young, J.T.N., & Tascab, M. (2017). Social support from outside the walls: Examining the role of relationship dynamics among inmates and visitors. *Journal of Criminal Justice, 52*, 57–67.

Miller, A.A., Therrien, W.J., & Romig, J.E. (2019). Reducing recidivism: Transition and reentry practices for detained and adjudicated youth with disabilities. *Education and Treatment of Children, 42*(3), 409–438.

Miller, J. (1976). *Toward a new psychology of women*. Boston: Beacon Press.

Miller, J., Caplan, J.M., & Ostermann, M. (2016). Home nodes, criminogenic places, and parolee failure: Testing an environmental model of offender risk, *Crime & Delinquency, 62*, 169–199.

Miller, K.M. (2006). The impact of parental incarceration on children: An emerging need for effective interventions. *Child and Adolescent Social Work Journal, 23*(4), 472–486.

Miller, K.M. (2007). Risk and resilience among African American children of incarcerated parents. *Journal of Human Behavior in the Social Environment, 15*(2/3), 25–37.

Miller, W.R., Benefield, R.G., & Tonigan, J.S. (1993). Enhancing motivation for change in problem drinking: A controlled comparison of two therapist styles. *Journal of Consulting and Clinical Psychology, 61*, 455–461.

Miller, W.R., & Rollnick, S. (1991). *Motivational interviewing: Preparing people for change*. New York: Guilford Press.

Mischkowitz, R. (1994). Desistance from a delinquent way of life? In E.G.M. Weitekamp & H.J. Kerner (Eds.), *Cross-national longitudinal research on human development and criminal behavior* (pp. 303–327). London: Kluwer Academic.

Mitchell, M.M., Spooner, K., & Yan Zhang, D.J. (2016). The effect of prison visitation on reentry success: A meta-analysis. *Journal of Criminal Justice, 47*, 74–83.

Mitka, M. (2004). Aging prisoners stressing health care system. *Journal of the American Medical Association, 292*, 423–424.

Morash, M. (2009). A great debate over using the Level of Service Inventory-Revised (LSI-R) with women offenders. *Criminology and Public Policy, 8*, 173–181.

Morash, M., Bynum, T., & Koons, B. (1998). *Women offenders: Programming needs and promising approaches*. Washington, DC: National Institute of Justice. Retrieved from www.ncjrs.gov/pdffiles/171668.pdf.

Morash, M., Haarr, R., & Rucker, L. (1994). A comparison of programming for women and men in U.S. prisons in the 1980s. *Crime and Delinquency, 40*(2), 197–221.

Morgan, K.D., Belbot, B.A., & Clark, J. (1997). Liability issues affecting probation and parole supervision. *Journal of Criminal Justice, 25*(3), 211–222.

Morgan, K.D., & Smith, B.L. (2005). Victims, punishment, and parole: The effect of victim participation on parole hearings. *Criminology & Public Policy, 4*(2), 333–360.

Morgan, K.D., & Smith, B.L. (2008). Impact of race on parole release decisions. *Justice Quarterly, 25*(2), 411–435.

Morris, N. (2002). *Maconochie's gentlemen*. New York: Oxford University Press.

Morrissey, J.P., Meyer, P.S., & Cuddeback, G.S. (2007). Extending ACT to criminal justice settings: Origins, current evidence, and future directions. *Community Mental Health Journal, 43*(5), 527–544.

Mossman, D. (1994). Assessing predictions of violence: Being accurate about accuracy. *Journal of Consulting and Clinical Psychology, 62*, 783–792.

Moult, B., Franck, L.S., & Brady, H. (2004). Ensuring quality information for patients: Development and preliminary validation of a new instrument to improve the quality of written health care information. *Health Expectations, 7*, 165–175.

Mueser, K.T., Bond, G.R., Drake, R.E., & Resnick, S.G. (1998). Models of community care for severe mental illness: A review of research on case management. *Schizophrenia Bulletin, 24*, 37–74.

Muftic, L.R., & Smith, M. (2018). Sex, parental incarceration, and violence perpetration among a sample of young adults. *Journal of Interpersonal Violence, 33*(2), 316–338.

Muhammad, M. (1996). Prisoners perspectives on strategies for release. *Journal of Offender Rehabilitation, 23*(1/2), 131–152.

Multi-Health Systems. (1995:1999). *Level of Service Inventory-Revised.* Tonowanda, NY: Multi-Health Systems.

Mumola, C.J. (2000). *Incarcerated parents and their children.* (NCJ 182335). Washington, D.C.: Bureau of Justice Statistics.

Mumola, C.J. (2007). *Medical causes of death in state prisons, 2001–2004.* (NCJ 216340). Washington, D.C.: Bureau of Justice Statistics.

Mumola, C.J., & Karberg, J.C. (2006). *Drug use and dependence, state and federal prisoners, 2004.* (NCJ 213530). Bureau of Justice Statistics.

Murphey, D., & Cooper, P.M. (2015). *Parents behind bars: What happens to their children?* Child Trends Organization. https://www.childtrends.org/publications/parents-behind-bars-what-happens -to-their-children.

Murray, J., & Farrington, D.P. (2005), Parental imprisonment: Effects on boys' anti-social behaviour and delinquency through the life-course. *Journal of Child Psychology and Psychiatry, 46*, 1269–78.

Murray, J., & Farrington, D.P. (2006). Evidence-based programs for children of prisoners. *Criminology and Public Policy, 5*(4), 721–736.

Murray, J., & Farrington, D.P. (2008). The effects of parental imprisonment on children. In M. Tonry (Ed.), *Crime and justice: A review of research* (Vol. 37, pp. 133–206). Chicago: University of Chicago Press.

Murray, J., Farrington, D.P., Sekol, I., & Olsen, R.F. (2009). Effects of parental imprisonment on child antisocial behaviour and mental health: A systematic review. *Campbell Systematic Reviews, 4*, 1–15.

Naffine, N. (1997). *Feminism and criminology.* Philadelphia: Temple University Press.

Nagin, D. (1998). Deterrence and incapacitation. In M. Tonry (Ed.), *The Handbook of Crime and Punishment* (pp. 345–368). New York: Oxford University Press.

Naser, R.L., & LaVigne, N. (2006). Family support in the prisoner reentry process: Expectations and realities. *Journal of Offender Rehabilitation, 43*(1), 93–106.

Naser, R.L., & Visher, C.A. (2006). Family members' experiences with incarceration and reentry. *Western Criminology Review, 7*(2), 20–31.

National Association of State Budget Officers. (2011). *State expenditure report: Examining fiscal 2009–2011 state spending*. Washington, D.C.: National Association of State Budget Officers. Retrieved from http://www.nasbo.org/Publications/StateExpenditureReport /tabid/79 /Default.aspx.

National Association of State Budget Officers. (2011). *State expenditure report, 2010*. Retrieved from http://www.nasbo.org/Publications/State-ExpenditureReport/tabid/79/Default.aspx.

National Association of State Budget Officers. (2020). *2020 State expenditure report: Fiscal years 2018–2020*. https://higherlogicdownload.s3.amazonaws.com/NASBO/9d2d2db1-c943-4f1b-b750-0fca152d64c2 /UploadedImages/SER%20Archive/2020_State_Expenditure_Report _S.pdf.

National Center for State Courts. (n.d.). *Mental health courts*. https: //www.ncsc.org/topics/alternative-dockets/problem-solving-courts /mental-health-courts/state-links.

National Center on Addiction and Substance Abuse. (2010). *Behind bars II: Substance abuse and America's prison population*. Retrieved from http://www.casacolumbia.org/templates/publications _reports.aspx.

National Coalition for the Homeless. (2009). *How many people experience homelessness?* Retrieved from http://www.nationalhomeless.org/fact-sheets/How_Many.html.

National Commission on Correctional Healthcare. (2002). *The health status of soon-to-be-released inmates*. (Vols. 1 & 2). Retrieved from http://www.ncchc.org/pubs/pubs_stbr.vol1.html and http://www.ncchc.org/pubs/pubs_stbr.vol2.html.

National Commission on Correctional Health Care, (2008). *Standards for health services in prisons*. Retrieved from http://www.ncchc.org/resources/2008_standards/intro.html.

National Conference of State Legislatures. (2021). *Felon voting rights*. https://www.ncsl.org/research/elections-and-campaigns/felon -voting-rights.aspx.

National Council on Alcoholism and Drug Dependence, Inc. (2015). Alcohol, drugs, and crime. https://www.ncadd.org/about-ncadd.

National Employment Law Project and In the Public Interest. (2016). *Reentry and employment for the formerly incarcerated and the role of*

American Trades Unions. Policy Brief. https://www.nelp.org/publication/reentry-and-employment-for-the-formerly-incarcerated-and-the-role-of-american-trades-unions/.

National Institute of Justice (NIJ). (2016). *Drug courts.* http://www.nij.gov/topics/courts/drug-courts/Pages/welcome.aspx.

National Public Radio. (2011). *Nation's jails struggle with mentally ill prisoners.* Retrieved from http://www.npr.org/2011/09/04 /140167676 /nations-jails-struggle-with-mentally-ill-prisoners.

National Research Council. (2014). The growth of incarceration in the United States: Exploring causes and consequences. Washington, D.C.: The National Academies Press.

Nelson, M., Deess, P., & Allen, C. (1999). *The first month out: Post-incarceration experiences in New York City*. New York: Vera Institute of Justice.

Nesmith, A., & Ruhland, E. (2008). Children of incarcerated parents: Challenges and resiliency, in their own words. *Children and Youth Services Review, 30*, 1119–1130.

Neuman, W. (1986). *The paradox of mass politics: Knowledge and opinion in the American electorate*. Cambridge, MA: Harvard University Press.

Newman, C. (1963). *Source book on probation, parole, and pardons.* Chicago: Thomas Books.

New York City Housing Authority. (2022, April). *NYCHA 2022 Fact Sheet.* Retrieved from https://www.nyc.gov/assets/nycha/downloads/pdf /NYCHA_Fact_Sheet_2022.pdf.

Nissen, L. (2006). Bringing strength-based philosophy to life in juvenile justice. *Reclaiming Children and Youth, 15*(1), 40–46.

Nixon, R. (1969, July 14). *Special message to the Congress on the control of narcotics and dangerous drugs.* [Speech]. Retrieved from *The American Presidency Project*, http://www.presidency.ucsb.edu/ws/?pid=2126.

Norcross, J.C., Krebs, P.M., & Prochaska, J.O. (2011). Stages of change. *Journal of Clinical Psychology, 67*(2), 143–154.

O'Brien, P. (2001). Making it in the "free world": Women in transition from prison. New York: SUNY Press.

O'Donnell, C., Lydgate, T., & Fo, W. (1971). The buddy system: Review and follow-up. *Child Behavior Therapy, 1*, 161–169.

O'Keef, M., Klebe, K., & Hromas, S. (1998). *Validation of the Level of Service Inventory (LSI) for community based offenders in Colorado: Phase II.* Denver, CO: Department of Corrections.

Office of Justice Programs. (1999). *Reentry courts: Managing the Transition from prison to community, A call for concept papers.* Washington, D.C.: U.S. Department of Justice. Retrieved from www.ncjrs.gov/pdffiles1/ojp/sl000389.pdf.

Olson, B.D., Jason, L.A., Ferrari, J.R., & Hutcheson, T.D. (2005). Bridging professional and mutual-help through a unifying theory of change: An application of the transtheoretical model to the mutual-help organization. *Journal of Applied and Preventative Psychology, 11*, 168–178.

Olson, D., Lurigio, A., & Alderden, M. (2003). Men are from Mars, Women are from Venus, but what role does gender play in probation recidivism? *Justice Research and Policy, 5*, 33–54.

Opsal, T. (2009). Women on parole: Understanding the impact of surveillance. *Women & Criminal Justice, 19*, 306–328.

Orr, K. (2014). CDCR to create special units for mentally ill inmates. https://www.capradio.org/articles/2014/08/29/cdcr-to-create-special-units-for-mentally-ill-inmates/.

Oudekerk, B., & Kaeble, D. (2021). *Probation and parole in the United States, 2019.* (NCJ 256092). Bureau of Justice Statistics.

Ouellette, H.M., Applegate, B.K., & Vuk, M. (2017). The public's stance on prisoner reentry: Policy support and personal acceptance. *American Journal of Criminal Justice, 42*(4), 768–789.

Owen, B. (1998). *In the mix: Struggle and survival in a women's prison.* Albany: State University of New York Press.

Owen, B., & Bloom, B. (1995). Profiling women prisoners: Findings from the national surveys and the California sample. *The Prison Journal, 75*, 165–185.

Page, J., & Schaefer, S. (2011). From risks to assets: Toward a strengths-based approach to juvenile justice reentry into the community. *CURA Reporter, 41*(1), 34–41.

Page, J., & Travis, J. (2010). *In our backyard: Overcoming community resistance to reentry housing (A NIMBY toolkit).* Washington, D.C.: Bureau of Justice Assistance. Retrieved from www.jjay.cuny.edu/TOOL_KIT_1-NIMBY_FINAL.pdf.

Pager, D. (2003). The mark of a criminal record. *The American Journal of Sociology, 108*(5), 937–975.

Pager, D. (2007). *Marked: Race, crime, and finding work in an era of mass incarceration.* Chicago: University of Chicago Press.

Palm, G.F. (1996). Planning for dads and kids time together. In J.K. Comeau (Ed.), *Family information services professional resource materials.* Minneapolis, MN: Family Information Services.

Palm, G.F. (2003). Parent education for incarcerated fathers. In J. Fagan & A.J. Hawkins (Eds.), Clinical and educational interventions with fathers (pp. 117–141). Binghamton, NY: Haworth Clinical Practice Press.

Palmer, T. (1975). Martinson revisited. *Journal of Research in Crime and Delinquency, 12*, 133–152.

Paparozzi, M. (2003) Probation, parole, and public safety: The need for principled practices versus faddism and circular policy development. *Corrections Today, 65*, 46 50.

Paparozzi, M.A., & Caplan, J.M. (2009). A profile of paroling authorities in America: The strange bedfellows of politics and professionalism. *The Prison Journal, 80*, 401–425.

Paparozzi, M.A., & Guy, R. (2009). Giant that never woke: Parole authorities as the lynchpin to evidence-based practices and prisoner reentry. *Journal of Contemporary Criminal Justice, 25*(4), 397–411.

Park, R.E., Burgess, E.W., & McKenzie, R.D. (1925; 1967). *The city: Suggestions for investigation of human behavior in the urban environment.* Chicago: University of Chicago Press.

Parke, R.D., & Clarke-Stewart, K.L. (2002, January). Effects of parental incarceration on young children. *National Policy Conference.* U.S. Department of Health and Human Services and The Urban Institute. Retrieved from aspe.hhs.gov/hsp/prison2home02/parke%26stewart.pdf.

Parsonage, W.H., Bernat, F.P., & Helfgott, J. (1994). Victim impact testimony and Pennsylvania's parole decision making process: A pilot study. *Criminal Justice Policy Review, 6*(3), 187–206.

Parsons-Lewis, H. (1972). Due process in parole-release decisions. *California Law Review, 60*(6), 1518–1556.

Patch, P.C., & Arrigo, B.A. (1999). Police officer attitudes and use of discretion in situations involving the mentally ill: The need to narrow the focus. *International Journal of Law and Psychiatry, 22*, 23–35.

Partnership for Responsible Drug Information. (2012). *Rockefeller drug laws information sheet*. Retrieved from http://www.prdi.org/rocklawfact.html.

Paternoster, R. (1989). Decisions to participate in and desist from four types of common delinquency: Deterrence and the rational choice perspective. *Law & Society Review, 23*(1), 7–40.

Pattillo, M., Weiman, D., & Western, B. (Eds.). (2004). Imprisoning America: The social effects of mass incarceration. New York: Russell Sage Foundation.

Pearson, F.S., Lipton, D.S., Cleland, C.M., & Yee, D.S. (2002). The effects of behavioral/cognitive-behavioral programs on recidivism. *Crime & Delinquency, 48*, 476–496.

Pease, K. (1982). Community service. *Justice of the Peace, 27*, 740.

Pelissier, B., & Jones, N. (2005). A review of gender differences among substance abusers. *Crime & Delinquency, 51*(3), 343–372.

Pelletier, E., & Evans, D. (2019). Beyond recidivism: Positive outcomes from higher education programs in prison. *The Journal of Correctional Education, 70*(2), 49–68.

Pennsylvania Department of Corrections. (n.d.). SCI Laurel Highlands. https://www.cor.pa.gov/Facilities/StatePrisons/Pages/Laurel-Highlands.aspx.

Pennsylvania Department of Corrections. (2020). Video visitation program. https://www.cor.pa.gov/family-and-friends/Pages/Video-Visitation.aspx.

Pennsylvania Department of Corrections. (2020–2021). FY 2020–2021 Budget. https://www.cor.pa.gov/About%20Us/Statistics/Documents/Budget%20Documents/Budget%20Testimony%202020-21.pdf.

Periman, D. (2011). Prisoner Reentry and the Uniform Collateral Consequences of Conviction Act. *Alaska Justice Forum, 27*(4), 1–11.

Peters, R.H., & Hills, H.A. (1997). *Intervention strategies for offenders with co-occurring disorders: What works?* Gains Center.

Petersilia, J. (1980). Criminal careers research: A review of recent evidence. In N. Morris & M. Tonry (Eds.), *Crime and justice: An annual review of research* (Vol. 2., pp. 321–379). Chicago: University of Chicago Press.

Petersilia, J. (1998). *Community corrections: Probation, parole, and intermediate sanctions*. Oxford: Oxford University Press.

Petersilia, J. (1999). A decade with experimenting with intermediate sanctions: What have we learned? *Perspectives, 23*(1), 39–44.

Petersilia, J. (2000). When prisoners return to the community: Political, economic, and social consequences. *Sentencing and corrections: Issues for the 21st century*. Washington, D.C.: National Institute of Justice. Retrieved from bcotn.org/…/csct/when_prisoners_return_to_communities%20.pdf.

Petersilia, J. (2001). Prisoner reentry: Public safety and reintegration challenges. *The Prison Journal, 81*(3), 360–375.

Petersilia, J. (2003). *When prisoners come home: Parole and prisoner reentry*. New York: Oxford University Press.

Petersilia, J. (2004). What works in prisoner reentry? Reviewing and questioning the evidence. *Federal Probation, 62*(2), p. 4–8.

Petersilia, J. (2005). From cell to society: Who is returning home? In J. Travis & C. Visher (Eds.), *Prisoner reentry and crime in America* (pp. 15–49). New York: Cambridge University Press.

Petersilia, J., & Turner, S. (1987). Guideline-based justice: Prediction and racial minorities. In T.M. Gottfredson & M. Tonry (eds.), *Prediction and classification: Criminal justice decision making* (pp. 151–181). Chicago: University of Chicago Press.

Petersilia, J., & Turner, S. (1991). An evaluation of intensive probation in California. *Journal of Criminal Law and Criminology, 82*, 610–658.

Petersilia, J., & Turner, S. (1993). Evaluating intensive supervision probation and parole: results of a nationwide experiment. *Research in Brief*. Washington, D.C.: National Institute of Justice.

Pettit, B., & Lyons, C.J. (2007). Status and the stigma of incarceration: The labor-market effects of incarceration, by race, class, and criminal involvement. In S. Bushway, M.A. Stoll, & D.F. Weiman (Eds.), *Barriers to reentry: The labor market for released prisoners in post-industrial America* (pp. 203–226). New York: Russell Sage Foundation.

Pettit, B., & Lyons, C.J. (2009). Incarceration and the legitimate labor market: Examining age-graded effects on employment and wages. *Law and Society Reviews, 43*, 725–756.

Pettus, C.A., & Severson, M. (2006). Paving the way for effective reentry practice: The critical role and function of the boundary spanner. *The Prison Journal, 86*(2), 206–229.

Pew Center on the States. (2011). *State of recidivism: The revolving door of America's prisons.* Washington, D.C.: The Pew Charitable Trusts. Retrieved from www.pewtrusts.org/.../wwwpewtrustsorg /.../State _Recidivism_Revolv....

Pew Charitable Trust. (2017). *Prison health care costs and quality: How and why states strive for high-performing systems.* https://www.pewtrusts.org/-/media/assets/2017/10/sfh_prison_health_care_costs_and _quality_final.pdf .

Phillips, S.D., Burns, B.J., Wagner, H.R., Kramer, T.L., & Robbins, J.M. (2002). Parental incarceration among youth receiving mental health services. *Journal of Child and Family Studies, 11*, 385–399.

Phillips, S.D., Erkanli, A., Keeler, G.P., Costello, E.J., & Angold, A. (2006). Disentangling the risks: Parent criminal justice involvement and children's exposure to family risks. *Criminology & Public Policy, 5*, 677–702.

Phillips, S.D., & Gates, T. (2011). A conceptual framework for understanding stigmatization of children of incarcerated parents. *Journal of Child and Family Studies, 20*, 286–294.

Phillips, L.A., & Lindsay, M. (2011). Prison to society: A mixed methods analysis of coping with reentry. *Journal of Offender Therapy and Comparative Criminology, 55*(1), 136–154.

Piehl, A. (2003). *Employment dimensions of reentry: Understanding the nexus between prisoner reentry and work — Crime, work, and reentry.* Retrieved from http://www.urban.org/publications /410856.html.

Pinaire, B., Heumann, M., & Bilotta, L. (2003). Barred from the vote: Public attitudes toward the disenfranchisement of felons. *Journal of Criminal Justice, 32*, 195–206.

Pinard, M. (2010). Reflections and perspectives on reentry and collateral consequences. *Journal of Criminal Law & Criminology, 100*(3), 1213–1224.

Pinta, E.R. (2001). The prevalence of serious mental disorders among U.S. prisoners. In G. Landsberg & A. Smiley (Eds.), *Forensic mental health: Working with offenders with mental illness* (pp. 1–10). Kingston, NJ: Civic Research Institute.

Piquero, A.R., Farrington, D.P., & Blumstein, A. (2003). The criminal career paradigm. (n M. Tonry (Ed.), *Crime and justice: A review of research* (Vol., 30, pp. 359–506). Chicago: University of Chicago Press.

Piquero, A.R., West,V., Fagan, J., & Holland, J. (2006). Neighborhood, race, and the economic consequences of incarceration in New York City, 1985–1996. In R.D. Peterson, L.J. Krivo, & J. Hagan (Eds.), *The many colors of crime: Inequalities of race, ethnicity and crime in America* (pp. 256–273). New York: New York University Press.

Pleck, J.H., & Masciadrelli, B.P. (2004). Paternal involvement by U.S. residential fathers: Levels, sources and consequences. In M.E. Lamb (Ed.), The Role of the father in child development, (4th ed., pp. 222–271). Hoboken, NJ: Wiley.

Poehlmann, J. (2005). Children's family environments and intellectual outcomes during maternal incarceration. *Journal of Marriage and Family, 67*, 1275–1285.

Poehlmann, J., Dallaire, D., Loper, A.B., & Shear, L.D. (2010). Children's contact with their incarcerated parents: Research and findings. *American Psychologist, 65*(6) 575–598.

Pogrebin, M.R., Poole, E.D., & Regoli, R.M. (1986). Natural deaths and unknown persons: The process of creating an identity. *Social Science Journal, 23*, 345–360.

Pollock, J. (1999). *Criminal women*. Cincinnati, OH: Anderson Publishing.

Pollock, J. (2002). *Women, prison, and crime*. (2nd Ed.). Pacific Grove, CA: Brooks/Cole.

Pollock-Byrne, J. (1990). *Women, prison & crime*. Pacific Grove, CA: Brooks/Cole.

Pompoco, A., Wooldredge, J., Lugo, M., Sullivan, C., & Latessa, E.J. (2017). Reducing inmate misconduct and prison returns with facility education programs. *Criminology & Public Policy, 16*(2), 515–547.

Post-Prison Education Program. (2022). Retrieved from https://www.postprisonedu.org/.

Powell, D.R., & Eisenstadt, J.W. (1988). Informal and formal conversations in parent discussion groups: An observational study. *Family Relations, 37*, 166–170.

Pratt, D., Piper, M., Appleby, L., Webb, R., & Shaw, J. (2006). Suicide in recently released prisoners: A population-based cohort study. *Lancet, 368*, 119–123.

Prochaska, J.O., & DiClemente, C.C. (1986). The transtheoretical approach. In J. Norcross (Ed.), *Handbook of eclectic psychotherapy* (pp. 163–200). New York, Brunner/Mazel.

Prochaska, J.O., & DiClemente, C.C. (2002). Transtheoretical therapy. In F.W. Kaslow & J. Lebow (Eds.), Comprehensive handbook of psychotherapy (Vol. 4, pp. 241–254). Integrative/Eclectic. New York: John Wiley & Sons.

Prochaska, J.O., DiClemente, C.C., & Norcross, J.C. (1992). In search of how people change: Applications to addictive behaviors. *American Psychologist, 47*(9), 1102–1114.

Purvis, M., Ward, T., & Willis, G. (2011). The Good Lives Model in practice: Offence pathways and case management. *European Journal of Probation, 3*(2), 4–28.

Quinney, R. (1974). *Critique of legal order*. Boulder, CO: Little Brown.

Rafter, N. (1985a). Gender, prisons, and prison history. *Social Science History, 9*(3), 233–247.

Rafter, N. (1985b). *Partial justice: Women in state prisons, 1800–1935*. Boston: Northeastern University Press.

Rafter, N., & Stanko, E. (1982). *Judge, lawyer, victim, thief: Women, gender roles, and criminal justice*. Boston: Northeastern University Press.

Rand, A. (1987). Transitional life events and desistance from delinquency and crime. In M.E. Wolfgang, T.P. Thornberry, & R.M. Figlio (eds.), From boy to man, from delinquency to crime (pp. 134–162). Chicago: University of Chicago Press.

Rapp, C.A., Saleebey, D., & Sullivan, W.P. (2005). The future of strengths-based social work. *Advances in Social Work, 6*(1), 79–90.

Rapp, R.C., Siegal, H.A., Li, I., & Saha, P. (1998). Predicting post-primary treatment services and drug use outcome: A multivariate analysis. *American Journal of Drug and Alcohol abuse, 24*, 603–615.

Razzano, D. (2001). *Virtual visits debut in Pennsylvania prisons*. Corrections.com. http://www.corrections.com/articles/9322-virtual-visits-debut-in-pennsylvania-prisons.

Redcross, C., Bloom, D., Azurdia, G., Zweig, J., & Pindus, N. (2009). *Transitional jobs for ex-prisoners: Implementation, two-year impacts, and costs of the Center for Employment Opportunities (CEO) prisoner reentry program*. Washington, D.C.: The Urban Institute. Retrieved from http://www.urban.org/publications/1001362.html.

Redlich, A.D. (2005). Voluntary, but knowing and intelligent? Comprehension in mental health courts. *Psychology, Public Policy and Law, 11*, 605–619.

Reichel, P., & Gauthier, A. (1990). Boot camp corrections: A public reaction. In R. Muraskin, (Ed.), *Issues in justice: Explaining policy issues in the criminal justice system* (pp. 73–96). Bristol, IN: Wyndham Hall Press.

Reichman, N. (1986). Managing crime risks: Toward an insurance based model of social control. *Research in Law, Deviance and Social Control, 8*, 151–172.

Reilly, K. (2013). Sesame Street reaches out to 2.7 million American children with an incarcerated parent. The Pew Research Center. https://www.pewresearch.org/fact-tank/2013/06/21/sesame-street-reaches-out-to-2-7-million-american-children-with-an-incarcerated-parent/.

Reisig, M., Holtfreter, K., & Morash, M. (2002). Social capital among women offenders: Examining the distribution of social networks and relationships. *Journal of Contemporary Criminal Justice, 18*(2), 167–187.

Reisig, M., Holtfreter, K, & Morash, M. (2006). Assessing recidivism risk across female pathways to crime. *Justice Quarterly, 23*(3), 384–405.

Remster, B. (2019). A life course analysis of homeless shelter use among the formerly incarcerated. *Justice Quarterly, 36*(3), 437–465.

Rettinger, L.J., & Andrews, D.A. (2010). General risk and need, gender specificity, and the recidivism of female offenders. *Criminal Justice and Behavior, 37*, 29–46.

Rhode Island Department of Corrections. (2012). *Rehabilitative services*. Retrieved from: http://www.doc.ri.gov/rehabilitative/prisonerreentry/Books%20Beyond.ph…

Rhine, E.E. (1996). Parole boards. In M. McShane & F. Williams (Eds.), *Encyclopedia of American prisons* (pp. 213–218). New York: Garland.

Rhine, E.E., Smith, W., & Jackson, R. (1991). *Paroling authorities: Recent history and current practice*. Waldorf, MD: St. Mary's.

Rhine, E.E., Smith, W., Jackson, R., Burke, P., & LaBelle, R. (1991). *Paroling authorities*. Laurel, MD: American Correctional Association.

Richards, S.C. (1995). *The structure of prison release: An extended case study of prison release, work release, and parole*. New York: McGraw-Hill.

Richardson, G.E. (2002). The metatheory of resilience and resiliency. *Journal of Clinical Psychology, 58*(3), 307–321.

Richie, B. (1996). *The gendered entrapment of battered, Black women.* London: Routledge.

Richie, B. (2001). Challenges incarcerated women face as they return to their communities: Findings from life history interviews. *Crime & Delinquency, 47*(3), 368–389.

Ridgway, J. (2010, February 15). *Incarceration nation. Mother Jones.* Retrieved from http://motherjones.com/mojo/2010/02/incarceration-nation.

Robbins, C.A., Martin, S.S., & Surratt, H. (2009). Substance abuse treatment, anticipated maternal roles, and reentry success of drug-involved women prisoners. *Crime & Delinquency, 55*(3), 388–411.

Roberts, D. (2002). *Shattered bonds: The color of child welfare.* New York: Basic Civitas Books.

Roberts, J., & Hugh, M. (2005). *Understanding public attitudes to criminal justice.* New York: Open University Press.

Rogers, S. (1981). *Factors related to recidivism among adult probations in Ontario.* Toronto, Canada: Ontario Ministry of Correctional Services.

Roman, C.G., & Travis, J. (2004). *Taking Stock: Housing, homelessness, and prisoner reentry.* Washington, D.C.: The Urban Institute. Retrieved from www.urban.org/uploadedpdf/411096_taking_stock.pdf.

Roman, C.G., & Travis, J. (2006). Where will I sleep tomorrow?: Housing, homelessness, and the returning prisoner. *Housing Policy Debate, 17*(2), 389–418.

Ronel, N., & Segev, D. (2014). Positive criminology in practice. *International Journal of Offender Therapy and Comparative Criminology, 58*(11), 1389–1407.

Rose, D., & Clear, T. (1998). Incarceration, social capital, and crime: Implications for social disorganization theory. *Criminology, 36*(3), 441–480.

Rose, D., & Clear, T. (2001). *Incarceration, reentry, and social Capital: Social networks in the balance.* Washington, D.C.: U.S. Department of Health and Human Services. Retrieved from http://aspe.hhs.gov/hsp/prison-2home02/Rose.htm.

Rose, D., & Clear, T. (2002). *Incarceration, reentry and social capital: Social networks in the balance.* Paper presented at From Prison to Home, Washington, D.C.

Rosen, D.L., Golina, C.E., Grodensky, C.A., May, J., Bowling, M., DeVellis, R.F., White, B.L., & Whol, D.A. (2015). Opt-out HIV testing in prison; Informed and voluntary? *AIDS Care, 27*(5), 545–554.

Ross, R., & Gendreau, P. (1980). *Effective correctional treatment*. Toronto, Canada: Butterworth.

Ross, T., Khashu, A., & Wamsley, M. (2004). *Hard data on hard times: An empirical analysis of maternal incarceration, foster care, and visitation*. New York: Vera Institute of Justice.

Rossman, S.B., Roman, C.G., Buck-Willison, J., & Morley, E. (1999). *Impact of the opportunity to succeed (OPTS) aftercare program for substance-abusers: Comprehensive final report*. Washington, D.C.: U.S. Department of Justice. Retrieved from www.ncjrs.gov/pdffiles1/nij/grants/230741.pdf.

Rothman, D. (1980). *Conscience and convenience: The asylum and its alternatives in Progressive America*. Boston: Little Brown.

Routhier, G. (2018). *State of the homeless 2018. Fate of a generation: How the city and state can tackle homelessness by bringing housing investment to scale*. Coalition for the Homeless.

Roy, K., & Dyson, O. (2005). Gatekeeping in context: Babymama drama and the involvement of incarcerated fathers. *Fathering: A Journal of Theory, Research, and Practice about Men as Fathers, 3*, 289–310.

Roy, K., & MacDermid, S. (2003). Families in society. In D. Bredehoft & M. Walcheski (Eds.), *Family life education: Integrating theory and practice* (3rd. Ed., pp. 59–67). Minneapolis, MN: NCFR.

Rubak, S., Sandboek, A., Lauritzen, T., & Christensen, B. (2005). Motivational interviewing: A systematic review and meta analysis. *British Journal of General Practice, 55*, 305–312.

Rubin, S., Weihofen, H., Edwards, G., & Rosenzweig, S. (1963). *The law of criminal correction*. St. Paul, MN: West Publishing.

Rumgay, J. (1998) *Crime, punishment and the drinking offender*. Basingstoke: Palgrave Macmillan.

Rumgay, J. (2002). Accountability in the delivery of community penalties: To whom, for what, and why? In A. Bottoms, L. Gelsthorpe & S. Rex, Sue (Eds.), *Community penalties: change and challenges* (pp. 126–145). Cullompton, UK: Willan.

Rumgay, J. (2004). Scripts for safer survival: Pathways out of female crime. *The Howard Journal of Criminal Justice, 43*, 405–419.

Runda, J, Rhine, E.E., & Wetter, R. (1994). *The practice of parole boards.* Lexington, KY: Association of Paroling Authorities International.

Rusche, G. (1933/1978) Labor market and penal sanction: Thoughts on the sociology of criminal justice. *Crime & Social Justice, 10,* 2–8.

Ryan, T.A. (1990). *Effects of literacy training on reintegration of offenders.* Paper presented at Freedom to Read, International Conference on Literacy in Corrections, Ottawa, Ontario, Canada.

Ryan, T.A., & McCabe, K.A. (1994). Mandatory vs voluntary prison education and academic achievement. *The Prison Journal, 74,* 450–461.

Sacks, S., Melnick, G., Bank, S., Friedmann, P.D., Grella, C., & Knight, K. (2007). CJDATS Co-Occurring Disorders Screening Instrument for Mental Disorders (CODSI-MD): A pilot study. *The Prison Journal, 87*(1), 86–110.

Saleebey, D. (Ed). (1992). *The strengths perspective in social work practice: Power in the people.* White Plains, NY: Longman.

Saleebey, D. (1996). The strengths perspective in social work practice: Extensions and cautions. *Social Work, 41*(3), 296–301.

Salisbury, E., Van Voorhis, P., & Spiropoulos, G. (2009). The predictive validity of a gender-responsive needs assessment: An exploratory study. *Crime & Delinquency, 55*(4), 550–585.

Sameroff, A.J., & Seifer, R. (1990). Early contributors to developmental risk. In J. Rolf, A.S. Masten, D. Cicchetti, K.H. Nuechterlein, & S. Weintraub (Eds.), *Risk and protective factors in the development of psychopathology* (pp. 52–66). New York: Cambridge University Press.

Sameroff, A.J., Barocas, R., & Seifer, R. (1984). The early development of children of mentally ill women. In N.F. Watt, E.J. Anthony, L.C. Wynne, & J. Rolf (Eds.), *Children at risk for schizophrenia: A longitudinal perspective* (pp. 482–514). New York: Cambridge University Press.

Sampson, R.J. (1988). Local friendship ties and community attachment in mass society: A multilevel systemic model. *American Sociological Review, 53,* 766–779.

Sampson, R.J., & Laub, J.H. (1993). *Crime in the making: Pathways and turning points through life.* Cambridge: Harvard University Press.

Sampson, R.J., Raudenbush, S., & Earls, F. (1997). Neighborhoods and violent crime: A multilevel study of collective efficacy. *Science, 277,* 918–924.

Saum, C.A., Hiller, M.L., & Houser, K.A. (2019). Exploring graduation and retention outcomes in an opioid specialty court. *Rehabilitation and Social Reintegration*, 223–263.

Sawyer, W. (2017). The steep cost of medical co-pays in prison puts health at risk. Prison Policy Initiative. https://www.prisonpolicy.org/blog/2017/04/19/copays/.

Scheff, T.J. (1979). *Catharsis in healing, ritual, and drama*. Berkeley: CA: University of California Press.

Schlager, M.D. (2008). Improving parole practice in New Jersey: A longitudinal analysis of organizational and attitudinal changes of parole officers. *Journal of Offender Rehabilitation, 47*, 271–289.

Schlager, M.D. (2009). The organizational politics of implementing risk assessment instruments in community corrections. *Journal of Contemporary Criminal Justice, 25*, 412–423.

Schlager, M.D., & Pacheco, D. (2011). An examination of changes in LSI-R scores over time: Making the case for needs-based case management. *Criminal Justice and Behavior, 38*, 541–553.

Schlager, M.D., & Simourd, D. (2007). Validity of the Level of Service Inventory-Revised (LSI-R) among African-American and Hispanic male offenders. *Criminal Justice and Behavior, 34*, 545–554.

Shlay, A.B., & Rossi, P.H. (1992). Social science and contemporary studies of homelessness. *Annual Review of Sociology, 18*, 129–160.

Schmidt, P., & Witte, A. (1988). *Predicting recidivism using survival models.* New York: Springer-Verlag.

Schneider, A.L., Ervin, L., & Snyder-Joy, Z. (1996). Further exploration on the flight from discretion. *Journal of Criminal Justice, 24*(2), 109–121.

Schneller, D.P. (1976). *The prisoner's family: A study of the effects of imprisonment on the families of prisoners.* San Francisco: R & E Research Associates.

Schram, P., & Morash, M. (2002). Evaluation of a life skills program for women inmates in Michigan. *Journal of Offender Rehabilitation, 34*, 47–70.

Schram, P., Koons-Witt, B., Williams III, F., & McShane, M. (2006). Supervision strategies and approaches for female parolees: Examining the link between unmet needs and parolee outcome. *Crime & Delinquency, 52*(3), 450–471.

Scroggins, J., & Malley, S. (2010). Reentry and the (unmet) needs of women. *Journal of Offender Rehabilitation, 49*, 146–163.

Seccombe, K. (2002). "Beating the odds" versus "changing the odds": Poverty, resilience, and family policy. *Journal of Marriage and Family, 64*(2), 384–394.

Senanayake, B., Wickramasighe, S., Eriksson, L., Smith, A.C., & Edirippulige, S. (2018). Telemedicine in the correctional setting: A scoping review. *Journal of Telemedicine and Telecare, 24*(10), 669–675.

Sered, S., & Norton-Hawk, M. (2019). Triple jeopardy: Women's employment struggles postincarceration. *Journal of Offender Rehabilitation, 58*(4), 261–280.

Seiter, R.P. (2002). Prisoner reentry and the role of parole officers. *Federal Probation, 66*, 50–54.

Seiter, R.P., & Kadela, K.R. (2003). Prisoner reentry: What works, what does not, and what is promising. *Crime & Delinquency, 49*(3), 360–388.

Seiter, R.P., & West, A.D. (2003). Supervision styles in probation and parole: an analysis of activities. *Journal of Offender Rehabilitation 38*(2), 57–75.

Seligman, M.E.P. (1998). Building human strength: Psychology's forgotten mission. *APA Monitor, 29*(1), 2.

Settles, T. (2009). Restorative reentry: A strategy to improve reentry outcomes by enhancing social capital. *Victims & Offenders, 4*, 285–302.

Severance, T. (2004). Concerns and coping strategies of women inmates concerning release: "It's going to take somebody in my corner". *Journal of Offender Rehabilitation, 38*(4), 73–97.

Shakur, S. (2004). *Monster: The autobiography of an L.A. gang member.* Santa Barbara, CA: Grove Press.

Shapiro, C., & Schwartz, M. (2001). Coming home: Building on family connections. *Corrections Management Quarterly, 5*(3), 52–60.

Sharp, S., & Marcus-Mendoza, S.T. (2001). It's a family affair: Incarcerated women and their families. *Women & Criminal Justice, 12*(4), 21–49.

Shaw, C.R., & McKay, H.D. (1942). *Juvenile delinquency in urban areas.* Chicago: University of Chicago Press.

Shearer, R. (2003). Identifying the special needs of female offenders. *Federal Probation, 67*(1), 46–51.

Shervington, W. (1974). Prison, psychiatry and mental health. *Psychiatric Annals, 4*(3), 43–60.

Shields, I., & Simourd, D. (1991). Predicting predatory behavior in a population of young offenders. *Criminal Justice and Behavior, 18*, 180–194.

Shlafer, R.J., Poehlmann, J., Coffino, B., & Hanneman, A. (2009). Mentoring children with incarcerated parents: Implications for research, practice, and policy. *Family Relations, 58*(5), 507–519.

Shollenberger, T.L. (2009). *When relatives return: Interviews with family members of returning prisoners in Houston, Texas*. Washington, D.C.: The Urban Institute. Retrieved from http://www.urban.org/publications/411903.html.

Shover, N. (1983). The later stages of ordinary property offender careers. *Social Problems, 31*(2), 209–18.

Shover, N. (1985). *Aging criminals*. Beverly hills, CA: Sage Publications.

Shover, N. (1996). *Great pretenders: Pursuits and careers of persistent thieves*. Boulder, CO: Westview Press.

Shover, N., & Thompson, C.Y. (1992). Age, differential expectations, and crime desistance. *Criminology, 30*(1), 89–104.

Sickmund, M., & Puzzanchera, C. (2014). *Juvenile offenders and victims: 2014 national report*. U.S. Department of Justice, Office of Justice Programs, Office of Juvenile Justice and Delinquency Prevention.

Siegal, H.A., Fisher, J.A., Rapp, R.C., Kelliher, C.W., Wagner, J.H., O'Brien, W.F., & Cole, P.A. (1996). Enhancing substance abuse treatment with case management: Its impact on employment. *Journal of Substance Abuse Treatment, 13*, 93–98.

Siegal, H.A., Rapp, R.C., Kelliher, C.W., Fisher, J.H., Wagner, J.H., & Cole, P.A. (1995). The strengths perspective of case management: A promising inpatient substance abuse treatment enhancement. *Journal of Psychoactive Drugs, 27*(1), 67–72.

Siegal, H.A., Rapp, R.C., Li, I., Saha, P., & Kirk, K. (1997). The role of case management in retaining clients in substance abuse treatment: An exploratory analysis. *Journal of Drug Issues, 27*, 821–831.

Siegel, J.A., & Williams, L.M. (2003). Risk factors for sexual victimization of women: Results from a prospective study. *Violence Against Women, 9*, 902–930.

Sieh, E.W. (2005). *Community corrections and human dignity*. Sudbury, MA: Jones & Bartlett.

Sigler, R. (1988). Role conflict for adult probation and parole officers: Fact or myth? *Journal of Criminal Justice, 16*, 121–129.

Sigler, R.T., & McGraw, B. (1984). Adult probation and parole officers -Influence of their weapons, role perceptions and role conflict. *Criminal Justice Review, 9*(1), 28–32.

Silber, R., Shames, A., & Reid, K. (2017). *Aging out: Using compassionate release to address the growth of aging and infirm prison populations.* Vera Institute of Justice.

Simon, R. (1975). *Women and crime*. Lexington, Mass.: Lexington Books.

Simon, J. (1993). *Poor discipline: Parole and the social control of the underclass*. Chicago: University of Chicago Press.

Simourd, D. (1997). The criminal sentiments scale-modified and pride in delinquency scale: Psychometric properties and construct validity. *Criminal Justice and Behavior, 27*, 645–663.

Simourd, D. (2004). Use of dynamic risk/need assessment instrument among long term incarcerated offenders. *Criminal Justice and Behavior, 31*, 306–323.

Simourd, D., & Malcom, B. (1998). Reliability and validity of the Level of Service Inventory-Revised among federally incarcerated sex offenders. *Journal of Interpersonal Violence, 13*, 261–274.

Simourd, D., & Oliver, M. (2002). The future of criminal attitudes research and practice. *Criminal Justice and Behavior, 29*, 427–446.

Skeem, J.L., Winter, E., Kennealy, P.J., Louden, J.E., & Tatar, J.R. (2014). Offenders with mental illness have criminogenic needs too: Toward recidivism reduction. *Law and Human Behavior, 38*, 214–224.

Slate, R.N., & Johnson, W.W. (2008). *The criminalization of mental illness: Crisis and opportunity for the justice system*. Durham, NC: Carolina Academic Press.

Slate, R.N., Buffington-Vollum, J.K., & Johnson, W.W. (2013). *The criminalization of mental illness* (2nd ed.). Carolina Academic Press.

Smart, C. (1998). Criminological theory: It's ideology and implications concerning women. In C. Smart (Ed.), *Law, crime and sexuality: Essays in feminism* (pp. 16–31). London: Sage Publications.

Smith, P., Cullen, F., & Latessa, E. (2009). Can 14,737 women be wrong? A meta-analysis of the LSI-R and recidivism for female offenders. *Criminology and Public Policy, 8*, 183–208.

Snedker, K.A., Beach, L.R., & Corcoran, K.E. (2017). Beyond the "revolving door?" Incentives and criminal recidivism in a mental health court. *Criminal Justice and Behavior, 44*(9), 1141–1162.

Snell, T. (1994). *Women in prison: Survey of state prison inmates, 1991.* (NCJ 136949). Washington, D.C.: Bureau of Justice Statistics.

Snook, J., & Torrey, E.F. (2018). America badly needs more psychiatric-treatment beds. *National Review*. https://www.nationalreview.com/2018/02/america-badly-needs-more-psychiatric-treatment-beds/.

Snyder, Z.K. (2009). Keeping families together: The importance of maintaining mother-child contact for incarcerated women. *Women and Criminal Justice, 19*(1), 37–59.

Snyder, Z.K., Carlo, T., & Mullins, M. (2001). Parenting from prison: An examination of a children's visitation program at a women's correctional facility. *Marriage and Family Review, 32*(3/4), 111–135.

Solomon, A.L., Johnson K.D., Travis J., & McBride, E.C. (2004). *From prison to work: The employment dimensions of prisoner reentry*. Washington, D.C.: The Urban Institute. Retrieved from www.urban.org/uploaded-pdf/411097_From_Prison_to_work.pdf.

Solomon, P., & Draine, J. (1995a). Issues in serving the forensic client. *Social Work, 40*, 25–33.

Solomon, P., & Draine, J. (1995b). One year outcomes of a randomized trial of case management with seriously mentally ill clients leaving jail. *Evaluation Review, 19*, 256–273.

Sommers, I., Baskin, D.R., & Fagan, J. (1994). Getting out of the Life: Crime desistance by female street offenders. *Deviant Behavior 15*, 125–149.

Sousa, L., Ribeiro, C., & Rodrigues, S. (2006). Intervention with multi-problem poor clients: Towards a strengths-focuses perspective. *Journal of Social Work Practice, 20*(2), 189–204.

Spelman, W. (2009). Crime, cash, and limited options: Explaining the prison boom. *Criminology and public policy, 8*(1), 29–77.

Spencer, L.S., & Fallon, C.M. (2012, August/September). Today's special needs call for new approaches. *Corrections Today*, 6–8.

Springer, D.W., Lynch, C., & Rubin, A. (2000). Effects of a solution-focused mutual ad group for Hispanic children of incarcerated parents. *Child and Adolescent Social Work Journal, 17*(6), 431–442.

Stall R., & Biernacki P. (1986). Spontaneous remission from the problematic use of substances: an inductive model derived from a comparative analysis of the alcohol, opiate, tobacco, and food/obesity literatures. *International Journal of Addiction, 21*, 1–23.

Stanton, A.M. (2000). *When mothers go to jail.* New York: Lexington Books.

Staudt, M., Howard, M.O., & Drake, B. (2001). The operationalization, implementation, and effectiveness of the strengths perspective: A review of empirical studies. *Journal of Social Service Research, 27*(3), 1–21.

Steadman, H.J. (1992). Boundary spanners: A key component for the effective interactions of the justice and mental health systems. *Law and Human Behavior, 16*(1), 75–86.

Steadman, H.J., Mulvey, E.P., Monahan, J., Robbins, P.C., Appelbaum, P.S., Grisso, T. Roth, L.H., & Silver, E. (1998). Violence by people discharged from acute psychiatric inpatient facilities and by others in the same neighborhoods. *Archives of General Psychiatry, 55*, 393–401.

Steadman, H.J., Redlich, A., Callahan, L., Robbins, P.C., & Vesselinov, R. (2011). Effect of mental health courts on arrests and jail days: A multisite study. *Archives of General Psychiatry, 68*(2), 167–172.

Steadman, H.J., Redlich, A.D., Griffin, P., Petrila, J., & Monahan, J. (2005). From referral to disposition: Case processing in seven mental health courts. *Behavioral Sciences & the Law, 23*, 1–12.

Steadman, H.J., Scott, J.E., Osher, F., Agnese, T.K., & Robbins, P.C. (2005). Validation of the Brief Jail Mental Health Screen. *Psychiatric Services, 56*(7), 816–822.

Stefanski, S. (2017). *The preliminary budget.* Retrieved from https://www.ibo.nyc.ny.us/iboreports/homeless-shelter-costs-continue-to-be-underbudgeted-in-future-years-preliminary-budget-2017.pdf.

Steffensmeier, D., & Allan, E. (1998). The nature of female offending: Patterns and explanation. In R.T. Zaplin (Eds.), *Female offenders: critical perspectives and effective interventions* (pp. 5–29). Gaithersburg, MD: Aspen Publisher, Inc.

Steiner, B., & Wooldredge, J. (2009). Individual and environmental effects on assaults and nonviolent rule breaking by women in prison. *Journal of Research in Crime and Delinquency, 46*(4), 437–467.

Stephan, J.J. (2008). *Census of state and federal correctional facilities.* (NCJ 222182). Washington, D.C.: Bureau of Justice Statistics.

Steurer, S.J., Smith, L.J., & Tracy, A. (2001). *Three state recidivism study.* Lanham, MD: Correctional Education Association.

Stringer, S.M. (2006). *Breaking parole: An analysis of the New York state Division of Parole's caseload management guidelines.* New York: Office of the Manhattan Borough President. Retrieved from www.mbpo.org/uploads/policy.../BREAKING%20PAROLE.pdf.

Strupp, H.M., & Willmott, D.J. (2005). *Dignity denied: The price of imprisoning older women in California*. San Francisco: Legal Services for Prisoners with Children.

Sturges, J.E., & Hardesty, K.N. (2005). Survey of Pennsylvania jail wardens: An examination of visitation policies within the context of ecosystem theory. *Criminal Justice Review, 30*, 141–154.

Substance Abuse and Mental Health Services Administration. (2015). *Screening and assessment of co-occurring disorders in the justice system* (Research Report No. SMA-15-4930). U.S. Department of Health and Human Services.

Sullivan, E., Mino, M., Nelson, K., & Pope, J. (2002). *Families as a resource in recovery from drug abuse: An evaluation of LaBodega de la Familia*. New York: VERA Institute of Justice.

Sung, H., Mahoney, A.M., & Mellow, J. (2011). Substance abuse treatment gap among adult parolees: Prevalence, correlates, and barriers. *Criminal Justice Review, 36*(1), 40–57.

Sutherland, R. (1939). *Principles of criminology*. Philadelphia: Lippincot.

Swank, G.E., & Winer, D. (1976). Occurrence of psychiatric disorder in a county jail population. *American Journal of Psychiatry, 133*, 1331–1333.

Swann, C.A., & Sheran-Sylvester, M. (2006). The foster care crisis: What caused caseloads to grow? *Demography, 43*(2), 309–335.

Swanson, C.G., Schnippert, C.W., & Tryling, A.L. (2014). Reentry and employment: Employer's willingness to hire formerly convicted felons in northwest Florida. In M.S. Crow & J. Ortiz Smykla (Eds.), *Offender reentry: Rethinking criminology and criminal justice* (pp. 203–223). Jones & Bartlett Learning.

Taheri, S.A., & Welsh, B.C. (2016). After-school programs for delinquency prevention: A systematic review and meta-analysis. *Youth Violence and Juvenile Justice, 14*, 272–290.

Talbott, J.A. (1975). Current clichés and platitudes in vogue in psychiatric vocabularies. *Hospital and Community Psychiatry, 26*(8), 530.

Tannenbaum, F. (1938). *Crime and the community*. Boston: Ginn Co.

Tartaglia, M. (2014). Private prisons, private records. *Boston University Law Review, 94*, 1690–1743.

Taxman, F.S. (1999). Unraveling "what works" for offenders in substance abuse treatment services. *National Drug Court Institute Review, 2*(2), 93–134.

Taxman, F.S. (2006, September). Assessment with a flair (purpose): Offender accountability in supervision plans. *Federal Probation*.

Taxman, F.S., Cropsey, K.L., Young, D., & Wexler, H. (2007). Screening, assessment, and referral practices in adult correctional settings: a national perspective. *Criminal Justice and Behavior, 34*(9), 1216–1234.

Taxman, F.S., Yancey, C., & Bilanin, J. (2006). *Proactive community supervision in Maryland: Changing offender outcomes*. College Park, MD: University of Maryland, Bureau of Governmental Research.

Taxman, F.S, Young, D., & Byrne, J. (2004). Transforming offender reentry into public safety: Lessons from OJP's reentry partnership initiative. *Justice Policy and Research 5*(2),101–128.

Taxman, F.S., Young, D., Byrne, J.M., Holsinger, A., & Anspach, D. (2002). *From prisoner safety to public safety: Innovations in offender reentry*. College Park, MD: University of Maryland, Bureau of Government Research. Retrieved from www.ncjrs.gov/pdffiles1/nij/grants/196464.pdf.

Taxy, S., Samuels, J., & Adams, W. (2015). *Drug offenders in federal prison: Estimates of characteristics based on linked data*. (NCJ 248648). Bureau of Justice Statistics.

Taylor, J.M. (1992). Post-secondary correctional education: An evaluation of effectiveness and efficiency. *Journal of Correctional Education, 43*(3), 132–141.

Taylor, J.M. (2004). Piecing together a college education behind bars. *Journal of Prisoners on Prisons, 13*, 74–91.

Taylor, K., & Blanchette, K. (2009). The Women are not wrong: It is the approach that is debatable." *Criminology and Public Policy, 8*, 221–229.

Teplin, L.A. (1984). Criminalizing mental disorder. The comparative arrest rate of the mentally ill. *American Psychologist, 39*, 794–803.

Teplin, L.A. (1994). The criminalization hypothesis: Myth, misnomer or management strategy. In S. Shah & B. Sales (Eds.), *Law and mental health: Major developments and research needs* (pp. 151–183). Washington, D.C.: Government Printing Office.

Tewksbury, R., & Connor, D.P. (2012). Inmates who receive visits in prison: Exploring factors that predict. *Federal Probation, 76*(3), 43–46.

Tewksbury, R., Erickson, D., & Taylor, J. (2000). Opportunities lost: The consequences of eliminating Pell grant eligibility for correctional education students. *Journal of Offender Rehabilitation, 31*(1/2), 43–56.

The 2010 Annual Homeless Assessment Report to Congress (2010). U.S. Department of Housing and Urban Development. Office of Community Planning and Development. Retrieved from www.hudhre.info/documents/2010HomelessAssessmentReport.pdf.

The Sentencing Project. (2022). *Incarcerated women and girls.* https://www.sentencingproject.org/publications/incarcerated-women -and-girls/.

Thombre, A., Montague, D.R., Maher, J.L. & Zohra, T. (2009). If I could only say it myself: Communicating with children of incarcerated parents. *Journal of Correctional Education, 60*(1): 66–90.

Thompson, A. (2008). *Releasing prisoners, redeeming communities.* New York: New York University Press.

Thorburn, K.M. (1995). Healthcare in correctional facilities. *Western Journal of Medicine, 163*(6), 560–564.

Thornton, D. (2002). Constructing and testing a framework for dynamic risk assessment. *Sexual Abuse: A Journal of Research and Treatment, 14,* 139–153.

Thorpe, T., MacDonald, D., & Gerald, B. (1984). *Follow up study: Sample of college inmate participants.* Albany, NY: New York State Department of Correctional Services.

Tillyer, M.S., & Vose, B. (2011). Social ecology, individual risk, and recidivism: A multilevel examination of main and moderating influences. *Journal of Criminal Justice, 39,* 452–459.

Tonry, M. (1996). *Sentencing matters.* Oxford: Oxford University Press.

Tonry, M., & Petersilia, J. (1999). Introduction. In M. Tonry & J. Petersilia (Eds.), *Prisons: Crime and justice: A review of research* (Vol. 26, pp. 1–12). Chicago: University of Chicago Press.

Torrey, E.F., Entsminger, K., Geller, J., Stanley, J., & Jaffe, D.J. (2008). *The shortage of public hospital beds for mentally ill persons: A report of the Treatment Advocacy Center.* Arlington, VA: Treatment Advocacy Center.

Torrey, E.F., Kennard, A.D., Eslinger, D., Lamb, R., & Payle, J. (2010). *More mentally ill persons are in jails and prisons than hospitals: A survey of states.* Treatment Advocacy Center.

Travis, J. (2000). But they all come back: Rethinking prisoner reenter. *Research in Brief-Sentencing and Corrections: Issues for the 21st Century.* Washington, D.C.: U.S. Department of Justice. Retrieved from www.ncjrs.gov/pdffiles1/nij/181413.pdf.

Travis, J. (2002). Invisible punishment: An instrument of social exclusion. In M. Mauer, & M. Chesney-Lind (Eds.), *Invisible Punishment: The Collateral Consequences of Mass Imprisonment* (pp. 15–36). New York: The New Press.

Travis, J. (2005). *But they all come back: Facing the challenges of prisoner reentry.* Washington, D.C.: Urban Institute.

Travis, L., & Cullen, F. (1984). Radical nonintervention: the myth of doing no harm. *Federal Probation, 48*(1), 29, 32.

Travis, J., Keegan, S., & Cadora, E. (2003, September). *A portrait of prison reentry in New Jersey.* Paper presented at the New Jersey Reentry Roundtable, Trenton, New Jersey. Retrieved from www.urban.org/UploadedPDF/410899_nj_prisoner_reentry.pdf.

Travis, J., & Lawrence, S. (2002). *Beyond the prison gates: The state of parole in America.* Washington, DC: The Urban Institute. Retrieved from www.urban.org/url.cfm?id=310583.

Travis, J., McBride, E.C., & Solomon, A.L. (2005). *Families left behind: The hidden costs of incarceration and reentry.* The Urban Institute.

Travis, J. & Waul. M. (2003a). *Prisoners once removed: The impact of incarceration and reentry on children, families, and communities.* Washington, D.C.: The Urban Institute.

Travis, J., & Waul, M. (2003b, September). *Prisoner reentry: National overview and New Jersey portrait.* Paper presented at the New Jersey Reentry Roundtable, Trenton, New Jersey. Retrieved from www.urban.org/UploadedPDF/410899_nj_prisoner_reentry.pdf.

Traylor, A.L., & Richie, B.E. (2012). Female offenders and women in prison. In J. Peterselia & K.R. Reitz (Eds.), *The Oxford handbook of sentencing and corrections* (pp. 561–583). Oxford University Press.

Tremblay, R.E. (1994, June/July). Desistance from crime: Towards a life-course perspective. Discussant Paper presented at the International Society for the Study of Behavioral Development, Amsterdam.

Turner, M., Cullen, F., Sundt, J., & Applegate, B. (1997). Public tolerance for community-based sanctions. *The Prison Journal, 77*(1), 6–26.

Turner, R.D., & Eichenlaub, M. (1998). *Long distance dads: Incarcerated fathers program*. Retrieved from www.portal.state.pa.us/.../server .pt?...parentname...parentid=24...

Turpin-Petrosino, C. (1999). Are limiting enactments effective? An experimental test of decision making in a presumptive parole state. *Journal of Criminal Justice, 27*(4), 321–332.

Tyler, J., & Kling, J. (2003, September). *What is the value of a "prison GED?"* Retrieved from http://www.nber.org/~kling/PrisonGED.pdf.

Tyler, J.H., & Kling, J.R. (2007). Prison-based education and reentry into the mainstream labor market. In S. Bushway, M.A. Stoll, & D.F. Weiman (Eds.), *Barriers to reentry: The labor market for released prisoners in post-industrial America* (pp. 227–256). New York: Russel Sage Foundation.

Uggen, C. (2000). Work as a turning point in the life course of criminals: A duration model of age, employment, and recidivism. *America Sociological Review, 67*, 529–546.

Uggen, C., & Kruttschnitt, C. (1998). Crime in the breaking: Gender differences in desistance. *Law & Society Review, 32*(2), 339–366.

Uggen, C., Larson, R., Shannon, S., & Pulido-Nava, A. (2020). *Locked out of 2020: Estimates of people denied voting rights due to a felony conviction.* The Sentencing Project.

Uggen, C., & Manza, J. (2002). Lost voices: The civic and political views of disenfranchised felons. In D. Dattilo, D. Weiman, & B. Western (Eds.), *Imprisoning America: The social effects of mass incarceration* (pp. 165–204). New York: Russell Sage Foundation.

Uggen, C., Manza, J., & Behrens, A. (2004). 'Less than the average citizen:' Stigma, role transition and the civic reintegration of convicted felons. In S. Maruna & R. Immarigeon (Eds.), *After crime and punishment: Pathways to offender reintegration.* (pp. 261–293). Portland, OR: Willan Publishing.

Uggen, C., Wakefield, S., & Western, S. (2005). Work and family perspectives on reentry. In J. Travis & C. Visher, (Eds.), *Prisoner reentry and crime in America* (pp. 209–43). Cambridge, UK: Cambridge University Press.

Ungar, M. (2006). Nurturing hidden resilience in at-risk youth across cultures. *Journal of the Canadian Academy of Child and Adolescent Psychiatry, 15*(2), 53–58.

Urban, N.B.L., Kegeles, L.S., Slifstein, M., Xu, X., Martinez, D., Sakr, E., Castillo, F., Moadel, T., O'Malley, S., Krystal, J.H., & Abi-Dargham, A. (2010). Sex differences in striatal dopamine release in young adults after oral alcohol challenge: A positron emission tomography imaging study with [11C] Raclopride. *Biological Psychiatry, 68* (8), 689–696.

U.S. Census. (2011). *Educational attainment.* Retrieved from http://www.census.gov/hhes/socdemo/education/.

U.S. Census Bureau. (2019). *Quick facts: United States.* https://www.census.gov/quickfacts/fact/table/US/PST045219.

U.S. Conference of Mayors. (2008). *Hunger and homelessness survey: A status report on hunger and homelessness in America's cities: A 25-city report.* Retrieved from usmayors.org/pressreleases/uploads/2011-hhreport.pdf.

U.S. Department of Education. (2009). *Partnerships between community colleges and prisons: Providing workforce education and training to reduce recidivism.* Jessup, MD: U.S. Department of Education. Retrieved from www2.ed.gov/about/offices/list/. . . /prison-cc-partnerships_2009.pdf.

U.S. Department of Education. (2015). Notice inviting postsecondary educational institutions to participate in experiments under the experimental sites initiative; Federal student financial assistance programs under Title IV of the Higher Education Act of 1965, as amended. 80 FR 45964. 45964-45966. 2015-18994. https://www .federalregister.gov/documents/2015/08/03/2015-18994/notice -inviting-postsecondary-educational-institutions-to-participate-in-experiments-under-the U.S. Department of Education. (2019). Notice inviting postsecondary educational institutions to participate in experiments under the experimental sites initiative; Federal student financial assistance programs under Title IV of the Higher Education Act of 1965, as amended. 84 FR 23779. 23779-23783. 2019-10811.https://www.federalregister.gov/documents/2019/05/23/2019-10811/notice-inviting-postsecondary-educational-institutions-to-participate-in-experiments-under-the U.S. Department of Education. (2020). Second Chance Pell. https://www2.ed.gov/news/newsletters/edreview/2020/0501.html.

U.S. Department of Education. (2021). *Issue paper: Prison Education programs.* Retrieved from https://www2.ed.gov/policy/highered/reg/hearulemaking/2021/pellforprisoneducation.pdf.

U.S. Department of Housing and Urban Development. (1997). *Meeting the challenge: public housing authorities respond to the "One Strike and You're Out" initiative.* Washington, D.C.: U.S. Department of Housing and Urban Development. Retrieved from www.ncjrs.gov/App/publications/Abstract.aspx?id=183952.

U.S. Department of Housing and Urban Development (2007). *Defining chronic homelessness: A technical guide for HUD programs.* Retrieved from www.hudhre.info/documents/DefiningChronic Homeless.pdf.

U.S. Department of Justice. (2002). *Reentry trends in the U.S.: Characteristics of releases.* Washington, D.C.: Bureau of Justice Statistics. Retrieved from http://bjs.ojp.usdoj.gov/content/reentry/reentry.cfm.

U.S. Department of Justice. (2002). *Reentry trends in the U.S.: Releases from state prison.* Washington, D.C.: Bureau of Justice Statistics. Retrieved from http://bjs.ojp.usdoj.gov/content/reentry/reentry.cfm.

Van Ness, D.W., & Strong, K.H. (2010). *Restoring justice: In introduction to restorative justice.* New York: Elsevier.

Van Voorhis, P. (1988). A cross classification of five offender typologies: Issues of construct and predictive validity. *Criminal Justice and Behavior, 15,* 109–124.

Van Voorhis, P., Bauman, A., & Brushett, R. (2012). *Revalidation of the Women's Risk Needs Assessment.* Pre-release results. University of Cincinnati.

Van Voorhis, P., Bauman, A., & Brushett, R. (2013a). *Revalidation of the Women's Risk Needs Assessment. Institutional results.* University of Cincinnati.

Van Voorhis, P., Bauman, A., & Brushett, R. (2013b). *Revalidation of the Women's Risk Needs Assessment. Probation results.* University of Cincinnati.

Van Voorhis, P., & Presser, L. (2001). *Classification of women offenders: A national assessment of current practices.* Washington, D.C.: National Institute of Corrections. Retrieved from static.nicic.gov/Library/021816.pdf.

Van Voorhis, P., Salisbury, E., Wright, E., & Bauman, A. (2008). *Achieving accurate pictures of risk and identifying gender-responsive needs: Two new assessments for women offenders.* Washington, D.C.: United States Department of Justice: National Institute of Corrections. Retrieved from static.nicic.gov/Library/022844.pdf.

Van Voorhis, P., Wright, E., Salisbury, E., & Bauman, A. (2010). Women's risk factors and their contributions to existing risk/needs assessment: The current status of a gender-responsive supplement. *Criminal Justice and Behavior, 37*(3), 261–288.

Van Wormer, K. (1999). The strengths perspective: A paradigm for correctional counseling. *Federal Probation, 63*(1), 51–59.

Van Wormer, K., & Boes, M. (1999). Social work, corrections, and the strengths approach. *Canadian Social Work, 1*(1), 98–111.

Vera Institute of Justice. (2020). *Second Chance Pell: A snapshot of the first three years.* https://www.vera.org/downloads/publications/second-chance-pell-snapshot-first-three-years.pdf.

Veysey, B.M. (1997). *Specific needs of women diagnosed with mental illnesses in U.S. jails.* Delmar, NY: National GAINS Center Policy Research. Retrieved from gains.prainc.com/pdfs/Women/Needs_of_Women_Mono.pdf.

Veysey, B.M., & Bichler-Robertson, G. (2002). Prevalence estimates of psychiatric disorders in correctional settings. In *The health status of soon-to-be-released inmates: A report to Congress* (Vol. 2, pp. 57–80). Chicago: National Commission on Correctional Health Care.

Viets, S.T., Clark, M.D., & Miller, W.R. (2002). What is motivation to change? A scientific analysis. In M. McMurran (Ed.), *Motivating offenders to changes: A guide to enhancing engagement in therapy* (pp. 15–30). New York: John Wiley & Sons.

Vilcica, R. (2018). Parole decision making: Testing for the punitive hypothesis in a large U.S. jurisdiction. *International Journal of Offender Therapy and Comparative Criminology, 62*(5), 1357–1383.

Visher, C.A. (2013). Incarcerated fathers: Pathways from prison to home. *Criminal Justice Policy Review, 24*(1), 9–26.

Visher, C.A., Debus, S., & Yahner, J. (2008). *Employment after prison: A longitudinal study of releasees in three states.* Washington, D.C.: The Urban Institute. Retrieved from www.urban.org/UploadedPDF/411778_employment_after_prison.pdf.

Visher, C.A., Debus-Sherrill, S.A., & Yahner, J. (2011). Employment after prison: A longitudinal study of former prisoners. *Justice Quarterly, 28*(5), 698–718.

Visher C.A., & Farrell, J. (2005). *Chicago communities and prisoner reentry.* The Urban Institute Justice Policy Center.

Visher, C.A., Kachnowski, V., LaVigne, N.G., & Travis, J. (2004). *Baltimore prisoners' experiences returning home.* Washington, D.C.: The Urban Institute. Retrieved from http://www.urban.org/url.cfm?ID=310946.

Visher, C.A., Knight, C.R., Chalfin, A., & Roman, J.K. (2009). *The impact of marital and relationship status on social outcomes for returning prisoners.* Washington, D.C.: U.S. Department of Health and Human Services. Retrieved from http://aspe.hhs.gov/hsp/09/Marriage&Reentry/rb.shtml.

Visher, C.A., LaVigne, N.G., & Travis, J. (2004). *Returning home: Understanding the challenges of prisoner reentry Maryland pilot study: Findings from Baltimore.* Washington, D.C.: The Urban institute. Retrieved from www.urban.org/uploadedPDF/410974_ReturningHome_MD.pdf.

Visher, C.A., & Travis, J. (2003). Transitions from prison to community: Understanding individual pathways. *Annual Review of Sociology, 29,* 89–113.

Vito, G., & Tewksbury, R. (2000). *Gender comparisons in drug testing probationer and parolees. Corrections Compendium, 25*(9), 1–5, 27.

Volavka, J., & Citrome, L. (2008). Heterogeneity of violence in schizophrenia and implications for long-term treatment. *International Journal of Clinical Practice, 62,* 1237–1245.

von Hirsch, A. (1976). *Doing justice: the choice of punishments.* New York: Hill & Wang.

Vose, B., Lowencamp, C., Smith, P., & Cullen, F. (2009). Gender and the predictive validity of the LSI-R. *Journal of Contemporary Criminal Justice, 24,* 459–471.

Wagner, P., & Jones, A. (2019). *State of phone justice: Local jails, state prisons and private phone providers.* The Prison Policy Initiative.

Wahler, E. (2006). *Losing the right to vote: Perceptions of permanent disenfranchisement and the civil rights restoration application process in the state of Kentucky.* Retrieved from www.sentencingproject.org.

Walker, S. (1998). *A History of American criminal Justice.* New York: Oxford University Press.

Walker, S. (2002). Crime and policy: A complex problem. In W.R. Palacios, P.F. Cromwell (Eds.), *Crime and justice in America: Present realities and future prospects* (pp. 25–41). Upper Saddle River, NJ: Prentice-Hall.

Walmsley, R. (2007). *World prison population list.* 7th ed. Kings College London, School of Law. London: International Center for Prison Studies.

Walsh, F. (1998). *Strengthening family resilience.* New York: Guilford.

Walters, S.T., Clark, M.D., Gingerich, R., & Meltzer, M. (2007, June). *Motivating offenders to change: A guide for probation & parole officers.* Washington, D.C.: U.S. Department of Justice. Retrieved from http://nicic.gov/library/022253.

Walters, S.T., Vader, A.M., Nguyen, N., Harris, T.R., & Ells, J. (2010). Motivational interviewing as a supervision strategy in probation: A randomized effectiveness trial. *Journal of Offender Rehabilitation, 49*, 309–323.

Walther, L., & Perry, J. (1997). The Vermont reparative probation program. *Journal on Community Corrections, 13*(2), 26–34.

Ward, T., Day, A., Howells, K., & Birgden, A. (2004). The multifactor offender readiness model. *Aggression and Violent Behaviour, 9*(6), 645–673.

Ward, T., & Maruna, S. (2007). *Rehabilitation: Beyond the risk assessment paradigm*. London, UK: Routledge.

Ward, T., & Stewart, C.A. (2003). The treatment of sex offenders: Risk management and good lives. *Professional Psychology: Research and Practice, 34*, 353–360.

Ward, T., & Svyersen, K. (2009). Human dignity and vulnerable agency: An ethical framework for forensic practice. *Aggression and Violent Behavior, 14*, 94–105.

Ward, T., Yates, P.M., & Willis, G.M. (2012). The Good Lives Model and the Risk Needs Responsivity Model: A critical response to Andrews, Bonta, and Wormith (2011). *Criminal Justice and Behavior, 39*(1), 94–110.

Warr, M. (1998). Life-course transitions and desistance from crime*. *Criminology, 36*(2), 183–216.

Watkins, E. (2017, November 20). *Bureau of prisons ending contracts with 16 halfway houses*. CNN. Retrieved from http://www.cnn.com/2017/11/20/politics/bureau-of-prisons-mark-inch-jeff-sessions/index.html.

Watson, A., Hanrahan, P., Luchins, D., & Lurigio, A. (2001). Mental health courts and the complex issue of mentally ill offenders. *Psychiatric Services, 52*(4), 477–481.

Watson, J., Solomon, A.L., LaVigne, N.G., Travis, J., Funches, M., & Parthasarathy, B. (2004). *A portrait of prisoner reentry in Texas.* Washington, D.C.: The Urban Institute. Retrieved from www.urban.org/uploadedpdf/410972_tx_reentry.pdf.

Weick, A., & Pope, L. (1988). Knowing what's best: A new look at self-determination. *Social Casework, 69*, 10–16.

Weick, A., Rapp, C., Sullivan, P., & Kisthardt, W. (1989). A strengths perspective for social work practice. *Social Work, 34*(4), 350–354.

Weinbaum, C., Lyerla, R., & Margolis, H.S. (2003, January 24). Prevention and Control of Infections with Hepatitis Viruses in Correctional Settings. *Morbidity and Mortality Weekly Report*, 52, 1–36.

Weisman, R.L., Lamberti, J.S., & Price, N. (2004). Integrating criminal justice, community healthcare, and support services for adults with severe mental disorders. *Psychiatric Quarterly, 75*(1), 71–85.

Weitekamp, E.G.M. & Kerner, H.J. (Eds.). (1994). *Cross-national longitudinal research on human development and criminal behavior*. Dordrecht, Germany: Kluwer Academic Publishers.

Welsh, W.N., & Zajac, G. (2013). A multisite evaluation of prison-based drug treatment: Four-year follow-up results. *The Prison Journal, 93*(3), 251–271.

Werner, E., & Smith, R. (1992). *Overcoming the odds: High-risk children from birth to adulthood.* New York: Cornell University Press.

Werner, E.E., & Smith, R.S. (2001). *Journeys from childhood to midlife.* Ithaca: Cornell University Press.

West, A.D. & Seiter, R.P. (2004). Social worker or cop? Measuring the supervision styles of probation & parole officers in Kentucky and Missouri. *Journal of Crime & Justice 27*(2), 27–57.

West, H., Sabol, W. & Greenman, S. (2010). *Prisoners in 2009.* (NCJ 230189). Washington, DC: U.S. Bureau of Justice Statistics.

West-Smith, M., Pogrebin, M.R., & Poole, E.D. (2000). Denial of parole: An inmate perspective. *Federal Probation, 64*(2), 3–10.

Western, B. (2006). *Punishment and inequality in America.* New York: Russell Sage Foundation.

Western, B. (2007). The penal system and the labor market. In S. Bushway, M.A. Stoll, & D.F. Weiman (Eds.), *Barriers to re-entry? The labor market for released prisoners in postindustrial America* (pp. 335–359). New York: Russell Sage Foundation.

Western, B., Kling, J., & Weiman, D. (2001). The labor market consequences of incarceration. *Crime and Delinquency 47*(2), 410–427.

Western, B., Schiraldi,V., & Ziedenberg, J. (2003). *Education and incarceration.* Washington, D.C.: Justice Policy Institute. Retrieved from www .prisonpolicy.org/scans/jpi/EducationandIncarceration1.pdf.

Wexler, H.K. (2003). The promise of prison-based treatment for dually diagnosed inmates. *Journal of Substance Abuse Treatment, 25*, 223–231.

Wheelock, D. (2005). Collateral consequences and racial inequality: Felon status restrictions as a system of disadvantage. *Journal of Contemporary Criminal Justice, 21*(1), 82–90.

Whiteacre, K. (2006). Testing the Level of Service Inventory-Revised (LSI-R) for racial/ethnic bias. *Criminal Justice Policy Review, 17*, 330–342.

Whitehead, J.T. (1985). Job burnout in probation and parole: Its extent and intervention implications. *Criminal Justice and Behavior, 12*, 91–110.

Whitmer, G.E. (1980). From hospitals to jails: The fate of California's deinstitutionalized mentally ill. *American Journal of Orthopsychiatry, 50*, 65–75.

Widom, C.S. (1989). The cycle of violence. *Science, 244*, 160–166.

Wilkinson, R. (2005, April). Engaging communities: An essential ingredient to offender reentry. *Corrections Today*, 86–89.

Williams, B., & Abraldes, R. (2007). Growing older: Challenges of prison and reentry for the aging population. In R. Greifinger (Ed.), *Public health behind bars: From prisons to community* (pp. 56–72). New York: Springer.

Williams, B.A., Lindquist, K., Hill, T., Baillargeon, J., Mellow, J., Greifinger, R., & Walter, L.C. (2009). Caregiving behind bars: Correctional officer reports of disability in geriatric prisoners. *Journal of the American Geriatric Society, 57*, 1286–1292.

Williams, L.C., Lindquist, K., Sudore, R.L., Strupp, H.M., Wilmott, D.J. & Walter, L.C. (2006). Being old and doing time. Functional impairment and adverse experiences of geriatric female prisoners. *Journal of American Geriatric Society, 54*, 702–707.

Wilson, D.B., Bouffard, L.A., & MacKenzie, D.L. (2005). A quantitative review of structured, group-oriented, cognitive-behavioral programs for offenders. *Criminal Justice and Behavior*, 32(2), 172–204.

Wilson, D.B., Gallagher, C.A., & MacKenzie, D.L. (2000). A meta- analysis of corrections-based education, vocation, and work programs for adult offenders. *Journal of Research in Crime and Delinquency, 37*(4), 347–368.

Wilson, W.J. (1997). *When work disappears: The world of the new urban poor*. New York: Vintage.

Wilson J.A., & Royo Maxwell, S. (2005). Prisoner reentry & recidivism. *Criminology & Public Policy, 4*(3), 479–526.

Wiltz, T. (2019). *Where 'returning citizens' find housing after prison.* The Pew Charitable Trust. https://www.pewtrusts.org/en/research-and-analysis/blogs/stateline/2019/04/23/where-returning-citizens-find-housing-after-prison.

Winerip, M., & Schwirtz, M. (2014, July 14). Where mental illness meets brutality in jail. *New York Times*, p. A1. https://www.nytimes.com/2014/07/14/nyregion/rikers-study-finds-prisoners-injured-by-employees.html#:~:text=Rikers%3A%20Where%20Mental%20Illness%20Meets%20Brutality%20in%20Jail,injuries%20to%20inmates.%20Richard%20Perry%2FThe%20New%20York%20Times.

Winnick, T., & Bodkin, M. (2008). Anticipated stigma and stigma management among those to be labeled "ex-con". *Deviant Behavior, 29*, 295–333.

Winnick, T., & Bodkin, M. (2009). Stigma, secrecy and race: An empirical examination of black and white incarcerated men. *American Journal of Criminal Justice, 34*, 131–150.

Winterfield, L., Coggeshall M., Burke-Storer M., Correa V., & Todd, S. (2009). *The effects of postsecondary correctional education: Final report.* Washington, D.C.: The Urban Institute. Retrieved from http://www.urban.org/publications/411954.html.

Wolf, J.G., & Sylves, D. (1981). *The impact of higher education opportunity programs: Post-prison experience of disadvantaged students: A preliminary follow-up of HEOP ex-offenders, final report.* Albany: New York State Education Department.

Wolf, N., Epperson, M., Shi, J., Huening, J., Schumann, B.E., & Sullivan, I.R. (2014). Mental health specialized probation caseloads: Are they effective? *International Journal of Law and Psychiatry,* 37(5), 464–472.

Wolff, N., Helminiak, T.W., Morse, G.A., Calsyn, R.J., Klinkenberg, D., & Trusty, M.L. (1997). Cost-effectiveness evaluation of three approaches to case management for homeless mentally ill clients. *American Journal of Psychiatry, 154*(3), 341–348.

Wolfgang, M.E., Thornberry, T.P., & Figlio, R.M. (1987). *From boy to man, from delinquency to crime.* Chicago: University of Chicago Press.

Wong, J.S., Bouchard, J., Gushue, K., & Lee, C. (2019). Halfway out: An examination of the effects of halfway houses on criminal recidivism.

International Journal of Offender Therapy and Comparative Criminology, 63(7), 1018–1037.

Wood, P., & Grasmick, H. (1999). Toward the development of punishment equivalencies: Male and female inmates rate the severity of alternative sanctions compared to prison. *Justice Quarterly, 16*, 19–50.

Yocum, A., & Nath, S. (2011). Anticipating father reentry: A qualitative study of children's and mothers' experiences. *Journal of Offender Rehabilitation, 50*(5), 286–304.

Young, D.S., & Smith, C.J. (2000). When moms are incarcerated: The need of children, mothers, and caregivers. *Families in Society: The Journal of Contemporary Human Services, 81*(2), 130–141.

Young, D.S., Taxman, F.S., & Byrne, J.M. (2002). *Engaging the community in offender reentry*. Washington, D.C.: U.S. Department of Justice. Retrieved from www.ncjrs.gov/pdffiles1/nij/grants/196492.pdf.

Zahn, M.A., Hawkins, S.R., Chiancone, J., & Whitworth, A. (2008). *The girls study group: Charting the way to delinquency prevention for girls*. Washington, D.C.: Office of Juvenile Justice and Delinquency Prevention.

Zamble, E., & Porporino, F.J. (1988). *Coping, behavior, and adaptation in prison inmates*. New York: Springer-Verlag.

Zamble, E., & Quinsey, V. (1997). *The criminal recidivism process*. New York: Cambridge University Press.

Zandbergen, P. A., Levenson, J.S., & Hart, T.C. (2010). Residential proximity to schools and daycares: An empirical analysis of sex offender recidivism. *Criminal Justice and Behavior, 37*, 482–502.

Zeng, Z. (2020). *Jail Inmates in 2018*. (NCJ253044). Washington, DC: Bureau of Justice Statistics.

Zgoba, K.M., & Jenkins, K. (2008). The influence of GED obtainment on inmate release outcome. *Criminal Justice and Behavior, 35*(3), 375–387.

Zigler, E., & Glick, M. (1986). *A developmental approach to adult psychopathology*. New York: Wiley.

Zingraff, M., & Randall, T. (1984). Differential sentencing of women and men in the U.S.A. *International Journal of the Sociology of Law, 12*, 401–413.

Index